THE EUROPEAN INHERITANCE

THE EUROPEAN INHERITANCE

EDITED BY

SIR ERNEST BARKER

SIR GEORGE CLARK

PROFESSOR P. VAUCHER

VOLUME III

OXFORD
AT THE CLARENDON PRESS

Oxford University Press, Amen House, London E.C. 4
GLASGOW NEW YORK TORONTO MELBOURNE WELLINGTON
BOMBAY CALCUTTA MADRAS KARACHI CAPE TOWN IBADAN
Geoffrey Cumberlege, Publisher to the University

FIRST PUBLISHED 1954
REPRINTED WITH CORRECTIONS 1955

PRINTED IN GREAT BRITAIN

PREFACE

THE origin of this work goes back to the war of 1939–45, and, in particular, to the winter of 1942–3. At the end of 1942 the British Minister of Education convened a Conference of the Ministers of Education of eight allied governments, then resident and active in London; and this Conference of Allied Ministers of Education continued to meet regularly afterwards. In February 1943 the Conference appointed a Books Commission, with the primary purpose of arranging for the supply of English books and periodicals, at the end of the war, to the member countries of the Conference which were then occupied by the enemy,[1] but also with the further purpose of considering the possibility of producing a work on history, 'of an objective character', which might be available for general use in the member countries and elsewhere. In pursuance of this further purpose the Books Commission proceeded to appoint (in March 1943) a History Committee, containing scholars drawn from all the member countries, to plan the production of such a work. The general plan of these volumes is the result of the deliberations of this Committee.

The scheme of the History Committee, as it eventually emerged, and as it was adopted and confirmed by the Conference of Allied Ministers of Education, was a scheme for the publication of a history of European civilization, to be called *The European Inheritance*, in seven chronological parts (from the beginnings of prehistory to the middle of the twentieth century), each part accompanied by maps and illustrations and by a number of appropriate historical documents. In submitting the scheme the History Committee proposed, and the Conference of Allied Ministers of Education agreed, that *The European Inheritance* should be a work of independent scholarship, independently published by a university press, under the direction of an editorial board which would choose and invite the individual contributors, and would thus be freely and solely responsible, along with the contributors, for the form and substance of the work. The Clarendon Press was accordingly approached,

[1] That purpose was achieved; and owing to the work of the Books Commission from 1943 to 1945 the occupied countries were able to obtain a very large number of books and periodicals for their university and public libraries. (Note by Professor Paul Vaucher.)

and agreed to publish the work; and an editorial board was then appointed (in March 1944), which in its eventual form consisted of Sir Ernest Barker (who had acted as Chairman of the Books Commission and of its Historical Committee), Dr. G. N. Clark (at the time of his appointment Regius Professor of History in Cambridge, and afterwards Provost of Oriel College, Oxford), and Professor Paul Vaucher, at that time cultural counsellor of the French government in London and afterwards professor in the university of Paris. (Professor Odlozilik, of the university of Prague, was originally a member of the Board, but when he went to the United States for service in an American university he relinquished his membership.) When these arrangements had been made, the Conference of Allied Ministers of Education, which had originally suggested the work, decided to ensure its freedom from even the slightest shadow of any political control by disclaiming all responsibility for its form and substance; and they accordingly passed the following resolution, to be inserted in each volume:

'This volume originated in a suggestion made by the Conference of Allied Ministers of Education early in 1943. The Conference subsequently approved the scheme of publication, but decided to ensure the independence of the editors and contributors by dissociating themselves from the preparation of the volume. While, therefore, the Conference agreed to the insertion of this prefatory note explaining the origin of the volume, it will be understood that they had no responsibility for either the form or the substance of the present work.'

Just as it was, in its inception, internationally planned, or at any rate planned on a European basis, so too in its execution the work has an international width. Naturally some of the scholars who have made their contributions to a work originally planned in Great Britain (though many continental scholars were long concerned in the planning) belong to the British Isles. The first part, on prehistory, is written by Professor Gordon Childe, Director of the Institute of Archaeology in the university of London, who has also studied and taught in the universities of Sydney, Oxford, and Edinburgh; part of the second part, dealing with the Greek and Roman inheritance, is from the pen of a veteran Cambridge scholar, Sir W. W. Tarn, and another part, dealing with the Hebrew inheritance, is written by a Cambridge Professor, originally trained in Oxford, who has lectured and taught in several English and several American universities, the Rev. C. H. Dodd; the fourth part, dealing with the sixteenth and seventeenth centuries, has been contributed by one of the two British editors. The contributors of three other parts all come from the continent of Europe: Professor Ganshof, of the university of Ghent, has written the section on the Middle Ages; Professor Vaucher (one of the editors) and Professor Mornet, both of the university of Paris, have collaborated in writing the part on the eighteenth century; and Professor Vermeil, of the same university, has contributed the part on the twentieth century. An American scholar, Mr. Geoffrey Bruun, born in Canada of British and Norwegian ancestry, has brought the perspective of the New World to his contribution on the development of Europe during the nineteenth century. The range of the contributors is wide: the reader will judge the depth of their scholarship and the lucidity of their exposition.

Two other things remain to be said in conclusion of this preface. The first is that the work has been planned to meet the needs of students in the upper forms of secondary schools and in the early years of university courses. (It is the hope of the editors that the original English version may be translated into other languages, and that the work may thus come to be used in the schools and universities of many of the countries of Europe, and even outside Europe.) The second is that in the third and succeeding parts the contributors have sought to deal not only with the internal history of Europe, but also with the history of Europe overseas, or, in other words, with the expansion of Europe. The work is not a history of mankind. But it is, at any rate, a history of European man, and of his influence on the rest of mankind. This is not to say, for a moment, that it has a European bias, or that it attempts to vindicate a particular eminence for the continent of Europe over other continents. It would not be 'objective history' if it had that bias or made that attempt. It is just a record of Europe and the overseas growth of Europe, set down by a number of scholars of European birth or origin, with the intention of communicating to the youth of Europe, as dispassionately and as justly as possible, some sense of the inheritance of Europe and the spread and the influence of that inheritance.

Detailed reference to authorities and sources is excluded by the plan of the three volumes, but the great debt which they owe to the labour of others will be apparent to scholarly readers, and this obligation the editors and authors gladly acknowledge.

E. B.

G. N. C.

P. V.

NOTE

The original conception of this work was due to Sir Ernest Barker, who also took the initiative during the late war in carrying it out, and has throughout borne the heaviest share of the editorial burden. We think it right that these facts should be recorded here, and we take this opportunity of thanking Sir Ernest for all the generous help and kindness which we have received from him.

G. N. CLARK

PAUL VAUCHER

8 *April* 1952

CONTENTS

VOLUME I

I. PREHISTORY

by V. GORDON CHILDE

II. I. GREECE AND ROME

by W. W. TARN

II. II. THE JEWS AND THE BEGINNINGS OF THE CHRISTIAN CHURCH

by C. H. DODD

III. THE MIDDLE AGES

by F. L. GANSHOF

VOLUME II

IV. THE EARLY MODERN PERIOD

by G. N. CLARK

V. 1. POLITICAL, ECONOMIC, AND SOCIAL DEVELOPMENT IN THE XVIIIth CENTURY

by PAUL VAUCHER

V. II. THE DEVELOPMENT OF LITERATURE AND CULTURE IN THE XVIIIth CENTURY

by DANIEL MORNET

VOLUME III

VI. THE NINETEENTH CENTURY (1815–1914)

by GEOFFREY BRUUN

VII. 1914–50

by EDMOND VERMEIL

VIII. REVIEW AND EPILOGUE

by ERNEST BARKER

DOCUMENTS

VOLUME I

VOLUME II

VOLUME III

LIST OF PLATES

VOLUME I

VOLUME II

This is one of the four miniatures painted, not earlier than 1477 and not later than 1482, for Mary of Burgundy in a Book of Hours which originally belonged to her father Charles the Bold. In the foreground a lady is reading—we must suppose that this is a portrait of the Duchess herself—and we see how a great lady lived, with her lap-dog, her large pearls, her brocaded work-bag, and her vase of cut flowers. The open window gives not on a natural scene but on her thoughts: there she is kneeling before the Madonna, who sits, attended by angels, before the altar of a church. The vertical lines of the late Gothic building and the overarching vault form a canopy; but the windows of the apse recede into the distance.

In a spacious and expensively appointed room, such as were seen in Venetian palaces at the time when it was painted (1502–7), the saint is represented with the expression and attitude conventionally appropriate to one receiving an inspiration. No doubt he is composing sacred music, of which specimens are shown in the foreground. At the back is a recess with an altar and its vessels, and a mitre and pastoral staff, between two doorways of Renaissance design, through one of which various scientific instruments are visible. Among the

With this decoration Bernini, the dominant figure of Italian baroque art, completed, in 1661, the interior of St. Peter's, the rebuilding of which had been proceeding ever since the foundation-stone was laid for Pope Julius II in 1507. Above the altar a cloud holds up a 'podium' or balcony with a holy relic, flanked by colossal statues of St. Athanasius, St. Gregory Nazianzen, and the two bishops, St. Ambrose and St. Augustine. On these there looks down the massive papal throne of bronze, which encloses an ancient chair encased in ivory, believed to be St. Peter's. Higher still, framed in gilded clouds and sheaves of rays, and surrounded by a host of angels, the daylight from a window of golden glass shines about a white dove, the symbol of the Holy Ghost.

VOLUME III

LIST OF MAPS

VOLUME I

I. PREHISTORY

II. I. GREECE AND ROME

II. II. THE JEWS AND THE BEGINNINGS OF THE CHRISTIAN CHURCH

III. THE MIDDLE AGES

VOLUME II

IV. THE EARLY MODERN PERIOD

V. POLITICAL, ECONOMIC, AND SOCIAL DEVELOPMENT IN THE EIGHTEENTH CENTURY

VOLUME III

VI. THE NINETEENTH CENTURY (1815-1914)

VII. 1914–50

VIII. REVIEW AND EPILOGUE

VI

THE NINETEENTH CENTURY

(1815–1914)

By

GEOFFREY BRUUN
Sometime Professor of History,
New York University

INTRODUCTION

THE nineteenth century was the great age of European expansion. For 300 years, following the voyages of Columbus, Da Gama, and Magellan, the shadow of the European hegemony had been moving across the oceans. For ten generations hardy explorers, traders, and colonizers had been hoisting sail in the harbours of the Old World to lay the broad foundation for empires overseas. Not until the nineteenth century, however, when western science 'put a girdle round about the earth', did the Europeans come into the plenitude of their imperial heritage. Their aggressive superiority and spectacular conquests eclipsed all historical prologues, though limited precedents might be found, for instance, in the spread of Hellenistic culture after the fourth century B.C. But Hellenistic civilization was circumscribed by its Mediterranean environment, whereas the hegemony of the modern Europeans expanded until all the continents of the earth yielded them some form of advantage. Between 1815 and 1914 the world entered a new era of global integration under the compulsion of western technology, an era that might, without undue exaggeration, be termed the European age. Before the nineteenth century closed European civilization dominated or impinged upon every segment of the globe, and all important groups of the world's population had taken the imprint of occidental culture or endured its pressure.

For the peoples of Europe the period between 1815 and 1914 was an era of such remarkable progress at home that it half-blinded them to the ever widening influence of their economy overseas. It was a period unmarred by any long or seriously debilitating wars, a century during which the cumulative energies of Europe could be turned to constructive enterprises, and surplus capital and population could find profitable outlets in other continents. Each generation enjoyed an increase in wealth and comfort, a widening of economic opportunity, an improvement in the standards of nutrition, health, and sanitation. With each decade new advances in technology speeded the mechanization of industry, new cities reared their anarchic skylines, new levels of production were attained in the factories and the mills. But the most significant indexes of progress were neither political nor economic; they were demographic. Throughout the nineteenth century the population of Europe increased at an average of three-fourths per cent. per year, a ratio of growth never before sustained by so vast a population for so long a period.

This phenomenal growth of population was a major clue to the European supremacy. General estimates agree that the population of Europe in 1815 was about 200,000,000; the nineteenth century saw this figure more than double, to reach a total of 460,000,000 by 1914. Other continents also recorded an exceptional rise in numbers during the same span of years, but the Europeans did better than hold their own. In 1815 the people living within the geographical confines of Europe constituted perhaps one-fifth of the world total; by 1914 they constituted one-fourth. To realize the singular nature of this triumph it should be noted that all the rival continents had a higher general birth-rate than nineteenth-century Europe. The Europeans altered the demographic balance of the globe, not by raising their birth-rate, but by lowering their death-rate.

The figures for Europe alone, however, fail to suggest the full scope of the European achievement in population growth. Between the fall of Napoleon in 1815 and the outbreak of the First World War in 1914 more than 40,000,000 emigrants left their European homes to settle in other continents. The consequences of this vast migration made the Europeans in large measure an extra-European stock. In 1815 there were less than 20,000,000 people of European birth or predominantly European blood beyond the seas. By 1914 the total had multiplied tenfold to almost 200,000,000.

This increase and dispersal of the Europeans during the nineteenth century was a fitting reflection of their imperial mood. By 1914 there were as many people of European descent outside Europe as there had been inside Europe a century earlier. Or, to state the fact another way, by 1914 one European in three was living overseas. As already noted, the 460,000,000 people in Europe at that date comprised one-fourth of the world population. If some 200,000,000 people of European blood living abroad are added, it becomes clear that there were nearly 700,000,000 people of European descent in 1914. The racial stock of this smallest of the continents, including its emigrant sons and their descendants, had come to constitute one-third of the human race.

Statistics such as these make it clear that a balanced chronicle of nineteenth-century Europe must transcend the narrow limits of the European stage. The major scenes of the drama were still enacted there, but the focus had widened to include a *magna Europa* beyond the seas. The day was definitely past when colonial annals could be treated as an epilogue to European events. The political ties that had once bound the New World to the Old were severed or slackened by 1815. Cities in the wilderness had grown to sovereign stature and become the nuclei of independent nations. Yet even the remotest frontier communities founded by European initiative knew themselves the offshoots of a living parent culture, as their nostalgic names so often testified. Their traditions and their techniques could be traced across the seas and down the centuries; their roots reached back to medieval monasteries that once dotted the expanding rim of Christendom; their defences recalled the Roman camps that marked the borders of an earlier *imperium*. By the nineteenth century the far-flung colonies of the Old World were rising to maturity as dominions or republics, but they were still the custodians of a common civilization and heirs of the European inheritance.

In the pages that follow the adventures of these European peoples overseas will be traced step by step with those of the Old World nations. The influence of Europe upon the world had been from the first an interdependent, a reciprocal process. As the Atlantic community evolved, European civilization became something vast and vague for which no satisfactory name could be found; but the spirit of this common western culture set the pattern of development in regions even more remote, in South Africa, Australasia, and the Far East. Upon Europe itself the exportation of ideas and techniques, of capital and population, had a continuous and increasing effect throughout the nineteenth century. The heavy investment of European capital helped to develop the resources of other continents and made Europe in a sense 'the world's banker', while the competition of the European powers for concessions and territory in Africa and Asia sometimes intensified local European tensions. The history of nineteenth-century Europe became a drama of rising pressures and competing policies that mounted to a climax within the framework of a precarious equilibrium. It was the fate of the twentieth century to inherit the violent and tragic denouement of these accelerating drives.

I

POLITICAL REACTION AND ECONOMIC PROGRESS (1815–30)

THE year 1815 rather than 1800 is the logical threshold to nineteenth-century Europe. The shocks of the French Revolution and the Napoleonic wars had cracked the rigid institutions of the old régime. When the tremors and the hammering subsided, the Europeans found themselves living in reconstructed quarters, half-ancient, half-impoverished, but with an ampler frame and more spacious corridors than the cramped architecture they had outgrown. The statesmen of the Restoration era, who repaired the shaken structure after Napoleon's fall, have been accused of planning for the past rather than the future of European society. It is a charge which liberal historians, wise after the event, often delighted to emphasize, but it is a charge that ignores almost entirely the mood and purport of the Restoration settlement.

For the reactionary statesmen who converged on Vienna in 1814 for probate of the revolutionary testament were neither antiquarians nor prophets; they were harassed diplomats bedevilled by the imperious problems of the present. Their object was to re-establish peace after a quarter of a century of arbitrary political engineering and almost incessant warfare; and they decided, humanly enough, that security might best be sought by invoking the counter-revolutionary principles of political immobility and dynastic permanence. Wherever old landmarks survived and could serve a useful purpose, they repaired them. But their basic aim was to restore not the injustices of the old régime but its remembered virtues, above all the benefits of stable government and the security of a state system in reasonable equilibrium.

Judged by these sober aims the diplomats who drafted the Vienna treaties were statesmen of ability. The general settlement that they devised was subsequently modified in detail, but for a hundred years it was altered within the orbit of their cautious formulas. The peace congress had been called, as its secretary Friedrich Gentz acknowledged, to divide among the victors the spoils taken from the vanquished, a delicate operation which it executed with due regard for reciprocal compensation and without unnecessary rancour or vindictiveness. After 1815 the great powers avoided an appeal to the sword for almost forty years; and when wars came they were wars for limited objectives, conflicts that could be localized and that were never permitted to reach ruinous and exhausting proportions. In spite of numerous defects the Vienna settlement can be seen in perspective as the portal to a century of progress, stability, and expansion. It opened the longest period unmarred by a general war that Europe had known since the Roman peace of the first and second centuries of the Christian era.

The pattern of European history after 1815 depended upon the interplay of three major factors, one political, one naval, and one economic. The political factor was the temporary ascendency of the four victorious powers, Britain, Austria, Russia, and Prussia. With France in eclipse these 'Big Four' were in a position to redraft the map of Europe in almost any form they could agree on as mutually acceptable. The second factor, equally significant in shaping any realistic settlement, was the naval supremacy of Great Britain. Nowhere on the globe was there a navy or an alliance of naval forces strong enough to defy the British mastery of the seas. The third factor, less obvious to most European diplomats, but potentially the most powerful of all as an arbiter of European destiny, was the mechanization of industry. The 'dark Satanic mills' were about to release their rhythmic energies, and the steam-engine was waiting to transform European economic life. To assess the influence of these three factors is far from easy, and the method adopted here will be to consider them individually in the order named.

The political reconstruction of the Continent was of primary concern to the governments of Austria, Russia, and Prussia. Austria, four times defeated by Napoleon's smashing campaigns, showed a surprising power of recuperation; and the selection of Vienna for the peace congress was a tribute to this revived prestige. The choice was also a tribute to the enterprise of Klemens von Metternich, the Austrian foreign minister, who displayed his social and diplomatic talents as cicerone to the assembled delegates. Metternich believed himself predestined 'to prop a falling house', and he feared with reason that the Habsburg realm would disintegrate if the national and liberal tides stirred up by the French Revolution rose again to inundate Europe. The empire on the Danube had become an historical anachronism in an age of national states; for although its area and population made Austria a great power, its society remained feudal and aristocratic and its disparate segments included Germans, Magyars, Poles, Czechs, Croats, Italians, and several lesser minorities. Yet the tincture of tradition was strong, the dynastic pride of the Habsburgs even stronger, and the collapse of the French *imperium* left Austria the predestined champion of the conservative forces. When Vienna played host to Europe in 1814–15 the receptions were as brilliant, the music as seductive, the women as beautiful, and the prestige of the Austrian court apparently as unassailable as ever. The Habsburg empire entered its final century in the golden glow of a St. Martin's summer that seemed like the return of spring.

Externally at least, Austria appeared little changed by the rude shocks of the revolutionary age. The distant Belgian provinces (the Austrian Netherlands) were permanently lost, but as compensation the Habsburgs kept the territories of the late Venetian Republic and the province of Lombardy. The Holy Roman Empire was not revived (that archaic fiction had been dissolved in 1806), but Austria assumed the lead in a new diplomatic creation, the German Confederation. This was a loose league of thirty-eight German states the governments of which sent delegates to a diet that met at Frankfort-on-the-Main. Hopes for more liberal institutions and a closer national union, which had fired many German hearts in the fervour of the *Freiheitskrieg*, were frustrated by this feeble compromise. Although the charter of the German Confederation promised 'a representative form of government' to the component states, Austrian pressure nullified this provision in action.

Prussia, like Austria, regained lost prestige at Vienna, and the territorial bargaining added part of Saxony and all of Swedish Pomerania to the Hohenzollern possessions. But the war efforts against the French had overtaxed the limited resources of the Prussian state, necessitating a decade or more of convalescence. So Prussia followed a cautious policy of retrenchment and recuperation after 1815, while Austria dictated to the lesser German states and set the tone of central European politics.

Russian interests were championed at Vienna by the Tsar

Alexander I in person. The personality of this 'crowned Hamlet' whom Napoleon characterized as a 'shifty Byzantine' baffled his contemporaries. It seemed incongruous that an autocrat of all the Russias should harbour genuinely liberal sentiments; yet Alexander had argued against hereditary monarchy with Napoleon, and he solicited information on the United States Constitution from Thomas Jefferson when the word republic was anathema to his princely colleagues. In the Tsar's heart the impulses of a humanitarian warred with the calculations of a statesman, and as late as 1820 he still dreamed of a liberal constitution for Russia. But the tug of tradition proved too strong, reaction triumphed, and after Alexander's death in 1825 his brother Nicholas I assured Metternich that no more flashes of mystical liberalism would confuse the eastern European horizon.

Tsarist Russia, like Austria and Prussia, had little to gain and much to lose if the revolutionary tide rose again. The hereditary monarchs at St. Petersburg, Vienna, and Berlin were tacitly united by similar interests and problems, for all had discontented minorities to control and all held segments of the dismembered Polish state. The 'fourth partition' of Poland, consummated at Vienna, allotted the lion's share to Russia, and Alexander created a constitutional Polish kingdom with himself as king. Since he also retained Finland, which his armies had overrun in 1809, and Bessarabia, which had been acquired from the Turks in 1812, Russia emerged from the revolutionary wars with more extensive conquests than any other continental power.

While the representatives of the 'Big Four' sat behind closed doors, subdividing Europe, the delegates of the secondary states haunted the antechambers. They knew that the fate of the smaller nations depended on two major issues: the desire to penalize those princes who had remained loyal to Napoleon overlong, and the desire to 'contain' France in future by blocking the likelier points of French expansion. Thus Denmark forfeited Norway, with its million inhabitants, to Sweden, the latter having possessed the foresight to desert the French cause early in 1812. Saxony, elevated to the status of a kingdom by Napoleon, lost two-fifths of its territory to Prussia. To block French expansion in the north-east three million Belgians and over two million Dutch were placed under the rule of William I of the house of Orange, to form the kingdom of the United

Netherlands. In the south-east a possible revival of French pressure was countered by guaranteeing the independence of Switzerland, and by strengthening the kingdom of Piedmont–Sardinia, where the house of Savoy was restored and granted the late republic of Genoa as an additional make-weight. Republics were definitely out of fashion with the peacemakers of 1815. Lombardy and Venetia became Habsburg provinces; at Naples a Bourbon claimant, Ferdinand I, was enthroned as King of the Two Sicilies; while in central Italy the papal states came once more under the temporal rule of Pope Pius VII. The principle of legitimacy likewise triumphed in the Iberian peninsula, Ferdinand VII regaining the Spanish throne and Portugal submitting to the house of Braganza.

The outstanding vindication of legitimacy, however, was the return of Louis XVIII to Paris, where he proclaimed his anxiety to re-weld the chain of time, broken by that 'fatal interlude', the French Revolution. The imperturbable Talleyrand, who had deserted Napoleon and rallied to the Bourbons, appeared at Vienna as the plenipotentiary of Louis XVIII, with legitimacy as his trump card. It would, he persuaded the 'Big Four', be a contradiction of principle to offer Louis XVIII a truncated kingdom: France must be restored to the Bourbons intact. The unexpected escape of Napoleon from his exile on Elba, and his brief recovery of power during the 'Hundred Days', proved that many Frenchmen were far from repentant, and this 'last flight of the eagle' stirred the Allies to a sterner mood. After Waterloo Napoleon was dispatched to St. Helena, French boundaries were further constricted, and an indemnity of 700,000,000 francs was levied upon the redoubtable and troublesome nation. But three years later, when it appeared that the Bourbon government was soundly entrenched, the armies of occupation withdrew, and France was permitted to join the four victor powers in a quintuple alliance.

Seven years after Waterloo the régime of Louis XVIII was offered a special chance to demonstrate its dependable conservatism. The Congress of Verona (with the British government dissenting) authorized Louis to send a French army into Spain to suppress liberal manifestations there and to buttress the shaken throne of that despicable Bourbon, Ferdinand VII. The pendulum of French foreign policy had travelled a full arc since the defiant day, thirty years earlier, when the First French Republic proclaimed a war against all kings. France was no longer 'the revolutionary nation', and the forbidden music of the *Marseillaise* seemed the fading echo of a fantastic dream. In 1821 Napoleon died on St. Helena. His son and heir, 'the Eaglet', raised in Vienna under Metternich's watchful eye, was the shadow of a great name, an unhappy youth destined to an early death. Legitimacy had triumphed, reaction was the order of the day, and Europe had apparently recovered from 'the poison of French ideas'.

Having vanquished Napoleon and re-established peace, the British, Russian, Austrian, and Prussian governments pledged themselves in 1815 to a twenty-year pact of friendship. Their spokesmen stressed their intention to preserve the peace settlement intact and to perpetuate the Concert of Europe through 'government by conferences.' At Aix-la-Chapelle (1818) the international machinery creaked, but it still functioned. But at the conference of Troppau and Laibach (1820–1) the British government was already at odds with its continental allies over the question of joint interference in the affairs of troubled nations. Metternich and his conservative colleagues were alarmed at the student agitation in German universities and the revolutionary outbreaks in Naples and Spain. Despite British dissent the governments of Austria, Prussia, and Russia endorsed the 'Troppau Protocol', declaring that any state that suffered a change of government through revolution would be excluded from the European Concert. When the three powers voted to intervene in Spain Britain declined to co-operate. George Canning, who had become British foreign secretary after Castlereagh's suicide (1822), withdrew England from the 'European Areopagus', and the Congress of Verona in that year marked the parting of the ways. Thus the Quadruple Alliance lost meaning before half its projected twenty years had passed, and the Tory government in London, hated by liberals at home, became the hope of liberals abroad.

This resumption by Great Britain of its traditional policy of isolation nullified the congress system. The exalted post-war mood of 1815 had evaporated already, and its most idealistic expression, the Holy Alliance proposed by Alexander I of Russia, was already dead. Alexander's messianic proposition to his colleagues, that 'the sole principle of force, whether between the said Governments or between their Subjects, shall be that of doing each other reciprocal service', had been accepted 'in principle' by most of his fellow princes, but it exerted no visible influence on their policies. By 1822 the remembered idealism and sacrifice of the war years had given way to the calculations and compromises of peace. Canning welcomed the return to a more realistic diplomacy of 'every nation for itself and God for us all', and Britain resumed an independent course in European and world affairs.

With this weakening of the European Concert the second factor listed earlier—the predominance of British sea power—became a decisive influence, especially when it operated against the conservative alliance. Within the heart of Europe the governments of Austria, Prussia, and Russia might work their will, but no state with a sea coast, or sea trade, or overseas colonies could ignore the British maritime pressure. Ferdinand VII of Spain learned this promptly when Canning granted conditional recognition (1822) to the governments set up by the rebellious Spanish colonists in South America, where the valiant labours of Simon Bolivar, the Liberator, and José de San Martin had established independent republics from Caracas to Chile. The conservative powers sympathized with Ferdinand's 'legitimate' claim to Spanish America; the Russian government offered him ships to carry a punitive force to the New World; but British aid to the rebels and British control of the seas made such an expedition impracticable. Trade with the new republics was already yielding the English rich rewards, and enterprising London bankers had found promising fields for investment in Latin America. They had no wish to see Spain reassert a rigid economic monopoly over its lost empire of nearly four million square miles and twelve to fifteen million inhabitants.

European colonial exploitation of the New World was at an end, and it was a New World nation, fittingly enough, that proclaimed this fact to the European cabinets. In his annual message to the Congress of the United States in 1823, President James Monroe declared it to be 'a principle in which the rights and interests of the United States are involved, that the American continents, by the free and independent condition which they have assumed and maintain, are henceforth not to be considered as subjects for future colonization by any European powers.'

The immediate incentive for this historic announcement was

a proposal from the Russian government to Britain and the United States suggesting that the three nations define their interests in the Pacific coast area of North America. But a more urgent motive inspiring Monroe was the fear that Spain, with the backing of the European alliance, might regain control over the South American republics that had so recently declared their independence. The political system of the European monarchies, the President emphasized, was essentially different from that of the Americas. 'We owe it, therefore, to candour', he wrote, 'and to the amicable relations existing between the United States and those powers to declare that we should consider any attempt on their part to extend their system to any portion of this hemisphere as dangerous to our peace and safety.'

This bold rebuke to the allied sovereigns by a fledgling republic would not by itself have blocked their intentions. The Monroe Doctrine became a cornerstone of United States foreign policy because it was reinforced by the might of the British fleet. Canning had, in fact, proposed a joint Anglo-American declaration, but the statesmen at Washington distrusted the British intentions. As issued, Monroe's message took the form of an independent gesture, important chiefly because of its later amplifications. The United States Congress passed no legislation ratifying it at the time, and the European powers affected to treat it with disdain. But the fact remained that Great Britain and the United States had both indicated their common, though independent, intention to preserve the liberty of the Spanish American republics. As an immediate consequence Spain forfeited all chance of regaining the colonial revenues that had so long sustained its failing economy. But there was a second result of much greater and more permanent significance. The exclusion of European pressure and European armies from the New World meant that for a century the United States was to be spared the cost of maintaining a large military establishment to defend its frontiers. The light taxes and the large measure of individual freedom that Americans came to prize so highly were not wholly the result of their free republican institutions. Rather, the development of those institutions was dependent upon the absence of strong and militant neighbours, and upon the security derived from political and geographical isolation. *Amerika, du hast es besser*, Goethe observed with his usual prescience, and he predicted a time when the New World nations would rival the achievements of the Old, and their argosies would glean the trade of both oceans through the severed isthmus of Panama.

Their freedom secured, the American republics were persuaded at first that they wished to live to themselves. 'In the wars of European powers in matters relating to themselves we have never taken any part', Monroe proclaimed, 'nor does it comport with our policy so to do'. But the severance of political bonds did not dissolve the cultural and economic ties that bound the Americas to Europe. By 1815 the United States had already waged several campaigns against the pirate fleets of Tripoli and Algiers in defence of its Mediterranean commerce; and ten years later the Mediterranean again captured American attention when the Greeks rose in rebellion against their Turkish masters. The creation of Philhellenic societies from Boston to Buenos Aires suggested that educated Americans had read Herodotus no less assiduously than their European cousins and were equally eager to identify the modern Greeks with the ancient Athenians and the Turks with the Persians. The cause of Greek independence made a powerful appeal to all men of classical training and of liberal impulses, a combination of sentiments certain to embarrass the conservative statesmen who were striving to hold Europe to a cult of immobility.

Metternich's first impulse was to let the Greek revolt burn itself out 'beyond the pale of civilization'. The Turkish sultan, Mahmud II, asked nothing better, and left his commanders in the Morea a free hand to make a solitude and call it peace. But the prolonged resistance of the Greeks won admiration throughout Christendom, and by 1827 Britain, Russia, and France had combined to arbitrate the six-year old struggle. When the Turks proved obdurate the naval forces of the three powers destroyed a Turco-Egyptian fleet in Navarino Bay, and in 1829 the treaty of Adrianople guaranteed the independence of Greece. The republic which the Greeks had proclaimed was subsequently transformed into a monarchy and a Bavarian prince crowned below the ruins of the Acropolis as Otto I, King of the Hellenes. Republics, it seemed, were still out of fashion. But a rebellion had been condoned, a government changed by violence, and a new national state created. Liberals took hope from this breach in the ramparts of conservatism, and the Greek revolt proved the opening tremor of a general political

The Battle of Navarino (1827)

eruption. One year after the treaty of Adrianople all Europe was ablaze with the revolutionary outbreaks of 1830.

The signal for this new series of popular insurrections came, aptly enough, from Paris. Louis XVIII had maintained a working balance between liberal and reactionary forces under a constitutional charter, but he died in 1824, leaving the throne to his stiff-necked brother, Charles X. Within five years Charles perpetrated a succession of blunders that recalled the ill-starred reign of James II in England. He sought to reward the old French nobility at the expense of the rising bourgeoisie, defied the Chambers by appointing reactionary ministers, and finally attempted a *coup d'état*, declaring the press censored, the Chamber of Deputies dissolved, and three-fourths of the electorate disfranchised. These ordinances of 26 July 1830 were Charles's last official edicts. Four days later Paris was in the control of an insurgent mob, the tricolour waved from Notre-Dame, and the king was in flight.

'Gentlemen, saddle your horses! France is in revolution again', exclaimed Nicholas I when word of the July days reached St. Petersburg. Metternich was less resolute. The news from Paris threw him into a mood of unwonted depression, and as Frederick William III of Prussia was as hesitant as ever the Troppau Protocol remained a dead letter. More imminent threats soon made joint intervention by the eastern powers a risky venture in any case, for the July revolution set off a chain reaction, igniting revolts in Belgium, Switzerland, Italy, the Germanies, and Poland. The Austrian, Russian, and Prussian governments could not afford to move into western Europe, where the liberals won and held important ground in the ferment of 1830–2. These liberal gains will be traced in the following chapter: they stretched out into the future. But in central and eastern Europe the weight of the past proved too heavy to lift, and the revolts of 1830 expired in bloodshed and frustration. All the major forces there, political, military, economic, and geographic, prescribed this negative outcome. After 1830 Europe was divided more positively than before into a progressive and a reactionary camp, into a western group of parliamentary governments and an eastern league of authoritarian monarchies. The main source of liberal strength was a powerful bourgeoisie; where no aggressive middle class could seize the reins of government the liberal drive collapsed.

It was logical that Britain and France should be the first powers to break away from the unenlightened rigidity of the Restoration programme. Britain forsook the European alliance in 1822 over the Spanish question. France defied the conservative monarchies in 1830 by a change of dynasty. Both nations were economically progressive; both had discarded the semi-feudal institutions and outmoded social distinctions of earlier centuries; both sympathized with less advanced neighbours who were seeking political emancipation and responsible government. There was, in the first half of the nineteenth century, a profound ideological conflict dividing liberal from conservative Europe, a conflict induced and intensified by the irresistible expansion of new economic forces. The peoples of north-western Europe, with the British in the lead, had developed institutions of representative government. But in central and eastern Europe the older system of monarchical despotism still fought to maintain itself; and the disposal of the national revenue, the command of the army, the censorship of the press, and the liberties of the individual remained in the hands of ministers who were responsible not to the nation but to the Crown. In the reactionary states of Europe the people remained subjects, in the liberal states they had become citizens.

Where the sceptre passed from an absolute monarch to a sovereign people the executive power devolved upon a ministerial cabinet responsible to a parliamentary majority. This political transition was the outward and visible sign of an economic and social revolution. It meant that the class structure inherited from the Middle Ages, the stratification of society into castes which set the privileged groups of nobles and clergy in opposition to the vast unprivileged majority, was yielding to an alternative class structure founded on a more dynamic economic system. The capitalist economy had created three new classes, a capitalist minority whose power and profits were derived primarily from investments, a 'middle class' dependent in part upon property and in part upon payment for services, and a proletarian majority whose members had almost no resources in land or savings and lived on wages. As the older privileged groups, the nobles and clergy, were supplanted and dispossessed, control passed to a new emergent aristocracy, the capitalists, who allied themselves with the upper bourgeoisie to establish a form of government that would safeguard their wealth and influence. The liberal philosophy that was formulated to justify this shift concealed an implicit contradiction, and involved a denial of justice that discredited the bourgeois synthesis. For the liberal creed preached the equality of all citizens before the law, but liberalism in practice too often concealed, behind a façade of democratic reforms, the concentration of the economic surplus in the hands of a narrowing minority. To hostile critics the evolution of the capitalist system appeared little better than the substitution of industrial serfdom for agrarian serfdom, and they insisted that government under the new régime remained what it had been under the old, 'the conspiracy of the few against the many'.

The rise of a capitalist economy in Europe may be seen as three consecutive phases of the same movement. The first period, from the close of the Middle Ages to the last years of the eighteenth century, was primarly an era of commercial capitalism. This was followed by an interval of about half a century during which industrial capitalism played a noteworthy part and many leading entrepreneurs increased their influence by investing their surplus wealth in the newly mechanized industries and in steam transportation. After 1850 the powerful role of the banks and financial agencies, which won a voice in business ventures through loans and the flotation of stocks, inaugurated the phase of finance capitalism that lasted into the twentieth century. It is obvious that no rigid dates can be assigned to mark the exact moment of transition from one phase to the next, but it is convenient to distinguish the forms that capitalist enterprise assumed in these successive periods.

The years from 1815 to 1830 fall within the period of industrial capitalism. As new inventions multiplied and the application of power revolutionized spinning and weaving, far-sighted factory owners made fortunes, and mushroom cities grew up around the mills. In seizing this golden opportunity British entrepreneurs enjoyed advantages that placed them half-a-century ahead of their continental competitors. The foreign export trade of Great Britain had trebled in the revolutionary period (1789–1815), and the profits were largely concentrated in the hands of men with the vision and initiative to ride the waves of the future. Iron and coal for an industrial civilization were available in England at convenient centres. The Enclosure Acts (over two and a half million acres were enclosed between 1802 and 1844) created larger and more efficient agricultural estates, but drove thousands of cottagers and small landholders to seek work in the towns, thus providing an abundance of cheap labour. British mechanics equalled and probably surpassed those of the Continent, and British capital was available to finance the new factories. In addition, Britain commanded raw materials, markets, and transportation routes. A dominant navy, an extensive colonial empire, and a merchant marine larger than all others combined, assured a constant influx of supplies and the ready export of manufactures to distant buyers. Lastly, to crown this unique combination of colonial, commercial, industrial, maritime, and naval leadership, Britain assumed the leading role in international finance, and London supplanted Amsterdam as the banking centre of Europe. By 1815 the Bank of England was the largest centre of deposit in the world, and when it resumed specie payments in 1819 its notes were the only negotiable paper that circulated throughout Europe at their face value in gold.

British economic leadership after 1815 increased the difficulties under which other European business groups laboured. France should have been an enterprising and redoubtable rival for world markets. But French commerce had been crippled by the long years of sea blockade, and did not recover until 1825 the volume of foreign trade it had enjoyed in 1789. French industry, free to exploit the European markets while Napoleon's power endured, suffered a sharp set-back with his fall, and could not compete favourably with the flood of British manufactures when peace unsealed the continental ports. French capital remained timid, French smelters still used wood, though coal was available, French manufacturers were satisfied with local customers when national markets alone could justify the installations and the investment required for large-scale production. The Revolution had cleared the ground, emancipated the bourgeoisie, abolished internal tariffs and bureaucratic obstructions. Yet France, a country of 200,000 square miles and 30,000,000 people (twice the area and population of Great Britain), could not meet the competition of English textiles or Russian wheat. French farmers and industrialists clamoured for more protection in order to hold their local markets, and then failed to meet even these limited demands. Lack of capital undoubtedly delayed the rise of large-scale industry in France. But a more alert and responsive government in Paris might have encouraged investors by limiting their liability and easing the law of bankruptcy, or have provided loans or subsidies to equip more efficient foundries and larger factories. In Belgium, where statesmen of greater vision directed the economic programme, the mechanization of industry made swifter progress, especially after the Belgians revolted against their forced union with the Dutch in 1830. While the French were still apathetic, Belgium led all Europe in railway construction, and the first lines were state enterprises, intelligently planned to stimulate trade and promote industry.

East of the Rhine the embryo industries produced by the age of steam faced the additional handicap of political separatism. For the Germanies still were divided into some thirty-eight fragments, and there could be no national market while this particularism endured. The advantages that would follow the adoption of a uniform currency, a uniform tariff policy, a uniform system of commercial law and weights and measures, predisposed the German business groups to favour political consolidation. When the reactionary settlement of 1815 postponed this hope indefinitely, the Prussian government took the lead in broadening the economic foundations for nationhood, despite opposition from Vienna and from some south German states. In 1818 all manufactured goods entering any of the scattered Hohenzollern domains were subjected to a moderate 10 per cent. *ad valorem* duty, while a heavy transit charge was imposed on merchandise passing *through* Prussian controlled areas. This economic pressure helped to persuade the governments of several adjoining German states that it would be advisable to enter the customs union. Within a generation the Zollverein included the greater part of north Germany, making the area a free internal market in which fiscal uniformity prevailed. All products entering this area were subject to the common tariff, the proceeds of which were distributed to the member states of the Zollverein in proportion to their population.

Outside the countries named—Britain, France, Belgium, the Germanies—the coming industrial transformation had carved few scars on the European landscape by 1830. Transportation and communication were still slow and costly, limited by the capacity of the stage-coach, the river barge, and the sailing ship. Four-fifths of the European people lived parochial lives in rural surroundings. Towns had outgrown their ancient walls but not their quaint, half-medieval aspect. City skylines were still dominated by the church spires, visible leagues away in clear weather, 'all bright and glittering in the smokeless air'. Even in England, where industrialism was most advanced, the pall of factory smoke had not yet spread its darkening canopy, and the urbanization of society, that was to turn four Englishmen out of five into town dwellers within a century, still lay in the future.

How little the nascent energies of the industrial age influenced the thought and culture of the time is apparent from its literature and art. The poets and philosophers who influenced European thought most powerfully after 1815 were critical, as always, of the society of their day, but when they projected a better world they prophesied the shape of things to come almost exclusively in terms of their own bookish preconceptions. Few thinkers showed any genuine interest or deep understanding for the current economic trends, the new forces that were changing European culture, predominantly agrarian since its immemorial origins, into an industrial civilization such as the world had never seen.

Major intellectual currents in the Restoration era were confused by petulant whirls and eddies and the prevailing mood was one of widespread disillusionment. Temporarily, it seemed as if all the glittering generalities of the eighteenth century were tarnished. The rationalist quest for a perfect, workable groundplan for society had miscarried. The revolutionary dreamers who had clutched at a syllogistic paradise for a regenerated humanity were discredited. As the vision splendid faded into the light of common day, Wordsworth composed a nostalgic dirge for the bright, misleading dawn of 1789,

> In which the meagre, stale, forbidding ways
> Of custom, law, and statute took at once
> The attraction of a country in romance.

Like most of his generation, Wordsworth had been sobered by experience, and he accepted the Restoration settlement as a necessary compromise, a sensible *mariage de convenance* contracted above the grave of a dream. Shelley might still insist with rapt defiance that poets were 'the unacknowledged legislators of the world', but by 1815 they were legislators without a mandate. The peoples of Europe had to learn anew to put their trust in princes and in the prosaic administrators the princes approved. Reformers with a blueprint for Utopia found no patrons at the Restoration courts. 'To the dreamers', Metternich recorded with pompous superfluity, 'I have never belonged.'

An incurable distrust of journalists, especially of writers with adventurous ideas, infected the official circles of Restoration society. Monarchs no longer honoured knights of the pen who attacked social abuses, as Frederick the Great and Catherine of Russia had once honoured Voltaire and Diderot. On the contrary, outspoken critics of State and Church after 1815 found themselves in difficulties with the censors and the secret police, and liberal professors were driven from their chairs in the universities. Even in England the 'panic of the French Revolution' inspired the Six Acts of 1819, which restricted public gatherings, authorized the seizure of seditious or blasphemous articles, and subjected pamphlets to a heavy stamp duty. In the outcome such attempts to control the press and to silence criticism had little measurable effect, but they undoubtedly intensified the febrile and frustrated mood of many European intellectuals in this winter of their discontent.

The spirit of Romanticism, already quickening European literature and art in the last quarter of the eighteenth century, reached its apogee in the decades after 1815. No check imposed upon political insurgence could halt the Romantic revolt; on the contrary it seemed as if ardent souls, denied the opportunity to act their dreams, applied themselves the more intensely to dream their actions. Romanticism was a coat of many colours; it matched the uniform of no one political party; but it met the needs of a generation shaken from its conventional certainties by the impact of prodigious events. Great collective efforts like the French Revolution leave a vacuum in their wake. The European imagination, wearied by contemporary realities, sought escape in the idealized historical novels of Walter Scott, in the dramas of Schiller, in the lyrics, ballads, and romances of fantasy-haunted writers, from Coleridge to Manzoni and from Herder to Heine, who saw a light that never was on land or sea. It is customary to speak of the Romantic movement as a revolt against the sterile truths of science and the rigidity of classical formulas, and the dictum is true in that Romanticism spoke the language of the heart and repudiated artificial patterns in favour of 'unpremeditated art'. Historically, however, it is more important to note that although the aspirations of the Romantic writers often triumphed over logic and reason they triumphed over little else. The heroes of Romantic tragedy, like their poetic creators, sought a life beyond life and a love beyond love, and they found themselves condemned to a common fate: frustration. When an entire generation takes such frustrated heroes to its heart, the historian is forced to seek the answer in social conditions rather than in aesthetic aims.

Georg Brandes, the Danish literary critic, related this mood of defeat, of abdication, to the effects of the French Revolution, suggesting that the removal of social barriers left ambitious and impressionable youths without an adequate excuse for failure in their quest for fame. In revenge, they found a scornful solace in repudiating the unappreciative world they could not conquer. Such an explanation is inviting, but it does not go deep enough. The generation that survived the French Revolution had watched a supreme assault of the human spirit break itself upon the ramparts of social inequality. All classes agreed by 1815 (though for divergent reasons) that the Revolution had been a failure, and such universal disillusionment craved its sublimation. The flame of revolt still burned secretly, 'like a lamp in a tomb', knitting a million readers in a vicarious kinship with those superb and tragic rebels, from Faust to Manfred, who defied destiny and scorned the world's incomprehension. The true altar of the Romantic poets was not the temple of the muses; it was an icy peak in the Caucasus, and their god was a tormented Titan. The Romanticism of the Restoration era was a Promethean cult.

Like most protest movements, the Romantic revolt was stronger in emotion than in logic and it produced singularly few works distinguished by structural integration and completeness. No new philosophy emerged in these years to justify the political settlement. The most influential thinker of the age, Georg Wilhelm Friedrich Hegel, evolved a synthesis of ideas that served both radicals and reactionaries as an arsenal of arguments. All political groups were equally impelled by the urge to find a satisfactory principle of authority, but it was a quest in which none succeeded. In England, liberal intellectuals digested the chill utilitarianism of Jeremy Bentham. In France some rationalists still attempted to found a secular society on a universal substructure of natural law, but they were in discredit. Scant attention greeted Auguste Comte's *Plan of the Scientific Operations necessary for the Reorganization of Society* (1822), and this early approach to the problem of scientific sociology had to await a climate of opinion more favourable to its acceptance. Across the Rhine, Friedrich Karl von Savigny indicted the French Civil Code as narrow and mechanical, and denounced the effort to extract social postulates from natural law in his essay *On the Vocation of our Age for Legislation and Jurisprudence* (1814). But Savigny offered no satisfactory alternative, for he concluded that the time was not yet ripe for a system of legislation based on a sound philosophic study of historical development.

In this general search for a principle of authority that would justify governments in exercising sovereign power the champions of the Restoration Settlement proved no more successful than their antagonists. If neither natural law as revealed by science and reason nor historical tradition embalmed in ancient statutes could provide an acceptable basis for social control, there remained only the older concept of divine law expressed in the Scriptures and in the dogmas of the Roman Catholic Church. This theocratic foundation had buttressed the canon and civil law of earlier centuries and was still available for those who would put their faith in it. Joseph de Maistre reformulated the Catholic traditionalist position in successive works culminating in *Du pape* (1819), but as he made papal supremacy the central doctrine of his system neither Protestant nor Catholic monarchs were willing to endorse an argument that subordinated their authority to that of the Pope. At the other extreme in the range of Catholic political speculation stood Félicité Robert de Lamennais, who denounced the rationalists for their adoration of science as the source of all truth and progress, and sought to revivify religion by urging liberal reforms within the Church. His anomalous blend of ultramontane tenets with pleas for free speech and a free press embroiled him with his fellow clericals in France, and in 1831 he carried his appeal to Rome. Pope Gregory XVI condemned his teaching, and Lamennais, defying the papal censure, thenceforth carried on his reforming efforts outside the Church.

A religious revival, a genuine spiritual quickening, touched all parts of Europe in these early decades of the nineteenth century, but the organized churches resisted rather than inspired it. Much of its strength was a carry-over from the humanitarian idealism of the revolutionary era, for humanitarianism was the only tenet of the revolutionary cult that survived undiscredited and undiminished. The Methodists in England, the Pietists in the Germanies, and the Society of Friends (Quakers) wherever they lived and worked, insisted on the need to improve social conditions, reform the jails and asylums, mitigate the penal laws, and abolish slavery and the slave trade. Antislavery agitation in Great Britain, which culminated in its abolition throughout the empire, owed much to the Christian zeal of the evangelical sects. Quakers and Methodists devoted themselves to many of the humanitarian aims that the legislation of the French Revolution had championed, but their humane programme was not an endorsement of the Revolution itself. On the contrary, the growth of the Nonconformist congregations, in England for example (where they came to include almost half the population), helped to inoculate the nation against revolutionary ideas. The rationalist assault had been delivered against institutions; the religious revival appealed to the conscience, and the popular preachers sought to regenerate society by converting the individuals who composed it. Where the Revolution had emphasized the rights of the citizen as the foundation of a just society, the religious revival stressed the duties of the Christian as the clue to the good life.

In their ultimate aims both the rationalists and the leaders of the religious revival were seeking a greater measure of social justice. Advocates of democracy saw it as the foreordained solution, arguing that when all citizens received the franchise governments would become truly popular because they would be truly representative. Across the Atlantic the principle that governments derive their just powers from the consent of the governed had already been firmly established by 1815, and democracy suffered no temporary set-back as in Europe. The faith that all adult (male) citizens should have a voice in choosing their legislators was vindicated in regular elections, and the rapid growth of population in the United States, from 8,000,000 in 1815 to 12,000,000 in 1830, demonstrated the practicality of popular republican institutions. The year 1828 brought the boisterous election of Andrew Jackson as seventh president, a notable triumph for the popular party that placed in the White House a son of the frontier whose heart was with the common people. In France the middle classes were gathering their forces for the overthrow of Charles X, and in England the period of Tory administration was drawing to a close. Repeal of the Test and Corporation Acts (1828) and the passage of the Roman Catholic Emancipation Act (1829) removed the civil restrictions and disabilities under which dissident religious groups had laboured. Throughout western Europe the forces of democracy were resuming their interrupted march, and the results were shortly to appear in the liberal victories of 1830–2.

II

LIBERAL GAINS AND ROMANTIC FRUSTRATIONS (1830–48)

THE French were no longer *la grande nation* after Waterloo; they were a defeated people saddled with an unpopular monarchy and sufficiently chastened to make the best of it. Every class and group, however, had a grievance. The old nobility and the higher clergy mourned their lost privileges. The middle classes distrusted the restored Bourbon dynasty and sought to hold and extend the legal and political gains the Revolution had brought them. A growing city proletariat demanded recognition and better living conditions. Chauvinists dreamed of a military revival that would regild the imperial eagles. The fact that these divided factions were held for fifteen years in a precarious balance did not augur that the old and the new France could be reconciled; it merely proved that momentarily the desire for order and stability overrode all other impulses. Throughout the Restoration period the Right and the Left, the Ultras and the Radicals, remained locked in opposition, manœuvring for advantage under a truce that neither accepted as permanent, while a group of moderates in the centre kept the system working. It was not a glorious period nor a memorable one, but it enabled the French people to recover from the exhaustion of war and to test the advantages of a limited, constitutional monarchy.

Charles X upset this restoration compromise by his refusal to play the limited role of a constitutional monarch. From his accession in 1824 he leaned steadily towards the Right, and when opposition mounted he attempted to distract the nation by dispatching a punitive expedition to seize Algiers (July 1830). This renewal of colonial expansion laid the cornerstone for later French empire in Africa, but at the time it failed to improve Charles's position or to appease the Parisians. Election returns presented the king with a defiant chamber that once again demanded the resignation of the unpopular Polignac ministry. Instead of yielding, Charles resorted to government by ordinance, dissolving the chamber, abridging the franchise, suspending the liberty of the press, and decreeing a new election. This violation of the charter (as the liberals understood it) provoked the Parisian populace to an immediate insurrection which the king had failed to provide against, and within three days he was in flight. The fate of another Bourbon had been settled on the barricades of Paris before the people of France could be consulted or even informed of the event.

It is significant that in this July crisis of 1830 the moderates counted until the last moment on a parliamentary victory to give them control of the ministry. They had no real wish for a revolution or a reversion to the discredited expedient of a republic, which was still associated with the Jacobin dictatorship. Swiftly rallying their forces, they nominated Louis Philippe of Orleans, head of a collateral branch of the royal house, to the vacant throne. These bourgeois politicians, who represented the propertied classes, dreaded the demands of an armed and victorious proletariat more than they feared the designs of a despotic king, and they manœuvred themselves adroitly into power between the opposing dangers. The middle classes welcomed Louis Philippe as a 'citizen king' who would reign but not govern, and they were determined to control the new régime by preserving their majority in the chamber of deputies.

In its outcome, the French Revolution of 1830 was less a revolution than a reaffirmation of the Charter of 1814. The charter was re-edited to eliminate ambiguous clauses and to redefine the French government as a limited monarchy, constitutional, representative, and responsible. The right to vote, though extended to 250,000 electors instead of 100,000, remained the prerogative of 'men of property', and this oligarchic group who possessed the franchise (numerically a mere one per cent. of the nation) spoke for France in terms of their own class interests. To placate the more radical elements of the populace the tricolour flag of the Revolution was substituted once again for the white flag of the Bourbon monarchy, and the ban on the singing of the Marseillaise was rescinded. At the same time, however, Louis Philippe made it clear that the July Monarchy would launch no revolutionary crusade against neighbouring states as the First French Republic had done. Reassured on this point, the European courts decided to recognize the new 'King of the French', and even Nicholas I of Russia addressed him as *Sire* although he declined to employ the more customary diplomatic greeting of *mon bon frère*.

The cautious foreign policy of the July Monarchy disappointed French republicans and chauvinists. Italian, German, and Polish revolutionaries who organized revolts in the hope of French support were likewise disillusioned. Outbreaks in Parma, Modena, and Rome were suppressed by Austrian troops. Agitation in the Germanies frightened a few princes into concessions, but firm counter-pressure by the Austrian and Prussian governments checked the liberal movement throughout central Europe, and by 1833 Metternich could congratulate himself that his system was 'triumphantly fireproof'. The Polish insurrection burned more fiercely, until internal divisions and lack of foreign aid doomed it, leaving Tsar Nicholas free to treat Russian Poland as a conquered country subject to martial law.

In Switzerland, the Iberian states, and Belgium, the reactionary powers could not intervene without risking war with France or Britain, and there the liberal groups improved their position. Most of the Swiss cantons established new constitutions by 1833, proclaiming the sovereignty of the people, the liberty of the press, and the equality of all citizens before the law. In Spain and Portugal disputes arose over the royal succession. England and France supported the Spanish regent, Maria Cristina, against her brother-in-law, Don Carlos, and the latter was sent into exile. Don Miguel, pretender to the Portuguese throne, shared the same fate after French and British pressure had set his niece, Maria II, on the throne in Lisbon. Both Iberian states were to be rent for years by civil strife, but liberals in general regarded the settlements reached there between 1830 and 1834 as victories for the western, constitutional powers. The reactionary governments of Austria, Prussia, and Russia, which favoured Don Carlos and Don Miguel, recalled their representatives from Madrid, while France and Britain entered into a 'quadruple alliance' with Spain and Portugal to preserve constitutional reforms.

The case of Belgium provided an even clearer test of strength between the absolutist (eastern) and constitutional (western) bloc. Unhappy in their forced alliance with the Dutch, decreed by the Congress of Vienna, the Belgian liberals rose in rebellion when they learned that the Parisians had dethroned Charles X. William I of the United Netherlands was extremely reluctant to lose half his kingdom, but the absolutist governments failed to aid him with military forces while the western powers supported the Belgian secessionists, and these circumstances decided the issue. Belgium was established as an independent state, and Leopold of Saxe-Coburg (a German prince who had become a British citizen) accepted the throne and married the daughter of Louis Philippe. This settlement was a tacit recognition that the fate of Belgium depended primarily on the attitude of France and Britain. At London the ambassadors of the five great powers (Britain, France, Austria, Prussia, and Russia) acknowledged the independence of Belgium and guaranteed its perpetual neutrality. The new state took its place among the nations as a constitutional monarchy under a charter that proclaimed the sovereignty of the nation, the supremacy of the legislative over the executive power, and the extension of the franchise on a broader base than the English or the French people enjoyed in 1830. The right to vote was still limited to a minority of the Belgian citizens with the requisite property qualifications, but there could be no question that the forces of liberalism had gained one more victory. Nor could there be any doubt that the British fleet (which blockaded Dutch ports until William I yielded) and the French military forces (which expelled the Dutch from Belgian territories) had made the independence of Belgium possible.

The electoral reforms introduced in France and Belgium in 1830–1 were sober compromises; no group except the extreme radicals had seriously proposed that the ballot should be granted to all adult citizens. Yet the fact that the franchise could be broadened at all without precipitating a social revolution made 1830 a turning-point in nineteenth-century history. For two generations the governing classes of Europe had been haunted by the memory of 1789, and fear that the smallest concession to popular demands would prove an invitation to chaos made conservative statesmen and churchmen uncompromising opponents of political change. Even in England, where the need to reform the electoral system had been emphasized by the younger Pitt in 1785, the 'panic of the French Revolution' postponed the project for nearly fifty years. After 1830 it could be postponed no longer.

Two major groups were working to reform the British parliamentary system when the news of the July revolution in France arrived to quicken their hopes. Whig leaders wanted a redistribution of seats in the House of Commons, for the shift of population from the south-east to the industrial north-west meant that a number of declining and half-depopulated boroughs still sent members of Parliament while large cities of recent growth, such as Liverpool and Manchester, lacked representation. The spokesmen who championed the working classes had more radical demands. They wanted an extension of the suffrage that would give a vote to the factory hands and the farm labourers, thus enabling them to elect their own delegates to Westminster to secure remedial legislation. When these two groups joined forces the long rule of the Tory party came to an end, and in 1831 the Whigs won a clear majority in the House of Commons for the first time in half a century. The electors had voted for reform, but the House of Lords refused once again to pass the bill sent up from the Commons. Rioting spread dangerously, and the deadlock was not broken until the Whig leader, Lord Grey, obtained an assurance from William IV that he would appoint sufficient new peers to outvote the opposition in the House of Lords. The threat sufficed, and in June 1832 enough recalcitrant Tory nobles and bishops abstained from voting to permit the Bill to pass the upper house.

The Reform Bill of 1832 reflected the divided aims of the groups that had secured its passage. Fifty-six boroughs that had previously returned 111 members were disfranchised, and thirty-two others lost one member each. The seats thus made available were redistributed, twenty-two large towns acquiring two each, twenty-one towns receiving one apiece, while the county membership was almost doubled. Separate bills were adopted to remodel the franchise on similar lines in Scotland and Ireland, but the measures did not establish equal electoral districts or anticipate future shifts in population. Though Lord Grey insisted that the Bill was 'final' it was in reality a moderate compromise that bitterly disappointed the radical leaders who had backed the Whigs in the expectation of far-reaching reforms. The franchise remained the privilege of the few, for it was limited to householders paying ten pounds annual rental, with freeholders, copyholders, and leaseholders likewise subject to a ten-pound qualification. The actual increase in the number of voters throughout the British Isles was not great; the Reform Bill extended the franchise to some 813,000 voters where less than 500,000 had possessed it previously. Political power still rested in the hands of the wealthier classes, and the real significance of the new dispensation was that it shifted control from the agricultural and commercial aristocracy that had monopolized it since 1689 to the newer industrial aristocracy and the upper bourgeoisie. England remained an oligarchy after 1832, but an oligarchy in which the economic interests of the manufacturers had come to outweigh the agrarian interests of the landed class.

Proof that the centre of political power had shifted and that a new balance had been achieved could be read in the legislation passed by the 'reformed' parliament. The victorious Whigs emerged as the 'Liberal party' and the Tories came to be known as 'Conservatives'. An attempt by the king, William IV, to appoint a Tory prime minister in defiance of the Whig majority (1834) was promptly rebuked on appeal to the electors, and the principle was finally established that no cabinet could remain in power if it lost the confidence of a majority in the popular chamber. The accession of Victoria in 1837 opened the longest and most glorious reign in British annals, and the young queen was tutored in the responsibilities of a constitutional monarch by the Liberal prime minister, Lord Melbourne. Despite occasional friction, the new balance of political forces worked effectively and became famous as the Victorian Compromise. The two-party system remained the rule with Liberal and Conservative cabinets alternating at irregular intervals but dividing almost equally the sixty-four years of Victoria's reign.

In 1835 the Whigs consolidated their victory by the Municipal Corporations Act, which enabled the same urban electorate that had secured the parliamentary franchise three years earlier to dominate the local administration in the industrial cities. A more definitive test of the political and economic ascendency of the manufacturing interests came in 1846. Great Britain was moving steadily towards free trade, and import duties on many raw products and even on manufactured goods had been reduced or abandoned in deference to the demands of the business classes. But the country landowners, who formed the strongest group in the Tory party, clung to the import tariff on grains which enabled them to market their crops without undue fear of foreign competition. The Anti-Corn Law League, led by Richard Cobden and John Bright, assailed the Corn Laws as unjust on the ground that they kept the price of bread high for the benefit of the landowners at the expense of the urban consumers. When the Tory leader, Sir Robert Peel (who had headed the Conservative ministry since 1841), introduced a bill to establish free trade in grain he split the Tory party. But the Whigs supported the measure and the Corn Laws were repealed (1846). Free trade had won, and the repeal of the Navigation Acts three years later was a logical corollary. As the leading industrial nation in a world where agriculture was still the dominant form of economy, the British could maintain a more lucrative balance of trade and sell more manufactured wares if they accepted food and raw materials in exchange without hindrance. For Britain, therefore, the abandonment of import and export duties was a logical and profitable step. It was less easy to convince other peoples, especially nations with a nascent industrial economy, that they would gain by the same policy. 'Free trade', the aphoristic Disraeli observed pointedly in 1843, 'is not a principle, it is an expedient.'

Many British employers had supported repeal because it meant cheaper bread for their workers. Toward other social measures, that might war with their profits, they showed less enthusiasm. An inadequate bill to shorten the hours of labour in textile factories was passed in 1833. Labour conditions in mills and mines were often appalling, but it was a Tory ministry that introduced further reforms, sponsoring a mines act in 1842 and further factory legislation in 1844. The humanitarian impulses of the age often took odd and contradictory forms, as exemplified by the abolition of slavery in 1833 with compensation of £20,000,000 to colonial slave owners, while a simultaneous bill provided a modest £20,000 annually for public education in Britain. Reform of the poor-laws (1834) reflected the conflict between economic and philanthropic motives even more clearly, for it established such a harsh régime in the workhouses that it made pauperism appear a crime. Such, indeed, it seemed to many employers, who lacked workers and considered that all indigent persons capable of work should be persuaded to seek it by convincing them that they would find conditions in the workhouses worse than in the factories.

When the British labouring classes saw that the Reform Bill of 1832 failed to increase their representation or influence—that it had on the contrary entrenched their employers more firmly in power—they renewed their agitation. Some turned to direct bargaining, and as the Combination Laws that restricted workers' unions had been repealed in 1825, a Grand National Consolidated Trades Union took rapid form and claimed 500,000 members by 1834. The alarmed government struck back sharply, organizers received severe prison sentences, and the union collapsed. Popular leaders then reverted to political reform, and by 1838 they had drafted a 'People's Charter' which the radicals united in presenting to Parliament. The famous Six Points of Chartism seem innocuous enough today, but in the 1830's and 1840's they were too extreme to please a legislature dominated by the propertied classes. The Chartists demanded universal manhood suffrage, secret ballot, annual elections, equal electoral districts, salaries for members of Parliament, and the abolition of property qualifications for those who stood for election. Despite widespread support the Chartists won no substantial concessions. Their final rally, in the stormy days of 1848, so frightened the authorities that the government appointed 170,000 special police to check the demonstrations. But the Chartist agitation had more sound than fury, and when the last monster petition was rejected by Parliament the movement collapsed.

Chartism was less an organized political drive than a protest movement the vigour of which fluctuated with economic conditions. British prosperity and business expansion between 1820 and 1848 was so remarkable that few malcontents could seriously challenge the advantages that accrued to the nation under middle-class rule. By 1840 Great Britain conducted 32 per cent. of the international trade of the world, more than three times as much as France which ranked second with 10 per cent. Had the British working classes been stirred by powerful revolutionary sentiments they would have rebelled after 1845, when poor harvests caused widespread wretchedness throughout Europe. The country most direfully affected by the famine of 1845–6 was Ireland, where the potato crop failed disastrously. Thousands starved and more thousands emigrated from that most distressful country. Between 1740 and 1840 the population of Ireland had quadrupled, rising from 2,000,000 to 8,000,000, thanks in part to the introduction of the potato. In the seventy years after 1845 the population fell almost 50 per cent. to 4,334,000 in 1914. No other European country suffered such a catastrophic decline, and the falling birth-rate and mass emigration that half-depopulated Ireland in the later nineteenth century is the most telling indictment that can be urged against British rule in the island that had served as the earliest testing-ground for British conquest and colonization and proved the least successful.

While the French and British experimented with electoral reform and a wider franchise after 1830, the statesmen of eastern Europe looked on with doubt and disapproval. A little democracy seemed a dangerous thing to the sober bureaucrats of Vienna, Berlin, and St. Petersburg, and they were not surprised to see the workers of Paris and London riot for further concessions. 'The mob is now rising against the bourgeoisie', Metternich remarked with the melancholy satisfaction of one who has seen his warnings rejected and then vindicated. A government that followed the shifting moods of an unpredictable electorate could not, in his opinion, maintain a consistent policy in domestic or foreign affairs. He noted without surprise that the Anglo-French accord of the early 1830's soon deteriorated and the two constitutional monarchies had drifted close to war by 1840 because their interests clashed in the eastern Mediterranean. Six years later a new Anglo-French crisis arose when Louis Philippe betrothed his youngest son, Anthony, to the Infanta Maria Louisa of Spain. The British foreign secretary, Lord Palmerston, appealed to Vienna for support, on the ground that a union of the French and Spanish dynasties would violate the treaty of Utrecht of 1713. Metternich replied suavely that Austria had never recognized the more recent settlement by which the Spanish throne had passed to Isabella II instead of the male heir, Don Carlos. It amused him to see two parliamentary powers at odds over the anachronistic issue of a dynastic marriage, and he did nothing to heal their estrangement. Palmerston, however, was a dangerous man to bait. Piqued at Metternich, he retaliated by encouraging the Italian liberals, who hoped to drive the Austrians from northern Italy. Such trifling was highly dangerous to peace when the fires of nationalist and republican insurrection smouldered throughout Europe. By 1847 Metternich found himself on the defensive, while the British cabinet opened negotiations with the newly elected Pope, Pius IX, whose Italian sympathies and zeal for reforms aroused the deepest concern at Vienna. A *rapprochement* between the British government and the Vatican, if sincere, was a portent singular enough to startle the absolutist monarchs.

An unreasoning fear of all political innovations dominated the conservative courts. To outward view the solid front presented by Austria, Prussia, and Russia in the 1830's and 1840's made these three powers appear a triangular fortress, serene and steadfast in a disordered world. But internal weaknesses and the expanding roots of a new economic system were cracking their rigid institutions. In Vienna the death of Francis I in 1835 bequeathed the Austrian throne to the incompetent Ferdinand I, and the real power passed to a council in which Metternich and Kolowrat were the most active members. No efficient administration existed in the Habsburg empire; there was no ministry, only ministers; and subordinate functionaries remained shackled by antiquated routines and their own invincible indolence. Austrian society possessed notable charms and virtues, a spirit of paternal benevolence and filial piety, a tradition of leisure and gaiety and good manners. There was a quaint affectionate devotion to the Habsburg family, there was a cultured and elegant aristocracy with a sense of *noblesse oblige*, there was a heritage of lavish art and lilting music that formed a unique contribution to the pattern of European culture. But the historic statesmanship that had built an empire on a foundation of fortunate marriages forsook the Habsburg counsels in the nineteenth century, and the divergent national aspirations of Germans, Magyars, Slavs, and Italians undermined the imperial structure. No common mood of patriotism appeared (as in neighbouring empires) to create an Austrian nation, and the half-autonomous kingdoms, duchies, and counties seemed as loosely knit as oriental satrapies when compared to the unified and centralized government of nineteenth-century France. Even Metternich had been known to admit that 'Asia begins on the Landstrasse'.

Few organs existed in the Habsburg lands through which zeal for reform or popular dissatisfaction could legitimately express itself. The provincial estates represented the privileged groups; jealous of their pretensions the members resented advice from Vienna, and resisted appeals from below. Endless instructions were drafted and pigeon-holed—on the need for fiscal reforms, on the condition of the peasants, on the tariffs that stifled trade, on the discontent of the workers in the rising factories of Bohemia. In Hungary, where a few hundred magnates ruled with feudal complacency, the diet debated and deferred the projects of Stephen Szechenyi for legal and economic changes, for railroads to the west and steamboats on the Danube. The more radical demands of Louis Kossuth, who challenged the higher nobility, advocating a free press and a more representative parliament, brought him three years' imprisonment (1837–40). An awakening spirit of nationalism, intensified by the spread of Romanticism with its glorification of the historic past, quickened the desire for complete autonomy. Magyar superseded Latin as the official language in the diet, and literate Hungarians repudiated German to cultivate the beauties of their native tongue. These were the decades when German philologists prepared dictionaries on the popular dialects of Europe, making pedantry the servant of minority movements and history the handmaiden of national revolts. The Hungarian renascence and the Slavonic revival fed upon the folklore of the people, renovated by the scholars and romanticized by the writers. Literary circles became the focal centres of popular discontent, but the reforms debated there with passionate impracticability were too often intellectual extravaganzas void of substance. Meanwhile, the bureaucratic fortress at Vienna stood proudly aloof in its majestic inertia, the dust on its parchment folios unstirred by the winds of doctrine blowing through the salons.

In Berlin the governing officials displayed more competence and energy, for they had been trained under that famous Prussian system which the great Frederick had made a model of efficiency for the chancelleries of Europe. Unfortunately, the Hohenzollern bureaucracy was vulnerable at the apex: to function at its best it needed a monarch with administrative genius. Two centuries earlier the year 1640 had opened the patient constructive rule of the Great Elector; in 1740, Frederick the Great had commenced his brilliant and historic reign; but in 1840 a Hohenzollern prince with courage and tenacity was lacking. When the timid and reactionary Frederick William III died in that year, the crown passed to a Romantic mystic, Frederick William IV, whose unstable moods were to end in chronic insanity.

At the outset of his reign Frederick William IV raised unfounded hopes of reform among his more liberal and patriotic subjects. He charmed those about him with seductive promises and then disappointed them with repeated postponements. Behind his pose of pseudo-liberalism, his humane religiosity, lay a deep ancestral distrust of popular movements and parliamentary rule. His secret ideal of government was a despotism founded on persuasion; he released political prisoners and then denounced them because they failed to recant, relaxed the censorship and then restored it because the journalists criticized him. Destiny had prepared a leading role for Prussia in the drama of German unification, but Frederick William IV hesitated to march with the times, and the military strength and economic ascendency of the Prussian realm made it certain that German union could not advance if Prussia held back. Frequent admonitions from Vienna and St. Petersburg increased Frederick's irresolution, but in 1847 he suddenly startled his admirers and his critics by convoking the provincial estates of the Hohenzollern domains to meet as a United Landtag. Liberal and national hopes ran high; but at the opening session the erratic monarch announced that his royal prerogatives must remain intact and that he would never permit the delegates to arrogate to themselves the authority of representatives of the people. This contradictory attitude typified the dilemma of the German nation. Historically and geographically the Germans stood between two worlds, the despotism of the past and the democracy of the future, the autocracy of Russian Tsardom and the bourgeois constitutionalism of Britain, France, and Belgium.

In St. Petersburg Nicholas I, Tsar and autocrat of all the Russias (1825–55), was plagued by no such inward conflicts. The mood of his reign was set in its opening year when he crushed the ill-fated Decembrist revolt inspired by a handful of liberal-minded army officers. The Polish uprising of 1830–1 hardened him in his conviction that any tampering with autocracy was a bid for rebellion, and he abrogated the constitution that Alexander I had granted to Russian Poland in 1815. Nicholas had a barrack-room mentality, but he was not a blind reactionary nor an insensate martinet like his grandfather Paul I. He exercised his responsibilities in the mood of a conscientious disciplinarian. To ensure order he created the famous or infamous 'Third Section' of the imperial chancery, a special division of secret police organized to combat agitation and ferret out conspirators. Where legal and financial reforms promised greater efficiency he favoured them; the fiscal system was reorganized and a new code of Russian law promulgated in 1832. Criticism was curbed and liberal discussion silenced, even in the universities, but this censorship was relaxed in the sphere of technical education which made some notable advances. Mechanics and engineers were imported from western Europe, and the first Russian railway was opened in 1838. But the department of government always closest to the Tsar's heart was the army. It was the major bulwark of that 'Nicholas system' which, under the consecrated formula of Orthodoxy, Autocracy, and Nationalism, defended Holy Russia from attack and from the contamination of 'western ideas'.

No influential middle class of the western European type existed in Russia, no mercantile or industrial oligarchy wealthy and powerful enough to fight for constitutional reforms and a representative assembly with a responsible ministry. But the tides of the age had definitely turned against the old formulas of monarchical absolutism; it was sometimes possible to resist, as Nicholas I succeeded in doing, but lesser monarchs were forced to obey the pressure. In Norway the *Storthing* abolished hereditary nobility in 1821. Fifteen years later it demanded further concessions, and Charles XIV of Sweden (the erstwhile Napoleonic general, Bernadotte) yielded in order to preserve the union of Norway and Sweden, easing the Act of 1814 that yoked the kingdoms. In Sweden likewise the intelligent monarch acknowledged the need for change; the educational system was expanded and liberalized, and the diet won control over the national revenues and asserted the principle of ministerial responsibility. In Denmark Frederick VI (1808–39) and Christian VIII (1839–48) still refused to compromise their absolutism by the grant of a constitution, but in the Netherlands the headstrong William I alienated his subjects so completely that they demanded legal restraints upon his power. Rather than accept a limited monarchy he abdicated in 1840 in favour of his more popular and more open-minded son, William II (1840–9). In Greece an insurrection forced Otto I, King of the Hellenes, to grant a constitution in 1843. In Switzerland a prolonged conflict between the conservatives and radicals, complicated by the rivalry of Catholics and Protestants, ended in 1847 with the victory of the Protestant cantons. The *Sonderbund* (a union of seven Catholic cantons formed in 1845) was dissolved, and the unity of the Swiss Confederation reaffirmed. The outcome was a victory of progressives over reactionaries, of those who favoured a stronger centralized confederation over those who wished to preserve cantonal autonomy.

Outside the Continent of Europe the development of greatest moment for the European peoples in these decades was the continued expansion of the United States of America. Between 1830 and 1850 its population almost doubled, rising from some twelve million to approximately twenty-three million. More extraordinary yet was the territorial expansion of the young giant of the west. The Louisiana Purchase of 1803 and the acquisition of Florida in 1819 had doubled its area, from 888,811 to 1,788,006 square miles. Between 1845 and 1848 the area almost doubled again to nearly 3,000,000 square miles. This sudden growth resulted from the annexation of Texas, a war with Mexico, and a treaty with Great Britain. Since 1836 Texas had maintained its independence of Mexican control, and in 1845 the United States Congress, by a simple majority vote, admitted 'the Republic of Texas' to the Union. A dispute with Mexico over the southern boundaries of the new state led to war the following year. When an expedition under General Winfield Scott occupied Mexico City the Mexican government abandoned the unequal struggle, ceding all claim not only to Texas but to New Mexico, Arizona, and California.

The United States election of 1844, which installed James K. Polk in the White House with a Congress pledged to 'the re-annexation of Texas', had been waged with a second expansionist slogan: 'Fifty-four Forty or Fight!' For years the United States (under the vague definitions of the Louisiana Purchase) had advanced a claim to the Pacific coast area as far north as 54° 40′ north latitude, the point that demarcated the southern limit of the Russian territory of Alaska. Three European powers, however, still nursed claims to the Pacific slope of the North American continent. The Russians had founded posts as far south as California; Spanish navigators had explored the coast northward to Arctic waters; and the British advanced a title to all the coastal area north of the forty-second parallel. The Anglo-American rivalry was eased in 1818 by an accord that set the forty-ninth parallel as a boundary as far west as the Rocky Mountains, but beyond the mountains the Pacific coast from 42° northward was left open to joint occupancy. In 1819 the

Spanish government resigned its tenuous claim on areas north of 42° to the United States; and in 1824 the Russians limited their southward advance to 54° 40′. American settlers now migrated in considerable numbers to the Oregon territory (there were 10,000 in the area by 1844), and the joint Anglo-American occupancy became impracticable. The difficulty was resolved by the Oregon treaty of 1846, which extended the boundary between the British and American lands westward along the forty-ninth parallel to the Pacific at the Gulf of Georgia. This clarification formally incorporated an area of 285,580 square miles within the boundaries of the United States. Added to the Texan territory assimilated in 1845 (390,144 square miles) and the Mexican cession of 1848 (529,017 square miles) these gains brought the United States an additional empire of 1,204,741 square miles in the three years from 1845 to 1848. This was almost one-third of the total area of Europe.

It was natural that the success of the democratic experiment in the New World should attract the attention of the Old: the Americans were heralds of the future. 'It appears to me beyond a doubt', Alexis de Tocqueville declared in 1835, 'that sooner or later we shall arrive, like the Americans, at an almost complete equality of conditions.' Tocqueville was the most profound observer to visit the United States in the first half of the nineteenth century, and his masterpiece, *La Démocratie en Amérique*, became a classic of liberal literature. 'I confess that in America I saw more than America', he wrote. 'I sought the image of democracy itself, with its inclinations, its character, its prejudices, and its passions, in order to learn what we have to fear or to hope from its progress.' His liberal sympathies did not blind him to the faults and weaknesses in American society. He noted the hold that negro slavery maintained in the southern states and the disparity of economic development between the north and south. Within a century, he predicted, the United States would contain over a hundred million people, divided into forty states, and he concluded that, in these circumstances, 'the continuance of the Federal Government can only be a fortunate accident'. He admired the Americans, but he was often distressed by their vulgarity and appalled by their rapacity. 'Sometimes the progress of man is so rapid that the desert reappears behind him.' Despite their zeal for education and self-improvement the people of this new nation lacked a high intellectual tradition: 'America has hitherto produced very few writers of distinction; it possesses no great historians, and not a single poet.' But Tocqueville admitted the vitality and independence of the press and the vigour of public discussion. 'It is difficult to imagine the incredible rapidity with which public opinion circulates in the midst of these deserts.'

The republics of Latin America interested contemporary Europeans to a much feebler degree than the Anglo-American experiment in democracy. Observers could not penetrate the confused social castes nor comprehend the frequent political reversals that punctuated Latin American annals. The population south of the Rio Grande was of mixed origin, 45 per cent. Indian, 30 per cent. mestizos, 20 per cent. white, and 5 per cent. negro. The achievement of independence had not been followed, as in the United States, by the formation of a federal union; Bolivar's project for a great Spanish American confederacy had already miscarried before he died in 1830. Separatist movements and civil wars produced a score of jealous republics jostling one another for elbow room in a continent twice the area of Europe; and militarism and clericalism, negligible factors in North American society, remained constant forces in the politics of the Latin American states. The destiny thus decreed for the peoples of Central and South America largely isolated them from the world and from one another, but this segregation permitted them to develop unique cultural variations, offshoots of the European grafts on the ancient American Indian stem. The outcome was to be a rich flowering of original and sometimes exotic art and craftmanship, but it was delayed—or rather due recognition of its novelty and variety was delayed—until the twentieth century.

The exodus of the Europeans into the semi-void areas of the globe, which lured the North Americans to the Pacific, also gained momentum in other regions after 1830—in Canada, Australasia, and north-eastern Asia. The vast half-continent that was to become the Dominion of Canada held slightly more than a million people in 1830, but by 1848 the number had doubled. Antagonism between the French and British elements, and conflicts between the governing councils (members of which were appointed) and the popularly elected provincial assemblies sharpened to the point of open rebellion in 1837. The following year the Earl of Durham was sent from England as governor-in-chief to assess the causes of the discontent. His statesmanlike *Report on the Affairs of British North America* (1839) advocated the union of Upper and Lower Canada (Ontario and Quebec) and the establishment of responsible government. In 1840 the British Parliament passed the Act of Union, creating a single legislature for the two provinces with equal representation for each. Responsible government, though not specifically provided for in the Act, was achieved through successive precedents established in the ensuing decade.

British efforts to colonize Australia and New Zealand did not take positive form until the nineteenth century. The selection of New South Wales in 1788 as a place of exile for deported convicts deterred voluntary emigration, and only a few thousand free colonists arrived in Australia before 1830. But the profits of sheep raising and of wheat farming began to attract the adventurous, and after 1837 the transportation of felons was rapidly abandoned. Progressive steps towards colonial self-government were crowned by the Australian Colonies Government Act passed by the British Parliament in 1850, and the several states received the right to establish their own legislatures, expand the franchise, and adjust their tariffs. Tasmania, settled in 1803, was separated administratively from New South Wales in 1825, and later gained responsible government. The islands of New Zealand were not placed under British sovereignty until 1840, when the first shiploads of colonists arrived, and a constitution was granted the settlers in 1846. The almost unchallenged supremacy enjoyed by the British navy in the nineteenth century guarded the new and feeble colonies against attack by stronger powers, and British troops were available when needed to drive back the thinly scattered aborigines. Thus by the mid-nineteenth century, the continent of Australasia had become, in unspectacular fashion, a section of the British world empire. In their aggregate, Australia, Tasmania, and New Zealand exceeded 3,000,000 square miles, and were roughly equivalent to the recently expanded limits of the United States of America.

In yet a third continent, where sparsely scattered peoples could offer no effective resistance to European armies, the march of conquest and colonization proceeded inexorably in the second quarter of the nineteenth century. Between 1828 and 1846 the Kirghiz Steppe, a region stretching east from the Caspian Sea, three times the area of France, came under Russian domination. Still farther to the east and north, Russian military garrisons, convoys of prisoners condemned to hard labour, and thousands of labouring peasants built a route of empire to the Pacific between the fiftieth and sixtieth parallels of north latitude. Small, scattered outposts had been dotting this bleak Siberian wilderness by imperial ukase since the seventeenth century, and hardy fur traders had crossed the Bering Strait to Alaska in the 1780's. But the consolidation of this vast Russian realm in northern Asia required a permanent population. In 1850 a fortified settlement erected to guard the mouth of the Amur river was named Nikolayevsk in honour of the reigning Tsar, and ten years later Vladivostok, 'Conqueror of the East', was founded on the Sea of Japan. Russia was building bases that would project the Muscovite power into the Pacific Ocean.

In their conquering march through other continents the Europeans accepted their success as proof of the superiority of their institutions, their religion, and their culture. Yet it is doubtful if these advantages would have carried them far without the engines provided by a dynamic technology. The revolution wrought in transportation and communication by steam and electricity gave nineteenth-century expansion an irresistible momentum, equipping it with new nerves and new sinews. The triumphs of western technology, however, depended in turn on the development of a scientific mentality, and the influences that shaped the mind and spirit of western man were imponderable. In the scientific revolution instruments of precision were more important than instruments of power, and the most extraordinary intellectual innovation of recent times, 'the invention of invention', was no product of the machines. It presupposed a philosophical reorientation, a basic change of attitude and belief in the mind of the modern European. Throughout earlier ages philosophical speculation had proceeded from abstract premisses; it had developed as a part of a high intellectual tradition; it remained remote from mundane economy, much as man himself remained (in his own eyes) a special creation, in the world but not of it. The nineteenth century deserves to be considered the first century of the scientific age because its leading thinkers not only accepted the unity of the natural order, but also came to accept the fact that man himself formed a part of that order, subject to its laws and limitations.

The most helpful clue to nineteenth-century thought is this concept of *continuity*. Not merely historical continuity (a convenient argument against social revolution), but faith in continuity as a law of nature, affirming the existence of graduated, unbroken relationships throughout the world of experience. *Natura nil facit per saltum.* Divergencies or apparent discrepancies in the natural order could be reconciled (it was believed) by closer observation and more precise experiments. The aim of science was to bridge the gaps in human knowledge, working towards that synthesis where contradictories coincide.

Three notable conclusions in three separate fields, advanced between 1830 and 1848, helped to confirm this faith in the unity and continuity of nature. Sir Charles Lyell's *Principles of Geology* (1830–3) suggested that it was not necessary to invoke supernatural agencies or a succession of 'catastrophes' to explain the irregularities of the earth's surface. They could have been produced, Lyell submitted, by geological forces still at work, although this view assumed a much greater age for the earth than the few thousand years ascribed it by the chronology of the Scriptures. Thirty years were to pass before Lyell ventured to publish his conclusions on a more controversial subject, *The Antiquity of Man*, but by 1838 the researches of Matthias Jakob Schleiden already offered striking evidence on the unity of all living organisms. Schleiden stressed the importance of the nucleus in cell growth and the indispensable role of the cell as the fundamental unit in the structure of plants and animals. A third illustration of the economy and uniformity of nature was drawn, almost simultaneously, from the inorganic kingdom. Michael Faraday had shown as early as 1831 the possibility of electromagnetic induction. In 1840 the classical experiments of James Prescott Joule demonstrated the mechanical equivalent of heat in electrical and chemical change (Joule's law). The equivalence of heat and mechanical energy had already been elaborated mathematically by Sadi Carnot (1824), and the general principle of the conversion of energy, which came to be known as the Law of the Conservation of Energy, was summarized by Hermann Ludwig Ferdinand von Helmholtz in 1847.

It was understandable that problems of thermodynamics should fascinate a generation of scientists newly introduced to the efficacy of the steam-engine. The first railway—the Stock-

Early locomotives in Lancashire (1829)

ton and Darlington—was opened in England in 1825. Four years later the earliest railways built in France and the United States began operation. Once instituted, the progress of the iron horse was spectacular; by 1848 all northern Europe had been joined together by metal links, and it was possible to travel by rail from Paris to Hamburg, Dresden, Berlin, Warsaw, and Vienna. The electric telegraph, developed in practical form by the American inventor, Samuel F. B. Morse, between 1832 and 1844, proved invaluable in regulating railway traffic. On the oceans the advent of steam and steel brought changes of equal moment. Iron for shipbuilding was first introduced at Glasgow in 1818 and the first screw propeller in 1836. The first all-steam crossing of the Atlantic (by the Netherlands steamer *Curaçao*) came in 1826. The Peninsula and Oriental Line established regular steamship service from England to Alexandria in 1839, and the first important transatlantic steamship line was founded by Samuel Cunard in 1840.

With technological achievements so widespread and so remarkable proclaiming the efficacy of applied science, it might be supposed that the literary interests of the age would have taken a practical bent. But the opposite was true; the intellectual impact of the new inventions was delayed; and the European mentality in the second quarter of the nineteenth century revealed a curious dichotomy. Science, with its rational and positivist approach, failed to capture the popular imagination. Romanticism, with its emphasis on the emotional, the imaginative, the supersensuous, and the supernatural, dominated literature and the arts, and the western world gave itself over to the pleasures of idealization and fantasy. The Germans and the British had already yielded to the new mood in the first quarter of the century, but the Latin peoples, more firmly wedded to neo-classical traditions, succumbed less readily. The growing popularity of Shakespeare in France after 1820 was a portent (as it had been in the Germanies fifty years earlier) that tastes were changing, and the disputes that raged over the virtues of Victor Hugo's *Hernani* on its presentation in 1830 proved that the Romantics could hold their own against the Classicists. In the subsequent decades the autobiographical novels of George Sand gained an extraordinary popularity in France and abroad. Her coterie included leading exponents of the Romantic movement from almost every field—Alfred de Musset in poetry,

Balzac in fiction, Chopin in music, Delacroix in painting, Lamennais in religion. The Romantic spirit was at once egoistic and contagious, and its dominant drive was the urge to escape—into the anguish of a great passion, into far countries, into utopian dreams, into the past. Colourful historical romances had already become the most popular form of literature when Sir Walter Scott died in 1832. The more widely read historians of the age—Lamartine, Michelet, Macaulay, Carlyle—united the heart of the poet to the skill of the novelist. Victor Hugo's prolific output, that made him the undisputed monarch of Romantic literature for half a century, was a miscellany of poems, novels, histories, and political tracts, as rich in eloquence as they were barren in constructive ideas.

By the middle of the century every national literature of the western world had felt the impact of Romanticism, although Germany, Britain, and France remained the mainsprings of the movement. In Russia Alexander Pushkin produced masterpieces in the Byronic style, in Italy Alessandro Manzoni's *I promessi sposi* (1827) took its place among the world's great romances, and in Spain and Portugal poets turned to Romantic themes under the inspiration of the French and German lyricists. Across the Atlantic the Romantic movement found its most individual expression in the fantastic melancholy of Edgar Allan Poe's verse, and in his prose *Tales of the Grotesque and Arabesque* (1840). In the field of the novel James Fenimore Cooper and Nathaniel Hawthorne completed their best work before 1850, and Herman Melville's classic, *Moby Dick*, appeared in 1851.

The fascination that rustic scenes, lonely ruins, misty mountains, and stormy skies held for the Romantic eye was early apparent in the landscapes of Caspar David Friedrich in Germany and John Constable and J. M. W. Turner in England. Romantic painting in France was heralded by Jean Géricault and best exemplified in the canvases of Eugène Delacroix. The sculptors remained generally faithful to classical formulas through the first half of the nineteenth century—it was the era of Canova and Thorvaldsen—but in architecture the Romantic idealization of the Middle Ages inspired a Gothic revival. Ruined cloisters were rehabilitated; country homes were laid out with Gothic doorways and draughty baronial halls; and a battle of the styles developed between the protagonists of the

Gothic revival and of the Classic tradition. In England the outstanding triumph of the Gothicists was represented by the Houses of Parliament (1840), and in France by the numerous reconstructions undertaken by Viollet-le-Duc, including the Sainte Chapelle at Paris and the walls of Carcassonne.

The music of the European peoples reflected the dominant influence of Romanticism throughout the nineteenth century. Its first quarter was the era of Beethoven, 'the Shakespeare of Music', of Carl Maria von Weber's fanciful operas, and of Schubert's exquisite songs. In all three composers the poetry and passion of the Romantic spirit could be heard transcending the more formal structure and regularity of the Classical idiom. Their deaths, within a few years of one another (1826–8), marked the transition to the second period of nineteenth-century music, a period distinguished by the work of Mendelssohn, Schumann, Chopin, Verdi, and, finally and pre-eminently, Wagner. Richard Wagner's prodigious influence on the modern opera was not yet widely felt by 1848, but his relationship to the Romantics was already evident in the style and themes of his *Tannhäuser* (1845) and *Lohengrin* (1848).

No one who ponders the art and literature of the time can fail to note how over-stimulated and confused the European imagination had become as the nineteenth century approached its middle point. The exaggeration, the mysticism, the cloudy perspectives, and the utopian dreams of the Romantic writers intensified the general mood of ardent aspiration for unattainable ends. It was a mood that largely ignored the world of practical affairs, a mood that was certain, when it invaded politics, to inspire idealistic programmes and feed upon extravagant promises. With the tide of liberalism rising throughout Europe and the social currents quickening toward revolution, it was almost inevitable that the journalists and poets, who had composed so many songs before sunrise, would be the first to harangue the masses from the barricades and proclaim Utopia in the forum. A new order was struggling to be born, but its self-appointed spokesmen had little understanding of its inner forces. The upheaval that impended in 1848 was to shake all Europe, prodigious in its prophecies but disappointing in its results, a fitting drama to close an age of Romantic frustration. Its defects were implicit in its leadership and in its appellation: it was to be 'the revolution of the intellectuals'.

III
THE STRESS OF NATION-BUILDING
(1848–67)

IN 1848 as in 1830 the signal for a new wave of revolutionary outbreaks went out from Paris. Discontent had mounted during the 'hungry forties' in France as elsewhere, and the policy of immobility perfected by the government of the citizen king exasperated its critics. Yet the February revolution, deceptively swift and easy when it came, took the nation by surprise. On the 23rd of that month, crowds rioted before the home of the unpopular minister François Guizot; someone fired a pistol, the troops responded with a volley, and the demonstrators paraded the bodies of the dead through the streets to inflame the populace. Twenty-four hours later Louis Philippe abdicated, while the Chamber of Deputies proclaimed France a republic and appointed a provisional government.

From its earliest hours the Second French Republic was a house divided against itself; and it did not stand. The Right Wing in the provisional government (headed by the poet and historian Alphonse de Lamartine) desired a moderate middle-class republic. The Left Wing (best represented by the journalist and historian Louis Blanc) wanted far-reaching social and economic reforms. Both factions, moderate republicans and radical socialists, had united to overthrow the inert ministry of Guizot (yet another historian), but they could not unite to found a stable republic. In the first weeks after the coup of February 1848 Louis Blanc's influence appeared too strong to challenge; he was the author of a programme for a new social order which he had outlined in his *Organisation du travail* (1840), and he had a large popular following. Pressed by the working men of Paris the provisional government established national workshops to assure jobs for all, and created a commission to reconcile the interests of employees and employers. But Paris was not France. The moderate republicans, relying on the more prudent mood of the nation, hastened the election of a national constituent assembly, and it was chosen by universal manhood suffrage on 23 April. The outcome was a clear vindication for the centre and right; the moderate republicans could count on 500 of the 900 deputies. The second largest group were the monarchists; but they were divided into some 200 Orleanists, about 100 Legitimists, and a few Bonapartists. The Left Wing followers of Louis Blanc won less than 100 seats.

In this register of national opinion the fate of the Second French Republic was already prefigured. The political revolution had been accepted by the nation as a *fait accompli*, but there was no real support for a social revolution outside the workers' *arrondissements* of Paris and the larger cities. The socialist agitators refused to accept the verdict of the electorate or to resign themselves to an insignificant minority role in the Constituent Assembly. Raising the cry 'bread or lead', the Parisian proletariat staged a new insurrection (23–26 June), and the terrified bourgeoisie acclaimed General Louis Cavaignac temporary dictator with orders to subdue the populace. He succeeded; thousands died; and the dream of class reconciliation that had been proclaimed at the *Fête de la Concorde* a few weeks earlier died with them.

'The red fool-fury of the Seine', as Tennyson termed it, had been repressed once more, and the assembly turned its attention to a constitution. A draft was adopted 4 November 1848; it provided for a single legislative chamber and a president, both elected by universal manhood suffrage. Memories of the plebiscites that built a throne for the first Napoleon disquieted a few shrewd deputies; but Lamartine rebuked them. 'Let God and the people decide', he insisted. On 10 December Prince Louis Napoleon Bonaparte, nephew of the great emperor, was chosen president as nominee of the 'Party of Order'. Although largely unknown, save for his name and the fact that he had twice attempted to seize power by still-born military coups, he received over 5,000,000 of the 7,000,000 votes cast. Eight years earlier, when the ashes of the first emperor were entombed in the Invalides, Louis Blanc had warned France against a Bonapartist restoration. 'It would be the despotism without the glory, the courtiers on our necks without Europe at our feet, a great name without a great man, in a word, the Empire without the Emperor.' On 10 December 1848, the shadow of dictatorship fell across France, only a shadow as yet, but still ominous. Louis Blanc, however, was no longer present to repeat his warning; he had been driven into exile after the June Days.

History was to repeat itself, although, as Philip Guedalla has pointed out, the steps by which the prince-president retraced his uncle's course were less an example of historical repetition than of historical plagiarism. He reformed the ministry to secure a cabinet devoted to his own person; he discredited the legislators by appealing over their heads to the people; he revived martial hopes while insisting that he sought only the victories of peace. The constitution forbade a second consecutive term for the president, and after failing to secure an amendment Louis Napoleon and his intimate advisers prepared a *coup d'état*. It was sprung on 2 December 1851; leading journalists and deputies of the opposition were arrested in the night; a popular rising in the Faubourg Saint Antoine was crushed with considerable bloodshed; martial law was proclaimed in disturbed provinces; and Louis Napoleon announced that he had saved the liberties of the people. A plebiscite was held three weeks later, and the voters supported Napoleon (after the nation had been admonished that the alternatives were acquiescence or anarchy) by a majority announced as 7,500,000 to 640,000. On 2 December 1852, one year after the *coup d'état* and exactly forty-eight years after the coronation of the first Napoleon, a *senatus consultum* was promulgated establishing the Second Empire.

The political wheel had swung full circle since the early months of 1848, and the French people, recoiling before the vision of socialism and anarchism, had flung themselves into the arms of a strong man. Four years after the impatient Parisians had ejected Louis Philippe because of the negative results of his domestic and foreign policies, they found themselves subjected to a dictatorship founded upon authoritarianism, militarism, and clericalism. France had not passed through these vicissitudes alone. Half the states of Europe evolved in comparable fashion as the romance of 1848 was translated into the reality of 1850.

News of the February revolution in Paris traversed Europe with remarkable speed, as if the newly developed electric telegraph had linked the nerve-centres of the nations and led them all to make a common response. In Vienna, capital of reaction, a crowd stormed into the diet on 13 March and then swept on to the Hofburg, where five demonstrators were killed in a collision with the imperial guardians of order. The feckless Ferdinand I, baffled by the violence of his 'good Viennese', hastened to appease them. Accepting the resignation of Metternich, who left Austria, the emperor abolished the censorship, approved the formation of a national guard, and promised his subjects a constitution. But the revival of popular disorders in May alarmed him more deeply; he fled with the imperial family to Innsbruck; and a committee of public safety assumed control in Vienna.

Throughout the Habsburg domains spontaneous uprisings rent the empire apart. The Hungarian diet adopted an independent constitution (March Laws, 1848), and once again Ferdinand gave tacit approval. The Croats organized a national committee pledged to work for autonomy. The Czechs demanded a constituent assembly, and a Pan-Slav congress assembled at Prague. Then the tide of revolution and separatism was hurled backward as rapidly as it had risen. Prince Alfred zu Windisch-Grätz, commanding the imperial regiments at Prague, overthrew the revolutionary Czech committee and set up a military government (17 June). The octogenarian Marshal Joseph Radetzky reasserted Austrian power in Lombardy and Venetia, advancing from his bases in the Quadrilateral (Mantua, Peschiera, Verona, and Legnano) to win a signal victory over the Sardinian army at Custozza, 24 July. By October the victorious military chiefs were dictating Austrian policy. Baron Joseph Jellachich, governor of Croatia, joined Windisch-Grätz before Vienna; they bombarded and occupied the capital (31 October), and executed the radical leaders.

In the face of these reverses the hope of reform faded, and the springtime promises extracted from the irresolute emperor became straw fetters to be brushed aside by the batons of the victorious marshals. Radetzky urged Ferdinand to resign in favour of his eighteen-year-old nephew, Francis Joseph, who ascended the imperial throne untrammelled by any constitutional commitments. The chief minister of the young emperor was Prince Felix von Schwarzenberg, a forceful diplomat who promulgated an emasculated constitution by decree, and spurred the generals on to complete the reconquest of Hungary. By January 1849, the imperial forces had re-entered Budapest. The defiant Hungarian diet, meeting elsewhere, proclaimed Hungary a republic with Louis Kossuth as president, but the new régime had little chance to survive in the wave of reaction sweeping Europe in 1849. Its fate was sealed by Nicholas I of Russia who dispatched an army to complete its destruction.

The Hungarian forces were overwhelmed at Temesvar, on 9 August; Kossuth escaped to Turkey; but a number of Hungarian patriots, captured by the Austrian and Russian forces, were hanged or shot in sanguinary reprisals. The Habsburg empire had been saved from dissolution at a tragic price. Hopes for a healthy reorganization of the monarchy, embodied by liberal thinkers in the still-born Kremsier Constitution of March 1849, had failed, and absolutism reappeared, softened by a few social reforms. With successive attempts at repair, none of which healed its fundamental weaknesses, the empire on the Danube was to survive until 1918, just two years longer than its new emperor, Francis Joseph (1848–1916).

In the German states as in the Austrian lands Liberalism, Authoritarianism, and Nationalism clashed in 1848 with negative results, producing a confused, three-sided contest. There was, however, one essential difference between the German states and the polyglot empire of the Habsburgs. German nationalism was a cohesive, not a disruptive, force; it was working to create, not threatening to dissolve, an empire. When Berlin was shaken by riots in March 1848, Frederick William IV outdid himself with promises, pledging his word that Prussia would be 'merged in Germany' under a national constitution. Two months later a German parliament of some 830 delegates, chosen by direct manhood suffrage, assembled at Frankfort-on-the-Main. This Frankfort Assembly faced a gigantic, possibly an insoluble, task. It sought to devise a constitution and government for a united Germany while four vital issues remained unsolved. (1) Should the new German Reich include the German provinces of Austria (the *Grossdeutsch* solution favoured by the Left) or omit them (the *Kleindeutsch* solution)? (2) Should non-German or part-German areas such as Prussian Poland, Bohemia, and Schleswig–Holstein be incorporated? (3) Should the new imperial constitution provide for a loose confederation of states or for a strongly centralized federal government? (4) Should the new Reich be a hereditary monarchy or a republic based upon the sovereignty of the people?

While the Frankfort delegates wrestled with these grave and intricate problems the march of events forced decisions upon them. The population of Schleswig and Holstein rebelled against Frederick VII of Denmark, and the Frankfort Assembly commissioned Prussia to intervene with armed forces, a patriotic rather than a parliamentary solution. When the recovery of Austria made it evident that the Habsburg court would oppose any Germanic union it could not dominate, the Frankfort Parliament reverted perforce to a *Kleindeutsch* formula, excluding Austrian provinces. The constitution adopted 27 March 1849 proposed a Federal Reich with a national parliament, under a hereditary emperor of the Germans, and Frederick William IV of Prussia was elected to this office. His refusal to accept an imperial crown from a popular assembly dealt a final blow to the entire project and discredited the Frankfort Parliament. Many moderate deputies went home in discouragement, and a radical minority adjourned to Stuttgart where their violent sessions were finally broken up by the Würtemberg soldiers (June 1849). The parliamentary approach to German unification had failed.

Had Frederick approved the constitution drafted by the Frankfort Parliament, he would have tacitly recognized the sovereignty of the German people. The jealousy of the Austrian court and the opposition of his brother-in-law, Nicholas I of Russia, reinforced his own innate distrust of democratic movements. But he still hoped to see a Germanic bloc take form in central Europe, embracing both Hohenzollern and Habsburg lands. Schwarzenberg at Vienna preferred to reconstitute the feeble diet of the German Confederation in which Austria had played a leading role. In the test of strength between the Berlin chancellery, with its plans for a Prussian Union, and the Austrian court with its determination to restore the settlement of 1815, Nicholas I gave his support to Vienna. Rather than risk war, Frederick William yielded, the tentative Prussian Union was dissolved, and the diet of the German Confederation reestablished. Hohenzollern diplomacy had suffered a reverse commonly termed the Humiliation of Olmütz, and the Russian Tsar had proved in 1850 that he would oppose liberal trends in Germany as resolutely as he had fought republicanism in Hungary in 1849.

All the fervour, the fighting, the compromising and constitution-making of 1848–9 ended in central Europe with a virtual restoration of authoritarian principles. Liberal and national hopes had miscarried so completely that a profound bitterness and disillusionment swept German intellectual circles. Some ardent reformers, like the young Carl Schurz, emigrated to the United States, persuaded that the flower of freedom could not blossom on the poisoned soil of Europe. Others, who remained, tried to find consolation in the meagre gains that had been achieved. In Prussia a limited constitution, elaborated after 1849, provided for a bicameral legislature with the lower house chosen by universal manhood suffrage. But the voters were divided into three classes according to their tax-paying ability, and the two wealthier groups, although they constituted only 17 per cent. of the electorate, chose two-thirds of the deputies. This Prussian Landtag could approve new laws, but it could not choose the ministers of the king; and the latter could rule by decree when the parliament was not in session.

For patriotic Germans the frustration of national hopes was a sharper disappointment than the miscarriage of liberal aspirations. It is significant that a majority of the Frankfort delegates had revealed, often unthinkingly, their willingness to compromise democratic principles in order to promote national aims; their tragedy lay in the fact that they achieved neither. The legend was later to find general acceptance that 1848 marked a turning-point in German destiny, and that the defeat of the Frankfort programme delivered the German people over to Bismarck and the cult of national egoism. Yet it seems clear that national egoism was already a dominant force in 1848. However eloquently the middle-class leaders at Frankfort might denounce autocracy, their votes proved that they were ever ready to invoke authoritarian aid, whether to secure Schleswig–Holstein, to hold the Polish provinces, to conquer Bohemia, or to crush the rebellious Slavs. The radicals allied themselves with the Pan-Germans whenever it was a question of preserving scattered German communities from absorption by the non-German majorities in the border regions.

The judicious Heinrich von Gagern, president of the Frankfort Parliament, spoke the thought of the majority when he proclaimed; 'What unity must we seek? That we live up to the destiny laid on us in the east; that we embrace as satellites in our planetary system those peoples in the Danube Basin who have no talent for and no claim to independence.' Such denial of self-determination to others by an assembly that rested its own authority on a popular mandate disclosed a paralysing contradiction in ideals. For the peoples with 'no claim to independence' were in revolt; they could be held only by force; and force lay with the generals. By January 1849 even the radicals at Frankfort were ready to applaud a deputy who declared: 'I would cheerfully renounce all our theorems and articles to found a great, powerful, and dominant Reich, led by Austria and her great generals, Radetzky, Windisch-Grätz, and Jellachich. . . . Let us first found real power, and then establish freedom, which is impotent without power.' For 'Austria' it is necessary to read 'Prussia'—the speaker was citing the right script in wrong characters. Yet his intuition was unerring. The German generation that came of age in 1848 rode forth on a romantic quest to rescue liberty. They turned back to marry power.

In Italy as in central Europe the hopes of 1848 were darkened by the events of 1849. The deferment of Italian political unity was the more surprising because the Alps and the sea made the peninsula a geographical entity. 'Italy is one nation', Napoleon I had pointed out thirty years earlier. 'Unity of customs, language, and literature must, at a period more or less distant, unite her inhabitants under one government, and Rome will without doubt be chosen by the Italians as their capital.' All roads led to Rome, but in 1848 the Italians had not yet decided which one they would follow. Giuseppe Mazzini, exiled after the Revolution of 1830, had dedicated himself and his 'Young Italy' to the dream of a unitary, secular republic. Vicenzo Gioberti, likewise in exile, proposed a confederation of all Italian states with the Pope as president. 'Italy is the true head of civilization and Rome is the ideal metropolis of the world', he wrote in his *Moral and Civil Primacy of the Italians* (1843). To many Italian Catholics, Gioberti's plan offered the most promising solution to the 'Roman Question' because it was improbable that the Pope would resign his temporal authority on any other terms, or willingly see Rome and the papal domains absorbed into a secular territorial state. A third programme for unification, intermediate between the two, proposed the formation of a national, monarchical state with the head of the house of Savoy as king of a united Italy. This plan found favour with many liberal intellectuals and business men who realized that Piedmont–Sardinia was the most advanced state in Italy economically and that Charles Albert of Savoy was in the best position to drive the Austrian garrisons from their positions in the Po valley.

Italy was already seething with unrest from Milan to Naples

when the news arrived in March 1848 that Metternich had fled from Vienna and Austria was in the throes of dissolution. Spontaneous uprisings in Venice and Milan drove out the Austrian whitecoats, and at Turin Charles Albert, with belated zeal, ordered the Sardinian army to support the national crusade. Popular enthusiasm at Rome and Naples moved Pius IX and Ferdinand II to send detachments to harry the retreating Austrians. *L'Italia farà da se*, Charles Albert proclaimed, and a wave of patriotic enthusiasm swept the peninsula. But events swiftly proved that Italy could not 'do it herself'. Divided counsels, dilatory tactics, and growing rifts among the revolutionary factions paralysed the patriotic cause. The papal and Neapolitan columns were recalled in May, and Radetzky, rallying the Austrian forces, defeated Charles Albert at Custozza (24 July 1848). The Italian operations had been weakened by dissension from the first; and as the weeks passed the moderate revolutionaries became dismayed by the increasing violence of the radicals. At Rome a popular insurrection drove Pius IX from the city, and a republic was proclaimed with Mazzini as its moving spirit and the tireless knight of liberty, Giuseppe Garibaldi, as its defender. But Naples had already yielded to reaction, and French and Austrian armies were preparing to dispute for control of a still divided Italy.

The Austrians moved first. On 23 March at Novara Radetzky inflicted a second and more crushing defeat on Charles Albert, who abdicated in favour of his son Victor Emmanuel II. In April a French expedition disembarked at Civita Vecchia and laid siege to Rome; the republicans were driven out, and Pius IX returned cured of his liberal sympathies. In May Austrian reinforcements restored the Grand Duke Leopold to power in Florence, and in July a second Austrian force bombarded Venice until the cholera-stricken city surrendered. By the close of 1849 the revolutionary movement had been crushed; Mazzini and Garibaldi were once more in exile; the military ineptitude and lack of unity that weakened the Italian revolutionaries had been revealed to the world and the republican cause completely discredited. Despite the presence of a French garrison at Rome that stayed to guard the papal possessions, the Austrian influence had been restored in Italy as effectively as in the Germanies.

The developments of 1848–9 taught the same lesson in

various forms throughout continental Europe. When faced with the alternative, a majority of the people would endure despotism and militarism rather than embrace the cause of revolution. There was, however, a discernible shift in the centre of authority; absolute monarchy was changing by revolution or by evolution to constitutional monarchy; the power of the hereditary land-owning aristocracy was in decline; and the power of the bourgeoisie was rising—was already, in Britain, France, and Belgium, the dominant influence in the state. But the franchise still rested upon tax or property qualifications, political power remained with the middle and upper classes, and though they might dispute on occasion they wielded it jointly in defence of their common interests. The essential clause in the bourgeois constitutions of the nineteenth century was the sacredness of private property. When this clause was called in question the typical bourgeois liberal reacted like a typical conservative. He might defend political equality in theory, but he would not promote economic egalitarianism in fact.

The most unmanageable factor in the bourgeois-dominated society was the industrial machine, for the machine was not only multiplying the profits of the factory owner, it was also multiplying the number of discontented proletarians. To meet this growing menace the first half of the nineteenth century produced no satisfactory solution. Most social thinkers of that age who recognized the problem at all preferred to expound romantic cures rather than to cope with economic realities. Their 'systems' were intellectual exercises that failed in application and earned for their advocates the derisive title of 'utopian socialists'. Most ideological of these major prophets of a new order was François Marie Charles Fourier (1772–1837). Fourier urged the organization of individual communities (*phalanstères*) of 1,620 members, each participant labouring according to his aptitudes and inclinations so that none would feel constrained and a spirit of complete harmony would prevail. Fundamentally, the pattern he advocated was a form of agrarian communism; and although attempts to apply it failed in France, several experimental colonies on Fourierist lines were founded in the United States. More realistic, in the sense that he accepted the decisive role of science and industry in modern society, was the socialism of Claude Henri de Rouvroy, Comte de Saint-Simon (1760–1825). His ideal order provided for a new social system of three classes: priests, savants, and industrials. The priests were to be at once moral leaders, artists, and guardians of the (Saint-Simonian) dispensation. The savants were to be scientists, teachers, and philosophers. The industrials, the most numerous class, were to be employed and cared for under a regimen that approximated to state socialism. The weakness of these schemes, and of others, less noteworthy, that attracted attention in the decades before 1848, lay in their assumption that human passions could be harmonized, and social antagonisms could be healed, by a philosophic formula. They were panaceas for perpetual peace drafted by doctrinaires while the opposing armies formed their lines for a century of social conflict.

The fundamental cleavage in European society had ceased, by the middle of the nineteenth century, to be the historical distinction between a privileged aristocracy and priesthood and the great body of unprivileged commoners. It had become instead a cleavage between those with property and those without, between those who owned the machinery of production and those who worked it, between employers and employees, in a word, between the bourgeoisie and the proletariat. This class conflict Karl Marx and Friedrich Engels exaggerated in memorable and dogmatic phrases in their *Communist Manifesto* of 1848 and later elaborated in the three volumes of *Das Kapital* (1867–95).

> The history of all hitherto existing societies [they wrote, in 1848] is the history of class struggles. . . . Society as a whole is more and more splitting up into two great hostile camps . . . Bourgeoisie and Proletariat. . . . The executive of the modern State is but a committee for managing the common affairs of the whole bourgeoisie. . . . Let the ruling classes tremble at a Communistic revolution. The proletarians have nothing to lose but their chains. They have a world to win.
>
> Working men of all countries, unite!

The Communist League, an international socialist organization that had commissioned Marx and Engels to draft this defiant proclamation, was disbanded in the reaction after 1848. For decades militant communism remained a shadow without much substance; Marx himself had described it as a spectre; yet it was a spectre that haunted Europe thenceforward. With the appearance of the Communist manifesto the era of utopian socialism declined. After 1848 socialists found that a change had come over the spirit of their dream, and the middle classes grew more acutely conscious of the rising threat from below. The frightened bourgeois had seen the proletarians throw up barricades; the barricades had fallen but the memory lived; and sober men of property sought for surer methods to restrain the restless masses. The middle classes realized somewhat late that ideas were weapons in the class war, and that in weakening the authority of organized religion they had reduced the influence of the clergy, the 'spiritual gendarmes' who might have guarded the populace against the infection of 'social heresies'. Ruling groups, even in Protestant countries, turned a more favourable gaze upon the Catholic Church after 1848. The Papacy concluded new concordats with the governments of Spain and Austria; Louis Napoleon strengthened the influence of the Church in France; and Catholic hierarchies were re-established in England (1850) and the Dutch Netherlands (1853). After the outbreaks of 1848, as in 1815, governments labouring to restore their shaken authority recognized that religion was an efficacious antidote to that revolutionary malady which had proved so dangerously contagious.

Another and more effective antidote to popular discontent was the rapid improvement in economic conditions that came after 1848. The poor crops, the hunger, and the unemployment of the 1840's had fostered revolt; the business expansion of the 1850's brought more prosperous times and some of the benefit filtered down to the depressed classes. Emigration overseas, a ready barometer of economic distress, had quadrupled in the ten years before 1850, but after that date it declined from a peak of some 400,000 annually to approximately 200,000. The causes of business fluctuations remained something of a mystery, but a sufficient body of statistics had accumulated by 1850 to demonstrate that world trade was increasing with unexampled rapidity—it was to double on an average once every twenty years throughout the remainder of the century. Economic progress, however, remained subject to disconcerting leaps and pauses. One explanation offered for the sudden expansion in the early 1850's was the discovery of gold deposits in California (1848) and in Australia (1851) which increased the supply of monetary gold, the world total rising 5 per cent. per annum from 1848 to 1857. Britain led the economic advance, exports from the United Kingdom increasing by one-third between 1850 and 1855; but mechanization of industry also made notable gains in France, and spread from its older centres in Prussia and Saxony to all the states of the Germanies. The mining of coal, smelting of iron, and construction of railways proceeded with extraordinary energy, and manufacturers' profits were magnified by the heavy expenditures of the British and French governments resulting from their war in the Crimea (1854–6). After the war ended, the period of prosperity culminated suddenly in 1857 with a sharp recession that affected Europe and America simultaneously, the first financial panic that may truly be called a world-wide economic crisis. It was evidence of the growing interdependence of world markets and an omen of the increasingly severe depressions that were to follow periods of over-expansion in the future.

During thirty-nine years, from 1815 to 1854, the great European powers had avoided any armed clash among themselves. This long peace was shattered by the outbreak of the Crimean War in 1854, and the seventeen years from 1854 to 1871 brought five separate conflicts each of which involved two or more great powers. Following this militant interlude there was to be another unusually long period of peace, from 1871 to 1914, during which no first-class powers engaged one another in battle on European soil.

France and Britain blundered into war with Russia in 1854 through a series of tragic misunderstandings, the responsibility for which was shared by all the governments concerned. Fear of the Muscovite giant haunted the dreams of British statesmen throughout the nineteenth century, for Russian encroachments were a growing threat to the Turkish empire, to Persia, and to British control of India. When the rigid Nicholas System preserved Russia unshaken through the revolutionary years 1848–9 the Tsarist empire emerged with prestige enhanced by its apparent strength and stability. While France, Austria, and Prussia were distracted by internal disorders, Russian forces moved into the Danubian principalities (Moldavia and Wallachia). Although this occupation of territories nominally subject to the sultan was undertaken with the latter's consent, and the Russian troops were withdrawn in 1851, the British, French, and Austrian governments watched with disquiet the

Pitmen hewing coal in a mine (1871)

growth of Russian influence in the Balkans. To diplomats in London and Paris especially the events of 1848–9 brought a sense of discomfiture. The Second French Republic could not pursue a firm foreign policy because it was at best a provisory régime, and the British, with a powerful navy but a negligible army, could not easily apply pressure against the eastern European powers. Palmerston's efforts to intercede on behalf of the Danes, the Hungarians, and the Italian liberals were rebuffed, while Nicholas of Russia used military and diplomatic pressure to influence developments in central Europe. The long-standing opposition between the autocratic (eastern) bloc and the liberal (western) nations thus furnished a strong argument for Franco-British unity.

France and Russia had conflicting interests in the Near East, where both powers claimed the right to protect Christian minorities and Christian pilgrims in the Holy Land. With the establishment of the Second Empire in 1852 this dispute became sharper, but Nicholas believed he could afford to ignore French protests. Since 1833 (treaty of Unkiar Skelessi) Russian influence had been dominant at Constantinople, and Russian diplomats had reached secret accords with the Austrian and British governments for the ultimate division of the Ottoman empire. The Anglo-Russian agreement had been formulated when the Tsar visited London in 1844, and confirmed though not clearly defined in a memorandum drafted by the Russian chancellor, Carl Robert Nesselrode. In 1852 the Russian diplomats still counted upon British willingness to accept Crete and Egypt as compensation if Russia annexed Turkish territory in Europe, but this scheme for an Anglo-Russian settlement of the Near Eastern question collapsed suddenly and irretrievably in March 1853. Without warning, the British foreign secretary informed the Tsar that the (still secret) accord drafted nine years earlier was unsatisfactory. In this reversal of policy the cabinet at London was influenced by two major considerations, the continued evasiveness of the Russians regarding the disposition to be made of Constantinople and the Straits, and a sharp though indirect warning through Brussels that if French interests were disregarded in the Near East a French army would occupy Belgium as compensation. Placed in a situation where they must alienate Russia or antagonize France, the British cabinet made a swift decision, sending a naval squadron to join the French

Mediterranean fleet at the entrance to the Dardanelles. The two maritime powers then advised the sultan's government to defy Russian threats.

Nicholas felt that he had gone too far to retreat with dignity; his army was already massed on the Turkish border. By July 1853 the Russians had once again overrun the Danubian Principalities; attempts by the Austrian court to arbitrate the issue broke down; and in September the British fleet moved on to Constantinople. Encouraged by this evidence of support, the Turks declared war on Russia, the allied navies entered the Black Sea, and on 28 March 1854, France and Britain declared war on Russia. Nicholas then accepted an ultimatum he had ignored earlier, and his forces, which had already crossed the Danube, were withdrawn from the Principalities, ending the Balkan phase of hostilities. But the Allies were not ready for peace; they transferred the scene of battle to the Crimean peninsula where an Anglo-French expeditionary force laid siege to the Russian fortifications at Sevastopol. In December 1854 Austria joined in a defensive and offensive alliance with France and Britain, but refrained from hostilities, and the siege of Sevastopol continued with heavy casualties until the Russians evacuated the city on 11 September 1855. Nicholas I had died the previous March and his successor, Alexander II, was a man of more pliant character. A threat from Vienna that Austria would enter the war persuaded the Russian government to accept peace, and the terms of settlement were arranged at the Congress of Paris, 25 February–30 March 1856.

Few wars in history had revealed more confusion of purpose, more incompetence in command, more costly casualties, and more negative results. The sultan preserved his empire for the moment and made promises of reforms which he did not fulfil. The Russians abandoned their conquests and agreed to neutralize the Black Sea, but evaded these restrictions after fourteen years. The Principalities were placed under a joint guarantee of the powers which was modified within a generation; and Britain, France, and Austria promised to guard and maintain the integrity of the Turkish empire, a pledge they all found it inexpedient to keep. For this inconclusive result over a quarter of a million men had died of battle or disease. The Concert of Europe had broken down, in part because Napoleon III had hoped to force a general reconsideration of the Vienna Settlement of forty years earlier. Indirectly, however, the Crimean War helped to promote two developments in international affairs that must be accounted benefits, though these grew out of the conduct of the war and had no relation to its causes. By the Declaration of Paris (1856) the powers established international rules to govern maritime blockade, protect neutral rights, and abolish privateering. The sufferings endured by the soldiers also awakened wide concern, and this helped to bring about the formation of the International Red Cross, established in 1864 by the Geneva Convention. The conscience of the western world had been shocked by the dispatches of war correspondents on the Crimean front who revealed the misery to which the troops were exposed from the icy weather, gangrene, pneumonia, typhus, and cholera. The commissariat and medical services of all the belligerents had proved shamefully inadequate, and four-fifths of the war deaths were the result of disease.

In the later phases of their war with Russia the British, French, and Turkish forces had been supported by 10,000 soldiers dispatched by the kingdom of Sardinia. This north Italian state had no real quarrel with Russia, but Victor Emmanuel II and his astute minister, Camillo di Cavour, hoped to win Anglo-French gratitude and to bring up the Italian question at the peace table. These hopes were not realized at the Congress of Paris, and Cavour then concentrated on winning the aid of Napoleon III with whom he entered into secret negotiations two years later. The emperor promised that if Austria attacked Sardinia a French army of 200,000 men would cross the Alps and Italy would be freed 'from the Alps to the Adriatic'. Louis Napoleon did not intend to promote a united kingdom of Italy; the plan provided that Piedmont–Sardinia might annex Lombardy–Venetia, Parma, Modena, and the Legations; that Tuscany, the Marches, and Umbria would be merged into a central Italian state; that the Pope would retain Rome and the Campagna; and the kingdom of Naples would remain intact. The four political segments might then be joined in a loose confederation with the Pope as president. On 23 January 1859, the French and Sardinian statesmen amplified their accord with a military convention. As compensation for the assistance promised, France was to receive Savoy and Nice from Sardinia.

In its execution the initial plan rapidly outran Napoleon's calculations. Cavour successfully provoked Austria, and the governing group at Vienna obligingly provided a *casus belli* by opening hostilities against the Sardinian kingdom at the end of April 1859. The first major battle took place on 4 June at Magenta; the Austrians withdrew in defeat; and a second sanguinary engagement at Solferino on 24 June induced both leading belligerents to consider peace. Napoleon III was depressed by the slaughter, disconcerted by the movement for national unification that was sweeping Italy, and fearful that Prussia might join Austria and attack France directly. Without consulting his Sardinian allies, the emperor concluded a truce with Francis Joseph at Villafranca on 11 July. Cavour was anxious that Sardinia should continue the fight alone; he therefore resigned from office when the more realistic Victor Emmanuel accepted the disappointing peace. Lombardy was transferred to Sardinia, but Venetia remained under Austrian control. After plebiscites, and amid great popular enthusiasm, Parma, Modena, the Romagna, and Tuscany were joined to the Sardinian kingdom. In their eagerness to win all Italy the partisans of union then turned to Naples and Rome. Garibaldi, with his famous thousand, disembarked in Sicily, secured the island in a few weeks, and crossed to Naples where he was welcomed as a liberator. He was about to march on Rome when Cavour, who had returned to office, forestalled such a brusque solution of the Roman question, fearing it might bring the Catholic powers to the aid of Pius IX. Piedmontese troops entered the domains of the Church and dispersed a papal force at Castelfidardo, but they spared Rome and moved south to unite with Garibaldi's hot-headed volunteers and take the initiative from them. By the close of 1860 Naples, Sicily, the Marches, and Umbria had joined the new kingdom of Italy. It was formally proclaimed on 17 March 1861, with Victor Emmanuel as king and the Piedmontese *Statuto* of 1848 as a constitution.

The stupendous exertions of these final months had overtaxed Cavour. He died on 6 June 1861, consoled by the assurance that *L'Italia è fatto*. Italy was made, but it was not yet complete. Rome remained a papal city defended by a French garrison, and the whitecoats still held Venetia. It was necessary for the Italians to fight the Austrians once more in 1866 (this time with Prussia as an ally) before the ancient republic of the doges could be added to the new Italian kingdom. Rome was not entered until the French garrison withdrew in 1870, after which the troops of Victor Emmanuel breached the walls and Pius IX shut himself in the Vatican, his temporal sovereignty wrested from him by the secular power. These later events were epilogues to the essential drama of Italian unification which had reached its climax in the deciding years 1859–61. The forces of Italian nationalism had triumphed over Austrian antagonism and papal resistance, and three men of different character but equal patriotism had prepared the victory, Mazzini the soul, Garibaldi the sword, and Cavour the brain of the *risorgimento*.

The part played by the kingdom of Piedmont–Sardinia in forging Italian unity revived the ardour of those nationalists who hoped to see Prussia play a comparable role in the Germanies. There too Austria stood for separatism and particularism, and it was clear from the events of 1848–50 that Austria would fight to prevent the organization of a German federal state under Prussian leadership. The realistic statesmen at Berlin were ready to settle the issue on the battlefield, and they were determined that Prussia, unlike Sardinia, should 'do it herself', for the price of French or Russian aid might prove too high. In 1859, while he was still regent, the new Hohenzollern ruler, William I (1861–88), appointed Albert von Roon minister of war and Helmuth von Moltke chief of staff, with instructions to strengthen the Prussian army. The opposition of the liberal majority in the Landtag almost halted the programme in 1862, but William found a leader for his council of ministers who was prepared to override parliamentary objections. The man he turned to was Otto von Bismarck, an arrogant, adroit, and unscrupulous statesman, who frankly avowed his contempt for Austrian ineptitude and for parliamentary vacillation, and insisted that the great questions of the day would be decided by 'blood and iron'.

In 1864 the reorganized Prussian army received its baptism of fire during a short war with the Danes. Frederick VII, counting on British and Swedish support, had sought to incorporate the duchy of Schleswig into the Danish kingdom, a policy reaffirmed by his successor, Christian IX. The status of Schleswig and Holstein was extraordinarily complicated; both were possessions of the Danish crown, but Holstein was a member of the

German Confederation. Resorting to arms, Austria and Prussia defeated the Danes and occupied both duchies, compelling Christian IX to relinquish them (peace of Vienna, 1864). Austria proceeded to administer Holstein while Prussia took Schleswig, a solution certain to provoke difficulties because Holstein was virtually an enclave within Prussian territory, and the Zollverein (the Prussian-dominated customs union) had been expanded in 1853 to embrace all non-Austrian German states. In October 1865 Bismarck secured a promise from Napoleon III that France would observe neutrality in the event of a war between Austria and Prussia, Napoleon accepting vague assurances of 'compensations'. With Russia Bismarck had already established cordial relations (he had served as ambassador to Saint Petersburg from 1859 to 1862), and in April 1866 he concluded an alliance with the Italian kingdom which was to annex Venetia if Austria were defeated. These diplomatic preliminaries completed, Prussia precipitated war by moving troops into the duchy of Holstein (June 1866).

Austria appealed to the diet of the German Confederation, and most of the German states took the Austrian side. But the issue was decided in a few weeks by the rapidity and success of the Prussian military moves. Moltke shattered the Austrian army in Bohemia in a single decisive battle at Königgrätz (or Sadowa) on 3 July 1866. Prussian breech-loading rifles proved their lethal efficiency against the Austrian muzzle loaders, and Moltke's use of railways for troop transport revolutionized strategy. The timing of the Prussian stroke had been masterly; for the Austrians, who had vanquished the Italian army decisively at Custozza on 24 June, could have recalled sufficient forces to change the military balance in the north if they had been given a few more days.

Bismarck made peace as swiftly as he had made war. The Italians received Venetia despite their military defeat at Custozza and a naval defeat at Lissa. Before Napoleon III could revise his diplomacy to match events (he had counted on a protracted war and an Austrian victory) the treaty of Prague was signed on 23 August 1866. The German Confederation was at an end, and Austria was excluded from Germany. All states north of the Main river joined a North German Confederation under Prussian leadership, and the south German states were left independent. When Napoleon III claimed some measure of compensation for France, his ambassador, Vincent Benedetti, imprudently put the French demands for Luxemburg and Belgium in writing. Bismarck revealed this proof of French aggressiveness to the diplomats of the south German states, Baden, Würtemberg, and Bavaria, which thereupon joined the Zollverein and concluded military alliances with Prussia. In their new independence (and isolation) their fear of France was greater than their distrust of Prussia.

At Paris the consequences of the Seven Weeks War of 1866 excited anger and mortification. Sadowa, it was now admitted, had been a defeat for the French because they were not there. Napoleon III had been guilty of costly miscalculations, not the least being his estimate of Bismarck, formed in 1862 when the latter was ambassador to Paris. After frequent conversations he concluded that the tall Prussian was 'not serious'. Bismarck had shown more insight. He decided that the enigmatic nephew of the great Napoleon was a sphinx without a riddle, 'a great, unrecognized incapacity'.

The Seven Weeks War settled the major problems of German unification; subsequent developments merely confirmed and extended that settlement. The constitution of the North German Confederation provided for federal union in which the component states retained their own administration but the federal government controlled foreign policy and the direction of the military forces. The King of Prussia became commander-in-chief and President of the Federation; in the federal council (Bundesrat) Prussia controlled seventeen of the forty-three votes and could block amendments as these required a two-thirds majority. The lower house (Reichstag), which was elected by universal manhood suffrage, provided a concession to liberal opinion without threatening Bismarck's ascendency; for the chancellor of the North German Confederation was to be responsible to the king of Prussia, not to the Reichstag, and this key post Bismarck reserved for himself. His quarrel with the Prussian parliament had been healed at the close of 1866 when a majority of the liberals approved a Bill of Indemnity, thus giving assent retroactively to acts they had declared arbitrary and illegal but now applauded when they saw them crowned with success.

For the Habsburgs the Seven Weeks War meant the end of their historic role in Italian and German politics. More than this, it meant that the bureaucrats at Vienna must face the necessity of reorganizing the internal administration of the Habsburg empire. Autocracy, restored after the revolts of 1848, had functioned for a decade; but the Italian war of 1859 and the defeat of Königgrätz in 1866 discredited the régime at Vienna and the army that was its mainstay. Francis Joseph could no longer evade the fact that he must surrender some of his prerogatives and modify the fundamental laws of the absolute monarchy.

The Compromise (*Ausgleich*) of 1867 was the consequence. Since 1860 the young emperor had experimented tentatively with a shadow parliament, a Reichsrath, but the Hungarian deputies withdrew in 1861 and the Czechs protested that it was another 'Germanizing' move of the imperial bureaucracy. Some form of decentralization, of federalism, appeared unavoidable, but if all the national minorities in the Habsburg lands were granted local autonomy the empire would be transformed into a confederation of eight or nine segments. The solution Francis Joseph adopted preserved the dominant position of the German minority in Austria and recognized that of the Magyar minority in Hungary. Under the Dual Monarchy established in 1867 Hungary became an independent kingdom with its own capital, its own parliament, and its own ministry. The two halves of the empire were linked by the fact that Francis Joseph was Emperor of Austria and King of Hungary, while such common problems as foreign affairs, defence, and finance were adjusted through delegations from the two parliaments. Tariff and economic issues were settled by an accord between Austria and Hungary renewable every ten years.

The gravest defect of the dual system was its failure to placate the minority peoples, especially the Slavs. Czech patriots demanded indignantly that the ancient kingdom of Bohemia be re-created and granted the same semi-independent status as Hungary. The Slovenes dreamed of uniting with Croats and Serbs to form an independent Yugoslav kingdom. Italian-speaking residents of Trieste and Istria looked towards Italy, and Rumanian nationalists in Bukovina towards Rumania. These discontented minorities made it very difficult for Francis Joseph to introduce genuine representative government lest the Germans in Austria and the Magyars in Hungary be outvoted by the combined opposition. In Hungary the Magyars limited the franchise to less than one-twentieth of the population.

The Poles living under Austrian rule were less dissatisfied

than most of their fellow Slavs. They realized that the reconstitution of Poland as an independent state was an almost unattainable ideal, and as Catholics they found some compensation in the fact that (unlike their Prussian and Russian brothers) they were subjects of a Catholic monarch. Furthermore, Francis Joseph allowed them a small degree of freedom in managing their own affairs and permitted them to keep alive their cultural if not their national aspirations. But perhaps the shrewdest policy adopted by the Austrian government was to subordinate the Ruthenians to the Poles. To maintain this relative superiority and hold their own against the Czechs the Poles accepted their own subordinationto Vienna.

In Russia as in Austria military defeats shook the prestige of the autocracy and the army and brought fundamental changes in the system of government. During the decade that followed the Crimean War the new Tsar, Alexander II (1855–81), introduced a series of reforms, the most important being the abolition of serfdom. Nine-tenths of the Russian soil was still in the possession of the state and the noble families in the middle of the century, and on this land lived 47,000,000 serfs, bound to the soil or to personal service. After cautious preparation Alexander issued an Emancipation Proclamation in 1861. All serfs gained their personal freedom, and those on the soil received farmland to work for themselves. The imperial government assumed responsibility for the compensation paid to the noble landholders, and as free peasants the former serfs were to reimburse the government by redemption payments spread over a period of forty-nine years. The solution had inevitable defects, and some critics complained that the serfs merely exchanged masters, becoming serfs of the state until they worked out their long redemption. Despite objections, Alexander held on his course; and while his zeal lasted he introduced other courageous reforms, seeking the approval of the 'westernizers' who wished Russia to imitate the more advanced institutions of the leading European states. New courts of justice were established in 1862, education was fostered, and local assemblies (zemstvos) were promised to each provincial district, the members to be elected by indirect suffrage (1864). Unfortunately, the outbreak of a revolution in Poland (1863) daunted the Tsar Liberator, and as his ardour for experiments declined the Slavophils regained their influence. They had always considered the civilization of Holy Russia a unique culture, and they believed that Russian society should be left to evolve according to its own social and religious patterns, and should not have western traditions forced upon it. By 1867 the ideals of Orthodoxy, Autocracy, and Nationalism were regaining their influence and the hope of further reforms waned, but the Emancipation edict remained the most momentous event in Russian national life in the nineteenth century.

To Great Britain the middle years of the nineteenth century brought domestic tranquillity, increasing prosperity, and a world-wide prestige. The bourgeois fear of radical working-class movements abated after 1848, partly because the trade-union leaders showed themselves prudent and moderate in their demands. The workers gained concessions from their employers by direct bargaining, and the collapse of the Chartist Movement left them apathetic on most political issues. On occasion, however, working-class pressure made itself felt and influenced government policy. Throughout the American Civil War of 1861–5 British upper-class opinion tended to favour the Confederacy, but radical and liberal groups regarded the Union forces as the forces of democracy. Even when the blockade maintained by the Union navy cut off shipments of American cotton and starved the British textile industry, the unemployed spinners of Manchester remained loyal to the Northern states and the anti-slavery cause. Relations between Washington and London grew dangerously tense on several occasions, especially when warships built for the Confederacy in British shipyards were allowed to escape to sea. But the British cabinet resisted the suggestions of Napoleon III for joint Anglo-French intervention and preserved, though it did not always scrupulously enforce, the policy of neutrality towards both belligerents which it had proclaimed in May 1861.

The nationalistic fever that accompanied the struggles for Italian and German unity also had repercussions on British political life. Garibaldi received an enthusiastic popular reception during a visit to England in 1864. When the North German Confederation took form in 1866, with a Reichstag elected by equal, secret, direct manhood suffrage, the great English champion of parliamentary reform, John Bright, pointed out that in Great Britain the franchise was still denied to five men out of six. 'What is it that we are now come to in this country', he demanded, 'that what is being rapidly conceded in all parts

A spinning-mill in the country (Northern Ireland)

Stone-paved streets and housing in a Lancashire cotton town (Bolton)

of the world is being persistently and obstinately refused here in England, the home of freedom, the mother of Parliaments?' With Palmerston's death in 1865 the political reins were slackened, and Earl Russell, who succeeded him as prime minister, introduced a mild reform measure in 1866. But the bill was rejected, and a Conservative cabinet took office, headed by Lord Derby and Benjamin Disraeli. Popular agitation moved Disraeli to introduce a new bill designed to add 100,000 borough electors to the rolls, and he blandly accepted liberal amendments that quadrupled this number. Further clauses redistributed fifty-eight parliamentary seats, and the revised Bill was passed in 1867. Reform measures for Scotland and Ireland followed the next year, and the British people advanced another stride on the road to democracy. The number of electors almost doubled, for 2,448,000 possessed the franchise after this Second Reform Bill became law. Thenceforth not only the middle class but also a considerable portion of the working classes were directly represented in the House of Commons.

The British Parliament did not legislate solely for the 31,000,000 inhabitants of the British Isles in 1867: it directed the destinies of an overseas empire of 200,000,000. Government at a distance, even when it is exercised with moderation and prudence, has inevitable defects. Of all the British imperial conquests, the vast subcontinent of India was the most profitable, complex, troubled, and vulnerable. British authority over the Indian states remained anomalous; some of them were independent allies of the Crown, some were vassals, some were annexed territories in which the administration had passed into the hands of British officials. After 1848 the vigorous administration of the Earl of Dalhousie (governor-general from 1848 to 1856) brought many improvements in public works, highways, railways, canals, bridges, irrigation schemes, telegraph and postal service. Dalhousie also sought to modify some of the more inhumane social and religious practices of India, notably suttee which Christian missionaries had denounced. Such administrative interference with time-honoured customs, and the more resolute subordination of the Indian princes to British control, aroused a deepening resentment. During Dalhousie's term of office the Punjab, Oudh, and six lesser states were annexed; and the governor-general was criticized for this vigorous imperialism when he returned to England.

In 1857 a serious mutiny broke out in Bengal among the native Indian troops (sepoys). Within a few weeks it spread through the Ganges provinces and central India, threatening British control, but the rebellion lacked organization and capable leadership. The daring and energy of the small British garrisons available checked it by the end of the year with the aid of loyal Indian forces, and the rebels were punished with drastic severity. Most of the great princes had remained neutral, and the masses of India were scarcely stirred from their apathy. But the warning produced a change in British policy. The Mogul empire at Delhi was broken up; the Mogul was exiled and his sons put to death; and the proportion of British to Indian soldiers was heavily increased. The authority previously exercised by the British East India Company was transferred to the Crown under a new cabinet member, the secretary of state for India, and the governor-general became the viceroy. The programme of modernization, annexation, and missionary activity, which had helped to arouse the revolt, suffered a set-back, but British power in India was not materially reduced. On the contrary, the administrative officials learned much from the rebellion, and the Better Government of India Act (1858) helped to place British control on a more extensive and more adequate foundation.

Throughout eastern Asia the European powers, Britain, France, and Russia in particular, made significant gains in the period 1848–67. The British extended their influence in Burma while the French secured the three eastern provinces of Cochin China. Joint action by the two powers against China led to the occupation of the port of Canton (1858) and the sack of Peking (1860), the extortion of indemnities and trade concessions, and the legalization of the opium traffic. In the same years Russia induced the Chinese government to cede extensive areas east and west of the Amur river. In the Malayan archipelago the Dutch completed their subjugation of Bali (1849), extended their control in Java, and divided Timor and neighbouring islands with the Portuguese.

In the Americas the most critical development in the third quarter of the century was the civil war in the United States, the longest and costliest struggle that racked a great power between 1815 and 1914. For several decades before 1860 sectional differences between north and south had grown sharper. The north-eastern states of the Union were dominated by commercial and industrial economy, while southern society remained essentially agrarian, with many large estates controlled by a planter aristocracy and worked by negro slaves. Successive attempts at a compromise on slavery, and especially on the problem of its extension to newly formed states in the west, failed to avert the 'irrepressible conflict', and the inauguration of Abraham Lincoln as president (4 March 1861) was followed by the secession of eleven southern states with a white population of 5,000,000. The advantages favouring the North indicated a swift decision, for the twenty-three states that remained in the Union had a population of 23,000,000 and contained the major financial, manufacturing, shipping, and railway resources of the nation. A blockade by Northern naval squadrons crippled the South by checking the export of cotton and the import of arms, and Union forces seized several coastal key points from Cape Hatteras to New Orleans. By 1863 the North had also secured control of the entire Mississippi valley, severing Texas, Arkansas, and Louisiana from the Confederacy. The Confederate armies fought brilliantly and desperately under the command of Robert E. Lee, who remained the outstanding military leader of the war, but Northern superiority in men and materials ultimately brought victory to the Union forces under General Ulysses S. Grant in the opening months of 1865.

On 14 April 1865 Abraham Lincoln was assassinated by a Southern fanatic shortly after his second inauguration. His stature as a statesman had grown steadily throughout the war years, and he was destined to take rank with Washington in the memory and affection of the American people. His rise from humble origins, his gaunt and homely appearance, his command of an English style that could range from uncouth frontier humour to a majestic biblical eloquence, the rare combination of compassion, shrewdness, faith, humility, and greatness in his character made Lincoln an enduring symbol of the democratic idea. He passed into history at the moment of victory, the Union saved, the slaves emancipated by his proclamation. His successor, Andrew Johnson, inherited the bitter and exacting problems of the Reconstruction era and had to cope with war-bred passions and prejudices while these were still unassuaged. Johnson's earliest act, after the capitulation of the last Confederate forces, was to proclaim a general amnesty for all ordinary persons involved in the rebellion (29 May 1865). Six months later, a thirteenth amendment was added to the Constitution, providing that 'Neither slavery nor involuntary servitude, except as a punishment for crime whereof the party shall have been duly convicted, shall exist within the United States, or any place subject to their jurisdiction.'

The American Civil War was the first major conflict in which railways helped to decide the outcome and mechanized industry revealed its startling potentialities for war production. European military observers learned important lessons on the effect of rifled artillery (which rendered many existing forts obsolete), on the importance of sea power and naval blockade, and on the colossal problems of transport and supply that had to be solved when nearly a million men were placed under arms. The cost of the war in men and money also provided grim warnings, for the total casualties on both sides reached almost half a million; the federal debt increased forty-fold in four years; and the Southern states were left devastated and prostrate by defeat, with the bonds and currency of the Confederacy reduced to worthless paper.

It was a curious comment on the partiality of most European observers that they ignored almost completely a second and more lethal war that ravaged another American republic in the 1860's. The militaristic state of Paraguay, a nation of over a million people ruled by the ambitious dictator, Francisco Solano López, took up arms against Brazil, Argentina, and Uruguay in 1865. The resulting five years' struggle virtually annihilated the Paraguayan people. Though exact figures are unavailable, it is probable that the toll from battles, reprisals, disease, and starvation reached three-quarters of a million dead. By 1870 estimates placed the surviving Paraguayans at 28,000 men and 200,000 women, a disproportion of one to seven. The republic, stripped of manpower, wealth, and half its territory, never recovered from its staggering losses in the War of the Allies.

Throughout the greater part of Latin America the decades after 1850 continued the familiar record of border disputes, civil wars, and military coups. The problems of centralization versus federalism, dictatorship versus parliamentarianism, clericalism versus secularism, and peons versus landlords, found no stable or enduring solutions. The most nearly tranquil states

Abraham Lincoln

Karl Marx

were the empire of Brazil, where a scion of the Portuguese royal house, Pedro II, maintained order throughout a long reign (1840–89), and Chile, where democracy made moderate progress under liberal presidents.

The history of Mexico in these years included one brief and tragic chapter, influenced in part by the contemporary civil war in the United States. The picturesque dictator, Antonio López de Santa Anna, was swept aside by a group of liberal reformers in 1855, and a remarkably able organizer of Indian blood, Benito Juarez, assumed leadership. For three years (1858–61) Juarez waged the War of the Reform, aiming at the secularization of Church property, reduction of military privileges, and improvement in the condition of the peons. He was elected president of the republic in 1861; but his repudiation of foreign loans and investments led to intervention by a European power, which judged it safe to ignore the Monroe Doctrine while the United States was weakened by civil conflict. Napoleon III dispatched a military force, predominantly French, which entered Mexico City and set up an empire (1864–7) under a Habsburg archduke who assumed the title Maximilian I, Emperor of Mexico. With the collapse of the Confederate cause in 1865, the State Department at Washington insisted that the United States would not recognize Maximilian and demanded the withdrawal of foreign troops from Mexico. Napoleon III was alarmed by events in Europe (the Austro-Prussian War impended) and disappointed at Maximilian's failure to liquidate the thousand-million-franc debt owed by the insolvent Mexican treasury. Accordingly, French forces were recalled in 1866; Maximilian remained to be captured and shot (19 June 1867); and Juarez returned to power. This outcome proved that the United States was prepared to enforce the Monroe Doctrine, brought discredit upon the French, and left Mexico with the perennial problems of the Church question, the land question, militarism, and foreign debts still unsolved.

Like the Mexicans, the people of the Canadian provinces felt the indirect repercussions of the American Civil War. Canadian export trade to the United States rose rapidly during the years 1861–5, stimulated by war demands and by a reciprocity agreement previously concluded in 1854. When the United States abrogated this treaty in 1866, the dislocation of their economy threw the Canadians back upon their own market.

They were also disturbed by the Russian cession of Alaska to the United States (1867), by the military power of their southern neighbour, and by Irish-American groups (Fenians) who raided some Canadian border towns to bring pressure to bear upon the British Parliament to free Ireland. Realizing that a common policy among their scattered provinces would provide the best answer to the problems of defence, economic development, internal communication, and immigration, the Canadians decided to establish a federal government, and the Dominion of Canada was created by the British North America Act passed by the British Parliament in 1867. The promise that railway connexions would be established helped to draw in the outlying provinces; Nova Scotia and New Brunswick joined in 1867, Manitoba in 1870, and British Columbia in 1869. The government of the new Dominion of Canada consisted of a senate and a lower house with a governor-general to represent the British Crown. Canada thus took its place as the first self-governing dominion in the British Commonwealth, a new nation of more than 3,000,000 people, with an area (still partly unexplored) that was later estimated at 3,000,000 square miles.

Throughout the years 1848–67, in the Americas as in Europe, the impulse towards nation-building appeared and reappeared as the dominant political trend of the period. From the Hungarian revolt to the Paraguayan holocaust the most sanguinary struggles were an expression of this desire to found or to expand a nation state. Russian expansion in the Near East produced the Crimean War of 1854–6; the spirit of the *risorgimento* ignited the Italian War of 1859; national aspirations roused the Poles to revolt in 1863; the desire of the Danish monarchs to consolidate their realm provoked the Danish War of 1864; Prussian plans for the unification of the Germanies precipitated the Austro-Prussian War of 1866. The exasperation that drove the people of the southern section to secede from the United States in 1861 proved less powerful than the will of the majority of the nation to preserve the Union. Whether the demands for independence and expansion were frustrated by superior forces, as in the case of the Hungarians, the Russians, the Poles, the Confederate states, and the Paraguayan republic, or whether the will to unity triumphed, as in Italy, Germany, the United States, and Canada, this desire to forge or to preserve the nation state

PLATE 45

Laying the Transatlantic Cable (1865)

revealed itself as the most powerful and imperious impulse agitating the western world.

The second political principle that shaped the age, the principle of parliamentary democracy, advanced more hesitantly and within narrower confines. In Great Britain it made substantial progress; in Italy, the North German Confederation, and the Austrian empire representative government won a varying measure of recognition; in the Netherlands, Denmark, Sweden, Switzerland, and Greece, constitutional reforms curtailed the prerogatives of the rulers and increased the powers of the popular chambers. But in France the democratic republic of 1848 was transformed into a virtual dictatorship by 1852; and in Russia the autocratic régime was only slightly softened by the concessions of Alexander II. The two outstanding reforms of this era, reforms that altered the legal status of more than 50,000,000 human beings, were the emancipation of 47,000,000 Russian serfs and more than 5,000,000 American negro slaves. These were notable triumphs for which the growth of humanitarian sentiment had prepared the way. Slavery was abolished in the British colonies in 1833, in the French in 1848, in the Netherlands East Indies after 1863, and in the Portuguese possessions between 1858 and 1878. Latin American governments anticipated or followed the European example, Colombia by stages after 1821, Mexico (1829), Argentina (1853), Venezuela (1854), Peru (1856), and Brazil (1871-88).

The progress of western technology in the period 1848-67 was marked by significant improvements in communication, metallurgy, and military weapons, a fitting anvil chorus to an age punctuated by such frequent and expensive wars. Railway and telegraph lines branched out rapidly. The first electric submarine telegraph was laid from Dover to Calais in 1851; six years later a transatlantic cable was completed, but a permanent service was not established until 1866. Urgent demands for better and cheaper steel and gun metal led Henry Bessemer to develop a method for decarbonizing molten pig-iron with an oxidizing blast (1856). Ten years later the regenerative gas furnace, improved by William Siemens in England and Pierre Martin in France, extended the use of the open-hearth process and inaugurated a veritable age of steel. The first ironclad warship was built for Napoleon III in 1859, and the civil war in the United States provided the first effective test of naval armour-plate in the historic duel of the U.S.S. *Monitor* and the C.S.S. *Merrimac* on 9 March 1862. Improvements in weapons included the rifling of artillery and small arms (1855), and the invention of the repeating rifle (1860), the machine-gun (1862), and the first efficient locomotive torpedo (1866).

In the intellectual world the most momentous event of the age was the publication of Charles Darwin's classic study, *On the Origin of Species by Means of Natural Selection*, in 1859. Darwin's theory reinforced the naturalistic currents in contemporary thought and was destined to influence not only the scientific, but also the social, historical, philosophical, and religious speculations of the following generation. But a theory that related man biologically to the anthropoid apes was too repugnant and too revolutionary to win rapid acceptance, and the vast majority of people in England and elsewhere shared Disraeli's reaction when he declared in 1864:

> What is the question now placed before society with the glib assurance which to me is most astonishing? That question is this: Is man an ape or an angel? I, my lord, am on the side of the angels. I repudiate with indignation and abhorrence those new-fangled theories.

IV

SCIENTIFIC MATERIALISM AND *REALPOLITIK* (1867–81)

THE forging of Italy and Germany into nation states altered the map of Europe and shifted the balance of power. Falling almost midway between 1815 and 1914 this climax of nation building separated the nineteenth century into two halves, with the year 1867 as an approximate watershed dividing the new Europe from the old. But political and military crises were not the only evidence of a significant demarcation. There were profounder trends, less sudden and dramatic but more fateful, steadily transforming the European inheritance, and they gained momentum when the flurry of the mid-century wars had passed.

At first glance the later half of the nineteenth century seems to differ so sharply from the earlier that the contrasts are more significant than the continuities. By 1867 the national centralized territorial state had become the triumphant political scheme of the age; the older federal ideal was largely discredited; and the Concert of Europe had retreated into the limbo reserved for diplomatic fictions. A technological revolution was remoulding the economic foundations of European and North American society. Industry superseded agriculture as the major economic activity of the western world, and town dwellers came to outnumber and outvote the rural population. The new industrialism gave impulsion to a new imperialism, and factory production created the wares and the weapons that enabled great powers to compete for the trade of a shrinking planet. On all levels of western society the rising material prosperity was the accepted yardstick of progress, and the thought of the age yielded to the dogmas of scientific materialism and *Realpolitik*. The prestige of the priests and the philosophers dimmed before that of the scientists, and the unsubstantial pageant of the romantic sunset was followed by the cold dawn of positivist philosophy and realistic art.

In the fourteen years between 1867 and 1881 this new Europe hardened into the definitive political matrix it was to retain until the First World War. The salient fact in the new international pattern was the ascendancy of Germany. Throughout the first half of the nineteenth century four great powers, Austria, Russia, Prussia, and France, had dominated the Continent, while Britain stood apart; but after 1867 this quadrilateral balance of power was a thing of the past. The political unification of Italy (1859–61) added a new state which counted (in area and population at least) as a fifth great power, and the creation of the North German Confederation (1867) doubled the strength and influence of Prussia. For France the consolidation of Italy and Germany involved an ominous risk, because it meant that thenceforth two first-class powers would be wedged against the French frontiers where previously there had been only divided secondary states. The formation of the North German Confederation shifted the diplomatic and military centre of Europe from Paris to Berlin, and those who failed to read this lesson aright had it thrust upon their attention promptly in a dramatic and terrible fashion.

In the summer of 1870 the Spanish Cortes invited a German prince, Leopold of Hohenzollern-Sigmaringen, to mount the throne at Madrid. Two years earlier a liberal insurrection had driven out the incapable Isabella II and opened a period of experiment and instability in Spain which was not to end until Isabella's son assumed the crown in 1875 as Alphonso XII. The invitation to Leopold was a makeshift expedient, but when news of it reached Paris in July 1870, it excited profound dissatisfaction there. The counsellors who surrounded Napoleon III foresaw a Prusso-Spanish alliance, and the French ambassador to Berlin, Vincente Benedetti, was instructed to insist that Leopold should decline the proferred crown. This was arranged, but the accommodation failed to placate French resentment. Benedetti in an interview pressed William I for further guaranties and apologies, but without success. Bismarck published an account of the interview in brusque phrases (the Ems telegram) that sharpened the antagonism on both sides, and the French council of ministers decided that Prussia must be humiliated even if it meant war. Relying upon unfounded assurances of Austrian and Italian aid the chambers supported a declaration of hostilities (19 July) while the Parisian crowds shouted 'On to Berlin'.

The Franco-Prussian War lasted six months and proved a shattering defeat for the French. No help came from Italy; the government of Victor Emmanuel seized the opportunity created

PLATE 46

Execution of French Communards in Paris (1871)

by the withdrawal of French troops at Rome to occupy the Eternal City. The Austrians waited (as the French had done in 1866) until the chance for effective intervention had passed. The Russian court preserved a benevolent neutrality towards Prussia, and welcomed the diversion created by the discomfiture of France because it permitted Russia to throw off the restrictions imposed by the treaty of Paris fourteen years earlier and to refortify the Black Sea bases. In London the Liberal cabinet headed by Gladstone was satisfied with promises from France and Prussia that the neutrality of Belgium would be respected. Bismarck published the injudicious demands for Belgian or Rhineland territory that Napoleon III had pressed in 1866, a revelation that weakened any British sympathy towards France and rallied the south as well as the north German states to the Prussian cause. By 2 September 1870 Napoleon was forced to capitulate at Sedan with 100,000 men, while a second French army of 173,000 under Marshal Bazaine surrendered at Metz on 27 October.

The news of Sedan overthrew the Second Empire. In Paris Republican leaders, headed by the energetic Léon Gambetta, proclaimed a Government of National Defence. But the war was already lost, and heroic efforts to raise new French armies prolonged the fighting without reversing the decision. German forces surrounded Paris and starvation forced the city to surrender on 28 January 1871. Two weeks later a newly elected French National Assembly met at Bordeaux and voted for peace. By the treaty of Frankfort (10 May 1871) France ceded Alsace and part of Lorraine, and pledged herself to pay an indemnity of 5,000,000,000 francs.

The tragic events of 'the terrible year' were not yet over. Radical leaders in Paris denounced the 'reactionary' Assembly that had made a humiliating peace, and the Parisian National Guard refused to surrender its arms. The assembly, which had moved to Versailles, decided to subdue the rebellious capital, and Adolphe Thiers, elected Chief of the Executive Power, pressed the attack while the German victors looked on. There was no unity of aim or of command among the Paris Communards, and their resistance was broken after weeks of bloody fighting that ended in blind massacre and reprisal. By June Thiers had restored order in Paris at a cost of 10,000 to 20,000 lives.

The Third French Republic, born in an hour of national defeat, survived almost by chance the vicissitudes of its early period. For five years the assembly hastily elected in 1871 clung to power; a majority of the members were monarchists, but they failed to unite behind a Legitimist, Orleanist, or Bonapartist pretender, and a general election in 1876 gave the republicans a majority in the Chamber of Deputies. Three years later they won control in the Senate also. Marshal MacMahon (who had replaced Thiers in 1873) resigned, and the national representatives chose a safe republican, Jules Grévy, to succeed him. By 1879, therefore, the Third French Republic had been consolidated as a moderately stable bourgeois régime. It was destined to survive until 1940, the most durable government the French people had known since the collapse of the ancient monarchy in the Revolution of 1789.

The Franco-Prussian War, which made France a republic, made Germany an empire. Leading German princes acclaimed William I of Prussia German emperor in the palace of Louis XIV at Versailles (18 January 1871) while the guns of Paris, a few miles away, were firing their last despairing volleys. Bismarck had rightly calculated that a common victory over an ancient foe would fuse the German nation. In structure, the new empire was an extension of the North German Confederation of 1867, with the four south German states (Bavaria, Würtemberg, Baden, and Hesse–Darmstadt) added. The imperial Bundesrat and Reichstag sat in Berlin, and Bismarck maintained his position as chancellor of the new Reich. His prestige was now almost unassailable. Under his leadership Prussia had won three wars in seven years, ended Danish, Austrian, and French interference in German affairs, and created a German empire of 41,000,000 people, the most powerful military state in Europe.

After 1871 Bismarck turned his chief attention to internal politics, labouring to consolidate the empire he had shaped. For eight years he waged a contest with the German Catholics because he believed it essential to reduce the influence of the Catholic orders and clergy, especially in education. But persecution failed in its purpose, and the Centre party, through which the Catholics defended their political and religious influence, grew stronger under attack. Meanwhile socialism was also gaining ground, until by 1878 Bismarck saw it as a greater threat than Catholicism. He therefore eased his struggle

(*Kulturkampf*) against the Catholic Church, opened negotiations with the new Pope, Leo XIII, and invited support from the Centre party. He had decided to embark on a radical change of policy.

While he was forging the empire Bismarck had leaned upon the National Liberals, and he found the middle-class business men and the professional groups loyal in their support. The National Liberals favoured German unity, but they also demanded free speech, a free press, free trade, and responsible parliamentary government. When Bismarck broke with them after 1878, he swung back to the conservative position more natural to him; he curbed the press, repressed the Socialists, and adopted a protective tariff. This reversal pleased the Prussian landowners and the great industrialists, but it 'turned the clock back' and split the National Liberal forces. By 1879 the new German Reich stood revealed as a militant, industrialized, authoritarian state in which powerful conservative groups would control the régime behind a façade of representative government. In France, almost at the same moment, the Third Republic took definitive form as a parliamentary bourgeois democracy in which the executive power and the conservative groups (Catholics, monarchists, militarists) were to be held in check and subordinated to the rule of parliament. Thus from St. Petersburg to Paris the political spectrum of Europe shaded from autocracy to parliamentarianism, preserving the gradations that had distinguished it since the Congress of Vienna.

In Great Britain the election of 1868 swept the Liberals into power under William Ewart Gladstone. This devout and humanitarian statesman dedicated his first ministry to domestic problems, to the reform of education, of the judicature, and of the army. But the issue nearest his heart was the ancient and envenomed Irish Question. 'My mission', he announced, 'is to pacify Ireland', and he laboured at it, in and out of office, for thirty years. The grievances the Irish nursed against England had a threefold root: religious, economic, and political. In 1869 Gladstone disestablished the (Episcopal) Church of Ireland, freeing Irish Catholics from the compulsion to support a church they did not attend. In 1870 an Irish Land Act improved the lot of the Irish tenantry, but it failed to provide the fair rent, fixity of tenure, and free sale demanded by the Tenant-Right League. Irish agitation and agrarian violence persisted, and the resentment of Irish landlords and Anglican clergy stayed the hope of further reforms. In 1874 the Conservatives carried the elections.

As Tory prime minister for the following six years Benjamin Disraeli dazzled the British public with a foreign policy reminiscent of the Palmerstonian era. His purchase of Suez Canal shares from the Khedive of Egypt (1875) gave Britain partial control of that vital waterway which had been completed in 1869 through French initiative. In 1876 an Act declared Queen Victoria 'Empress of India', and the flattered sovereign made Disraeli Earl of Beaconsfield. But the resumption of imperialism carried its risks and penalties. In Egypt Britain and France assumed joint responsibility for straightening out the Khedive's finances; but the condominium ended with Britain in charge. In 1877 the British annexed the South African Republic (in breach of an earlier understanding with the Dutch settlers) and provoked a revolt of the Transvaal Boers, complicated by local wars with the Kaffirs and Zulus. In India a Second Afghan War broke out in 1878. These, however, were distant and peripheral threats. The real crisis in foreign affairs during Disraeli's second ministry was the revival of Anglo-Russian tension over the Near Eastern question. It brought the two powers as close to war as they could come and still avoid it.

A free outlet to the Mediterranean Sea or the Indian Ocean was a logical goal of Russian imperialism, but it meant the subjugation of Turkey or Persia. By 1870 all the signs indicated that Russian ambitions for conquest were reviving. The restrictions imposed after the Crimean War were repudiated, internal reforms languished, and Alexander's officials turned to reorganize the army and expand the programme of military training. The Balkans were seething; insurrections against Turkish misrule broke out in Herzegovina and Bosnia in 1875, spread to Serbia, and were followed by an uprising in Bulgaria (1876) which was repressed in murderous fashion by the Turkish irregulars (the 'Bulgarian Atrocities'). Russia could no longer be restrained, and by 1877 the Tsar's forces were fighting their way towards Constantinople, where the British Mediterranean fleet cast anchor in February 1878 to forestall them. Once again the Russians had overreached themselves, for the terms they exacted from the Turks were rejected by Britain and Austria. With deep reluctance Alexander II agreed to refer the entire Balkan question to a general international conference.

Gladstone speaking in the House of Commons

The Congress of Berlin of 1878 was the most notable diplomatic assembly since that of Vienna sixty-three years earlier. All six European great powers were represented, and the settlement was a typical example of reciprocal compensation. Russia kept southern Bessarabia, Batum, Kars, and Ardahan. Austria received a mandate to occupy Bosnia and Herzegovina. Britain occupied Cyprus. Greece obtained Thessaly, and Bulgaria was left partly autonomous and partly tributary. Serbia, Rumania, and Montenegro became independent. The French (not yet recovered from their defeat in 1870) were put off with a promise of Tunis, and the Italians with vaguer promises respecting Albania. Disraeli and Salisbury returned from Berlin with the announcement that they had achieved peace with honour, but subsequent developments threw doubt on their statesmanship. In extending Austrian influence in the Balkans they had prepared the way for an Austro-German *Drang nach Osten*. But no premonition of this future peril dimmed the jingoistic mood of the British public in July of 1878. It was Disraeli's hour, all the sweeter because the Russians were bitter with frustration.

At St. Petersburg deep official resentment over the Berlin settlement was reflected in the press, but it was directed, somewhat illogically, against Bismarck rather than Disraeli. The Russians felt themselves the dupes of their neighbours' ingratitude. They had aided the Habsburg monarchy in 1849, yet Austria had favoured France and Britain in the Crimean War; they had adopted a benevolent neutrality towards Prussia in 1870–1, yet at the Congress of Berlin Bismarck had looked on while they were robbed of their Turkish conquests. It seemed a shabby return for so much altruism, and Alexander II wrote a heated rebuke to William I. Bismarck hoped the Russian indignation would burn itself out, but he wasted no time on explanations or regrets. Turning to Vienna he arranged an Austro-German Alliance (1879) that was in substance a defensive pact against Russia or France or both. Then, after relations between Berlin and St. Petersburg improved again, the eastern powers reaffirmed their earlier friendship, and Prussia, Austria, and Russia concluded a secret accord suitably known as the Three Emperors' League (1881). If any one of the partners became involved in war with a fourth power (Turkey excepted) the other two promised friendly neutrality. The Three

Emperors' League was renewable every third year; it lapsed within the decade; and its chief interest is the clue it provides to Bismarck's 'nightmare of coalitions' that might be formed against Germany. He would have neutralized Britain by similar diplomacy if he could. In 1882 he did succeed in drawing Italy into the Austro-German agreement, transforming the Dual into a Triple Alliance. For Germany the value of this elaborate and negative Bismarckian System was that it left France isolated. If the French chauvinists undertook a war of revenge to reconquer Alsace–Lorraine they would have to fight it alone.

For two decades after 1878 international tensions in Europe tended to relax. This easing of the pressures nearer home left the great powers more freedom of action overseas, and the last twenty years of the nineteenth century found them competing more keenly for unclaimed areas of Africa and Asia. After 1900, when almost all Africa and the more vulnerable portions of Asia had been pre-empted, the international pressure in Europe mounted once more. These developments will be discussed more fully in a later chapter.

Across the Atlantic the United States, like the leading European powers, took on its modern aspect in the decades after 1865. The war between the states had given machine industry an extraordinary impetus and speeded up the construction of railway and telegraph lines. The first transcontinental railway from the Atlantic to the Pacific was completed in 1869; three more followed within twenty years. By 1876 refrigerator cars were rushing chilled meat from Kansas City to New York, whence refrigerated ships carried it to Europe. Barbed wire conquered the Great Plains, separating herds and guarding grain lands, and chilled steel rollers were invented to mill the mounting wheat crops. The integration of the American economy, and its expansion to match the margins of a continental market, provided the most dynamic development of the Reconstruction era: American 'Big Business' leaped from its cradle with steel sinews and a giant's appetite. High wages encouraged the introduction of machinery; there was a shortage of manpower although the population was rising at an unprecedented rate. By 1880 the American nation had passed 50,000,000, outstripping in population every great power of that day except Russia.

This phenomenal American business prosperity threw a strain on democratic institutions that bent and almost broke them.

Western farmers were angered by the unfair monopolistic practices of railways and flour-mills, and sought vainly for legislation to bring them under control. State legislatures were suborned by bribery, and the administration of President Grant was disfigured by revelations of corruption that forced Congressmen from office and drove members of the cabinet to resign. Inflation and over-expansion finally took their toll, and in 1873 a panic shook the financial centres of the United States and Europe, reflecting (as the earlier panic of 1857 had done) the increasing interdependence of the international economy. But the resiliency of American business enterprise was proved by its vigorous recovery. Europe needed the agricultural products of the New World, gold flowed to the United States, business confidence returned, and in 1879 the Treasury resumed specie payments.

To the Dominion of Canada, unified by the Act of Confederation of 1867, the subsequent decade brought no radical changes. Discontent among the half-breeds of Manitoba excited them to a brief rebellion, easily repressed (1869–70). Projects for a transcontinental railway were bogged down in political scandals until a new charter organized the Canadian Pacific Railway Company and the line was completed in 1885. As in the United States the population shifted westward and increased steadily, reaching 4,324,810 by 1881.

To the Latin American peoples the period brought one notable conflict, the War of the Pacific (1879–83), in which Chile defeated Peru and Bolivia, emerging as the dominant power of the Andean region. A ten-year revolt in Cuba (which had remained under the Spanish Crown) ended in 1878 with promises of reform from Madrid that were not kept. The United States, which had sought to purchase the island earlier, did not intervene; and when the people of Haiti invited annexation (1870) the United States Senate showed equal restraint by rejecting the proposal. More surprising was the negative attitude in Washington in 1878, when the republic of Colombia granted a French company (headed by Ferdinand de Lesseps) a ninety-nine-year lease with exclusive rights to build an inter-oceanic canal across the isthmus of Panama. Not until twenty years later, after De Lesseps's company had foundered, and plans for an alternative Nicaraguan canal had miscarried, did the United States government undertake the Panama venture in a conviction that 'manifest destiny' prescribed it.

American initiative lagged in cutting the isthmus because the people of the United States were slow to recognize their nation as a power in the Pacific. The westward movement was so swift that it outstripped calculation. In the west coast states (Washington, Oregon, and California) the population multiplied tenfold in thirty years; by 1880 it was well over one million. American pressure, naval and commercial, had begun to influence the ancient empires of east Asia for a generation before the American people were awake to this new responsibility. The part played by the United States navy in the awakening of Japan was a striking illustration of this absent-minded imperialism.

Proud, feudal, and self-sufficient, the Japanese people had rejected contacts with Europeans since the expulsion of Christian missionaries early in the seventeenth century. Save for a single restricted Dutch trading post at Nagasaki, Japan remained isolated from the rest of the world until the middle of the nineteenth century; but then the policy of exclusion was abandoned with startling results. In 1853 and 1854 American warships visited Edo Bay, and Commodore Matthew Calbraith Perry extorted a treaty that opened two Japanese ports to American trade. Britain, Russia, and the Netherlands promptly secured similar privileges, and the Japanese ruling nobility was split over the question of accepting or rejecting foreign intercourse. Western technological supremacy decided the issue; in 1864 an allied expedition of British, French, Dutch, and American frigates shelled the Japanese defences at Shimonoseki; and in 1865 the four powers secured broader trade conventions. The demonstration of western weapons and their irresistible effect wrought a revolution in Japanese thought and politics.

For generations the authority of the Japanese emperor (Mikado) had been eclipsed by that of the Shogun, a hereditary official with extraordinary powers. In 1868 a young, capable, and realistic emperor, Mutsuhito (1867–1912), reasserted the imperial dignity, moved his capital to Tokyo, and opened a new period in Japanese history. The Shogun resigned, the feudal warlords surrendered their semi-independent powers, and the xenophobia of the preceding period was officially abandoned. Instead of rejecting all things occidental, the statesmen of the new régime imitated and adopted western institutions. The Japanese navy was remodelled on that of Great Britain; the army leaders studied and incorporated Prussian methods; the educators borrowed American practices. Japanese law courts and codes introduced French and German procedures; new legislation was approved in constitutional fashion by an elected diet and chamber of peers comparable to European parliaments. No less remarkable was the rapid reorganization of Japanese industry. Students travelled abroad to observe and master western business methods, and returned to plan railways, shipyards, factories, banks, hotels, department stores, and newspapers in their homeland. Seldom in history had a nation devoted itself to such sedulous imitation since the Japanese themselves adopted Chinese culture and customs fifteen centuries earlier. Europeans observed the furious awakening of the island kingdom with an amused tolerance, and Arthur Sullivan and W. S. Gilbert, in their light opera *The Mikado* (1885), created a mythical picture of Japan that was a source of innocent merriment. The awakening of Europe to the real significance of the Japanese revolution was to come later.

The outstanding characteristic that the Japanese borrowed from Europe, and the problem which the nineteenth century posed for the twentieth century to answer, was that of a runaway technology. The age of steam and steel, of a coal economy and machine production, achieved its first centenary in the western world around 1870. The preceding century had seen a stable agricultural and commercial society transformed by the dynamics of industrialism. The designation 'Industrial Revolution' frequently applied to this social and economic transformation is far from satisfactory, though it has persisted for want of a more exact designation. The central fact in the rise of nineteenth-century industry was not the invention of machinery (machines of exceptional ingenuity and flexibility had been perfected earlier), but the application of a cheap and plentiful source of power for driving the machines. One pound of coal, when efficiently burned, yielded more energy than a human being expended in a day's work, and the steam-engine was a more dependable servant than the older machines run by wind, water, or animal power. The classic example of the expansion that might be wrought by power-driven machinery was the revolution in the British textile industry. In the decade 1810–20 this industry provided employment for 250,000 workers, but only one in twenty-five laboured in a factory. Sixty years later the number of workers was approximately the same, but all had by then abandoned home looms for factory labour. The social and environmental revolution that overtook these textile workers and their dependents had, inevitably, produced significant and often adverse changes in their mode of life. But this was not the most arresting fact in the transition to machine production. The consideration which brought about the change to the factory system was the fact that it increased the output per worker twelvefold. By 1880 the same number of textile hands (approximately 250,000), using power-driven machinery, were turning out as much fabric as 3,000,000 workers could have produced under the domestic system.

That modern machine industry was built on coal was testified by the rate of its consumption. Between 1670 and 1770 the annual European coal production increased only threefold. Between 1770 and 1870 (the century of the Industrial Revolution) it rose thirtyfold. But this first century of industrialism, impressive and even revolutionary though its effects proved, was only a prologue. After 1870 (until European economy was dislocated by the First World War) the average increase in coal production *each decade* was greater than the total increase for the preceding century. After 1870, therefore, it became increasingly evident that western civilization was geared to a runaway technology.

Such a spurt in the progress of industrialism, after the movement had been steadily accelerating for a hundred years, indicates that after 1870 western economy entered a new phase, a 'New Industrial Revolution'. There was unquestionably a quickening of the tempo, a broadening of research, a constellation of inventions that made the 1870's a decade of unparalleled expansion. Before it closed scientists and engineers had begun to challenge the reign of King Coal by demonstrating the commercial possibilities of two alternative sources of energy. By 1881 the production of petroleum already exceeded 3,000,000 tons annually, and the oil industry had been born. More significant still, newly perfected dynamos in electric power plants were generating current for light circuits and other commercial purposes. The age of oil and electricity was at hand, with its incredible instruments of power and precision, waiting to transform the living standards of the western world. The dawning era could not fail to be an age of industry, but it proved to be much more than that. The rapid increase in human powers and potentialities that dazzled western man in the last quarter of the nineteenth century was more than a second industrial revolution. It would be more accurate to say that the new era brought a technological revolution, and to call the period that opened about 1870 the technological age.

The new instruments of power and precision that appeared in the early years of this technological era read like a catalogue of scientific marvels. Between 1867 and 1881 the telephone, microphone, electric lamp, gramophone, internal combustion engine, and electric tram-car made their first appearance. Advances in dry-plate photography, elementary colour photography, and motion pictures opened new avenues of research. The rotary perfecting press and the typewriter speeded labour in printing shop and office. Nor was mechanization confined to industry. The improved reaper and binder enabled the farmer to expand his acres while chemical fertilizers increased the yield. Transportation costs fell while the speed and regularity of the carriers improved; the airbrake solved the problem of deceleration; and railroad tunnels through the Alps (Mont Cenis, 1871; Saint Gothard, 1882) reduced the journey from Italy to Germany or France from days to hours. The Suez Canal, which enabled vessels to pass from the Mediterranean to the Red Sea and Indian Ocean, and the first transcontinental railway to cross the United States, were both opened in the same year (1869).

Man's growing mastery over his physical environment, his victories over time and space, were matched in this period by his discoveries about himself. Charles Darwin's treatises *On the Origin of Species by Means of Natural Selection* (1859) and *The Descent of Man* (1871) gave a profound impulse to the study of biology and anthropology. Gregor Mendel's researches into the mechanics of heredity (1865) were overlooked for a generation, but Francis Galton emphasized the role of inheritance in the mental development of human beings (1867), and Wilhelm Wundt demonstrated the interdependence of mind and body in his *Principles of Physiological Psychology* (1872). The concept of evolution and the principle of natural selection were applied to human customs and institutions by Walter Bagehot (1873). Interest in the new theories concerning man's origin and development spread rapidly among scientifically inclined laymen and were popularized by forceful writers and lecturers such as

Thomas Henry Huxley in England and Ernst Haeckel in Germany.

Nothing brought the scientists more prestige than advances in medicine and surgery: people in every station were fascinated by the report of new victories over pain, disease, and death. Antiseptic surgery, introduced by Joseph Lister (1865), directed attention to the importance of bacteria as agents of infection. Louis Pasteur and Robert Koch gave a shrewd blow to the immemorial belief in spontaneous generation by proving that germs were not merely the concomitants but the cause of great plagues. Within half-a-dozen years the bacteriologists, working with tireless zeal, identified the bacillus of leprosy, the malaria parasite, the bacteria of anthrax, and the germs of tuberculosis, diphtheria, and Asiatic cholera. A dramatic inoculation by Pasteur (1885) saved the life of a boy who had been bitten by a mad dog and marked the first sure step in the conquest of hydrophobia. Physicians could now recognize the enemies that hitherto they had fought in the dark, and could safeguard possible victims of many deadly diseases by the administration of serums and antitoxins. A new branch of medicine had come into being, the science of immunology.

Every hypothesis of the scientists, when vindicated by experiment, advertised the efficacy of their methods and invested the positivist approach with greater authority. Chemists and biologists, physicists and geologists did not stop to ponder (as the speculative philosophers had so often done) imponderable essences and unverifiable generalities; they handled the stuff of life and the building blocks of matter. When Dmitri Mendeleeff first published his Periodic Law of the Elements (1869), arguing that they would be found, when ranged according to their atomic weights, to display a certain periodicity, so that each eighth element revealed somewhat similar properties, his table won attention as a further proof that nature was intelligible to those who accepted her pronouncements. A strong conviction had grown up that everything in the physical universe was behaving in a rational manner and that it was man's disorderly mind that had led him to misread her. The major obstacle to the progress of science, many rationalists insisted, was the heritage of conceit and superstition that induced men to prefer a flattering illusion to an unflattering truth. The march of scientific discovery had been achieved through the depersonalization of myths. Among the myths that would ultimately be discredited, or so some agnostics proclaimed, were many articles of the Christian faith, especially those that involved a belief in miraculous events and appeared to contradict natural laws and the natural order.

This growing conflict between rationalism and religion, between the scientist and the theologian, was sharpened by the controversy over the Darwinian theory of biological evolution. Fundamentally, however, the dispute was deeper and more ancient. It was the recurrent argument between the materialist, who believes that the facts of the universe can be sufficiently explained by the existence and nature of matter, and the transcendentalist who asserts the primacy of spiritual over empirical truth. In 1864 Pope Pius IX issued a famous encyclical, *Quanta cura*, and in an accompanying syllabus he warned the faithful against 'the principal errors of our time'. It was not true, the syllabus emphasized, that God did not exist, or that all action by God upon man and upon the world was to be denied. Nor was it true that human reason, without any regard to God, was the sole arbiter of truth or falsehood, or that the miracles narrated in the Holy Scriptures were poetic fictions and the Testaments contained mythical inventions.

Had the papal warning paused with this condemnation of philosophical materialism and agnosticism it might have excited less comment, but Pius went on to rebuke those anticlericals and nationalists who insisted upon the supremacy of the secular State, and those liberals who favoured the separation of Church and state and advocated the establishment of secular education. The final clause of the syllabus (number 80) specifically rejected the idea that the Roman Pontiff could or should reconcile himself with progress, liberalism, or modern civilization, and this declaration seemed to many to set the Roman Church squarely athwart the intellectual and political currents of the age. Although the syllabus of errors was not proclaimed as dogma, and leading Catholic apologists hastened to explain that it should be considered as an admonition evoked in part by contemporary developments in Italy, it aroused a sharp debate on the nature and extent of the papal authority. The dispute was not softened but intensified when the Vatican Council defined the dogma of papal infallibility (1870). This twentieth oecumenical council of the Roman Catholic Church (the first general council since the sixteenth century) declared it to be a dogma 'divinely revealed' that the Roman Pontiff, when he spoke *ex cathedra*, possessed 'that infallibility with which the Divine Redeemer willed that His Church should be endowed for defining faith and morals'. This proclamation marked the high point in the pontificate of Pius IX. Before the close of 1870 the forces of the new Italian kingdom had occupied Rome, the council had adjourned, and Pius was 'the prisoner of the Vatican'. In Great Britain, France, and especially in Germany, criticism of the papal claims was acute and prolonged. A liberal group in the German empire, who became known as the Old Catholics, refused to be bound by the decision of the council, and Bismarck supported their revolt, opening a struggle between state and Church in Germany (the *Kulturkampf*) that lasted throughout the 1870's.

A widening rift divided those who accepted religious dogmas as literal, unchanging truths and those who admitted that all the great prophets, including Jesus, had been influenced by the social and intellectual conditions of their environment. Biblical scholars who came to feel that the Old and New Testaments should be evaluated by the same methods that historians used to determine the credibility of secular records dedicated themselves to what was known as the Higher Criticism. In Germany David Friedrich Strauss laboured until his death in 1874 to prove that many passsages in the Gospel narratives should be regarded as embodying 'myths' rather than facts. In France Joseph Ernest Renan compiled an erudite *History of the Origins of Christianity* in eight volumes (1863–83) to show that the religious ideas of the Hebrew prophets and the Church Fathers changed and evolved as the world about them changed. It was an error, Renan believed, to ascribe a dogmatic finality to the judgements they had formulated under the influence of temporal conditions.

The same realistic approach gave a new vigour to historical interpretation. By assuming that the literature, the art, the social customs, and the religious practices of a people were contingent on the level of its culture, the force of inherited traditions, the soil, climate, and food supply, critics set up a naturalistic foundation and a frame by which to measure man's achievements. The French critic and historian Hippolyte Adolphe Taine esteemed this method so highly that it led him to a scientific determinism. He believed that individuals and nations could be anatomized with precision because their thoughts and actions were the inescapable consequence of heredity and environment.

The mood of realism that dominated the second half of the nineteenth century had clearly manifested itself in literature and art by 1870. In fiction the new spirit had already stamped the work of Nikolai Gogol, 'the father of Russian realism', who died in 1852. The same year opened the long literary career of Leo Tolstoy, a career that was to touch its zenith with the publication of *War and Peace* (1866), at the same moment that Feodor Dostoievski completed his *Crime and Punishment*. Literary realism came of age in France with Gustave Flaubert's *Madame Bovary* (1857), although Flaubert did not regard himself as a realist and was dismayed when the work was attacked on the grounds of indecency. The earliest novels of the Goncourt brothers appeared in the 1860's, and Émile Zola, the leading exponent of naturalism, commenced his prolific writing in this decade. In England Charles Dickens's prodigious output continued until his death in 1870. His blend of realism and sentiment, his genius for characterization that often verged on caricature, and his sympathy for the poor and unfortunate had made him the most popular English novelist since Sir Walter Scott. The reaction against early Victorian idealization and sentimentality, already presaged in the satirical novels and parodies of William Makepeace Thackeray, found more sober and conscientious expression in the works of George Eliot (Mary Ann Evans). George Meredith's first success, *The Ordeal of Richard Feverel*, dated from 1859, and Thomas Hardy's series of mordant novels commenced with *Desperate Remedies* in 1871. In drama the outstanding realist of the later nineteenth century was the Norwegian, Henrik Ibsen, whose assaults on bourgeois complacency awakened a succession of reverberations from the presentation of *Pillars of Society* (1877) to *When We Dead Awaken* (1899).

To dumbfound the bourgeois and shock his prudish conventionality was not difficult in an age that made a cult of respectability. The poet and artist were expected to idealize rather than to imitate nature, and those who repudiated academic rules and sought a fresh and more natural approach to their subject-matter invited critical censure. The Pre-Raphaelite Brotherhood (Holman Hunt, Dante Gabriel Rossetti, John Everett Millais) were relatively innocuous as painters, but when their literary colleagues turned to verse, Rossetti, Algernon Charles Swinburne, William Morris, and others were attacked in the *Contemporary Review* as 'The Fleshly School of Poetry' (1871). The Pre-Raphaelites were realists in their earnest wish to depict life honestly, but realists in very little else; their enthusiasm for medieval art forms and their search for ideal beauty linked them to the Romantic tradition. In France they found a more virile counterpart in the Parnassian School led by Leconte de Lisle and Sully-Prudhomme. The Parnassians strove more consciously and more successfully to adapt their art to the rational and scientific spirit of the age while freeing it from the excessive emotionalism, mysticism, and subjectivism of the Romantic era.

America produced two noteworthy writers of realistic literature in Mark Twain (Samuel Langhorne Clemens) and Walt Whitman. Twain's masterpieces were his picaresque novels, *The Adventures of Tom Sawyer* (1876) and *The Adventures of Huckleberry Finn* (1884), which recaptured, with robust humour and colloquial idiom, the memories of his boyhood in Missouri. Walt Whitman is more difficult to classify; an intense individualist, exuberant, mystical, and romantic in his celebration of democracy, he also produced many passages of gusty blank verse stamped with a stark and authentic realism. At his worst his unrestrained *mélange* of names and images degenerated into banality and his verse read 'like a hardware catalogue'.

The revolt against the pomp and prettiness of academic art influenced European painting from the middle of the nineteenth century onward, and the feud between the academicians and the heretics lasted until its closing decades. Artists who repudiated religious and neo-classical themes to paint ungainly nudes and naturalistic landscapes were rejected by the salons and largely ignored by the public. Gustave Courbet was the first painter who frankly invited the charge of realism. His contempt for precedent and allegory was supreme: 'Show me an angel', he mocked his critics, 'and I will paint one.' His genre pictures captivated young art students in the 1850's and 1860's, and he stood with Edouard Manet in his revolt against the sterile mannerisms of the French salon masters. As painters, however, Courbet and Manet diverged, and the latter became a leader of the impressionist school. Manet's scenes had the sharp focus and arresting fidelity of a photograph, and within its limits his technique remained unsurpassed. But Realism and Impressionism both had limitations, the limitations implicit in the artist himself. If he painted only what he saw, and if what he saw was the reflection of light on the surface of things, that was seldom enough. When the impassioned quarrels that shook the studios and cafés of the Latin quarter for half a century finally died away, the painter who came closest to apotheosis was one who had been little regarded: Paul Cézanne.

A friend of Zola, drawn like the novelist to the realistic creed in art, Cézanne patiently analysed and then outgrew the Realists and Impressionists. He laboured to find the geometric in nature, to 'give architecture to the universe', and his experiments in technique laid the foundations for Post-Impressionism and Cubism. His landscapes repelled his contemporaries, but later admirers were to acclaim him as a master who saw beneath the surface and gave an organic structure, a solidity and richness, to natural objects. And what was more important, they came to recognize that his effects were achieved not by slavish imitation but by an intense and arduous *re-creation* of nature.

This rediscovery that the artist was himself the most important element in his art, and that the thinker not only perceived but also imposed form on the objective world, had a significance beyond the sphere of aesthetics. Nineteenth-century thought had been dominated by an increasing faith in the order and continuity of natural processes. The principle of the conservation of matter and the conservation of energy reinforced the tenets of positivism, and materialistic explanations prevailed over theological or metaphysical arguments concerning the nature of the universe and of man. Before the nineteenth century closed, however, investigators on the frontiers of science began to detect some disturbing aberrations that challenged several of the 'immutable' laws upon which the positivists had rested their case. The orderly and self-sufficient universe that had been posited was already dissolving when the century closed, and new thinkers were preparing, like Cézanne, to re-create nature. But the story of this revolution in philosophy and physics belongs to the twentieth century.

V

THE FRUITS OF INDUSTRIALISM AND IMPERIALISM (1881–98)

By the close of the nineteenth century mechanized industry had become the most powerful force shaping western civilization. The machines outstripped the intention of their builders, economic materialism overshadowed the age, and Emerson's prophetic warning that 'Things are in the saddle and ride mankind' turned to sober truth. For machine production was dynamic and expansive; its energies outgrew control, transformed the structure of European society, and invaded remoter regions. The primary function of the machines was to pour out a flood of cheap, standardized commodities, but their influence did not end when this primary function was fulfilled: the multiplication of factories brought a rise in the urban proletariat until the armies of socialism threatened the bourgeois state. The quenchless hunger of the iron slaves for more raw materials and wider markets launched the industrial powers on a new campaign of colonial imperialism. The progress of industrialism in the final decades of the nineteenth century bore a direct relation to the growth of the proletariat and the pressure of imperialism, and for all three developments power-driven machinery provided the principal moving force.

In peace or war industrial machinery had become the indispensable instrument, the essential gauge of power. Area and population were no longer the most significant indices of a nation's economic productivity or war potential. Warfare itself was becoming industrialized, and a new ratio of strength had emerged that made manpower insufficient in battle unless it was backed by the tireless energy and prodigious output of a mechanized industry. In this new world of competing imperialisms no nation that lacked a well-developed factory system could long sustain the role of a great power.

This new dispensation by the god of the machine, this revision in the prerequisites of power, had not been fully grasped by political or military observers when the nineteenth century closed. In retrospect it becomes clear that three leading nations had far outrun their rivals in the race to exploit the advantages of an industrial economy. Great Britain had been the 'workshop of the world' for a hundred years, but by 1900 Germany and the United States had cut down the British lead. The resources and industrial equipment of these three countries—Britain, Germany, and the United States—placed them in a special category. They were the super-powers. France, Russia, Austria, and Italy were all great powers but they occupied a secondary position; their industry was not adequate to their needs, although France almost approached the requirements of a super-power. The third category included the remaining states of Europe and the world, from highly industrialized but numerically weak nations like the Belgians with 7,000,000 population, to numerically strong but industrially negligible empires like the Chinese with possibly 300,000,000 people. Japan, though it attracted attention to itself by defeating China in 1894, was still an unpredictable factor in the later decades of the nineteenth century. It was shortly to reveal the awe-inspiring rapidity with which modern technology could alter the industrial and military status of an energetic nation.

Not only the possession of industrial machinery but the manufacture and export of machines became an index of power by 1880. Britain, the United States, and Germany were then the principal exporters; together they produced four-fifths of the machinery sold in the international market. The three increased their virtual monopoly up to the First World War, but among themselves there was a significant reversal of rank. In 1880 the order of precedence was Great Britain, Germany, the United States. By 1913 it had become Germany, the United States, Great Britain. This relative decline in the value of British machine exports was an ominous portent for Great Britain. For the British built almost half their machinery for sale abroad, whereas the Germans sent only one-fourth of theirs out of the country and the Americans only one-tenth. In terms of *total* production the discrepancy between the three leading competitors for world markets had become highly impressive. By 1913 the United States was building one-half the industrial machinery of the world, Germany one-fifth, and Britain one-eighth. The fact that the Americans kept nine-tenths of their enormous output of machines at home obscured their extraordinary progress towards industrialization, and the rivalry between Britain and Germany for world trade appeared the most acute. In reality, however, both Germany and Britain had been outstripped in the industrial race by the young giant of the west when the twentieth century opened.

In the 1880's and 1890's the Anglo-German trade rivalry developed into a duel of titans in which the arithmetic of power recorded a succession of German gains. In 1880–4 German steel mills produced only half as much steel as the British; by 1900 they were producing 20 per cent. more. British exports of cotton manufactures dropped between 1880 and 1900, while German exports doubled. British pig-iron production and consumption remained almost stationary during these twenty years, but German output and consumption increased over 100 per cent. This rivalry in metals and textiles, the strongest branches of British trade, provided a real challenge, but the competition of the German merchant marine stirred the British people even more deeply. Although German shipping tonnage on register remained only one-sixth that of Britain from 1880 to 1900, the lower freight rates on German ships lured manufacturers—and even some British manufacturers—to ship their wares through Hamburg. 'The Germans', *The Times* admitted in 1886, 'are beginning to beat us in many of the qualities which are the factors of commercial success.' Other British observers, however, remained more optimistic. In 1901 the London *Daily Telegraph* could still declare with confidence: 'What is gone is our monopoly. What is not gone is our supremacy. There is no decadence.' The opening of the twentieth century found Britain still in the lead with 21 per cent. of international trade. Germany came second with 12 per cent., the United States third with 11 per cent., and France fourth with 8 per cent. In the next thirteen years world trade doubled and the percentages shifted, but of the four leading powers only the United States made a relative gain. When the First World War commenced the figures stood: Britain 17 per cent., the United States 15 per cent., Germany 12 per cent., and France 7 per cent. Yet it was still the (now stationary) German share of international trade that most Englishmen viewed with alarm rather than the more rapid American expansion.

Fortunately for Great Britain the movement of commodities across political frontiers was not the only important index of economic strength. Nine-tenths of the international financial transactions were still carried on in pounds sterling, because the pound remained the most stable unit of exchange. The profits from banking, insurance, and foreign investments brought Great Britain an 'invisible' income that helped to pay for the excess of imports over exports and preserved British financial leadership. Between 1880 and 1913 British investments abroad multiplied threefold, until a quarter of the national wealth had been exported. The French foreign investments were only one-half and the German only one-third the British total. Furthermore, almost 50 per cent. of British capital exported went to develop regions within the empire and could be safeguarded with fair success. The rate of interest on foreign investments was generally high, but the risk of loss was often high also. When, as sometimes happened, foreign borrowers defaulted on their debts, British, French, or German bondholders might press their government to help them to collect. A considerable share of the capital exported went to politically weak and economically retarded countries and paved the way for the march of imperialism. Small nations in need of financial aid and technological equipment, impoverished peoples whose leaders borrowed heavily from the bankers of London, Paris, or Berlin, might find themselves reduced to a condition of economic vassalage. Their country might even forfeit its political independence and become a protectorate of the great power to which its resources had been pledged.

As business profits mounted and the capital available for investment increased, those with money to lend placed it with investment brokers and might remain almost entirely ignorant of the good or evil that it wrought in domestic or foreign ventures. Investors and bondholders were usually satisfied if their return remained sufficiently high, and they did not inquire too strictly whether the corporation that paid them dividends rewarded its staff equitably or whether the interest they drew from a mine in South America or a trading company in Africa represented a reasonable profit or a pitiless extortion. The widening gulf that separated the rich from the poor, the owners of capital from the workers, increased the evils of 'absentee landlordism' in the capitalistic system. The effect, inevitably, was to depersonalize and dehumanize the relationship between the bondholder and the 'bondservants' whom he might never see.

Within the factory system itself this shift towards finance capitalism weakened the older paternalistic relation between the employer and his workmen. In the early years of the industrial revolution most mills and factories began as private enterprises, and many remained under the direction of a single family for generations. The profits that arose from the business were usually put back to provide for expansion, and a small responsible group of shareholders, closely connected with the business and often personally known to the employees, retained ownership and control. But this type of family industry was outgrown as the nineteenth century advanced. Larger, more impersonal aggregations of stockholders, protected by the statutes governing limited liability companies, tended to supplant the family firm or partnership. In England after the Companies Act of 1844, in France after 1867, in Germany after 1870, corporations with an active board of directors and hundreds or thousands of shareholders multiplied rapidly. Ownership was more widely distributed while management was steadily centralized. Control of a company, or of an entire industry, might come to rest with a handful of men or with a single 'captain of industry' who won a commanding influence. Local shopkeepers felt the encroachment of the chain stores; small foundries and ironworks were swallowed up by the gigantic steel combinations. Free business enterprise, which permitted the development of business corporations, was itself threatened by the tightening monopoly secured by a few aggressive firms. In law the corporation had only the rights of a legal person, but in fact it was potentially immortal and capable of unlimited expansion. An aggressive corporation might absorb or crush its competitors until it dominated a field of economic activity so completely that free business enterprise within that field became a fiction.

A parallel development that sometimes facilitated such concentration of control within an industry was the rise of finance capitalism. In order to expand its activities, or to buy out a competitor, a company might borrow the necessary capital from a firm of bankers, who thus acquired an interest in the company. Occasionally the bankers insisted that a member of their staff be elected chairman of the company in order to watch over the investment. One German bank, for example, had directors on the boards of 200 corporations before 1914. The influence that a great investment trust, with headquarters in London, Berlin, Paris, or New York, might gain in this way could decide events in distant continents, but its activities were a mystery to the man in the street and might extend beyond the ken and the control of local legislators.

By 1900 the growth of large business combinations, known variously as pools, trusts, or cartels, had become a problem to jurists and politicians. Some corporations with monopolistic tendencies became so powerful that it was feared they might evade government control and pursue their quest for profits at the expense of the public welfare and the national interest. Yet it was also recognized that, through the benefits of centralization, they often improved the methods of mass production, stimulated new industries, provided new forms of employment, and promoted prosperity. Men who acquire power are often admired and criticized at the same time. The courage, initiative, and foresight of the business leaders who built vast financial pyramids, developed the resources of a wilderness, and gambled with lives and gold on engineering feats that involved great risks but dazzling rewards, fascinated the new age. Admirers saw these titans as architects of prosperity who asserted humanity's right of eminent domain to exploit the resources of the planet, and, if need be, to enforce the benefits of civilization upon reluctant and unprogressive peoples. But to hostile critics who distrusted the aims and deplored the methods of these international financiers and captains of industry they appeared ruthless and predatory, the 'robber barons' of the modern world. The legal devices and financial legerdemain that obscured the operations of 'big business' were too complex for the common man to grasp, and it was easy for political agitators to play upon his distrust of the 'capitalists' and to magnify their power. Like the god Mercury, patron of commerce, they seemed to abstract the fatness of the fields and the fruits of other men's labour by secret and invisible means.

The nineteenth century closed with all the energies of a dynamic industrial civilization rising to a crescendo. In the economic sphere concentration and centralization appeared to be the dominant principles of the age—concentration of capital, of industry, of population, of power. Throughout Europe and North America the formation of pools, cartels, combines, corporations, trusts, and other devices for merging the directorates of varied business interests, tightened and centralized the control of economic life. The concentration of population was even more noteworthy than the concentration of wealth. In England

and Belgium one-half the people were urban dwellers in 1850, three-fourths in 1900. In Germany, where the census had recorded only eight large cities (100,000 inhabitants or more) in 1871, there were thirty-three by 1900 and forty-eight by 1910. Large cities grew faster than small ones, and the towns devoured the villages. By 1900 one out of twenty-five Frenchmen lived in Paris, one out of twenty Germans in Berlin. In England and Wales one-tenth of the inhabitants had been drawn into the vortex of London. Even in the United States, with 3,000,000 square miles to disperse in, nearly one-half the population was concentrated on one per cent. of the land area, and the ten largest cities held one-eighth of the nation.

This expansion of the modern city was closely linked to the growth of the factory system. Modern industry was essentially dynamic, cumulative, and expansive. Under machine production, the unit cost of an article declined as the standardized output rose. It was more profitable, therefore, to aim at a larger and larger body of consumers, to expand production and constantly invade new areas. Steam power assured cheap and regular transportation (the railway mileage of the world quadrupled between 1870 and 1900), and the decline in shipping charges brought into being for the first time in history a world market and a world economy. Raw materials could be brought to the machine from other continents and manufactures exported halfway around the world at rates that allowed them to compete profitably with local wares.

The consequence was sharper competition, and this in turn demanded increased efficiency and production to lower the selling price. Small firms with a limited trade often went under, while large industries branched out, some of them growing to gigantic proportions. In Germany the minor industrial plants (those employing five workmen or less) declined by half between 1880 and 1914, while the larger factories (employing fifty or more workers) doubled in number. A majority of the German industrial labourers were still occupied in small plants at the earlier date, but thirty years later two-thirds were in large factories. The number of industrial units had declined, they were fewer but larger, and they employed four times the total of workers recorded for 1880. Such continued herding of millhands and factory help into fewer but larger combines was common to all the industrialized countries. In general it promoted efficiency, multiplied production, and lowered costs. But it had other effects not intended by the employers and less gratifying to them. In a large company with thousands on its pay-roll the cleavage between the management and the workers tended to widen. The workers became conscious of themselves as a class with separate interests, differing demands, and specific grievances. And they could unite more effectively for collective bargaining as their numbers rose and their working conditions brought them together.

One logical result was the rapid growth of labour unions. By the last quarter of the nineteenth century the laws against workers' organizations had been relaxed. The skilled craftsmen were the first to form craft unions to promote the welfare of their members. Later, many of these unions hastened to federate in large industrial unions, and by 1900 trade union membership reached 2,000,000 in Great Britain and about 1,000,000 in Germany and the United States. The unskilled labourers were more hesitant about organizing, but once their movement began to progress in the 1880's it developed rapidly. Miners, dockers, and factory hands turned to collective bargaining, and large industrial unions appeared in Europe, the United States, and the British self-governing dominions.

With the rise of powerful unions, labour ceased to be a 'commodity' in the world of industry and became in some sense a partner. The workers demanded a more substantial share of the profits and enforced their demand by the threat to strike. Their claims for higher wages had justification, especially after 1895, for prices and living costs, which had been relatively low for twenty years, began a long climb. The rise in real wages between 1880 and 1900 was only 20 to 25 per cent. in Great Britain, Germany, and France, whereas the average worker's productive capacity, thanks to the machines, increased more rapidly, and the proportionate wealth of the capitalist employer rose more rapidly still. The industrial labourer, whose efforts were essential to production, was persuaded that he did not receive a just share of the benefits and profits which the mechanism of industry had made available.

In addition to bargaining directly with their employers, working men could carry their fight into the field of politics; when they did so socialism became an acute political issue. Throughout the later nineteenth century the vote was extended to a larger and larger electorate in all democratic countries, and the disinherited classes grew more powerful when they found that they could oppose the weight of numbers to the influence of privileged minority groups. In the German empire and the French Republic universal manhood suffrage had been granted by 1871; in Switzerland it was embodied in the Federal Constitution of 1874; in Great Britain it was virtually in force after the Reform Acts of 1884–5 which raised the electorate from 3,000,000 to 5,000,000. Spain (1890), Belgium (1893), and Norway (1898) adopted it, and the government of the Netherlands enfranchised all adult males who paid one florin in taxes (1896). An Italian law of 1882 allowed the vote to all males over twenty who had a primary school education and could meet a small property qualification, and universal manhood suffrage followed in 1912. In Austria and Hungary political democracy was delayed by the determination of the German and Magyar minorities to retain their ascendancy, and in most of the Balkan states it was absent or inoperative. Neither the Russian nor the Ottoman empires had a national franchise or even a constitution in 1900, but the Russians were to secure a representative assembly, the Duma, in 1906, and the Young Turks adopted universal manhood suffrage, nominally at least, after their successful revolution shattered the reactionary régime of Abdul Hamid II in 1908.

Had the millions of citizens with low incomes and little or no property been united by their poverty they could have carried all elections against the wealthy few. In Prussia, for instance, on the eve of the First World War, the few thousand persons with fortunes that averaged 5,000,000 marks were outnumbered 400 to 1 by the great majority whose worldly wealth averaged less than 25,000 marks *per capita*. For Great Britain comparable statistics suggest that there were 5,000 citizens whose wealth exceeded £100,000, but seven Englishmen out of eight had an average of £100 or less—one-thousandth as much. Political equality did not appear to have brought economic equality nearer, but the unpropertied majority were not of one mind on tariffs, capital levies, and taxes on income, inheritance, or surplus profits. Farmers wanted a fair price for their crops and often welcomed import duties that excluded foreign shipments of grain. City workers, on the other hand, might agitate for the abolition of 'corn laws' in the hope that with free importation the price of bread would fall. Some labour groups felt that their interests set them more sharply against one another than against their employers with whom they shared one common concern: the promotion of the particular industry or enterprise on which all depended for a livelihood.

A conflict of aims divided the urban and rural classes in almost every country. The rural worker tended to remain individualistic, conservative, and orthodox in his religious faith. The urban worker was more readily won to collectivism, more willing to join a union, and more susceptible to materialistic and agnostic doctrines. Cleavages in the ranks of the 'expropriated classes' also developed because of professional pride. Trained mechanics and skilled artisans regarded themselves with reason as the aristocracy of labour and resisted the levelling dogmas that invoked a mechanical equality for all members of society. Every farmer with an acre of land, every worker who owned his home, every foreman promoted to a position of responsibility, had an advantage to safeguard. In addition there was a large middle-class army of white-collar workers, store and office clerks, small shopkeepers, small business men and members of various professional groups, who all enjoyed a social if not an economic status that set them apart from the ranks of organized labour.

These divisions and differences within the working classes help to explain why the socialist parties that were formed in the 1880's and 1890's grew very slowly at first. A period of preparation and education was needed before the masses could become conscious of themselves and of their common ideals and aims. This emergence of the masses, this increasing emphasis on the rights of the common people, slowly shifted the centre of gravity in European society. But it revealed itself first and most positively in the spread of popular education, in the growth of trade unionism, in the formation of co-operative organizations, before it invaded the political arena and compelled the older parliamentary groups to make way for a 'people's party' powerful enough to claim a share in the government.

Until the end of the nineteenth century the lower classes improved their condition chiefly by adopting some of the liberties and benefits that the middle class had already won. There was a steady diffusion through the submerged levels of European society of democratic ideals, liberty of thought and action, economic and educational opportunity, and finally political representation. The growth of craft unionism and then of industrial unionism has already been noted: it enabled the workers to improve their bargaining power and to secure better wages and working hours from their employers. But the spread of popular education and the formation of co-operative societies were equally important as signs of a proletarian awakening. Taking the year 1900 as an approximate dividing line, it may be said that before that date most European workers still sought to improve their condition within the framework of an existing bourgeois democracy. After that date an increasing proportion of the unpropertied classes passed over to the socialist camp. They had come to the decision that the prevailing social and political order was fundamentally iniquitous and that it must be overthrown or radically transformed. This change in attitude was a shift from an evolutionary to a revolutionary philosophy, though many cautious radicals still preferred to shut their eyes to this fact and to think of a socialist revolution as something that could be effected gradually and by constitutional means.

A central tenet of the capitalist creed was the sanctity of private property. So long as wealth continued to beget wealth and large fortunes remained in the possession of a small minority the accumulation of unearned increments could not fail to perpetuate the economic inequality. Recognition of this fact helped to inspire the co-operative movements that developed strongly in the later nineteenth century. Their founders hoped to subordinate the spirit of competition and profit-making to the general benefit of the members. Consumer co-operatives grew up within the capitalistic system, and the profits of distribution were passed on as dividends to the shareholders. As all who participated were encouraged to purchase a share in the enterprise, all were in some sense employers and employees, capitalists and workers. Producers' co-operatives were in general less numerous and less successful than consumers' co-operatives, but both had the same purpose and inspiration, to dissolve the distinction between capital and labour by fusing the two together. Farmers organized agricultural co-operatives to assemble, grade, pack, preserve, transport, and market their produce. From their contributed capital they founded rural credit banks to minister to their individual needs. In the fields of manufacture and commerce producers' co-operatives turned to processes in which labour was an important element, the making of furniture, clothing, shoes, or soap, and the distributing of them through their own retail stores. In general, prices were fixed at the prevailing levels, and profits were distributed to members in proportion to their share certificates. The co-operative movement spread to all the European countries, and to America, Asia, and Australia. In 1895 an International Co-operative Alliance was formed to advise and encourage new groups. Essentially, the movement was an attempt to develop semi-collectivist cells within the body of a capitalist society, and the members were almost all people of modest circumstances who were seeking a better way to protect themselves from what they regarded as the exploitation of the middleman and the financier.

Fraternal orders or friendly societies of a myriad aims and types also took root, and they multiplied more extensively than the co-operatives. Like the trade unions and the Rochdale Society of Equitable Pioneers (the most permanent form of co-operative store), the 'friendly society' owed much to British initiative. After 1860 the laws governing free associations were simplified throughout western Europe, and lodges, working mens' clubs, and national and international brotherhoods sprang up spontaneously. Their purposes, as defined in their charters, ranged from the convivial to the grim, from social entertainment to care of the maimed, the sick, the blind, and the orphaned, and to burial of the dead. Many societies, and these the most important, offered mutual insurance benefits to their members, to help them in facing sickness, accidents, old age, and other dark eventualities that haunt the poor. In Great Britain friendly societies counted 7,000,000 members by 1885 and 14,000,000 by 1910. On the continent of Europe the movement was less pronounced, but various organizations with similar aims, co-operative credit associations, working men's benefit clubs, and Catholic health, welfare, and insurance circles, made notable gains in funds and membership during the closing decades of the century.

A mutual benefit association, if it remained active and solvent, had a steadying influence on its working-class members. They gained a hardier sense of social solidarity, and they looked with more favour on the laws safeguarding private property because their individual premiums and expected benefits were a form of capital investment. Most men become more conservative when they have something to conserve. In Britain, where *laissez-faire* ideals were strong, many workers created insurance funds on their own initiative; in Germany, with its paternalistic traditions, the state assumed this responsibility after 1883. Bismarck was determined to curb the socialists, but he recognized the validity of their demands for social justice. The industrial and the agricultural labourer, living on a minimum wage, could seldom make adequate provision against sickness, disability, and old age. The worker who ceased to work ceased to earn and might become destitute within a few weeks or months. It was therefore both prudent and humanitarian for the state to introduce a system of compulsory insurance that would provide aid in advance for the unemployed, the aged, the sick, and the disabled.

Germany was the first great power thus to experiment with social insurance on a national scale. A Health Insurance Law, adopted by the Reichstag in 1883, offered a maximum of thirteen weeks of medical care in any one year to its beneficiaries. The workers bore two-thirds and the employers one-third of the cost. In 1884 an Accident Insurance Law followed, wholly supported by dues collected from the employers, and in 1889 the structure was crowned by an Old Age and Invalidity Law. For the maintenance of this last the workers, the employers, and the government all contributed, and the magnitude of the state insurance programme was soon revealed in the official reports. Between 1885 and 1900 some 50,000,000 benefit claims were paid under the sickness, accident, and age disability clauses.

Impressed by the German experiment, other nations introduced similar legislation before the century ended. Health insurance acts, old age pensions, and compensation for workers injured at their trade, were enforced in Austria–Hungary, Denmark, Norway, Belgium, Switzerland, Italy, and France. Even in Great Britain, where the prejudice against state intrusion into business and industrial management remained powerful, a Workmen's Compensation Act was passed in 1897. The British measure restricted compensation to accidents not caused by the 'gross carelessness of the worker', a provision that threw many cases into litigation. In the United States all forms of state insurance for the working classes lagged, partly because of the higher economic status of the average worker, but chiefly because of the individualistic philosophy that dominated the American way of life. The Australians and New Zealanders, in striking contrast to most English-speaking nations, anticipated European labour legislation; the colony of Victoria set up boards to fix industrial wages in 1885, and the New Zealand Labour party after 1890 embarked on a daring social programme to break up large land holdings, limit private fortunes by a progressive income tax, and protect industrial workers through strict factory laws. The eight-hour day was established by law in 1897 and old age pensions in 1898.

This flood of labour legislation, so swift and so wellnigh universal in the western world, made the 1890's a significant decade in social history. The spirit of the times was obviously changing. Workers' hours, wage rates, health, safety, protection, disability risks and old age pensions were ceasing to be a matter of private concern. The business philosophy of free economic enterprise and unregulated competition, in which the employee and employer met on a basis of voluntary contracts with a minimum of government supervision and regulation, had been tried and found wanting. The state was stepping in, not merely to mediate between capital and labour, but to enforce compulsory arbitration, compulsory insurance, compulsory wage rates, and compulsory pensions to the aged and disabled worker and his dependents. Within a generation this drift towards state socialism was to become an almost irresistible current, driving the peoples of Europe towards a more and more explicit regulation of their social and economic life.

The decline of *laissez-faire* and the growth of economic regimentation could also be measured by the rise of tariff walls that obstructed the free flow of trade and intensified the spirit of economic nationalism. The 1880's brought a powerful swing towards protectionism. To protect themselves from the serious competition of British manufactures and American wheat, European industrialists and farmers urged their governments to fence the national field, and the politicians, always interested in additional revenue, responded promptly by raising import duties. Russia, Spain, and Italy had already increased their tariff legislation by 1878; Germany turned resolutely towards protection in 1879; France and Austria imposed additional rates on imported manufactures in 1881. After 1885 a second wave of protectionist sentiment swept Europe, Germany leading with higher duties on many agricultural products, France matching the measures immediately, Italy following in 1887, and Sweden in 1888. When Switzerland forsook free trade in 1891, only Great Britain, Belgium, and Holland remained loyal in principle to the *laissez-faire* commercial policy that had been so widely endorsed earlier in the century. The United States, where the industrial interests had been in the ascendant since the Civil War, guarded the vast American market with jealous vigilance, erecting a tariff wall in the 1880's that was higher than any in Europe. Even the British dominions broke with *laissez-faire* traditions to follow the general trend, levying import duties on goods from all countries including Britain.

The last quarter of the nineteenth century was a period of unbridled imperialism. All the great powers sought new conquests, and all except Austria–Hungary fought colonial wars to extend their possessions on other continents. One-fifth of the land area of the globe and one-tenth of its inhabitants were gathered into the expanding domains of the European conquerors within a generation, a rate of imperialist encroachment unsurpassed in history. It was the climax of five centuries of European expansion overseas; by 1900 European civilization overshadowed the earth; and Joseph Chamberlain summarized this denouement in a sentence: 'The day of small nations has long passed away; the day of Empires has come.'

Africa, four times the area of Europe, was parcelled out in a generation. The race to establish protectorates throughout its little-known hinterland quickened after 1881 when the French secured Tunis. Disorders in Egypt afforded an excuse for British occupation of Alexandria a year later, but Anglo-Egyptian forces required fifteen years to subjugate the Sudan. The daring journeys of David Livingstone, Henry M. Stanley, Savoignan de Brazza, Herman von Wissman, and other African explorers revealed the riches and wonders of the Dark Continent. An 'African fever' seized the imagination of the Europeans as they read of strange safaris from the Saharan sands to the South African veldt and from river-haunted lowlands to the mist-hung Mountains of the Moon. Adventurers made 'treaties' with native kings, diplomats bluffed and gambled to maintain inflated claims, and colonial ministers exchanged notes in a mood of rising exasperation.

In 1884, at the initiative of Bismarck and the French premier Jules Ferry, fourteen nations sent delegates to Berlin for a conference on African affairs. Rules were adopted for the suppression of slavery, the free navigation of the Niger and the Congo, and the definition of 'effective occupation'. The powers recognized the Congo Free State (subsequently a Belgian possession) and prepared to delimit their rival spheres of influence. Britain, France, Germany, Italy, Belgium, Portugal, and Spain came into possession of vast hinterlands which lay behind the coastal ports they had established, and the areas they claimed were expanded swiftly until all Africa had been delimited. Maps of an empty continent changed to a Joseph's coat of coloured patches, ending the vague romantic cartography described by Swift, wherein

> . . . geographers, in Afric-maps,
> With savage-pictures fill their gaps;
> And o'er unhabitable downs
> Place elephants for want of towns.

More than once, in the late nineteenth century, competition for African territory brought some of the great powers close to hostilities. The French annexation of Tunis in 1881 antagonized the Italians (who coveted the site of ancient Carthage) and drove them into an accord with Germany and Austria (Triple Alliance, 1882). An Anglo-French encounter in the Upper Nile Valley (Fashoda Affair) excited both nations in 1898 to a dangerous degree. Franco-German disputes over Morocco provoked a series of crises between 1905 and 1912, crises that were resolved by compromises but increased the international tension.

With the native African peoples the infiltrating Europeans could not avoid a number of local and limited conflicts. The years from 1880 to 1900 were filled with muted echoes of obscure clashes in desert and jungle, as the Riffs, Senegalese, Hovas, Tuaregs, Ashantis, Basutos, Zulus, Matabeles, and other stubborn tribes fought vainly against the conquering whites. Only the Abyssinians maintained their independence, repulsing in 1887 and 1896 the Italian expeditionary forces that pushed inland from Eritrea. In almost all areas in which the Europeans established control they checked tribal warfare, improved communication and transportation, and sought to curb disease. It is easy to prove that in the protectorates established by the various European governments the officials were not always equal to their great responsibilities and their treatment of the native Africans was sometimes selfish and arbitrary. But to leave Africa and its peoples to unsupervised exploitation by commercial adventurers and the operations of mining and trading companies that would have extorted their own terms from the native rulers and administered their concessions to please themselves might have been incalculably worse.

The pressure of European expansion, regulated or unregulated, was certain to affect all Africa by the close of the nineteenth century. In 1878 little more than one-tenth of the Continent was under the control of European governments; by 1914 they controlled nine-tenths. The largest single bloc was subjugated by the French. Stretching from Algeria to the Ivory Coast and from Senegal to the Anglo-Egyptian Sudan this French African empire had expanded until it constituted an area twenty times the size of France, exceeding in territorial extent even the total of all British African possessions.

The fairest test of the effects of European rule on the Dark Continent would be a comparison of vital statistics before and after the completion of the European hegemony. Unfortunately, nothing that can even loosely be regarded as census statistics are available. By sifting and analysing data from various sources, however, enough evidence has been accumulated to suggest that the native population of Africa before 1880 had been stationary or almost stationary for centuries. More dependable evidence indicates that between 1880 and 1914—the period during which European governments extended their control over most of the continent—the population increased by about one-third. Such a trend suggests that so far as health and life expectancy were concerned European rule brought the Africans very definite benefits.

In South Africa, where the British were to fight the severest colonial war resulting from the 'new imperialism', the chief resistance came not from native tribes but from the descendants of European settlers. Cape Town had been founded by the Dutch in 1652 but the Cape Colony passed under British control during the Napoleonic Wars, and by 1826 its boundaries had been extended to the Orange river. The Boers, as the Dutch colonists were called, resented British interference, and in 1835 some 10,000 of them began a 'Great Trek' northward, setting up a republic beyond the Vaal river. War between the British and Boers in 1842 and 1848 was followed by an attempt at delimitation of territory. The British recognized the independence of the Transvaal area where the Boers established the South African

Republic (Sand River Convention, 1852). The lands north of the Orange river were also left to them and the Orange Free State emerged there after 1854.

The discovery of diamonds (1867) between the Vaal and Orange rivers, and the location of rich gold mines in the Transvaal (1886) altered the economic picture. The British annexed the diamond fields, which had been under the authority of the Orange Free State, in 1871, and six years later they pressed on to annex the South African Republic. The pressure of imperialism had swept aside the Sand River Convention. Boer resentment, already aroused by the British policy of protecting the African natives, became intense, while the British were affronted by the legal and political discrimination to which foreigners (Uitlanders) were subjected in the Boer republics. The proclamation of a German protectorate over an adjacent stretch of the south-west African coast (1884) increased British apprehension, while the agitation of the Uitlanders alarmed the Boers.

In 1890 the vigorous British imperialist Cecil Rhodes, who had made a fortune in the diamond fields, became prime minister of the Cape Colony. He dreamed of a Cape-to-Cairo railway that would traverse Africa from south to north on British territory, but he found a stubborn opponent in the Boer leader, Paul Kruger. Kruger had fought (1880) to make the South African Republic (Transvaal) independent again after Great Britain annexed it in 1877, and in 1883 he became its president. In 1895 Rhodes's friend Dr. Leander Starr Jameson led 600 men into the Transvaal to aid a revolt of the Uitlanders there. Forewarned, the Boers captured the raiders. After four more years of abortive negotiations war broke out in 1899, with the South African Republic and the Orange Free State allied against the British empire.

For two and a half years the Boers maintained the unequal struggle, finally yielding to forces that outnumbered them five to one and accepting British sovereignty in May 1902. They were promised eventual representative government and a grant of £3,000,000 to repair their shattered farms. The outcry against British aggression that arose throughout the civilized world left the British people in a chastened mood, for they had been brought to realize their diplomatic isolation, their unpopularity, and their military unpreparedness. The South African War greatly weakened if it did not altogether destroy the spirit of aggressive self-confidence that had inflamed British pride in the later nineteenth century. Five years after the war ended the Transvaal and the Orange River colony were granted responsible government, and in 1909 the British and Boer provinces were united as a self-governing dominion, the Union of South Africa.

Asia with its far larger population (one-half the human race in 1880) seemed destined to share the fate of Africa in these decades of advancing imperialism. The British already controlled India; their patrols were clashing with Russian outposts in Persia and Afghanistan; Tibet and the Yangtse valley were designated as potential spheres for their activities; and upper Burma was annexed as a province of India in 1886. By 1883 the French completed their conquest of Indo-China from Cambodia to Tonkin; the Chinese province of Yunnan was open to their penetration, and the territory of Kwangchowan became theirs on lease in 1898. In the north the Russians were building a railway across Manchuria and waiting only for the collapse of Chinese authority to press into Mongolia and Sinkiang. China, the torpid dragon, seemed destined to die the death of a thousand cuts. It writhed in its sleep but could not rouse itself to repel the gnawing tactics of its numerous foes.

Even the Japanese, adopting European formulas of imperialism along with European technology, joined the race for Chinese concessions. Attacking their huge but inert neighbour in 1894 they detached Korea, annexed Formosa, and almost secured the Liaotung peninsula. But this last-named prize was also of interest to the Russians, the Germans, and the French, and these powers 'persuaded' the Japanese to restore it to China. The successes won by the Japanese in the Sino-Japanese war of 1894 precipitated a further rush for concessions. All the powers demanded, and all except Italy received, additional leases, treaty ports, commercial privileges, and indemnities, until their greed finally aroused the Chinese to resistance. In 1900 a secret society, the 'Literary and Patriotic Order of Harmonious Fists' (anglicized as Boxers), murdered missionaries and traders and besieged the European legations. This ill-planned attempt to expel the 'foreign devils' from China brought swift and indiscriminate reprisals. An international army marched on Peking, sacked the palace of the reactionary Empress Tzu Hsi who had encouraged the Boxers, and levied a heavy indemnity.

Among the twelve powers that collaborated in this resettlement of Chinese affairs were Japan and the United States.

Unlike most of the other participants that took a share in crushing the Boxer Rebellion, the United States held no territory and claimed no sphere of influence on the mainland of Asia. But the Americans had come into possession of the Philippine islands in 1898 after a brief war with Spain, and had annexed the Hawaiian islands the same year. Although the immediate cause of the Spanish-American War had been a revolt of the Cubans (who were speedily liberated from Spanish domination) the conflict marked a turning-point in American and world affairs. For it signalized the emergence of the United States as a world power, despite the fact that the American people were slow to realize that their long-cherished isolation was at an end. Still absorbed in the gigantic task of exploring and exploiting their own continent, they had attempted to shun adventures beyond the seas. With the acquisition of the Philippines and Hawaii, however, they (or at least their government) recognized the need for a two-ocean navy and an inter-oceanic canal at Panama to permit the speedier reinforcement of either fleet. The Pacific had become an ocean of destiny: the opening of the twentieth century found the battleships of six great powers—Britain, France, Germany, Russia, Japan, and the United States—cruising in Far Eastern waters. Of these watchful guardians of oriental affairs, the two powers most vitally interested in the status of China were Japan and Russia, for both had territory bordering on the Sea of Japan. Their rivalry for a dominant influence in north China was to bring the two into armed conflict by 1904.

The progress of western technology, which had changed man's way of life more radically in the nineteenth century than in the preceding two thousand years, continued to accelerate as the century ended. Newer metals, copper, tin, zinc, aluminium, were in rising demand for a machine-dominated economy, but iron still ruled the industrial world. Between 1880 and 1900 the steel production of the globe soared from 4,000,000 to 28,000,000 metric tons, the output of pig iron from 18,000,000 to 39,000,000. With iron available in quantity, engineers applied it to novel structural purposes, notably bridge building and architecture. The Forth Bridge, the Brooklyn Bridge, the Eiffel Tower, and the first skyscrapers in Chicago and New York were completed in the 1880's. The compound steam turbine, perfected by Sir Charles Parsons in 1891, revolutionized steam engineering and raised the power available for electric generators and ocean transport. Electricity opened new paths in industry and metallurgy, providing power for lathes and elevators, reducing metals in the electric furnace, welding them with the electric arc, refining and plating them by electrolysis. The inorganic chemists created new commercial products in their laboratories almost overnight, the most spectacular being the German development of synthetic dyes from coal-tar residues. British manufacturers began the production of cheap wood-pulp paper; a French scientist exhibited the first artificial silk made from cellulose at the Paris Exposition of 1889; and German chemists learned to fix the nitrogen of the air and to synthesize the nitrates indispensable for fertilizers—and for explosives.

In pure as distinguished from applied science (the distinction was rapidly dissolving in actuality) the most fateful advances of this period were made in the study of radioactivity. Although the full significance of the advance was not realized immediately, Wilhelm Konrad Röntgen (German) opened a new era in physics with his detection of X-rays in 1895. The following year Antoine Henri Becquerel (French) discovered that uranium gave off rays similar to those observed by Röntgen, and in 1898 Pierre Curie (French) and Marie Curie (Polish) isolated radium. This international quest into the secrets of matter had been precipitated by Heinrich Hertz (German), whose investigation of the electromagnetic theory of light first propounded by Clerk Maxwell (British) enabled him to demonstrate the existence and measure the velocity of electromagnetic waves as early as 1886.

That such abstract calculations and experiments, seemingly as remote as the stars from the world of practical affairs, had in fact a direct commercial utility was swiftly demonstrated by Guglielmo Marconi. This Irish-Italian inventor utilized 'Hertzian Waves' (as radio waves were still called) to transmit messages, and wireless telegraphy was born (1895). Within three years messages had been successfully transmitted across the English Channel and within six across the Atlantic Ocean. It was a foretaste of the marvels that might be expected from the new science of telecommunication.

The impact of the new technology was changing the face of

nature and the fate of man, but the esoteric formulas of the scientists remained arcana to the multitude. Natural science had made incalculable strides in the century and a half since Benjamin Franklin drew electricity from the heavens by flying a kite in a thunderstorm. The promethean fire of heaven had been harnessed to drive man's engines, to hurl his words across the ocean, and to probe the secrets at the heart of matter. To express the laws, compute the relations, and classify the phenomena detected by physicists and chemists, the mathematicians had elaborated their discipline throughout the nineteenth century, adding novel refinements to the laws of motion divined by Sir Isaac Newton and exploring the possibilities of non-Euclidean geometry. Modern mathematics, the most original creation of the human mind, had become an international language, the language, as Galileo had boldly insisted four centuries earlier, in which Nature wrote her secrets. Yet it remained, like the hieratic symbols of the ancient priesthoods, a script that only a small company of initiates could decipher. The scientists formed a select and emancipated fellowship. Segregated by their intent specialization, dedicated to their recondite mysteries, they had outdistanced the lagging march of western civilization.

Nineteenth-century society was fascinated by the triumphs of its scientists and technicians, but it was a fascination of the mind only; the heart remained loyal to an older religious and humanist tradition. 'We admire with awe', Matthew Arnold admitted to the heralds of a new scientific order,

> We admire with awe
> The exulting thunder of your race;
> You give the universe your law,
> You triumph over time and space!
> Your pride of life, your tireless powers,
> We laud them, but they are not ours.

European thought was still dominated by literary patterns that had been reaffirmed with the Renaissance and perpetuated for five centuries by the rule of the graphocracy. As Inspector of Schools, Arnold fought for the ancient literatures against the intrusion of the new sciences into the curriculum. Emphasis on the literary classics as the core of conventional instruction had made education almost synonymous with book learning, hardening the European mind to the cast of a typographical culture.

When, in the later nineteenth century, the still unlettered majority were invited to share the cake of culture, they were prescribed the type of liberal education admired by a leisured class. Instruction proceeded almost entirely on the intellectual plane with scant regard for the practical problems the pupils must face in later life in the field or factory, office or shop, nursery or kitchen, where most of them were destined to labour.

With literacy as the accepted yardstick, the progress of popular education in the nineteenth century was measured by the decline in the percentage of illiterates. Statistics are incomplete and standards variable, but it seems reasonably clear that a majority of the European people were still unable to read and write when the century closed. Figures available for England show one-third of the men and one-half the women illiterate in 1840; in France and Belgium one-half the adult citizens were in the same condition in 1850; in Germany and the Scandinavian states standards were higher; but in Italy, Spain, Portugal, Austria, Russia, and the Balkan countries only one person in ten could be accounted literate in 1860.

The progress of political democracy made popular education a critical issue, for it appeared dangerous to give the franchise to citizens unable to read and write. James Madison, fourth president of the United States, emphasized this predicament with the trenchant warning that 'popular government without popular education is the prologue to a farce or a tragedy'. Almost all European governments made some provision for free public schools at the primary level during the last third of the nineteenth century, Austria–Hungary (1868–9), Great Britain (1870), Germany (1872), Switzerland (1874), Italy (1877), the Netherlands (1878), Belgium (1879), and France (1878–82). Illiteracy declined with remarkable rapidity. By 1900 it had fallen below 5 per cent. in Germany, Scandinavia, Britain, and France, thus ceasing to be a serious problem in north-western Europe. Southern and eastern Europe still presented a darker picture. One-third of the population of Austria–Hungary, one-half of the Italians, two-thirds of the Spaniards and Portuguese, and four-fifths of the Balkan and Russian peoples were unable to read and write when the nineteenth century ended. This meant, taking Europe as a whole, that one-half of the population remained illiterate. In the United States the rate of illiteracy for those over ten years of age fell from 17 per cent. to 10 per cent. between 1880 and 1900, but in Latin America it remained in general exceptionally high, exceeding 90 per cent. in Mexico, Brazil, and Bolivia.

The unprecedented increase in the total reading public throughout western Europe and North America created an ever-widening field for popular journalism to exploit. The number of newspapers in Europe doubled between 1880 and 1900. New inventions—the linotype, monotype, straight-line press, automatic feeder and binder, half-tone photo engraving, and colour presses—reduced costs and multiplied circulation, aided by the substitution of wood-pulp for rag paper. News gathering was speeded by the more rapid transmission of mail and the extension of telegraph and telephone lines. With millions of readers gleaning their knowledge of current events from the penny newspapers, the techniques of propaganda and advertising evolved rapidly and public opinion was given capricious turns. Politicians learned to heed and sometimes to manipulate the oracle of the press; and the right to speak and write freely on public questions became a cardinal principle of the democratic faith.

Under this growing stimulus printing and publishing activities expanded phenomenally. In Germany, long a leader in the book trade, the printing plants doubled their output in twenty years. Wherever literacy increased, new public libraries, reading rooms, book shops, and book stalls strewed volumes, periodicals, and pamphlets before the public, catering to its shifting caprices. The heritage of European civilization, in so far as it could be contained in books, was brought within reach of the literate classes, a liberation and an invitation to learning that speeded the democratization of western culture. The common man became aware of a world beyond his former limited horizon, and he acquired a knowledge of social and national questions that prepared him more adequately for the role of an active citizen. Literacy thus provided an indispensable foundation for the spread of democracy in the western world. For as Nicolai Lenin learned in his earliest attempts to arouse the Russian masses, without literacy 'there can be no politics, there can be only rumours, gossip, and prejudice'.

The literature of the late nineteenth century was a mirror in which coming developments cast their shadow before. At the bottom of their inkwells writers saw in cloudy vision the coming disintegration of the bourgeois synthesis, beheld the genii of science, obedient yet terrifying, rise like an incalculable cloud, and deepest of all caught the pale reflection of their own disenchanted faces, each man seeking the riddle of his inner real self. These three recurrent themes—social justice, science, and the inner self—provide a clue to the mood of European literature at the close of the nineteenth century.

A conviction that society had outgrown the drawing-room politics of the Victorian Compromise, and that the genteel tradition in art left too much unsaid about life, had inspired the realist revolt of the 1860's and 1870's. But writers like Émile Zola and Henrik Ibsen, however just their insight and pitiless their pens, were not made to lead a popular revolution. A vital proletarian literature did not develop until socialism had become a more powerful political force. Yet a warning that all was not for the best in the best possible of bourgeois worlds had been sounded by Henry George in *Progress and Poverty* (1879); it was repeated more movingly by Gerhard Hauptmann in *The Weavers* (1892), and echoed from the underworld dives depicted in the early stories of Maxim Gorki. In Britain the formation of the Fabian Society in 1883, which enlisted the support of Sidney Webb and George Bernard Shaw, was a prophetic step, for its members aimed at 'the reorganization of society by the emancipation of land and industrial capital from individual and class ownership . . .'. From his earliest novels and plays, published in the 1880's and 1890's, Shaw revealed his ability to make socialism dangerous by making it amusing. He set himself to puncture by his incisive ridicule the inflated pretensions of British superiority, bourgeois superiority, and masculine superiority, and few of those who laughed at his thrusts realized that the deflation of these confident premisses would loose the fountains of the social deep.

Modern technology, that was casting its shadow across so many fields of man's endeavour in the late nineteenth century, affected the manufacture of books more rapidly than it influenced the minds of their authors. The high literary tradition continued to feed itself upon the past, and the masters of *belles lettres* ignored as long as possible the vulgar intrusion of the machines. Even in popular journals the space devoted to scientific inventions and discoveries remained inadequate to their importance when the century closed, partly because the methods and personalities of the scientists were difficult to simplify or to dramatize. But adventure stories with a pseudo-scientific background grew in favour (Jules Verne had raised this type of writing to respectability in the 1860's), and romances laid in the brave new world to be created by science vied with the historical novel in popular appeal. By a strange liaison the new science fiction became involved with utopianism, and a hybrid literature emerged that combined social fantasy with scientific features. Samuel Butler's *Erewhon* (1872) depicted an ideal commonwealth in a manner that made the book a satire on contemporary England. Edward Bellamy's *Looking Backward* (1887), written in a more popular and kindly vein, sold a million copies. William Morris's *News from Nowhere* (1891), Herbert George Wells's *War of the Worlds* (1898), and similar products of sociological idealism enjoyed wide popularity. On the continent one of the most influential novels of this genre was *Freiland, ein soziales Zukunftsbild* (1890), an imaginary account of the foundation of a socialistic colony in equatorial Africa, written by the Austrian journalist and economist Theodor Hertzka.

That bourgeois society was sick some of its own more discerning sons had detected for themselves before 1900. From Scandinavia to Spain writers turned their attention increasingly to social criticism as the nineteenth century neared its close, but there is space to mention only a few representative names. In Norway Björnstjerne Björnson, in Denmark Georg Brandes, in Holland Edward Douwes Dekker and his disciples who founded *De Nieuwe Gids* in the 1880's, in France Émile Zola and Anatole France, in Germany Nietzsche, Hauptmann, and the feminist Louise Otto-Peters, in Italy Edmondo De Amicis, in Spain Ricardo Macías Picavea and Ángel Ganivet—all were disturbed by the symptoms of decadence that they discerned around them, but few supplemented their diagnosis by a constructive programme for social recuperation.

Meanwhile there were growing indications of a coming revolt against positivism, intellectualism, and scientific determinism. Science was turning sensitive artistic natures back upon themselves, verifying Coleridge's dictum uttered early in the century that 'Poetry is not the proper antithesis to prose but to science'. Poetry and science could not, in truth, be easily reconciled. It is one of the singular lacunas of modern literature that the epic achievements of the scientists have never been celebrated fittingly in epic verse. The wonder-workers who created enough legends to stock a modern mythology, who bent the lightning to their will, weighed the sun with a slide rule, and exorcized invisible armies of death with the wave of a test-tube, found no bards to praise them in immortal song.

This dichotomy in western culture between the makers of things and the makers of songs ran deeper than a chance intellectual estrangement. The generation that came of age in the 1890's was ripe for disillusionment. It had grown to maturity in an era of great material achievement but in an atmosphere chilled by what Disraeli had well termed 'the frigid theories of a generalizing age'. It was the first generation to realize sharply that science had plunged humanity down an unknown road. A shock went through the confident ranks as the vanguard slowed, seeking the milestones that were not there. The literature of the period records this faltering of morale, the change from inherited optimism to introspective doubt that came with *la fin du siècle*, as if a chill wind had struck from the untravelled wastes of the new century.

Modern man was outgrowing the intoxication of his triumphs and feeling the weight of his desolate and incommunicable singularity. Like the enigmatic hero of Joseph Conrad's early novel, *Lord Jim* (1900), he still obeyed an inherited pattern of conduct. But he was an exile from his own past, an unwitting victim of dark powers, an eternal wanderer, 'excessively romantic' and 'inscrutable at heart'. Like Lord Jim he seemed destined to pass away under a cloud, leaving no one certain what it was he sought.

'Within!' This challenge, raised by Miguel de Unamuno to rally his fellow Spaniards after the defeats of 1898, had a wider, an international significance. 'Those who cannot remember the past are condemned to repeat it', George Santayana warned almost at the same moment. The admonitions were well timed. To take bearings for the road ahead the Europeans had to resurvey the road behind and to reappraise themselves and their traditions. The intellectual confusion of the age resulted in great part from the schism between theology and science, and a number of ardent minds set themselves to seek a reconciliation that would make man 'whole' again. After 1885 the idealist schools of philosophy attracted new converts. Several leading scientists, notably the French mathematician Henri Poincaré, suggested that scientific laws might prove to be relative and statistical, and that mental processes were not reducible to the same terms as physical phenomena. This belief found its ablest defender in Henri Bergson, who insisted in his *Essai sur les données immédiates de la conscience* (1889) that subservience to the external world deadened the mind by reducing its activities to a standardized, mechanistic pattern.

The concept of relativism weakened the position of the positivists and determinists. Walter Pater, who died in 1894, had already observed this trend. 'To regard all things and principles of things as inconstant modes or fashions', he admitted, 'has more and more become the tendency of modern thought.' Those who craved certitude were moved to seek it in other disciplines than science; some turned to 'art for art's sake', and some to religion. Leo XIII, who had succeeded the obdurate Pius IX in 1878, welcomed the opportunity presented by the shift in opinion. Without compromising Catholic tradition, he suggested the possibility of reducing the discrepancies between the religious and the rationalist interpretations of history, and he threw open the Vatican archives to accredited scholars in the faith that with deeper understanding contradictions might be found to harmonize. Ecclesiastics stressed the social welfare of the masses as a field in which Church and state had a joint interest. Sceptics were reminded that the opposition between science and religion was not absolute, and that the careers of Gregor Mendel and Louis Pasteur showed that it was possible to be a great scientist and a good Catholic at the same time. The close of the nineteenth century not only brought a Catholic revival in literature; it found the Church functioning with renewed vigour on many fronts, to the surprise of agnostics who had been prepared, a generation earlier, to predict its imminent collapse.

Those who were indifferent to religion sought other clues to the riddle of the inner self. In the naturalistic atmosphere that western man had come to breathe during this materialistic age the neurotic turned to psychology for relief, and the artist became, almost inevitably, something of a psychologist. He found no lack of pathological subjects. The uprooting of millions caused by the migration to the cities, the falling birth-rate that weakened family life and changed the only child from an

anomaly almost to a norm, the precarious eco
the wage-earner, all combined to destroy the em
of the average citizen. Lonely in a crowd he c
thoughts upon himself.

This narcissistic drive, this subjectivism, soo
in art. Expressionism, the practice of giving fr
one's inner thoughts and sensations, became a
nique; the term was first applied to a style of pai
to literature and drama. The interior monolo
of consciousness' novel, the search for new sy
unique personal vocabulary, revealed the gro
of the newer writers with inner states of tho
The psychological novel was not new but it
new stage of refinement. Henry James, who
long series of novels, dramas, and essays in the
his characters with unrivalled subtlety and psy
In the 1880's Maurice Barrès commenced a tr
gave the significant title *Le Culte du moi*, incre
psychological individualism, and in *Les De*
coined a term that fittingly described the man
of his generation.

Philosophy as well as psychology lent it
against a strictly intellectual and rational exp
ence. The tenets of Pragmatism, as elabora
Peirce (who introduced the word about 187
James, suggested that the true is 'only the ex
of thinking' and that will and interest rather
of logic determine man's rationalizations an
fied form the Pragmatic principle that an id
could be readily assimilated with Darwinism
those which helped the individual or the gro
unceasing struggle for existence. Business
cited the doctrine of the 'survival of the fitt
for unregulated competition, and found its
fittest survive a pleasing reflection on their
there were other more dangerous implica
and Pragmatism, for these philosophies mig
port the conclusion that will-power (volu
power (energism) counted more effectivel
vive than the dictates of reason or the refin
arguments offered comfort to the depresse

implied that victory in the social struggle might be decided, not by logic or legal casuistry, but by mass determination and naked force. Nietzsche had stressed the amoral nature of power, insisting that the born leader, the superman, must act with the impersonal ruthlessness of a natural force because he was 'beyond good and evil'. The leaders of a militant proletariat, aspiring to social control, digested the conclusion. To wield power it was necessary to be ruthless.

Ideas are weapons, and the circulation of ideas like those of Marx and Nietzsche were storm warnings. An era of profound social upheavals was approaching. The nineteenth century had seen European society sweep forward like a mighty river broadening and deepening with each decade, turbulent at times but reasonably obedient to its dikes and never catastrophically destructive. The vigorous and intelligent rule of a benevolent bourgeoisie had favoured a remarkable degree of social order, and the *pax Britannica* had helped to preserve a balance of power among the nations. Wealth, population, standards of living, popular education, and public health had made advances never equalled hitherto by any empire on any continent. Though the force of organized religion had declined, the spirit of humanitarianism had expanded; no age had done more for the common man, or shown more respect for the sanctity of treaties and of contracts. But the nineteenth century, with its order and security, was near its close. Such golden centuries have been rare in the annals of mankind, and no two have ever followed in immediate succession.

VI

RISING SOCIAL PRESSURES AND THE BALANCE OF POWER (1898–1914)

WHEN the twentieth century opened in 1901 the European powers had been at peace for thirty years, and there had been no general European war in eighty-five years. All the leading nations except Russia had created the machinery for parliamentary government, although in Germany and Austria–Hungary this machinery did not always function and ministries might defy a majority of the popular representatives and remain in office despite votes of no confidence from the lower chamber. Grave problems existed, social and internal tensions were increasing, but faith in progress and reason was strong, and most people believed their political machinery adequate to resolve the strains by timely readjustments. In this they were mistaken. The problems were not solved. In 1914 the disruptive forces within European society escaped control and the continent was plunged into a disastrous struggle that reduced its population and left its economy shattered. The outbreak of this First World War marked the close of an historical epoch. When the relative equilibrium that had endured since 1815 broke down in 1914, the 460,000,000 inhabitants of Europe entered a new era of violent conflicts, economic collapse, and social revolution. Those who survived learned to look back with regret to the years before 1914 as a happier age of decency and order and security.

It is difficult for readers of a later generation to retrace the history of the European nations from 1898 to 1914 without feeling at each step the approach of a tragic denouement, a climax unintended and unforeseen by the actors of the drama. In retrospect, this sense of dramatic irony tends to invest all the decisions taken in those closing years with a quality of doom and to make the outcome appear inescapable. Such a reading is of course a falsification, a dramatization, of the past. But it is not a falsification to affirm that after 1900 signs multiplied in Europe that a grave climax could not be long postponed. The driving forces of European economy had begun to slip their yokes; their masters, reduced to servants, understood these growing forces too imperfectly to curb their acceleration; the political and diplomatic controls were no longer adequate to the increasing strains. Technology, industry, political and economic nationalism were all generating powerful but uneven and sometimes contrary thrusts. In a word, European civilization was threatened by a growing disparity between 'strong physics and weak sociology'.

In such a society there were two principal areas where friction could accumulate sufficiently to set off an explosion. Deepening class antagonism within each troubled nation might lead to a revolution. National rivalry between the more and more heavily armed states might precipitate a war. As it happened, no important European government was overthrown by an internal upheaval in the decades before 1914, largely because the statesmen in every country made adroit concessions to the discontented masses. This search for social justice was the most significant drive in the domestic politics of the European peoples from 1898 to 1914. In the pragmatic sense the quest for social justice was successful: revolutions were avoided. How they were avoided can be explained only by analysing each state separately, because no two had identical patterns or programmes.

In Great Britain the political pattern from 1895 to 1914 broke into two parts, a decade of Conservative rule (1895–1905) followed by a period of Liberal ascendancy (1906–14). The Conservatives came to power in 1895 with the aristocratic Robert Cecil, Marquess of Salisbury, as prime minister and the forceful Joseph Chamberlain as colonial secretary. Chamberlain headed a splinter group of 'Liberal Unionists' who had deserted Gladstone and the Liberal party to join the Conservatives because they were determined to preserve the union with Ireland. A mood of nationalism and imperialism was stirring the British people. The Diamond Jubilee of Queen Victoria in 1897 was celebrated with great pomp, reminding them of the unparalleled progress and prosperity Great Britain had known through the queen's long reign. Chamberlain tried to direct this pride and elation into a positive programme, demanding closer imperial ties with all parts of the empire, larger armaments, and an intrepid foreign policy. In Africa the ardent apostle of Anglo-Saxon supremacy, Cecil Rhodes, predicted an all-British railway from Cairo to Cape Town, a project that fired the imagination of the expansionists. 'I would annex the planets if I could', Rhodes declared with characteristic ardour.

The South African War (1899–1902), for which Britain proved unprepared, dissipated some of this enthusiasm for imperialism, for although the Boer farmers were finally defeated the war was costly to Britain in money and prestige. To raise more revenue and cement the empire more solidly Chamberlain proposed a protective tariff with imperial preference. But import duties on food and manufactures, which might have built an economic fence around the empire and helped British manufacturers to compete against the 'protected' industries of Germany and the United States, would also have raised the cost of living for British workers. Tariff Reform was hotly discussed and the issue split the Conservative party, now under the lead of Arthur James Balfour. In 1905 the Liberal leader, Sir Henry Campbell-Bannerman, took office at the head of a new ministry, and an election in 1906 confirmed the Liberal ascendancy. The British electorate had repudiated Tariff Reform and turned away from the nationalist-imperialist-protectionist programme Chamberlain had propounded.

The Liberal government, in alliance with the Labour party, attacked the social question energetically. In 1906 a Workmen's Compensation Act laid the responsibility for the workers' welfare squarely upon the employers, establishing compensation benefits for those workers who were injured or incapacitated at their labour. An Old Age Pensions Act (1908) set up annuities for workers reaching the age of seventy, the funds to be drawn from the national exchequer. In 1909 a Minimum Wage Law established boards to fix the basic remuneration for certain poorly paid occupations, and this measure was extended to include the vital coal industry with its million workers three years later.

'The root trouble of our social system', declared David Lloyd George, who became chancellor of the exchequer in 1908, 'is the precariousness of living.' In 1911 he introduced a National Insurance Act to provide compulsory insurance for workers against sickness, invalidity, and unemployment. The beneficiaries were required to contribute premiums towards some of these funds, but a heavy share of the load fell upon the employers and the national treasury.

To balance the expanded budget Lloyd George proposed extra levies, in particular a graduated income tax, an increased inheritance tax, and a special assessment on the 'unearned increment' resulting from rising land values when such rises profited the owner unduly. This Lloyd George budget of 1909 passed the Commons, but was defeated in the Lords. Thereupon the Liberal government that had sponsored it appealed to the electorate and was returned to office with a reduced majority. The budget became law, and after a second appeal to the voters the House of Lords was shorn of its power to block financial measures, though it could still hold up other bills for as long as two years (Parliament Act of 1911). The will of the popular majority had triumphed against the conservative groups, but class antagonism had been sharpened in the struggle. More serious still, a crushing burden had been imposed on the treasury and the taxpayers. Coming at a time when international tensions were increasing, this diversion of revenue to social services created difficulties, because it reduced the sums available for imperial defence. This other side of the picture—the problem of national security as contrasted with the problem of social security—will be examined later.

The adoption of these 'Liberal Reforms' in Great Britain after 1905 was in some sense a 'peaceful revolution'. The Liberals were the traditional reform party, but they were driven leftward after 1906 by labour pressure. The British working classes had been disposed to neglect politics until 1901, but in that year a judicial ruling of the House of Lords (Taff Vale Judgment) imperilled the trade unions and rallied workers to the newly-founded Labour party. In the elections of 1906 this party won twenty-nine seats in the House of Commons and increased them to forty-two in 1910. The Liberal cabinet wished to hold the support of these Labour members, and it adopted Labour (that is Socialist) proposals. Hitherto Great Britain had lagged behind most advanced continental countries in social legislation, but after 1906 it caught up and even surpassed them in such innovations as unemployment insurance.

In the Third French Republic a turning-point in the long struggle between Right and Left was reached in the Dreyfus Affair. Captain Alfred Dreyfus, a French Jew, was pronounced guilty of treason by a military court in 1894 and sentenced to life imprisonment in the penal colony on Devil's Island. Four years later the accumulation of evidence pointing to his innocence forced a reopening of his case despite the haughty opposition of the French high command. The French people were profoundly stirred, dividing into Dreyfusards and Anti-Dreyfusards.

The final dramatic revelation that Dreyfus was the victim not merely of a judicial error but of a sustained conspiracy discredited a number of army leaders, anti-Semitic journalists, and other prejudiced groups that had insisted upon his guilt. The parties of the Right were repudiated at the polls, and a 'republican bloc' based on the Centre and Left won control of the Chamber of Deputies and dominated French politics after 1899.

The army staff had long been a stronghold of royalist, reactionary, and Catholic sentiment: it was now republicanized. The authority and influence of the Catholic Church in France was weakened by an Associations Law (1901) that dissolved the religious orders engaged in teaching: public education was laicized. The concordat of 1801, that had governed the relations of Church and State in France for a century, was abrogated (Separation Law, 1905), and the state assumed the ownership of all Church property. In practice, the law was eased, and religious congregations continued to use the churches for worship by arrangement with the local authorities. The principal consequences of the reform crusade were the divorce of religion and politics, the triumph of the republic over its Catholic and royalist opponents, and the virtual elimination of royalism as a vital force in French political life.

The weakening of royalism, militarism, and Catholicism brought a relative strengthening of socialism. The Republican Bloc needed support from the Left for its attack on the citadels of the Right, and it bought this support by a series of social reforms. A Factory Law reduced the working day to eleven hours (1900), then to ten hours (1906), and finally to eight hours for minors (1907). Some measure of compensation for workers injured or disabled at their trade was authorized in 1898, and successive pension laws provided aid for the indigent aged until almost all occupations had been covered by 1910.

To most French workers these limited concessions did not appear sufficient. Socialist agitation mounted steadily. Ideological disputes divided the various socialist groups, but they managed to elect a total of 50 members to the Chamber of Deputies in 1890, 54 in 1906, 76 in 1910, and 101 in 1914. A United Socialist party was organized in 1905.

French workers were more interested in politics than the British and more revolutionary in temper than the Germans.

Their labour unions (*syndicats*) used the strike as a political as well as an economic weapon, and their leaders spoke of the day when the solidarity of the working classes would be such that a nation-wide strike would force the bourgeois government to abdicate. To link the various *syndicats* under a unified command a *Confédération Générale du Travail* was created in 1895, and in 1906 its leaders called a general strike for an eight-hour day. The government of the French Republic found itself facing an organization (the C.G.T.) so powerful that it threatened to become a state within the state. But the people of France as a whole, while sympathetic towards labour, were not ready for a working-class revolution: 'the heart of the French bourgeois is on the left,' as André Siegfried was to note wittily, 'but his pocket book is on the right.' The cabinet, headed by the energetic Georges Clemenceau, ordered the police to arrest leading syndicalist officials, and the strike was abandoned. Four years later a graver crisis faced the government when the railway workers walked out, but the cabinet mobilized army reservists to run the trains, and once more the threat of a paralysing strike that would make the labour committee a virtual dictatorship was frustrated. Thereafter, syndicalism as a revolutionary force tended to decline, although membership in the C.G.T., which rose from 200,000 in 1906 to 400,000 in 1912, reached 500,000 in 1914.

In Germany the rapid evolution of the Social Democratic party was more impressive than the slow growth of the Labour party in Britain or the doctrinaire debates of the United Socialists in France. Bismarck's repressive laws against the socialists were allowed to lapse after 1890, when the new emperor, William II, relieved the Iron Chancellor of his office. William was talented, ambitious, impulsive, and inept. His ideal of government was a sort of paternal despotism founded on popularity; he wanted to be admired by his subjects; and he believed that he could charm the German masses into obedience without coercion. But his successive chancellors—the conscientious Caprivi, the septuagenarian Prince von Hohenlohe, the pliant Prince von Bülow, the earnest but ill-starred Bethmann-Hollweg—were not men of Bismarck's stamp. German imperial policy in the Wilhelmian era lacked the unity of direction Bismarck had maintained, becoming more erratic and confusing as rival policy-making cliques jockeyed for power. The ambiguity in the German constitution that left the imperial chancellor and his ministry responsible to the emperor but condemned them to work out legislation with a frequently hostile Reichstag remained unresolved. And policies none too well co-ordinated at best were in constant danger at critical moments from William's headstrong interference and love of histrionic gestures.

In the Reichstag the forces of opposition were headed by the Social Democrats. As the acceleration of German industry multiplied the legions of urban workers, the strength of the Social Democratic party mounted surprisingly. By 1912 it had 110 deputies in the Reichstag, the largest single political bloc, representing some 4,250,000 electors. Twice in 1913 the Social Democrats joined with other dissidents to muster a majority vote, declaring that the Reichstag lacked confidence in the government. But the chancellor did not resign. Nor did the opposition force the issue: few German socialists were revolutionaries. They had extorted a number of concessions for the workers from 1890 onwards—limitation of working hours, improvement in factory conditions, expansion of the old age, sickness, and accident insurance acts, an imperial department of labour—and they had become more cautious as they saw themselves drift within sight of attaining power by constitutional means.

The authoritarian structure of the German state made power a reality for the party that could grasp it, and the Social Democrats were prepared to preserve the system if they could direct it. The basic rift in German political life was a rift between the impotent many and the powerful few; landlords, manufacturers, bankers, bureaucrats, military leaders shaped the national policies in a manner that seemed selfish and monopolistic to the masses. The Social Democrats fought, therefore, to limit great fortunes by imposing inheritance and income taxes, to cut the agrarian profits of the great landowners by lowering the tariff on imported food, to pare the dividends of the corporations and the employers by ensuring higher pay, easier hours, and more favourable working conditions for servants, labourers, and factory hands. They fought, also, to curb the control of the militarists by reducing the annual armament appropriations, for they believed with good reason that the army high command was the citadel of German conservatism. The army had never been democratized; its higher offices were reserved for the Junkers, members of the landed nobility and particularly of the aristocracy of east Prussia. Before 1914, 30 out of 32 commanding generals in the German army, and 37 out of 44 lieutenant-generals, were of noble birth. Against such class favouritism the Social Democrats were pledged to fight. But how were they to democratize the army without weakening it? And might not the officers of the high command prefer to provoke a war, in order to demonstrate their value and capacity, rather than wait until the Social Democratic party climbed to power, curtailed their appropriations, and cancelled their privileges?

In Italy, as in most of Europe, the parties of the Left gained ground in the opening years of the twentieth century. Since the unification of the kingdom two generations earlier, the Chamber of Deputies had contained a Right and a Left grouping, with the leaders of the Right coming as a rule from the industrial north and those of the Left from the south. But this sectional affiliation, and all other distinctions between the rival parties, were of less significance than the fact that both played politics, practised favouritism, and coveted the spoils of office. They alternated in power rather than in policy, and neither maintained a high standard of political honesty or efficiency. From 1896 to 1903 the Right was in power; then the Left forces, dominated by Giovanni Giolitti, took office and controlled Italian politics until the First World War.

Illiteracy, high taxes, low wages, emigration, and lack of essential raw materials such as coal and iron, made it difficult for Italy to play the ambitious role of a great power. Between four and five million Italians sought new homes in North and South America between 1860 and 1914. Unfortunately, those who remained were swayed by an enthusiastic nationalism that easily degenerated into chauvinism. Their political leaders found it convenient to distract popular attention from ills at home by references to *Italia irredenta* (the 'unredeemed' areas including Istria, Trieste, and the Trentino, still held by the Austrians) and to the need for an overseas empire comparable to that of France or Britain. An attempt to conquer Abyssinia ended in a catastrophic military defeat in 1896. Discontent and lawlessness spread among the impoverished peasants of Naples and Sicily, and syndicalist organizers with a frankly revolutionary programme appealed to the poorly paid industrial workers of Milan and other northern cities. A general strike at

Milan (1904) stirred up so much violence that the army was called upon to suppress it.

Imitating the social remedies already initiated by Bismarck in Germany the Italian parliament adopted old age pensions and compulsory insurance against sickness and accidents as early as 1898. Trade unions were legalized, and many public utilities taken over by the municipal or national authorities. But these palliatives failed to relieve the popular discontent or to improve the feeble condition of the national finances. In 1912 the (fourth) Giolitti ministry decided to abolish the literacy and property qualifications limiting the suffrage, and the electorate was expanded from 3,000,000 to 8,500,000 adult males. An election the following year brought a sharp rise in the socialist representation, the number of socialist deputies leaping from forty-one to seventy-eight. It was apparent that in Italy, as in Britain, France, and Germany, the ascendancy of the liberal bourgeoisie was threatened by the rising power of the proletariat. But in Italy the Catholic Church, although it was still officially unreconciled with the national government, exerted a powerful restraining influence over the masses and combated the spread of socialist doctrines. In the election of 1913 it was significant that the representation of the Catholic groups rose from fourteen to thirty-five deputies, a larger proportionate increase than that achieved by the socialists.

Spain at the opening of the twentieth century was still in many respects a land of the old régime. The monarch wielded considerable personal power; the Church and the Catholic religious orders retained a privileged position, great wealth, and a decisive influence over education; a few aristocratic families possessed princely domains while landless peasants starved; and the army pursued its own policies, defying the civil government. The army officers knew that their support was indispensable to the king, the debonair but shallow Alphonso XIII. Spanish economic development was slow, with manufacturing, mining, and railway construction largely dependent on foreign capital; and the last relics of the once vast Spanish colonial empire in America and the Philippines were lost to the United States in 1898. Sectionalism, always strong among the Basques and Catalonians, weakened the unity of the nation, while anarchist and syndicalist doctrines spread among the urban workers. Some half-hearted attempts at reform were made between 1898 and 1914, but the clerical question, the land question, the labour question, and the army question continued to resist solution. Spain was obviously drifting towards a social upheaval of unpredictable gravity in which the army, with its preference for military dictatorship, was likely to determine the outcome.

In Portugal parallel conditions prevailed and revolution came more swiftly. Charles I (1898–1908) was selfish and extravagant; he was assassinated in 1908; and his successor, Manuel II, was dethroned by a naval revolt in 1910. Portugal became a republic with a constitution resembling that of France, but apart from some anti-clerical edicts the new régime did little to change the basic pattern of Portuguese politics or to improve the condition of the people. Spain and Portugal together had a population of 26,000,000 in 1914, and the Portuguese empire in Africa and the East Indies was twenty times the area of Portugal itself, yet the Iberian peoples exerted less political, economic, and military influence in Europe and the world than their history and their numbers warranted. But despite the severance of all political ties their linguistic and cultural traditions still affected the lives of 50,000,000 people in Latin America, and Spanish remained, after English and Russian, the most widely spoken of the European languages.

Belgium and the Netherlands, like Portugal, possessed overseas empires many times their own area, and like Portugal they relied upon British friendship and naval supremacy because without the *pax Britannica* their possessions would have been highly vulnerable. Belgian progress in the nineteenth century proved remarkable and consistent. The constitutional monarchy established after Belgium broke away from the Netherlands in 1831 functioned smoothly; peace, order, and industrial expansion brought a phenomenal development of metallurgy and manufacture; and the Belgian population increased to almost 8,000,000 by 1914, making Belgium the most densely populated country in Europe. The Liberal (bourgeois) party, that controlled Belgian politics from 1849 to 1884, was weakened by the rise of socialism, but the beneficiary of the resulting split was the Catholic party, which achieved parliamentary leadership and controlled the cabinets from 1884 to the First World War. Social legislation, especially after 1900, established old age pensions, legalized trade unions, regulated factory work, and improved the living conditions of the urban classes.

The Netherlands, likewise a constitutional monarchy, had a slightly smaller population than Belgium (6,250,000 in 1914), and Dutch economy was less highly industrialized. Dutch social and political institutions were also less democratic. Until 1887 the electorate did not exceed 150,000; it was doubled in that year, and doubled again in 1896, but it still fell far short of universal suffrage. There was widespread dissatisfaction among the unenfranchised, and minor social reforms did little to allay it. Serious strikes dislocated the railway and shipping services in 1903, and the government, faced with a failure of transport and trade, broke the workers' resistance by calling out the troops. Yet, despite labour trouble at home and repeated insurrections among the native peoples in their populous Indonesian empire, the Netherlanders remained prosperous, ranking fifth in foreign trade and seventh in merchant tonnage among the nations of the world until the outbreak of the First World War.

The Swiss Confederation had an area (16,000 square miles) somewhat larger, and a population (4,000,000) somewhat smaller, than that of the Netherlands in 1914. But Switzerland had no sea-coast, no navy, and no colonies, preserving its independence by prudent diplomacy, with three great powers —Germany, France, and Italy—pressing its frontiers. It lacked many of the characteristics commonly thought essential to a national state: centralization of government, and unity of speech, institutions, and religion. The twenty-two Swiss cantons were sovereign units linked by a loose federal tie. The population was almost evenly divided between the Protestant and Roman Catholic faiths. Two-thirds of the people spoke German, but in five cantons French was the accepted tongue, and in one Italian. Circumspect in their relations with foreigners who visited the Alpine resorts in profitable numbers, vigilant in defence, and industrious in manufacture, commerce, and farming, the Swiss remained peaceful and progressive. A constitution adopted in 1874 provided for universal manhood suffrage, free compulsory education, and religious toleration. In two respects Swiss democracy was the most advanced in Europe by 1914: the electors could demand a plebiscite on any important legislative measure that came before the federal parliament (the referendum), and could initiate legislation on any proposal made by 50,000 or more electors (the initiative).

The smaller countries of Europe, it is interesting to note,

tended to conform to a norm or pattern by the beginning of the twentieth century. They had in general about one-eighth of the population and area of the great European powers. They owed their continued existence as sovereign states less to their own innate capacity for defence than to the mutual jealousies of strong neighbours, which preserved them from absorption in order to maintain the European balance of power. This held true of the three northern states, Denmark, Sweden, and Norway. The Scandinavian countries, like Switzerland, Belgium, and the Netherlands, occupied an area of equilibrium equally vital and equally vulnerable to three powerful neighbours, for Britain, Germany, and Russia all had interests in the Baltic.

The Scandinavian nations remained at peace throughout the nineteenth century (save for the Danish War of 1864) and evolved along constitutional lines as limited monarchies, setting an admirable example of political stability, economic enterprise, and high culture. The Danes devoted themselves with particular success to agriculture and dairy farming, the Norwegians built up a maritime tonnage that ranked fifth in the world by 1914, and the Swedes developed their machine and metallurgical industries with notable success. The union of Sweden and Norway under one crown, approved by the Congress of Vienna, was dissolved peaceably after almost a century when Norway became an independent kingdom under a Danish prince in 1905. Norway was one of the earliest European states to establish woman suffrage (1907 and 1915); Denmark followed, liberalizing the voting procedure by constitutional amendments between 1901 and 1915; and Sweden adopted proportional representation and universal manhood suffrage after 1907. All three Scandinavian countries lost heavily by emigration between 1850 and 1914, some 350,000 Danes, 800,000 Norwegians, and 1,500,000 Swedes leaving their homelands during this period.

In contrast to the Baltic nations, with their relatively high literacy, peaceful intercourse, and political stability, the Balkan peoples remained largely illiterate, economically backward, and politically unstable into the twentieth century. The Near Eastern question—the problem of organizing the liberated sections of the Balkan peninsula as the Turkish tide receded, and ultimately the dilemma of deciding which great power would control Constantinople if the Turks were expelled from

Europe entirely—had precipitated several acute crises during the nineteenth century. The solution achieved, if it could be considered a solution, was to erect the Balkan provinces into sovereign states as they were successively detached from the sultan's suzerainty. By the opening of the twentieth century three independent kingdoms (Greece, Serbia, and Rumania), and one autonomous but not yet wholly independent kingdom (Bulgaria), had been carved from the shrinking empire of Turkey-in-Europe.

Greece, which had thrown off the Turkish yoke in 1829, was burdened by an excessive foreign debt, insufficient resources, and a rising population (about 2,500,000 in 1900). The kingdom, enlarged by the addition of the Ionian islands in 1864 and Thessaly in 1881, had an area of almost 25,000 square miles, which was increased to 28,000 in 1913 by the annexation of Crete. The poverty prevailing among the peasant population and dislike of military service prompted some 15,000 Greeks to emigrate annually after 1900.

Serbia, which likewise had a population of about 2,500,000 in 1900, was at that date an inland kingdom of 19,000 square miles. Guaranteed autonomy in 1829, the Serbs forced the withdrawal of the last Turk garrisons in 1867 and became entirely independent in 1878. Serbia was constantly shaken by the plots of pro-Austrian and pro-Russian factions; the arbitrary rule of Alexander I (1889–1903) ended in his assassination; and his successor Peter I, of the rival Karageorge dynasty, linked Serbian policies with those of Russia, stimulating the Pan-Slav hostility towards Austria that already agitated the Serb people.

Rumania was the largest and most populous of the Balkan states when the twentieth century opened, a country exceeding 50,000 square miles in area, with 6,000,000 inhabitants. Formed from the Danubian principalities, Moldavia and Wallachia, when these became autonomous (1861), Rumania was recognized as independent in 1878, losing Bessarabia to Russia while gaining the Dobruja in exchange. The Rumanians were more Latin than Slavonic, and considered themselves descendants of Roman colonists who settled in ancient Dacia.

Below Rumania and south of the Danube lay the kingdom of Bulgaria, with an area of 37,000 square miles and 4,000,000 people. The Congress of Berlin set up autonomous principalities of Bulgaria and eastern Rumelia in 1878, and these were united seven years later. The Bulgars did not assert their complete independence from Turkey until 1908.

Balkan politics could not well be tranquillized while Austrian and Russian agents strove to manipulate the unstable régimes and utilize the factional feuds to promote policies devised at Vienna and St. Petersburg. Half the inhabitants of the Austro-Hungarian empire were Slavs; they were dissatisfied because they were exploited economically and politically by the dominant German and Magyar groups; and they were susceptible to Pan-Slav propaganda calling for the formation of a Slav bloc in south-eastern Europe. This threat kept the Austrian and Hungarian statesmen in a state of nervous apprehension, but they hesitated to mollify the Slav subjects of Francis Joseph by democratic reforms and concessions, and could only oppose a blind opposition to the expansionist dreams of the Balkan nations, especially the Serbs. The Habsburg empire was a weakening anachronism, but it had the support of Germany, the leading military power of Europe, and could thus assume the risk of defying Slav agitation and Russian pressure.

The Russian government, in the opening decade of the twentieth century, had difficulties and distractions of its own. The impact of the industrial and technological revolutions struck Russian society while it was still in many respects half-feudal and half-medieval. An energetic reformer, Serge Witte, recognized the disadvantages under which Russia laboured because of its retarded economy: as late as 1913 Russian foreign trade was less than that of Belgium, although Russia had twenty times the population and six hundred times the area of that small but highly industrialized state. Witte became minister of finance in 1893, and laboured for ten years to expand Russian factories, railways, mines, arsenals, shipyards, and banks, in order to make the Tsar's empire capable of sustaining the role of a great power in peace and war. But his policies were attacked by the Slavophils, who feared western influences, and when Witte appealed to the zemstvos (provincial assemblies) in 1902 a majority of the replies criticized his economic policies. Tsar Nicholas II thereupon removed him from office, ignoring the fact that the criticism had been levelled even more directly against the autocratic political system that denied Russia a national parliament and a responsible ministry.

There was justice, however, in the claim of the conservatives that the progress of industry, which Witte had fostered, increased the opposition to the Tsar's régime. The urban workers, collecting in the expanding factory towns, organized labour unions and adopted revolutionary slogans. Russia was still a predominantly agricultural country, but industrial workers could be organized much more effectively than peasants, and by 1914 one-seventh of the population had gathered into the cities. Witte had planned to placate this rising proletariat with social legislation, promising accident insurance, pensions, and similar benefits, but the discontent increased after his dismissal. Economic progress also strengthened the Russian bourgeoisie, hitherto limited in numbers and without political power, and the business classes favoured liberal reforms in government and a system of national representation.

Thus the dangers of revolution rose rapidly in Russia after 1900. The peasants had long been discontented; the intellectuals were persistently critical; the small middle class envied the parliamentary influence which their class commanded in western Europe; the workers, increasingly class-conscious and aggressive, read Marxist pamphlets and preached socialism. Finally, the subject nationalities of the Tsar, the Finns and Poles in particular, were antagonized by the policy of 'Russification' whereby the Slavophils and nationalists strove to extend the Russian language and Orthodox religion throughout the empire. So long as the revolutionary factions remained weak and divided the secret police found it possible to repress them; anarchism and terrorism had been sternly checked after Alexander II was assassinated in 1881. But no police force could cope with the class movements and rising social pressures that developed after 1900. The ancient formula of Orthodoxy, Autocracy, Nationalism, was losing its appeal as the pervasive influences generated by liberalism and industrialism leavened Russian society. Any reverse that exposed the lethargy and inefficiency of the bureaucracy to public condemnation, and focused the widening discontent on the officials responsible, was certain to produce a crisis for the régime.

The crisis came in 1905 after military and naval disasters in the Far East had revealed the extent of Russian unpreparedness and incapacity. How the Russo-Japanese War tilted the international balance of power will be discussed later. Its effect upon the internal balance in Russia itself, already so precarious, was to stir up a popular outburst that came as near to overturning the régime as a revolution can come without succeeding. The hated minister of the interior, Viacheslav Plehve, was assassinated; workers who attempted peacefully to petition the Tsar were repulsed with volleys that killed seventy (Bloody Sunday, 22 January 1905); the St. Petersburg unions organized soviets to direct the popular movement; and Nicholas II realized that until he could recall his best troops from Manchuria he must make concessions or lose his throne. Dismissing his reactionary advisers, he restored Witte to favour and promised a constitution and a popular national assembly, with guarantees of civil liberties (October Manifesto, 1905).

This capitulation satisfied the moderates who believed the Tsar would keep his promises. The more progressive liberals organized the Constitutional Democratic party and demanded a constituent assembly, while the Social Democrats and radical working men rejected the Tsar's programme entirely. But the October Manifesto served its purpose. It postponed the crisis and it split the ranks of the opposition. Throughout the winter of 1905–6 the military forces returned from Manchuria, to repress the working-class demonstrations in St. Petersburg with much bloodshed and to restore order in the provinces. Witte secured large loans from France and Britain (the French had a military alliance with the Russian government and wanted to maintain it), and this financial aid tided the Tsarist régime over its crisis. When the promised assembly (the Duma) met in May 1906, Nicholas II was in a sufficiently strong position to chasten it, and to insist that the promises he had made in his October Manifesto assured the Russian people a national parliament but did not compromise the absolute powers he had inherited.

This first Duma had been elected by what amounted to universal manhood suffrage, but the radical parties had declined to participate and the Constitutional Democrats (Cadets) emerged with the largest representation. Even they were bitterly disappointed, for the 'Octobrists' who had placed their faith in Nicholas found that he did not wait for the Duma to meet but issued a set of fundamental laws for the empire on his own initiative. When the deputies of the nation criticized them as insufficient he dismissed the Duma for its contumacy. The more audacious members adjourned to Viborg in Finland and drafted a manifesto urging the Russian people to refuse taxes until their liberties were assured, but the gesture aroused slight response. A second Duma, elected in 1907, proved even more recalcitrant than the first. Nicholas therefore revised the franchise, increasing the representation of the propertied groups while decreasing that of the workers and peasants: the result, not surprisingly, was a third Duma more amenable to his wishes.

Russian autocracy had survived the most critical test it had yet faced. From 1907 until the First World War there was an uneasy political truce while the reactionaries congratulated themselves on the Tsar's firmness and the revolutionaries analysed their mistakes. Some cautious reforms were attempted in social legislation and education, economic progress continued, and the compromise with autocracy represented by a legislative assembly that could not legislate served its anomalous purpose. In Peter Stolypin the Tsar found a minister with the character and skill to manage the tamed Duma, but Stolypin was assassinated in 1911. A fourth Duma, elected in 1912, discussed but failed to attack the vital issues—the land question, the labour question, a responsible ministry, the energetic development of Russian resources—and it was still in session when Russia was engulfed in the First World War. The moment was approaching when military defeats would unleash a revolution that could not be held in check, a revolution that Tsardom could not survive.

In the new world of the Americas the United States was the only country that had developed an industrial economy to match that of Europe. There too, by 1900, mushroom cities had drawn men from the forest and the farm to the mill and the workshop. In the first decade of the twentieth century American economic expansion rapidly quickened its pace, and the phenomenal gains which it made showed the unlimited productive capacity of American factories. Iron production rose 50 per cent. within ten years; coal production doubled; oil production trebled. As in Europe, the expanding industries tended to amalgamate, and corporations or 'trusts' took shape, dominating and in some cases almost monopolizing an entire field of manufacture, mining, or transportation. Steel trusts, oil trusts, and electric power trusts were followed by combinations to control a single raw commodity, such as copper, lead, or coal, or to 'corner' the market by organizing the facilities that went to a single item of merchandise such as plate glass or wire nails. Even before 1900 this concentration in manufacturing, transportation, and finance had proceeded so rapidly that it threatened to nullify the system of free economic enterprise. Great millionaire corporations, with their headquarters in the eastern cities, became so powerful, and in some cases so unscrupulous, that they bought out or made bankrupt lesser competitors. Subsidiary enterprises were absorbed by securing 51 per cent. of their stock, and a small number of financiers and industrialists could acquire vast influence through interlocking directorates whereby they determined the policies of several companies operating in allied enterprises. The growth and centralization of power through business combinations advanced so swiftly that the United States had already surpassed Great Britain, France, and Germany in this respect when the twentieth century opened.

In the organization of labour, on the other hand, the United States lagged behind the leading European countries. The American Federation of Labour, formed in 1886 with 150,000 members, increased its membership to almost 3,000,000 by 1914, but it lacked political power and representation. The division of political authority between the state legislatures and the federal Congress made it difficult to adopt any uniform and far-reaching programme of labour legislation. Laws passed in one state to raise wage rates or limit profits might defeat their aims by driving manufacturers to move their factories or incorporate their companies in another state where the laws were more favourable to them. Only a federal act that could be enforced throughout the nation was likely to provide a charter for labour, but even federal acts could miscarry. In 1890, for instance, the Congress enacted an Anti-Trust Law which declared illegal 'every contract, combination in the form of trust or otherwise, or conspiracy in restraint of trade or commerce among the several states or with foreign nations'. This loose wording left the interpretation of the act to the courts which ruled (1895) that it forbade labour union leaders to call a strike if this involved 'restraint of interstate commerce'. Yet two years later, when the question arose whether the act applied to mergers or combinations of railway companies, the court ruled that it did not. Labour leaders became convinced, not without reason, that organized justice, or at least the interpretation of the statutes, favoured 'Big Business'. They continued to work for remedial legislation, shorter hours, higher pay, safety devices in mines and factories, and compensation for workmen injured at their trade, but the progress made was slow and unsatisfactory.

One reason for this delay was the absence in the United States of an active and effective socialist party, to match the Labour party in Great Britain and the united socialist groups in France and Germany. Although an American socialist party was organized in 1901, it did not play a significant role in politics until the election of 1912, when its candidates obtained almost one million votes. Even this defection from the ranks of the two established parties, the Republicans and the Democrats, could not be interpreted as a real revolt of American labour. There was, it is true, a widespread dissatisfaction with the 'Big Business' interests and their monopolistic methods, and an equally wide criticism of American foreign policy, which had taken an imperialist turn after 1900. But the swing towards the left, discernible in the American elections of 1910 and 1912, was much less vehement than the leftward trend in European politics that marked the decade before 1914.

From the foundation of the republic the electors in the United States had shown a strong preference for the two-party system. The Northern victory in the Civil War left the Republican party in the saddle, and from 1865 to 1900 the Democratic party won only two presidential elections. In 1900 a Republican victory placed William McKinley in the White House; his assassination in 1901 brought the Vice-President, Theodore Roosevelt, into office. Roosevelt was energetic, popular, and progressive. He was re-elected in 1904, and in 1908 the Republicans won again, placing William Howard Taft in power as 26th President. But signs of defection and opposition were appearing within and without the Republican ranks. In the election of 1910 the Democrats secured a majority in the House of Representatives. The electors had grown increasingly critical of the 'Old Guard' leadership of the Republican party; it was attacked on the ground that it had proved too lenient towards the trusts, had maintained an excessively high tariff, and had pursued an aggressive policy of interference in Latin America. When Taft was nominated for re-election in 1912 Roosevelt split the Republican organization and ran as candidate of a 'Progressive' insurgent group, bidding for popular support by advocating more explicit anti-trust laws, abolition of child labour, and similar reforms. But the Republicans, even 'progressive' Republicans, were identified in the public mind with business interests, and the Democratic candidate, Woodrow Wilson, won the three-cornered election.

Wilson believed that he had a popular mandate to carry through a programme of domestic reforms. He created a Department of Labour, approved a reduction in the tariff rates, and increased public control over the banking system. An amendment to the Constitution (1913) empowered Congress to levy a federal income tax. A stricter law on combinations (Clayton Anti-Trust Act) curbed monopolistic practices in business, prohibited interlocking directorates in large corporations, and specifically excepted labour unions from its provisions, reversing the court decision of 1895. After 1914 friction with Mexico and increasing involvements arising from the war in Europe partly diverted Wilson's attention from domestic affairs, and the strength of the Democratic following declined. But the Democrats had now identified themselves with a policy of social reform. This was highly significant for the future, because the trend of the age was towards political control of the national economy and social legislation to improve the condition of the common man. The half-century in American history that preceded Wilson's victory in 1912 had been a period of Republican ascendancy with business expanding freely under a minimum of control; the period that followed 1912 was to see the Democrats in power for the greater part of the time with increasing federal control over business activities. The social and economic life of the nation was to be increasingly regimented in peace and war to a degree that most nineteenth-century Americans would have found almost inconceivable.

In British North America the opening years of the twentieth century brought mounting waves of immigration and rapid expansion in the central and western regions of the dominion. The provinces of Alberta and Saskatchewan were admitted (1905) and a second transcontinental railway completed in 1914. Canada sent two contingents to fight with the British in the South African War, but the Canadian Senate rejected a bill to contribute three Dreadnoughts to the imperial navy (1913). Economic and financial ties with the mother country remained close; a preferential tariff with Britain was adopted in 1898, while a treaty for trade reciprocity with the United States was opposed by a majority of the Canadian electors in 1911.

In Latin America the history of the various republics continued to follow the pattern set in the nineteenth century; no profound changes marked the years from 1898 to 1914. A revolution in Mexico (1911) opened a period of disorder and civil war. The government of Colombia failed to grant the United States permission to build a canal across the isthmus of Panama (1903), whereupon the province of Panama seceded from Colombia, was promptly recognized by the United States as an independent republic, and granted the lease desired. The canal was completed in 1914. But the high-handed methods adopted by the United States government, which landed armed forces to maintain order in Cuba, the Dominican Republic, Haiti, Nicaragua, and at other points in Central America and the Caribbean, aroused opposition among Latin Americans against the 'Colossus of the North'. Inter-American relations were strained and unsatisfactory in the years preceding the First World War, but efforts were made to improve them. Occasional congresses called to promote friendly understandings and arbitrate disputes led to the formal creation (1910) of the Pan-American Union, an agency of conciliation which included the diplomatic representatives of all the American republics.

The southern hemisphere, which had hitherto supported only an insignificant fraction of the population of the globe, began to play a more impressive part in world affairs by the opening of the twentieth century. In the Argentine Republic a population of 1,700,000 (1869) was multiplied fivefold in half a century to reach 9,000,000 by the First World War, largely through the influx of Spanish and Italian immigrants. The Union of South Africa, created in 1909, had over a million inhabitants of European descent. In the South Pacific the Commonwealth of Australia, proclaimed in 1901, had a population of four millions by 1914, almost exclusively of European blood; while New Zealand, which acquired dominion status in 1907, contained a million white settlers by that date. The determination of the Australians and New Zealanders to preserve white supremacy led them to exclude immigrants who came from the more densely populated continents of Asia and Africa, and they were prepared to enforce this determination by arms if necessary. Australia established the nucleus of a navy in 1908 and adopted military conscription in 1911; New Zealand likewise provided for universal military training and contributed to the support of the British fleet.

From these new dominions rising to nationhood in the Antipodes, attention must now be turned back to Europe itself. During the two decades before 1914 a fateful game was played out on the European chess-board, a game that seems in retrospect one of the most deadly tournaments ever waged by Old World diplomats. It is important to recall again that the successive decisions on international problems taken between 1894 and 1914 were often manœuvres of the moment. No one could foretell how firmly the alliances then formed would work, nor predict that they would hold fast under strain. Yet the trend of international events had its own inexorable logic, dividing Europe more and more definitely into two opposing camps. The balance of power, invoked by statesmen as the surest guarantee of peace, became instead a mechanism so delicately interlocked that it made almost inevitable (as an alternative to general peace) a general war. The diplomatic history of the period from 1894 to 1914 is the story of how the six great powers of Europe came to be ranged in two rival systems of alliances, with the tension between the systems growing until it became unendurable.

From the date of its proclamation in 1871 the German empire was the leading military state of Europe. Bismarck was haunted by the fear that German security might be threatened by a coalition of powers; he was persuaded that France would be the logical core of such a coalition; and he worked for twenty years to keep France diplomatically isolated. His agreements with Austria and Italy (the Triple Alliance) and his understanding with Austria and Russia (the Three Emperors' League), so long as they remained in effect, left France no important continental ally. But Bismarck's dismissal in 1890 was followed by the decline and ultimately by the collapse of his system. In 1890 the German foreign office decided not to renew the Reinsurance treaty with Russia; this agreement had been made, in 1887, because Russia declined to prolong the Three Emperors' League, and it provided primarily that neither power would join in an attack against the other. The Russians were willing to renew this guarantee, and the attitude of the German foreign office puzzled and alarmed them. Prompt French overtures to

St. Petersburg for a Franco-Russian military alliance had little result at the moment, but the French were persistent. Early in 1894 a convention was concluded binding France to aid Russia and Russia to aid France if either were attacked by Germany. This new agreement was to remain in force as long as the Triple Alliance endured, an admission that it was intended as a counterweight to the understanding then uniting Germany, Austria, and Italy. But the Franco-Russian convention had a second purpose. Both members were competing with Great Britain at a number of points, the French in North Africa and south-east Asia, the Russians in the Near East, Persia, and Afghanistan. As France and Russia had no sharp conflict of aims at any point, they could afford to strengthen one another in resisting British pressure.

In London the Franco-Russian pact aroused misgivings, and relations between Britain and France remained fretful until they reached a crisis in 1898. The discovery that a French expedition from Equatorial Africa had penetrated to the valley of the upper Nile at Fashoda brought both powers close to a state of war until the French withdrew their outpost. This peaceful solution was fostered by the new French foreign minister, Théophile Delcassé, whose seven years of service in that office were to be largely devoted to cementing an Anglo-French accord. At the moment the British were still satisfied with their 'splendid isolation', but their attitude changed steadily in the next few years. The South African War brought home to them the cost of military unpreparedness. The death of Queen Victoria in 1901 and the retirement of Salisbury in the next year were followed by a change of mood in British diplomacy. Edward VII distrusted his nephew, William II, and was sympathetic towards the French. But a much more powerful factor in changing the British attitude was the German naval programme. Commencing in 1898 the Germans undertook the construction of a High Seas Fleet, and on New Year's Day 1900 the Kaiser announced his intention of making the German navy equal to the German army. At the same time the minister of marine, Admiral Alfred von Tirpitz, revealed the conviction behind this naval programme by uttering a significant prophecy. 'In the coming century', he warned, 'the German people must be either the hammer or the anvil.'

The boasts of indiscreet German writers and the information

compiled by the British naval intelligence agents strengthened the belief in England that Germany rather than France or Russia would prove the chief threat to British naval security in the foreseeable future. German plans called for the launching of fourteen battleships between 1900 and 1905, with twelve more laid down, a rate of building that would make Germany the second naval power of the world by 1906. German naval strength, moreover, could be concentrated in the North Sea while British warships were scattered throughout the oceans of the globe. That the British admiralty recognized the threat which this implied is clear from the measures adopted after 1902. By an understanding negotiated with Japan in that year, Britain and Japan agreed that both would maintain in the Far East 'a naval force superior in strength to that of any third power'. The basic fact in this Anglo-Japanese accord was that it ruled out the danger of a Russo-Japanese alliance which would have placed the British Far Eastern squadron in grave danger. Britain was seeking to minimize the risk of a hostile combination in that distant area so that new ships under construction might be kept at home.

The second major move the British made to concentrate their navy in home waters came in 1904. Anglo-French relations had been improving steadily for two years; the differences between the two powers in Africa were smoothed away by an agreement that left Egypt a sphere of British influence while France acquired paramount control in Morocco; and this happy reconciliation was celebrated by the conclusion of the *Entente Cordiale* in 1904. The *Entente* was not a treaty of alliance, but it established a friendly understanding, and it left the British reasonably confident that they need not fear an attack by the French in the Mediterranean. It had the further advantage that it reduced the danger of a Franco-Russian war against Britain, and thus left the admiralty in London free to turn its main attention to the growing threat presented by the German High Seas Fleet at Kiel. The first specific British plans for the disposition of torpedo craft in the event of a war with Germany were issued in the summer of 1904.

Meanwhile developments in the Far East were changing the precarious balance of power in a manner at once swift and unforeseen. On 4 February 1904 the Japanese made a sudden attack on the Russian naval base at Port Arthur, bottling up the

Russian Far Eastern fleet. Japanese armies were landed to besiege the port and a large-scale war developed as the Russians brought up reinforcements. The initiative and energy of the Japanese astonished European observers, and the astonishment mounted as the Japanese compelled Port Arthur to capitulate after a year's siege and defeated a second Russian army at Mukden. With command of the sea the Japanese could supply their forces readily, while the Russians had to fight at the end of the Trans-Siberian railway. A struggle waged so far away did not involve any other European powers directly. But the fact that France was the tacit ally of Russia and Britain of Japan made both nations aware of the advantage Germany would derive if they became involved. This realization helped to stimulate the *Entente* reached by France and Britain shortly after the outbreak of hostilities in the Far East. Germany, meanwhile, displayed a friendly neutrality towards Russia, and the Kaiser went so far as to promise the Tsar that Russia could count upon German aid if Britain went to the assistance of the Japanese.

The Japanese, however, were doing very well by themselves. With internal revolts crippling the Russian war effort, the Tsar's government played its last card by sending the Russian Baltic fleet to Far Eastern waters to re-establish naval control; it reached the Straits of Tsushima in May 1905, and was totally destroyed by the Japanese. Not since the Battle of Trafalgar one hundred years earlier had the world seen such an overwhelming naval disaster. The Russians had now lost every battle in this one-sided war. They made peace in September 1905, at Portsmouth, New Hampshire, after President Theodore Roosevelt had offered his mediation to hasten this result. Russian and Japanese forces were withdrawn from Manchuria, which was restored to China, but the Japanese won virtual possession of Korea, annexed the southern half of Sakhalin island, and took over the Russian lease of the Liaotung peninsula.

The threat of revolution within Russia made peace a necessity for the Tsar's harassed government. Had the war continued the outcome might have been less unequal, since the Russians had built up an army of a million men in Manchuria, the Japanese lines were widely extended, and the financial strain of a major conflict was exhausting Japanese resources. There was bitter disappointment in Tokyo because the peace terms failed to include a financial indemnity.

In Europe the revelation of Russian weakness set up a dangerous oscillation in the balance of power. The French, with their one certain ally temporarily enfeebled, felt themselves gravely threatened by the might of Germany. In Berlin the fear of a two-front war dissolved as it became evident that Russia would require several years for recovery. The advisers who surrounded William II believed the moment ripe for Germany to take a bold stand, to extort concessions from France in the colonial field and to press the Austro-German drive in the Near East. From 1905 to 1914 the tension in Europe was to mount steadily and the issues that revealed this tension may be summarized under three heads, the colonial question, the naval question, and the Balkan question.

The first German move, undertaken in 1905, involved the colonial question and might be described as exploratory. It was designed to test the reality of the Anglo-French *Entente*. The French received a sharp warning from Berlin that German interests in Morocco had been ignored and compensation must be provided. Delcassé put his trust in British support and wished to defy the German threat. But his colleagues in the French cabinet lacked his confidence; Delcassé was forced to resign the post of foreign minister which he had filled for seven years; and France yielded to the German demands for an international conference on the Moroccan problem. Diplomatic representatives of all the great powers met at Algeciras in January 1906, but only the Austrians supported the German stand. The conference declared Morocco an independent sultanate; but it also recognized the right of the French to exercise 'police power' in the area. This ambiguous concession left the way open for further expansion of French influence, which continued to spread (as German diplomats noted) 'like an oil stain'.

Algeciras marked a rebuff for Germany. Even the Italians failed to stand by the Triple Alliance, for Delcassé had succeeded before his fall in reconciling French and Italian conflicts in the Mediterranean. Instead of weakening the Anglo-French *Entente* the dispute over Morocco strengthened it. While the conference was still in session French and British military experts discussed secret plans for landing 100,000 British troops in France if war came.

In reality colonial disputes were less dangerous than they appeared, chiefly because no colonial issue could affect the vital interests of all the great powers. Russia was not likely to risk war to support French claims in the Congo, nor Austria to mobilize for the defence of German trade in Morocco. This fact helps to explain why the Moroccan difficulties were settled peaceably not once but three times. In 1908 a second dispute arose there when the French seized three German deserters from their foreign legion, invading the German consulate at Casablanca to arrest the fugitives. This 'Casablanca Affair' was submitted to a board of arbitration. In 1911, when French troops in Morocco marched into Fez, the Germans protested again. But Britain stood behind France; the crisis passed; and France emerged with a virtual protectorate over Morocco, buying Germany off with the cession of 100,000 square miles of the French Congo.

The Anglo-French *Entente* had grown stronger under strain. From 1906 to 1909 French policy was directed by the resolute and irascible Georges Clemenceau, who maintained Delcassé's policy of co-operation with Britain. Furthermore, British distrust of Russia was largely dissipated by the outcome of the Russo-Japanese War, and Clemenceau's mediation hastened an Anglo-Russian accord concluded in 1907. Rivalry between the two powers in the Middle East was reduced by establishing joint spheres of influence in Persia, while Russia recognized the preponderant interest of the British in the Persian Gulf and Afghanistan. No formal alliance yet bound Britain, France, and Russia, but they were clearly drawing together. The revival of Russia as a military power was hastened by the French government, which authorized loans of several thousand millions of francs to aid the Tsar and hasten Russian rearmament. The years 1906–7 thus brought the first clear indication that Europe was dividing into two major systems of alliances with three great powers on each side: a Triple *Entente* was coming into being to offset the weight of the Triple Alliance.

These same years 1906–7 saw the second major issue, the naval question, take a more acute form, for Britain launched the first Dreadnought in 1906. The revolutionary features of this new capital ship rendered all existing navies (including the British) obsolete. As late as 1900 effective battle-range was considered to be about 2,000 yards, or a little more than one mile. In reality the invention of smokeless powder, improved fire control, and more accurate range-finders made effective action possible at four or five times that distance. British naval experts had been pondering these new possibilities when the Russo-Japanese War provided practical demonstrations of long-range firing. Their answer was the Dreadnought, which was protected by eleven-inch armour, carried ten twelve-inch guns, and was equipped with turbine engines that gave it a speed of twenty-one knots. It was better protected, faster, and twice as heavily armed as any warship then afloat, and its appearance opened a new epoch in naval competition. Architects and strategists grasped the costly truth that the war fleets of the world would have to be rebuilt, and in this new race the British were only one year ahead because the Dreadnought had been constructed in twelve months. Only a general agreement among the leading powers to limit their building programmes could avert a deadly and extravagant race. But, despite talks on naval limitation at the Hague Peace Conference in 1907, at a London Naval Conference in 1908, and at Berlin in 1912, no solution acceptable to both the Germans and the British could be found. Without such an accord, Britain and Germany, as the leading sea powers of the world, were condemned to watch one another's naval appropriations and outbid them. It was this naval rivalry, more than any other factor, that focused British attention on Germany as the predestined foe.

The third international issue noted above, the Balkan question, was less clear-cut but even more hazardous. All the great powers were interested in the affairs of the Near East, and for the Austrians and Russians the Balkan peninsula and the Straits were vital areas. Austro-German influence there had been growing since 1900; and in 1908 Austria stole a march by annexing Bosnia and Herzegovina, still nominally part of the sultan's empire, but under Austrian administration since the Congress of Berlin of 1878. Russian protests proved ineffectual, and the Serbs, who were ready to start a war over this Austrian absorption of their fellow Slavs, were warned to keep the peace. The Balkan crisis of 1908 passed because neither France nor Britain was ready to back Russia in meeting the Austrian coup. But there was grave anxiety at Paris and London over the *Drang nach Osten*, the Austro-German drive to the east. The construction of a railroad through the Balkans to Constantinople and thence to Bagdad promised to draw Turkey and the Persian

Gulf within the range of German imperialism. Neither Britain nor Russia could permit Constantinople and the Straits to pass under German control, and France likewise had interests to guard in the Levant.

The Ottoman empire was ready to fall apart and no plans had been concerted by the powers for a peaceful division of the sultan's legacy. The British had already occupied Egypt; the French were established in Algeria, Tunis, and Morocco. In 1911 the Italians invaded Tripoli and annexed it; they had bargained for French and British acquiescence by tacit promises not to stand by the Triple Alliance in the event of a general war, and had then won the consent of the Germans and Austrians for their venture by renewing the alliance before it expired. For a year the Ottoman government at Constantinople refused to admit the loss of Tripoli, but events forced it to conclude peace with Italy in October 1912. A new danger had arisen. The evident weakness of Turkey had inspired the Balkan states, Serbia, Greece, and Bulgaria, to open an attack on the sultan's empire, with the proud announcement that they intended to drive the Turks from their last foothold in Europe.

This First Balkan War of 1912 brought speedy victories to the allies; Serbian forces overran most of Albania while the Bulgarians advanced on Constantinople. Then the great powers called a halt. Austria would not permit the Serbs to keep Albania, Russia opposed the Bulgarian claims to Thrace. A temporary settlement, worked out at London in May 1913, broke down immediately because Bulgaria attacked its late ally, Serbia, and was attacked in turn by Greece, Rumania, and Turkey. Within a few months Bulgaria was stripped of almost all its recent gains. The great powers, intervening once again, forced the Serbs and Greeks to abandon Albania, which was set up as an independent principality. Austrian opposition had been thrown into the scale against the creation of a greater Serbia, with an outlet on the Adriatic Sea, because the Austrian government was insecure. Half the inhabitants of the Habsburg empire were Slavs; many of them were discontented; and the emergence of a Pan-Slav state or a Slav Confederation in the Balkans would, it was feared, dissolve the crumbling frontiers of the Austro-Hungarian realm. The Pan-Slav dream, with Russia in the background, was a nightmare to the diplomats at Vienna and Budapest.

Around the Balkan cockpit, like gamblers that have staked more than they can afford to lose on their favourites, the great powers watched and wrangled through the struggles of 1912 and 1913. With each shift in fortune the odds increased; the ledgers of Europe told the story of these final years of tension with bleak impersonality. Since 1871 the European peoples had been living under an 'armed peace' that grew more costly to maintain with each passing decade. Military and naval expenditures doubled between 1880 and 1900, then doubled again between 1900 and 1910. For the sixteen-year period from 1898 to 1914—the period covered in this chapter—the annual armament bill of the great powers rose 140 per cent. Standing armies were increased after every crisis, and Germany, as the leading military power, set the pace. When France and Russia became allies in 1894 German forces were raised from 487,000 to 557,000. When France and Britain established their *Entente* in 1904 the German standing army rose to 605,000. In 1910 it was 617,000; in 1911, 631,000; in 1912, 666,000; in 1913, 761,000; in 1914, 820,000. The French countered in 1913 by extending the period of military service, and the peace-time strength of their army was advanced to 750,000. Russia followed the trend the same year by planning an increase in effectives from 1,300,000 to 1,800,000 men. Great Britain, without a system of military conscription, had less than 300,000 men in the regular army, and of these 110,000 were stationed in the colonies and protectorates. In addition, there was a volunteer force, the Territorials, the members of which had received short periods of training and could be mobilized for national defence. This was a small army for a great power, but the British placed their trust in the Royal Navy as the shield of their empire and their island.

On the sea the *Entente* nations, Britain, France, and Russia, held an unquestionable superiority. The Russian navy was the least powerful of the three and could undertake only local defence in the Baltic and Black Sea. The French battleships, by agreement with the British, were concentrated in the Mediterranean, where they could outmatch any likely combination of Austrian and Italian forces. In the North Sea the British Grand Fleet faced the German High Seas Fleet with a decisive margin in all major categories. The British had sixty-four battleships against forty, ten battle cruisers to four, and a two-to-one advantage in light cruisers, torpedo-boats, and destroyers.

The German bid for naval power, opened in 1898, had produced the second most powerful navy in the world by 1914. But the British had strained their resources to maintain their ascendancy, and they could face the German challenge with confidence. If war came between the Triple Alliance and the Triple *Entente*, the *Entente* powers could control the seas of the world with British aid. But could they count on British aid? No formal treaty bound Britain to France or Russia; yet the French had left their North Sea coast almost undefended by an agreement with Britain which assumed that the British navy would defend it. These naval agreements, and the disposition of the French and British fleets, were based upon the reality of an Anglo-French alliance; it was the denial that such an alliance existed which constituted a fiction. The British people still preferred to believe that, if a general war developed on the continent, they were at liberty to proclaim their neutrality, but their neutrality was already compromised almost beyond redemption.

By 1914 all the diplomats knew that 'peace was at the mercy of an accident'. The implications of the interlocking alliances, the irreversible momentum that would be released the moment the great powers mobilized, were clear to the generals and the statesmen. Mobilization, they reminded one another fatalistically, meant war. But forty years of general peace in Europe had lulled the peoples into a false dream of security; they went about their affairs in happy ignorance while the anvil chorus quickened and the continent echoed to the march of armed millions engaged in their annual manœuvres. Each year produced its diplomatic crisis; each year the foreign ministers blustered and dissembled and compromised; each year the crisis passed. The diplomats knew how closely they were circling the maelstrom of war, but they were caught in the current and they had no policy that looked beyond the moment. They grappled with each emergency as it arose, improvising solutions while time ran out and the hour approached when no new solution could be improvised.

On 28 June 1914 the Archduke Franz Ferdinand, nephew of the Emperor Francis Joseph and heir to the Austrian throne, was shot while on a tour of inspection in Sarajevo, Bosnia. The assassin was a Bosnian youth who had obtained weapons and aid from the Serbian 'Union or Death' society, a terrorist organization formed to agitate against Austria. Officers in the Serbian bureau of military intelligence had encouraged the plot and rumours of it had reached some Serbian cabinet members who failed to counteract it or to warn the Austrian government. Convinced that Serbian officials were implicated, although satisfactory proof of this was not yet in their hands, the statesmen at Vienna determined to teach the Serbs a lesson that would humble them and discourage further plotting. After waiting four weeks to complete its preparations and obtain an assurance from Berlin that Germany would stand firmly behind it, the Austro-Hungarian government presented an ultimatum to Serbia on 23 July. The Serbs accepted most of the conditions within the forty-eight hours allowed them, but simultaneously they began mobilization. Russia supported them, France supported Russia, and ten days later Europe was at war. The crisis for which no peaceful solution could be improvised had arrived.

THE NINETEENTH CENTURY (1815–1914)

DOCUMENTS

I. POLITICAL REACTION AND ECONOMIC PROGRESS (1815–30)

I

The Holy Alliance, 26 September 1815. Preamble

THEIR Majesties, the Emperor of Austria, the King of Prussia, and the Emperor of Russia, in view of the great events which the last three years have brought to pass in Europe and in view especially of the benefits which it has pleased Divine Providence to confer upon those states whose governments have placed their hope in Him alone, having reached the profound conviction that the policy of the powers, in their mutual relations, ought to be guided by the sublime truths taught by the eternal religion of God our Saviour, solemnly declare that the present act has no other aim than to manifest to the world their unchangeable determination to adopt no other rule of conduct, either in the government of their respective countries or in their political relations with other governments, than the precepts of that holy religion, the precepts of justice, charity, and peace. These, far from being applicable exclusively to private life, ought on the contrary directly to control the resolutions of princes and to guide their steps as the sole means of establishing human institutions and of remedying their imperfections.

E. HERTSLET (ed.), *The Map of Europe by Treaty* (London, 1875), i. 317.

II

The Quadruple Alliance, 20 November 1815. Preamble

In the name of the most Holy and Undivided Trinity. The purpose of the alliance concluded at Vienna the 25th day of March, 1815, having been happily attained by the re-establishment in France of the order of things which the last criminal attempt of Napoleon Bonaparte had momentarily subverted, their Majesties the King of the United Kingdom of Great Britain and Ireland, the Emperor of Austria, King of Hungary and Bohemia, the Emperor of all the Russias, and the King of Prussia, considering that the repose of Europe is essentially interwoven with the confirmation of the order of things founded on the maintenance of the royal authority and of the constitutional charter, and wishing to employ all their means to prevent the general tranquillity (the object of the wishes of mankind and the constant end of their efforts) from being again disturbed, desirous, moreover, to draw closer the ties which unite them for the common interests of their peoples, have resolved to give to the principles solemnly laid down in the treaties of Chaumont on the 1st of March, 1814, and of Vienna of the 25th of March, 1815, the application the most analogous to the present state of affairs, and to fix beforehand by a solemn treaty the principles which they propose to follow, in order to guarantee Europe from dangers by which she may still be menaced; for which purpose the high contracting parties have . . . [agreed to] . . . discuss, settle, and sign the conditions of this treaty. . . .

E. HERTSLET (ed.), *The Map of Europe by Treaty* (London, 1875), i. 372–3.

III

George Canning defines the Position of Great Britain, 1823

It is perfectly true, as has been argued by more than one honourable member in this debate, that there is a contest going on in the world between the spirit of unlimited monarchy and the spirit of unlimited democracy. Between these two spirits, it may be said that strife is either openly in action, or covertly at work, throughout the greater portion of Europe. . . .

. . . .

Our station, then, is essentially neutral; neutral not only between contending nations, but between conflicting principles. The object of the government has been to preserve that station, and for the purpose of preserving it, to maintain peace. By remaining at peace ourselves, we best secure Portugal; by remaining at peace, we take the best chance of circumscribing the range, and shortening the duration, of the war which we could not prevent from breaking out between France and Spain. By remaining at peace we shall best enable ourselves to take an effectual and decisive part in any contest into which we may be hereafter forced against our will.

R. THIERRY, *The Speeches of the Right Honourable George Canning, with a Memoir of his Life* (London, 1836), v. 126–9.

IV

The Monroe Doctrine

. . . In the wars of the European powers in matters relating to themselves we have never taken any part, nor does it comport with our policy so to do. It is only when our rights are invaded or seriously menaced that we resent injuries or make preparation for our defence. With the movements in this hemisphere we are, of necessity, more immediately connected, and by causes which must be obvious to all enlightened and impartial observers. The political system of the allied powers is essentially different in this respect from that of America. This difference proceeds from that which exists in their respective Governments; and to the defence of our own, which has been achieved by the loss of so much blood and treasure, and matured by the wisdom of their most enlightened citizens, and under which we have enjoyed unexampled felicity, this whole nation is devoted. We owe it, therefore, to candour and to the amicable relations existing between the United States and those powers to declare that we should consider any attempt on their part to extend their system to any portion of this hemisphere as dangerous to our peace and safety. With the existing colonies or dependencies of any European power we have not interfered and we shall not interfere. But with the Governments who have declared their independence and maintained it, and whose independence we have, on great consideration and on just principles, acknowledged, we could not view any interposition for the purpose of oppressing them, or controlling in any other manner their destiny, by any European power in any other light than as the manifestation of an unfriendly disposition toward the United States.

PRESIDENT JAMES MONROE, Annual Message to the United States Congress, 2 December 1823; J. D. RICHARDSON, *A Compilation of the Messages and Papers of the Presidents, 1789–1897* (Washington, 1896–9), ii. 217.

V

A Protest Against Political Reaction

XCVI

Can tyrants but by tyrants conquer'd be,
And Freedom find no champion and no child
Such as Columbia saw arise when she
Sprung forth a Pallas, arm'd and undefiled?
Or must such minds be nourish'd in the wild,
Deep in the unpruned forest, 'midst the roar
Of cataracts, where nursing Nature smiled
On infant Washington? Has Earth no more
Such seeds within her breast, or Europe no such shore?

XCVII

But France got drunk with blood to vomit crime,
And fatal have her Saturnalia been
To Freedom's cause, in every age and clime;
Because the deadly days which we have seen,
And vile Ambition, that built up between
Man and his hopes an adamantine wall,
And the base pageant last upon the scene,
Are grown the pretext for the eternal thrall
Which nips life's tree, and dooms man's worst—his second fall.

XCVIII

Yet, Freedom! yet thy banner, torn, but flying,
Streams like the thunder-storm against the wind;
Thy trumpet voice, though broken now and dying,
The loudest still the tempest leaves behind;
Thy tree hath lost its blossoms, and the rind,
Chopp'd by the axe, looks rough and little worth,
But the sap lasts,—and still the seed we find
Sown deep, even in the bosom of the North;
So shall a better spring less bitter fruit bring forth.

GEORGE GORDON, LORD BYRON, *Childe Harold's Pilgrimage*, Canto IV (1818).

VI

Addresses to the German Nation

These addresses have in the first place appealed to you, and they will appeal to the entire German nation, in so far as it is possible at present to assemble the nation around a speaker by means of a printed work, to reach a definite conclusion and to be resolved in their own minds on the following issues:

1. Whether it is true or false that there is a German nation, and that its continued existence in its singular and independent form is at the present time in jeopardy;
2. Whether it is worth the effort, or not worth the effort, to preserve this nation;
3. Whether there is any certain and thorough method of maintaining it, and what this method is.

JOHANN GOTTLIEB FICHTE, *Sämmtliche Werke*, ed. by J. H. FICHTE, vol. vii (Berlin, 1846), p. 448. Translated by GEOFFREY BRUUN.

VII

Metternich meditates on Government

There is a rule of conduct common to individuals and to states, established by the experience of centuries as by that of everyday life. This rule declares 'that one must not dream of reformation while agitated by passion; wisdom directs that at such moments we should limit ourselves to maintaining'.

Let the monarchs vigorously adopt this principle; let all their resolutions bear the impression of it. Let their actions, their measures, and even their words announce and prove to the world this determination—they will find allies everywhere. The governments, in establishing the principle of *stability*, will in no wise exclude the development of what is good, for stability is not immobility. But it is for those who are burdened with the heavy task of government to augment the well-being of their people. It is for governments to regulate it according to necessity and to suit the times. It is not by concessions, which the factious strive to force from legitimate power, and which they have neither the right to claim nor the faculty of keeping within just bounds, that wise reforms can be carried out. . . .

PRINCE RICHARD METTERNICH (ed.), *Memoirs of Prince Metternich*, translated by MRS. ALEXANDER NAPIER, vol. iii (London, 1881), pp. 470–1.

VIII

Democracy in America

The emigrants who fixed themselves on the shores of America in the beginning of the seventeenth century severed the democratic principle from all the principles which repressed it in the old communities of Europe, and transplanted it unalloyed to the New World. It has there been allowed to spread in perfect freedom, and to put forth its consequences in the laws by influencing the manners of the country.

It appears to me beyond a doubt that sooner or later we shall arrive, like the Americans, at an almost complete equality of conditions. But I do not conclude from this that we shall ever be necessarily led to draw the same political consequences which the Americans have derived from a similar social organization. I am far from supposing that they have chosen the only form of government which a democracy may adopt; but the identity of the efficient cause of laws and manners in the two countries is sufficient to account for the immense interest we have in becoming acquainted with its effects in each of them.

It is not, then, merely to satisfy a legitimate curiosity that I have examined America; my wish has been to find instruction by which we may ourselves profit. Whoever should imagine that I have intended to write a panegyric will perceive that such was not my design; nor has it been my object to advocate any form of government in particular, for I am of opinion that absolute excellence is rarely to be found in any legislation; I have not even affected to discuss whether the social revolution, which I believe to be irresistible, is advantageous or prejudicial to mankind; I have acknowledged this revolution as a fact already accomplished or on the eve of its accomplishment; and I have selected the nation, from among those which have undergone it, in which its development has been the most peaceful and the most complete, in order to discern its natural consequences, and, if it be possible, to distinguish the means by which it may be rendered profitable. I confess that in America I saw more than America; I sought the image of democracy itself, with its inclinations, its character, its prejudices, and its passions, in order to learn what we have to fear or to hope from its progress.

ALEXIS DE TOCQUEVILLE, *La Démocratie en Amérique*, translated by HENRY REEVE (1835), author's preface to the first part.

IX

Heinrich Heine analyses the Situation in France, 1842

The Parisian bourgeoisie are obsessed by a nightmare apprehension of disaster. It is not fear of a republic but an instinctive dread of communism, of those sinister fellows who would swarm like rats from the ruins of the present régime. No, the French bourgeoisie would not be alarmed by a republic of the earlier variety, nor even by a little Robespierrism. They would easily reconcile themselves to that form of government and stand watch over the Tuileries regardless of whether the building housed a Louis Philippe or a Committee of Public Safety. For what the bourgeoisie want above all is order and protection—protection of their existing property rights—and these are objectives that a republic should be able to guarantee as surely as a monarchy. But as already noted these shopkeepers sense instinctively that today a republic might no longer represent the principles of the seventeen nineties. It might become the instrument through which a new unacknowledged power would seize control, a proletarian party preaching community of goods. The bourgeoisie are therefore conservatives by external necessity, not by inward conviction. Their politics are motivated by fear.

Will this restraining fear persist very long? May not the national giddiness confuse these cautious heads some day or other and send them spinning once more into the whirlpool of revolution? I do not know. It is possible. In fact the election returns in Paris are a constant reminder that it is more than possible, it is probable. The French have short memories and easily forget even the dangers they have the best reasons to fear. This explains why they so often appear as the actors, nay more, as the principal protagonists, in the vast tragedy which the dear Lord has staged on Earth. . . .

HEINRICH HEINE, *Sämmtliche Werke*, 4 volumes, edited by O. J. LACHMANN (Leipzig, 1887), iv. 296. Translated by GEOFFREY BRUUN.

X

Giuseppe Mazzini instructs the Members of Young Italy

Young Italy is a brotherhood of Italians who believe in a law of *progress* and *duty*, and are convinced that Italy is destined to become one nation—convinced also that she possesses sufficient strength within herself to become one, and that the ill success of her former efforts is to be attributed not to the weakness, but to the misdirection of the revolutionary elements within her—that the secret of force lies in constancy and unity of effort. They join this Association in the firm intent of consecrating both thought and action to the great aim of reconstituting Italy as one independent sovereign nation of free men and equals.

Life and Writings of Joseph Mazzini (London, 1890), i. 96.

XI

Proclamation of the Cracow Poles, 1846

We are twenty million strong. If we rise as one man nothing can stand in our path. We will gain such freedom as has never been known on earth. We will win for ourselves a society in which each one of us shall enjoy worldly goods according to his merits and capabilities. There shall be no special privileges of any kind, and every Pole shall find security for himself and his family. Anyone physically or morally handicapped by his birth shall receive without any humiliation the help of the whole community. Land conditionally held by the peasants shall become their own unconditional property. Usury, serfdom and all kinds of feudal dues shall be abolished without compensation. Sacrifices made for the nation's sake shall be rewarded by distribution of the nation's wealth.

From henceforth there shall be no distinction amongst us; we are brothers, the sons of one mother, our country, and one Father—in

Heaven. Let us pray for His aid, and He will bless our aims and grant us the victory. But that He may hear our prayers, let us not soil ourselves by drunkenness and pillage; let us not foul our blessed weapons by despotic behaviour or by the murder of members of other creeds, other nations; for it is not against the people that we fight but against their oppressors.

FRANÇOIS FEJTÖ, *The Opening of an Era, 1848* (London, Allan Wingate, 1948), pp. 364–5.

XII

Manifesto of the Communist Party, 1848

. . . . . .

Hitherto, every form of society has been based, as we have already seen, on the antagonism of oppressing and oppressed classes. But in order to oppress a class, certain conditions must be assured to it under which it can, at least, continue its slavish existence. The serf, in the period of serfdom, raised himself to membership in the commune, just as the petty bourgeois, under the yoke of feudal absolutism, managed to develop into a bourgeois. The modern labourer, on the contrary, instead of rising with the progress of industry, sinks deeper and deeper below the conditions of existence of his own class. He becomes a pauper, and pauperism develops more rapidly than population and wealth. And here it becomes evident, that the bourgeoisie is unfit any longer to be the ruling class in society, and to impose its conditions of existence upon society as an over-riding law. It is unfit to rule, because it is incompetent to assure an existence to its slave within his slavery; because it cannot help letting him sink into such a state that it has to feed him, instead of being fed by him. Society can no longer live under this bourgeoisie; in other words, its existence is no longer compatible with society.

The essential condition for the existence and for the sway of the bourgeois class is the formation and augmentation of capital; the condition for capital is wage-labour. Wage-labour rests exclusively on competition between the labourers. The advance of industry, whose involuntary promoter is the bourgeoisie, replaces the isolation of the labourers, due to competition, by their revolutionary combination, due to association. The development of modern industry, therefore, cuts from under its feet the very foundation on which the bourgeoisie produces and appropriates products. What the bourgeoisie therefore produces, above all, are its own grave-diggers. Its fall and the victory of the proletariat are equally inevitable.

KARL MARX and FREDERICK ENGELS, translated by SAMUEL MOORE, edited by FREDERICK ENGELS, 3rd edition (London, 1888), Part I.

XIII

The Romantic Movement

The Children of the Poor

Take heed of this small child of earth;
He is great: he hath in him God most high.
Children before their fleshly birth
Are lights alive in the blue sky.

In our light bitter world of wrong
They come; God gives us them awhile.
His speech is in their stammering tongue
And his forgiveness in their smile.

Their sweet light rests upon our eyes.
Alas! their right to joy is plain.
If they are hungry, Paradise
Weeps, and, if cold, Heaven thrills with pain.

The want that saps their sinless flower
Speaks judgment on sin's ministers.
Man holds an angel in his power.
Ah! deep in Heaven what thunder stirs,

When God seeks out these tender things
Whom in the shadow where we sleep
He sends us clothed about with wings,
And finds them ragged babes that weep!

VICTOR HUGO, *Œuvres complètes, Poésie, vol. xiii, L'Art d'être grand-père*, pp. 239–40 (Paris, 1882). Translated by ALGERNON CHARLES SWINBURNE.

III. THE STRESS OF NATION-BUILDING (1848–67)

XIV

An abridged list of Decrees issued by the Provisory Government of the Second French Republic, March–April 1848

The abolition of royalty under any form whatsoever.
The proclamation of the Republic.
Dissolution of the Chamber of Deputies.
The National motto shall be *Liberté, Égalité, Fraternité.*
Reorganization of the National Guards, dissolved by the preceding régime.
Abolition of former titles of nobility.

The right to work and the establishment of national communal workshops open to all unemployed citizens.

Creation of a government commission for the workers, under the direction of Louis Blanc, to conciliate the interests of workers and employers.

The convocation of a National Assembly.

J. B. J. PAILLIET, *Constitutions Américaines et Françaises* (Paris, Alphonse Delhomme, 1848), pp. 448–56. Translated by GEOFFREY BRUUN.

XV

Nicholas I helps to crush the Hungarian Revolt, 1849

The insurrection in Hungary has of late made so much progress that Russia cannot possibly remain inactive. A temporary insufficiency of the Austrian forces, divided as they are on many points, has favoured the progress of the insurrection. . . . The Austrian Government being for the moment unable to oppose a sufficient power to the insurgents, it has formally requested His Majesty the Tsar to assist in the repression of a rebellion which endangers the tranquillity of the two empires. It was but natural that the two Cabinets should understand one another on this point of common interest, and our troops have, consequently, advanced into Galicia to coöperate with Austria against the Hungarian rebellion. . . .

Manifesto of TSAR NICHOLAS I of Russia, 27 April 1849; *The Annual Register for 1849* (London, 1850), pp. 333–4.

XVI

To a Foiled Revolter or Revoltress

1. Courage! my brother or my sister!
   Keep on! Liberty is to be subserved, whatever occurs;
   That is nothing that is quelled by one or two failures, or by any number of failures,
   Or by the indifference or ingratitude of the people, or by any unfaithfulness,
   Or by the show of the tushes of power—soldiers, cannon, penal statutes.
2. What we believe in waits latent forever through Asia, Africa,

Europe, North and South America, Australia, Cuba, and all the islands and archipelagoes of the sea.

3. What we believe in invites no one, promises nothing, sits in calmness and light, is positive and composed, knows no discouragement,
Waits patiently its time—a year—a century—a hundred centuries,

. . . . . .

9. Did we think victory great?
So it is—But now it seems to me, when it cannot be helped, that defeat is great
And that death and dismay are great.

WALT WHITMAN, *Leaves of Grass* (Boston, 1860–1), pp. 394–6.

XVII

The Declaration of Paris, 1856

The Plenipotentiaries of Great Britain, France, Austria, Russia, Sardinia and Turkey who signed the Treaty of Paris of March 30th, 1856 . . . have adopted the following solemn Declaration:

1. Privateering is, and remains abolished;
2. The Neutral Flag covers Enemy's Goods, with the exception of Contraband of War;
3. Neutral Goods, with the exception of Contraband of War, are not liable to capture under Enemy's Flag;
4. Blockades, in order to be binding, must be effective, that is to say, maintained by a force sufficient really to prevent access to the coast of the enemy.

The Governments of the Undersigned Plenipotentiaries engage to bring the present Declaration to the knowledge of the States which have not taken part in the Congress of Paris, and to invite them to accede to it.

Convinced that the maxims which they now proclaim cannot but be received with gratitude by the whole world, the undersigned Plenipotentiaries doubt not that the efforts of their Governments to obtain the general adoption thereof will be crowned with full success.

The present Declaration is not and shall not be binding, except between those Powers who have acceded, or shall accede, to it.

E. HERTSLET (ed.), *The Map of Europe by Treaty* (London, 1875–91), ii. 1282–3.

XVIII

Napoleon III and Cavour Plan a War. Plombières, 20 July 1858

The Emperor . . . began by saying that he had decided to support Sardinia with all his forces in a war against Austria, provided that the war was undertaken for a non-revolutionary cause, and that it could be justified in the eyes of diplomacy and still more of public opinion in France and Europe.

The question of a cause presented the chief difficulty. . . .

. . . . . .

We passed to the important question: what would be the aim of the war? The Emperor readily admitted that the Austrians must be driven completely out of Italy. . . . But then, how is Italy to be organized? After long debate, we agreed in general on the following points, while recognizing that they might be modified by the events of the war. The valley of the Po, Romagna and the Legations will constitute the kingdom of Upper Italy under the house of Savoy. The Pope would keep Rome and its environs. The rest of the papal states are to form, with Tuscany, the kingdom of Central Italy. The borders of the kingdom of Naples would not be affected. The four Italian states would form a confederation like the Germanic Confederation, and the Pope would be given the presidency to console him for the loss of the best part of his states.

This arrangement seems to me completely acceptable. For your Majesty, as sovereign by right of the richest and strongest segment of Italy, would be sovereign in fact of the whole peninsula. . . .

After we had settled the future destiny of Italy, the Emperor asked me what France would get and if your Majesty would cede Savoy and the county of Nice. . . .

A report by Cavour to Victor Emmanuel II, 24 July 1858. *Lettere di Camillo Cavour, raccolte ed illustrate da* LUIGI CHIALA, vol. iii (Turin, 1884), pp. ii–iv. Translated by GEOFFREY BRUUN.

XIX

Alexander II decides to liberate the Russian Serfs, 3 March 1861

In considering the various classes and conditions of which the State is composed we came to the conviction that the legislation of the empire, having wisely provided for the organization of the upper and middle classes, and having defined with precision their obligations, their rights, and their privileges, has not attained the same degree of efficiency as regards the peasants attached to the soil. . . .

These facts had already attracted the notice of our predecessors of glorious memory and they had taken measures for improving the conditions of the peasants; but among those measures some were not stringent enough, insomuch that they remained subordinate to the spontaneous initiative of such proprietors who showed themselves animated with liberal intentions; and others, called forth by peculiar circumstances, have been restricted to certain localities or simply adopted as an experiment. . . . We thus came to the conviction that the work of a serious improvement of the condition of the peasants was a sacred inheritance bequeathed to us by our ancestors, a mission which, in the course of events, Divine Providence called upon us to fulfil. . . .

Having invoked the Divine assistance, we have resolved to carry this work into execution.

The Annual Register for 1861 (London, 1862), pp. 207–9.

XX

Bismarck lectures the Prussian Budget Committee, 1862

Our blood is too hot; we choose to wear armour that is too heavy for our slight body; but we should wear it nevertheless. The eyes of Germany are not fixed upon Prussia's liberalism, but upon her armed might. Bavaria, Würtemberg, and Baden may try out liberal experiments; no one will assign them Prussia's role. Prussia must conserve and maintain her strength for the favourable moment—a moment which has once already slipped by. Prussia's boundaries, as set by the Vienna treaties, are not satisfactory for a healthy state life. The great questions of the day will not be settled by speeches or by majority votes—that was the mistake of 1848 and 1849—but by blood and iron!

H. KOHL (ed.), *Die politischen Reden des Fürsten Bismarck*, 12 vols. (Stuttgart, 1892–4), vol. ii, pp. 29–30. Translated by GEOFFREY BRUUN.

XXI

The Gettysburg Address, 19 November 1863

Fourscore and seven years ago our fathers brought forth on this continent a new nation, conceived in liberty, and dedicated to the proposition that all men are created equal.

Now we are engaged in a great civil war, testing whether that nation, or any nation so conceived and so dedicated, can long endure. We are met on a great battle-field of that war. We have come to dedicate a portion of that field as a final resting-place for those who here gave their lives that that nation might live. It is altogether fitting and proper that we should do this.

But in a larger sense, we cannot dedicate—we cannot consecrate—we cannot hallow—this ground. The brave men, living and dead, who struggled here, have consecrated it far above our poor power to add or detract. The world will little note nor long remember what we say here, but it can never forget what they did here. It is for us, the living, rather, to be dedicated here to the unfinished work which they who fought here have thus far so nobly advanced. It is rather for us to be here dedicated to the great task remaining before us—that from these honoured dead we take increased devotion to that cause for which they gave the last full measure of devotion; that we here highly resolve that these dead shall not have died in vain; that this nation, under God, shall have a new birth of freedom; and that government of the people, by the people, for the people, shall not perish from the earth.

ABRAHAM LINCOLN, *Complete Works*, edited by J. G. NICOLAY and JOHN HAY (New York, 1894), ii. 439.

XXII

William Ewart Gladstone advises Parliamentary Reform, 1866

. . . You cannot fight against the future. Time is on our side. The great social forces which move on in their might and majesty, and which the tumult of our debates does not for a moment impede or disturb—those great social forces are against you; they are marshalled on our side; and the banner which we now carry, though, perhaps, at some moment it may droop over our sinking heads, yet it soon again will float in the eye of heaven, and it will be borne by the firm hands of the united people of the three kingdoms, perhaps not to an easy, but to a certain and to a not distant victory.

The Annual Register for 1866 (London, 1867), Part I, p. 135.

IV. SCIENTIFIC MATERIALISM AND *REALPOLITIK* (1867–81)

XXIII

The Liberal Faith

So complete was my father's reliance on the influence of reason over the minds of mankind, whenever it is allowed to reach them, that he felt as if all would be gained if the whole population were taught to read, if all sorts of opinions were allowed to be addressed to them by word and in writing, and if by means of the suffrage they could nominate a legislature to give effect to the opinions they adopted. He thought that when the legislature no longer represented a class interest, it would aim at the general interest, honestly and with adequate wisdom.

JOHN STUART MILL, *Autobiography* (London, 1873), p. 106.

XXIV

Charles Darwin on the Descent of Man

The main conclusion arrived at in this work, and now held by many naturalists who are well competent to form a sound judgment, is that man is descended from some less highly organized form. The grounds upon which this conclusion rests will never be shaken, for the close similarity between man and the lower animals in embryonic development, as well as in innumerable points of structure and constitution, both of high and of the most trifling importance—the rudiments which he retains, and the abnormal reversions to which he is occasionally liable—are facts which cannot be disputed. They have long been known, but until recently they told us nothing with respect to the origin of man. Now, when viewed by the light of our knowledge of the whole organic world, their meaning is unmistakable. The great principle of evolution stands up clear and firm, when these groups of facts are considered in connection with others, such as the mutual affinities of the members of the same group, their geographical distribution in past and present times, and their geological succession. It is incredible that all these facts should speak falsely. He who is not content to look, like a savage, at the phenomena of nature as disconnected, cannot any longer believe that man is the work of a separate act of creation. . . .

CHARLES DARWIN, *The Descent of Man* (London, 1871), ii. 385–6.

XXV

Social Darwinism, 1873

. . . Our habitual instructors, our ordinary conversation, our inevitable and ineradicable prejudices tend to make us think that Progress is the normal fact in human society, the fact which we should expect to see, the fact which we should be surprised if we did not see. But history refutes this. The ancients had no conception of progress; they did not so much as reject the idea; they did not even entertain the idea. Oriental nations are just the same now. Since history began they have always been what they are. Savages, again, do not improve; they hardly seem to have the basis on which to build, much less the material to put up anything worth having. Only a few nations, and those of European origin, advance; and yet these think —seem irresistibly compelled to think—such advance to be inevitable, natural, and eternal. Why then is this great contrast? . . .

In solving, or trying to solve, the question, we must take notice of this remarkable difference, and explain it, too, or else we may be sure our principles are utterly incomplete, and perhaps altogether unsound. But what then is that solution or what are the principles which tend towards it? Three laws, or approximate laws, may, I think, be laid down, with only one of which I can deal in this paper, but all three of which it will be best to state, that it may be seen what I am aiming at.

First. In every particular state of the world, those nations which are strongest tend to prevail over the others; and in certain marked peculiarities the strongest tend to be the best.

Secondly. Within every particular nation the type or types of character then and there most attractive tend to prevail; and the most attractive, though with exceptions, is what we call the best character.

Thirdly. Neither of these competitions is in most historic conditions intensified by extrinsic forces, but in some conditions, such as those now prevailing in the most influential part of the world, both are so intensified.

These are the sort of doctrines with which, under the name of 'natural selection' in physical science, we have become familiar; and as every great scientific conception tends to advance its boundaries and to be of use in solving problems not thought of when it was started, so here, what was put forward for mere animal history may, with a change of form but an identical essence, be applied to human history. . . .

WALTER BAGEHOT, *Physics and Politics* (London, 1912), pp. 41–44.

XXVI

The Definition of Papal Infallibility, 18 July 1871

Concluding paragraphs

Therefore faithfully adhering to the tradition received from the beginning of the Christian faith, for the glory of God our Saviour, the exaltation of the Catholic religion, and the salvation of Christian people, the Sacred Council approving, we teach and define that it is a dogma divinely revealed: that the Roman Pontiff, when he speaks *ex cathedra*, that is, when in discharge of the office of pastor and doctor of all Christians, by virtue of his supreme Apostolic authority, he defines a doctrine regarding faith or morals to be held by the universal Church, by the divine assistance promised to him in blessed Peter, is possessed of that infallibility with which the divine Redeemer willed that his Church should be endowed for defining doctrine regarding faith or morals; and that therefore such definitions of the Roman Pontiff are irreformable of themselves, and not from the consent of the Church.

But if any one—which may God avert—presume to contradict this our definition: let him be anathema.

W. E. GLADSTONE and PHILIP SCHAFF, *The Vatican Decrees* (New York and London, 1875), pp. 166–8.

V. THE FRUITS OF INDUSTRIALISM AND IMPERIALISM (1881–98)

XXVII

Social Insurance

Speech by Bismarck in the German Reichstag, 15 February 1881

At the opening of the Reichstag in February, 1879, the Emperor, while referring to the law of October 21, 1878 [an act to repress the German Socialists], expressed the hope that this Assembly would cooperate in ameliorating social ills by means of legislation. A remedy cannot be sought only through the repression of Socialistic excesses. It is necessary at the same time to have a definite advancement in the welfare of the working classes. The matter of first importance here is the care of those workers who are incapable of earning a living. On behalf of these, the Emperor has advised that a bill be laid before the Bundesrat to insure workers against the consequences of accidents, and it is hoped that this bill will satisfy a need felt by employees and employers alike. His Majesty trusts that this measure will receive the approval of the Federal Governments, and that it will be accepted by the Reichstag as a supplement to the legislation that guarantees protection against Social-Democratic movements. Previous provisions for guarding workers against the risk of falling into helplessness through incapacity caused by accident or age have not proved adequate, and the inadequacy of such provisions has been a main contributing cause in driving the working classes to seek help by joining Social-Democratic movements.

The draft of a bill on a closely connected problem has been brought to the same stage. It is designed to regulate the relationships of the guilds, and to strengthen the efforts of individual workers employed at the same handicraft by bringing them together in bonds of union. This will increase their efficiency and raise their moral stamina. . . .

H. KOHL (ed.), *Die politischen Reden des Fürsten Bismarck*, 12 vols. (Stuttgart, 1892–4), vol. viii, p. 314. Translated by GEOFFREY BRUUN.

XXVIII

The Triple Alliance of Germany, Austria–Hungary, and Italy, 1882

Article I. The High Contracting Parties mutually promise peace and friendship, and will enter into no alliance or engagement directed against any one of their States.

They engage to proceed to an exchange of ideas on political and economic questions of a general nature which may arise, and they further promise one another mutual support within the limits of their own interests.

Article II. In case Italy, without direct provocation on her part, should be attacked by France for any reason whatsoever, the two other Contracting Parties shall be bound to lend help and assistance with all their forces to the Party attacked.

The same obligation shall devolve upon Italy in case of any aggression without direct provocation by France against Germany.

Article III. If one, or two, of the High Contracting Parties, without direct provocation on their part, should chance to be attacked and to be engaged in a war with two or more Great Powers non-signatory to the present Treaty, the *casus foederis* will arise simultaneously for all the High Contracting Parties.

Article IV. In case a Great Power non-signatory to the present Treaty should threaten the security of the states of one of the High Contracting Parties, and the threatened Party should find itself forced on that account to make war against it, the two others bind themselves to observe towards their Ally a benevolent neutrality. Each of them reserves to itself, in this case, the right to take part in the war, if it should see fit, to make common cause with its Ally.

. . . . . .

Article VI. The High Contracting Parties mutually promise secrecy as to the contents and existence of the present Treaty.

A. F. PRIBRAM, *The Secret Treaties of Austria–Hungary, 1879–1914* (Cambridge, Mass., Harvard University Press, 1920), i. 65 ff.

XXIX

France and Russia prepare a Military Convention, 1892–4

France and Russia, inspired by a common desire to preserve peace and having no other object than to meet the exigencies of a defensive war, provoked by an attack of the forces of the Triple Alliance against either of them, have agreed upon the following provisions:

1. If France should be attacked by Germany, or by Italy supported by Germany, Russia will employ all her available forces to fight Germany. If Russia should be attacked by Germany, or by Austria supported by Germany, France will employ all her available forces to fight Germany.

2. In the event that the forces of the Triple Alliance, or of one of the Powers belonging to it, should be mobilized, France and Russia, at the first news of this event, and without any preliminary agreement, will mobilize immediately and simultaneously their entire forces, and will move them as close as possible to their frontiers.

3. The available forces to be employed against Germany shall be 1,300,000 men furnished by France, and 700,000 or 800,000 furnished by Russia. These forces shall be engaged so completely and so promptly that Germany will be forced to fight simultaneously in the East and in the West.

4. The General Staffs of the armies of the two countries will consult together at all times to prepare for and to facilitate the execution of the above-mentioned measures. They shall exchange, in time of peace, all information in their possession, or which shall come into their possession, concerning the armies of the Triple Alliance. Methods of corresponding in time of war shall be studied and prepared in advance.

5. France and Russia will not conclude peace separately.

6. The present convention shall have the same duration as the Triple Alliance.

7. All the clauses above enumerated are to be kept completely secret.

France, Ministère des Affaires Étrangères, *Documents diplomatiques*: 'L'Alliance Franco-Russe' (Paris, Imprimerie Nationale, 1918), No. 71.

XXX

A Defence of British Colonialism

. . . Though there is little that is glorious in most of the great Empires mentioned in history, since they have usually been created by force and have remained at a low level of political life, we observe that Greater Britain is not in the ordinary sense an Empire at all. Looking at the colonial part alone, we see a natural growth, a mere normal extension of the English race into other lands, which for the most part were so thinly peopled that our settlers took possession of them without conquest. If there is nothing highly glorious in such expansion, there is at the same time nothing forced or unnatural about it. It creates not properly an Empire, but only a very large state. So far as the expansion itself is concerned, no one does or can regard it but with pleasure. For a nation to have an outlet for its superfluous population is one of the greatest blessings. . . .

JOHN ROBERT SEELEY, *The Expansion of England* (London, Macmillan & Co., 1883), p. 296.

XXXI

A German comment on Colonial Rivalry, 1890

Deutschland wach auf!

English diplomacy works darkly and swiftly. On 18 June 1890, the Anglo-German Treaty on Africa exploded like a bomb and took the world by surprise. At the stroke of a pen the prospect of a great colonial empire for Germany was annulled. . . . Faced with this situation men of every party, feeling themselves Germans first of all, will want to take matters into their own hands. We hope that the Reichstag, by an overwhelming majority, will tell the Government: This treaty with England is inimical to our interests and an affront to our honour. . . . At our Kaiser's call we will step into the ranks, we will let ourselves be led, silent and obedient, against the enemy's guns. But in return we may demand a reward worthy of the sacrifice: that we take our share of the world as a conquering nation and do not ask it as a concession granted by another nation in its munificence.

Germany, Wake Up!

O. BONHARD, *Geschichte des Alldeutschen Verbandes* (Berlin, 1920), p. 2. Translated by GEOFFREY BRUUN.

XXXII

Friedrich Nietzsche Advocates a Super-Race

Now that the 'herd-animal' has become the prevalent type in Europe, is it not time to train, consciously and artificially, an antithetic type, and to inculcate in it the contrary virtues? Might not democracy itself find a justification and a goal if someone appeared who could utilize and build upon it? Ultimately, in addition to slavery (the novel and admirable climax toward which European democracy is headed) a superior strain might be produced. This higher breed of dominant Caesarian spirits would use democracy as a platform, brace themselves upon it, and lift themselves above it. The new race would then achieve things hitherto thought impossible, attain to a vaster perspective, and fulfil its earthly destiny.

FRIEDRICH NIETZSCHE, *Der Wille zur Macht*, Fragment 954 (1888). Translated by GEOFFREY BRUUN.

Nietzsche's notes for 'The Will to Power'—a work in which he planned to give systematic expression to his doctrines—were composed a few months before madness overtook him in January 1889.

VI. RISING SOCIAL PRESSURES AND THE BALANCE OF POWER (1898–1914)

XXXIII

Social Pressure

. . . Whereas . . . every war is but an outrage (*attentat*) against the working men, . . . a bloody and terrible means of diverting them from their demands, the Congress declares it necessary, from the international point of view, to enlighten the working men, in order that in case of war they may reply to the declaration of war by a declaration of a revolutionary general strike.

Statement of policy by the Congress of the *Confédération Générale du Travail* (1908). LOUIS LEVINE, *Syndicalism in France* (New York, Columbia University Press, 1914), p. 189.

XXXIV

Some Fruits of Imperialism, 1900

The old century is very nearly out, and leaves the world in a pretty pass, and the British Empire is playing the devil in it as never an empire before on so large a scale. We may live to see its fall. All the nations of Europe are making the same hell upon earth in China, massacring and pillaging and raping in the captured cities as outrageously as in the Middle Ages. The Emperor of Germany gives the word for slaughter and the Pope looks on and approves. In South Africa our troops are burning farms under Kitchener's command, and the Queen and the two Houses of Parliament and the bench of bishops thank God publicly and vote money for the work. The Americans are spending fifty millions a year on slaughtering the Filipinos; the King of the Belgians has invested his whole fortune on the Congo, where he is brutalizing the negroes to fill his pockets. The

French and Italians for the moment are playing a less prominent part in the slaughter, but their inactivity grieves them. The whole white race is revelling openly in violence, as though it had never pretended to be Christian. God's equal curse be on them all! So ends the famous nineteenth century into which we were so proud to have been born.

WILFRID SCAWEN BLUNT, *My Diaries*, 2 vols. (London, Martin Secker, 1919–20), vol. i, p. 464.

XXXV

Law Separating Church and State in France, 9 December 1905

Title I

1. The Republic assures liberty of conscience. It guarantees the free exercise of religions subject only to the restrictions enacted below in the interest of public order.
2. The Republic does not recognize nor pay nor subsidize any religion. Consequently, commencing on 1 January next following the promulgation of the present Law, all expenses relative to the exercise of religions shall be omitted from the budgets of the state, the departments, and the communes. . . .

Title II

3. On the promulgation of the present Law the agents who administer the public lands shall proceed to compile an inventory describing and evaluating: (1) the personal and landed property of the [religious] establishments; (2) the property, owned by the state, departments, and communes, the use of which the establishments have enjoyed.
4. Within one year . . . the personal and landed property of the . . . public religious establishments shall be transferred . . . to the associations . . . which are to be formed under the provisions of Article 19. . . .
11. Ministers of religion . . . over sixty [years of age], who have performed ecclesiastical duties paid by the state for thirty or more years, shall receive an annual pension. . . .

. . . . . .

Title IV

18. Associations formed to provide for the cost, maintenance, and public exercise of a religion must be organized in accordance

with . . . the Law of 1 July 1901 [the Associations Act which decreed that all religious orders or congregations in France, including those instructing the young, must obtain a specific authorization from the government].

19. These associations must have for their exclusive purpose the exercise of a religion and be composed at least: In Communes of less than 1,000 inhabitants of seven persons . . . of 1,000 to 20,000 . . . of fifteen persons . . . of more than 20,000 . . . of twenty-five adult persons. . . .
The associations may receive . . . donations and collections . . . They shall not . . . receive subventions from the state, departments, or communes. . . .

. . . . . .

TITLE V

30. . . . Religious instruction shall not be given to children between the ages of six and thirteen, enrolled in the public schools, except outside class hours.

Bulletin des lois de la République française, xiie série, Partie principale, No. 2663 (Paris, 1905), pp. 1697–1707. Translated by GEOFFREY BRUUN.

XXXVI

The Franco-British Entente, 1904

Article 1. His Britannic Majesty's Government declare that they have no intention of altering the political status of Egypt.

The Government of the French Republic, for their part, declare that they will not obstruct the action of Great Britain in that country. . . .

Article 2. The Government of the French Republic declare that they have no intention of altering the political status of Morocco.

His Britannic Majesty's Government, for their part, recognize that it appertains to France, more particularly as a Power whose dominions are conterminous for a great distance with those of Morocco, to preserve order in that country, and to provide assistance for the purpose of all administrative, economic, financial, and military reforms which it may require.

. . . . . .

Article 9. The two Governments agree to afford to one another their diplomatic support, in order to obtain the execution of the clauses of the present Declaration regarding Egypt and Morocco. . . .

Great Britain, *Parliamentary Papers*, ciii (London, 1911), Cd. 5969 (Treaty Series, 1911, No. 24), pp. 162–5.

XXXVII

The Austro-Hungarian Ultimatum to Serbia, 23 July 1914

. . . .

It is clear from the statements and confessions of the criminal authors of the assassination of the twenty-eighth of June, that the murder at Sarajevo was conceived at Belgrade, that the murderers received the weapons and the bombs with which they were equipped from Serbian officers and officials . . . and, finally, that the dispatch of the criminals and of their weapons to Bosnia was arranged and effected under the conduct of Serbian frontier authorities.

The results brought out by the enquiry no longer permit the Imperial and Royal Government to maintain the attitude of patient tolerance which it has observed for years toward those agitations which centre at Belgrade and are spread thence into the territories of the Monarchy. Instead, these results impose upon the Imperial and Royal Government the obligation to put an end to those intrigues, which constitute a standing menace to the peace of the Monarchy.

In order to attain this end, the Imperial and Royal Government finds itself compelled to demand that the Serbian Government give official assurance that it will condemn the propaganda directed against Austria–Hungary, that is to say, the whole body of the efforts whose ultimate object it is to separate from the Monarchy territories that belong to it; and that it will obligate itself to suppress with all the means at its command this criminal and terroristic propaganda.

. . . .

The Imperial and Royal Government awaits the reply of the Royal Government by Saturday, the twenty-fifth instant, at 6 p.m., at the latest.

MAX MONTGELAS and WALTER SCHUCKING (editors), *Outbreak of the World War, German Documents Collected by Karl Kautsky* (New York, Oxford University Press, 1924), Supplement I.

VII

1914–50

By

EDMOND VERMEIL

Emeritus Professor of the University of Paris

INTRODUCTION

Man mag es ein Glück heissen, wenn junge Leute nicht einsehen, dass jetzt eigentlich niemand geboren werden kann, der dem Tag und der Stunde gewachsen wäre.[1]

GOETHE

§ 1. *Statement of the problem*

In the period between the two world wars of the twentieth century an historian can readily discern three categories of events, which emerge more and more clearly with the unfolding of the great drama which may aptly be called 'the second Thirty Years War'.

First and foremost in the general scheme a sort of world system is seen to take shape, resulting from earlier disturbances. Europe, weakened by wars and revolutions, and enclosed henceforth between the Atlantic and the natural frontiers of Russia, loses her traditional pre-eminence. She yields in favour of two great continental powers which have grown up in the east and the west. Out of the 1917 Revolution is born a new Russia which, excluded from Europe by the play of mutual enmities, stretches its tentacles out to the Middle and the Far East. North America, a participant in both world wars, withdraws in the interval between them into isolation from the League of Nations, and turns her attention to the large-scale development of her agriculture and industry. The states of South America suffer many vicissitudes, and only attain organization after innumerable attempts. As for Africa, all that it now expects is to see its natural riches exploited by Europe in the hour of her own grave danger.

Secondly, we have to note how Europe, tiny Europe, develops meanwhile in the social, economic, and political fields. She restricts herself within a perimeter drawn by the nations—differing in size and tendencies—which are grouped around defeated and dismembered Germany. As soon as Italian fascism appears in 1922, Hitler's party fortifies its positions, tries a first *putsch* in 1923, suffers a momentary eclipse, and in 1930 wins its first electoral victory. There is now no obstacle that can stand in its way. Supported by Italy, Spain, and Japan, and confronted in the west by appeasing powers, Hitler takes advantage of the

[1] It may be counted a matter of good fortune if the young are unaware that nobody can now be born into the world who is equal to the day and the hour.

'balkanization' of the south-east, and casts his horrible shadow on the perimeter states to hurl himself later in conquest on Austria and Czechoslovakia. At last, in the Second World War, he attacks Poland and the Scandinavian states, and then gambles on the decisive adventure: the crushing of the western powers and the destruction of Russia, the two ultimate objectives of the Pan-Germanic programme. Germany has never seemed so close to world dominion; but never, too, has she seemed so close to irreparable defeat as when the Allied victory sets up, on her shattered soil, the four-power occupation of the Russians, Americans, English, and French. Europe now has to solve again the problem of Germany's relations with the perimeter states. Under pressure from both Russia and America, Europeans can no longer solve it by themselves and their own resources; for the tragedy of Germany, partitioned by the line of the Elbe, is bound up with the tragedy of the whole world.

After the disappearance of the old absolute monarchies Europe was thus a sort of battleground where democracy and fascism engaged in a fight to the death. On the spiritual and intellectual level (and here we reach the third of our categories) the drama took the form of a struggle between traditional humanism, the basis of a future international order, and aggressive nationalism, hammering out its own savagely Machiavellian ideology based on absolute dictatorship in a totalitarian state. The League of Nations, an institution belonging to the 'old Europe', reproduced the essential features of its humanism, which was based on the tradition of classical antiquity, on the Christianity of the confessions which sprang from the Reformation, on liberal and parliamentary democracy, and lastly on socialism as expressed in the various internationals—all of them forces united in a common respect for human personality. By breaking away from the League soon after the coming of Hitler, Germany unleashed the opposing ideologies and hastened the breakdown of the Geneva organization. We have to ask ourselves how, in this tragic age, new problems were forced on the attention of Europe; how science, philosophy, and religion, teaching, the press, and the arts became agents or victims of the profound dualism which split and ravaged the Old World at the time of the world wars.

In each of the three fields which we have just mentioned the stages of development are no less clearly marked. First of all, after the First World War there were the years 1919–23 which followed the armistice and its immediate consequences, with their inevitable train of difficulties and vicissitudes. A paradoxically hopeful period followed between 1924 and 1928; a period of much lending and borrowing, when the world seemed to be returning to a normal exchange of goods, and even Germany, after Locarno, seemed about to join the League of Nations and take her place in the community of Europe. But in 1929, just at the turn of the decade, the terrible world crisis intervened. It is true to say that it split the whole western world into two. From 1930 to 1936 its cruel repercussions were felt simultaneously by all peoples in every continent. From 1937 to 1939 they culminated in the events which led up to the declaration of war. And from 1939 to 1945 the second world conflagration brought to a close that series of events which the followers of Hitler termed *faits accomplis*.

§ 2. *A general review of the period*

The Europe whose history ends for us with this new Thirty Years War was founded, soon after the middle of the nineteenth century, on the unification of Italy, the building up of the Austro-Hungarian monarchy, and the creation of the Bismarckian empire. At the turn of the century these three states, united in the Triple Alliance, were to cause the emergence of an opposing group, in which Great Britain, France, and Tsarist Russia came together in the Triple Entente, eventually joined by Rumania. The clash between these two organized coalitions gave rise to the First World War.

The history of European diplomacy between 1900 and 1914, as revealed by a detailed study of facts and problems, follows a scheme which is relatively simple but inexorable in its development. It includes the progressive breakdown of the Triple Alliance; the gradual strengthening of the Triple Entente; various attempts at *rapprochement*, or conversely at breaking away, between the members of one group and those of another; conflicts between the opposing powers which become more and more irreconcilable; the movement of the central empires, under the influence of serious diplomatic defeats, towards the risking of a war of aggression which would also be a fight for existence.

In all this the Franco-German quarrel plays a secondary role. The front of the stage is occupied by Anglo-German rivalry and the conflict between the central empires and Russia. On the west, England and France against Germany; on the east, the deadly struggle between the Slav and the German. Germany is therefore certain of having to fight on two fronts. This general grouping suggests the idea of a force which, starting in Germany, pushes westward, eastward, and southward at the same time, and tends to cut Europe into two parts so that the German Reich may establish its sovereign rule. Armed with a huge industrial machine which enables her, as long as she maintains a flourishing export trade, to import the raw materials necessary to build up a formidable army and navy, the Germany of William II and the ruling caste becomes alive to the possibilities revealed by a more and more extravagant nationalism. Nourished by religion, philosophy, and science, and flattering the ambitions of the landed aristocracy and the higher bourgeoisie of industry and trade, Pan-Germanic ideas, with their origins rooted in German romanticism, culminate in a continental and colonial programme which counts for victory on British neutrality, and more especially on the crushing of two military powers at once: in the west France, already defeated by Germany in 1871; in the east Tsarist Russia, which had just been beaten by Japan at the opening of the twentieth century.

Germany and her allies would accordingly appear to have driven themselves into war. From the point of view of the central empires the general conflagration was inherent in, and demanded by, the situation of 1914 when seen in its reality. Actually, the Triple Alliance was involved by its own fault, and as the result of a solidarity which hardly concealed serious weaknesses and profound disagreements. This is a responsibility which falls entirely on the Alliance, without taking into account the effective steps which it may have risked at the last moment to set hostilities in motion. To develop an economic system which is irresistibly impelled by its own dynamic force to try new ventures; to maintain the most powerful army in the world and also a considerable battle fleet; to fail to achieve all diplomatic objectives in consequence of forcing threatened states to unite together more and more closely—may not all this be regarded as laying oneself open to an irresistible temptation to make use of force?

This conception of Austro-German responsibility seems psychologically correct. As they showed themselves to the world, especially from 1900 to 1914, the faults of German diplomacy are related to those of the German character as a whole. The danger was not to be found in an implacable will carrying out its aim with a mixture of determination, tenacity, and moderation, in accordance with a clearly conceived and exactly defined plan. It lay rather in a curious mixture of narrow nationalism and ambitious universalism, of mysticism and brutality, of astute adaptability and stiff rigidity. Bismarck had shown a relative wisdom which permitted him, without giving Europe too much cause for anxiety, to maintain the edifice he had erected in the middle of the old continent; but his successors had found their task overwhelming. They had managed badly a people which was at once industrious and impulsive. All the errors implied by a long-standing national maladjustment meet together, as it were in a single focus, in this vital conception of German responsibility.

It would be easy to give an analogous demonstration in the field of internal politics. It would not be difficult to show that the western parliamentary democracies found far better solutions to the problems of government than Bismarck's Reich. In Germany, as many excellent observers have noted, even on the very eve of the war power lay in no one's hands. The emperor and the ruling class were no longer capable of exercising it, and by the terms of the constitution the Reichstag was not empowered to do so. This explains why the Reich was unable to withstand the giddy confusion of war.

It would be equally easy to show how, during hostilities, Bismarck's system must, and did, fall rapidly to pieces. Disintegration set in simultaneously on federal, administrative, political, economic, and social levels. Whether in the relations between the central power and the states, or in those between emperor, government, and Reichstag, or in the matter of finding some reconciliation between the demands of the bourgeoisie and those of the proletariat, and between the claims of soldiers and those of civilians, we always find the same 'pluralism', the same danger of incoherence in a gigantic collective effort, doomed thereby to eventual defeat.

Germany lost and deserved to lose the First World War. Russia and North America shared with the European Allies in bringing about her resounding defeat. American intervention, at the time of Ludendorff's great offensive launched on a single front in 1918, compensated for the inevitable Russian default.

How is it possible to assess the heritage bequeathed to the Old

World by this great catastrophe? It was soon summed up in the will to revenge of a nation justly punished by the treaty of Versailles, but left with her political unity intact, with her means of power quickly restored to her by the Allies themselves, and with a free hand for action in Europe, now more partitioned than ever after the disappearance of the Dual Monarchy. But let us not forget the fears awakened by the spectre of social revolution lifting its head since 1917 in defeated Russia. These fears, widespread in Europe, where the League of Nations was ineffectual, were used by Germany to help her rearmament campaign, and to aid her attempt to achieve, under a compact dictatorial régime, supreme power in the Old World.

I
THE NEW WORLD SITUATION

§ 1. *The Americas*

To the west of Europe, and beyond the Atlantic, the two halves of the American continent present an amazing contrast. In spite of the variety of elements which compose them, the U.S.A. and Canada are the offspring of northern Europe. They reproduce tendencies towards federation and democracy which are copied more or less faithfully from parliamentary models to be found in the mother continent. Comparatively independent of the U.S.A., the republics of Central and South America look rather towards Spain and the Spanish tradition which they carry on overseas. As a general rule, they have leanings towards the fascist dictatorships, military or civilian, on which the white man relies, when in command of the government, in order to discipline the native and mixed immigrant populations.

(*a*) *The United States*. After making sure of final victory in 1918, North America was not equal to the task of making sure of peace. The Wilsonian gospel, which summed up the whole tradition of democratic liberalism in its fourteen points, was not able to rebuild a world shattered by four years of bitter fighting. It was not a sufficient achievement to bring about a surrender. To establish peace on a solid foundation, it would have been necessary to reconcile the two terms of a contradiction which was insoluble by its very nature. On the one hand there was Germany, determined not to admit her unique responsibility, and pinning her hopes to the Wilsonian gospel in her wish to escape all discriminatory punishment and to receive the equality of treatment which was her ultimate object. On the other hand there were the demands of the European allies, who could not agree to absolute equality between victors and vanquished when the treaty of Brest-Litovsk had shown them, almost prophetically, the pitilessly harsh conditions which Germany would have imposed on them if she had won the day on the western battlefields.

The U.S.A. was not able to arbitrate in this fundamental conflict. President Wilson had not the necessary physical resources to defend his ideals and his cause, nor had he, what was even more essential, the unstinting support which he hoped for from the American public. In Congress he had a Republican majority against him, haunted by fears of bolshevism and of future class wars, and seeking refuge in a protective isolationism.

The U.S.A. had not yet grasped the significance of the gulf which had arisen in the Old World between western humanism and German ideology. After pouring out material and military aid, America withheld the moral support which would have been so precious. Even if she had supported Wilson, she could certainly not have foreseen either the tragic struggle which was fated to take place, under cover of Wilson's principles, between unrepentant Germany and the European democracies, or the later rise of fascism and the complicity of the European middle classes in the Italian and German régimes. When the Washington Conference met in October 1921, to settle the problem of debts, the United States was confronted with a Europe in which the two most powerful nations, Britain and France, could not agree, and with an Asia in a state of ferment and an Africa full of unrest. When America demanded the settlement of the debts contracted by her former allies, how cruel was the contrast between her economic prosperity and the distress of the mother continent, already forced to submit to the supremacy of the dollar. It is a fact that the U.S.A. granted to Europe and Germany many more dollars than she received in payment of their debts. But then she was taking the place of the mother continent, formerly the world's creditor. Economic and financial supremacy was passing across the Atlantic and moving from east to west.

The world was about to enter the President Coolidge era, the phase in American history when the industry of the U.S.A., putting all its efforts into large-scale production, worked unremittingly for a relatively restricted population—and that *vis-à-vis* a Europe the population of which had increased in a single century by 300 million persons.

The question of prohibition arose in the U.S.A. because the government wished to increase the productivity of labour and the purchasing power of the wage-earners. From this period also dates the racial feeling, springing from religious and Puritan sources, which, fostered by the First World War, set American Protestantism against everything foreign to itself. Faced with the danger of communism, the U.S.A. rallied round its *élite* and retreated even farther into isolationism.

Europe had been almost entirely 'balkanized' by the treaty

of Versailles. She had become a collection of small states. She was therefore more than ever at a disadvantage in comparison with a continent which was in the process of organizing both its agricultural and industrial production and its internal trade for the whole of its area. Americans believed, too, that they could not only build a self-sufficient economic system for themselves, but that they could also, returning to the European world, rebuild the economy of Germany, by means of the Dawes and Young plans, and make a final peace settlement by the Kellogg pact of 1928. At a time when President Hoover, elected by the Republican party, was triumphing in four years of incredible prosperity, the Americans had not the least idea of the terrible crisis about to burst upon them. Nor did they suspect that they were responsible for the first electoral victory won by Hitler in September 1930. After sowing the seeds of the Second World War in Germany, they were not to emerge from their crisis for many a long year to come.

The 1929 crisis affected agricultural conditions before bursting on the industrial and financial scene. This cataclysm, suddenly putting a stop to the loans of which America had been generous to Europe, once more held up communications between the Old World and the New. The great drama spread from the U.S.A. to Europe and South America, that is to say to the whole capitalist world. It was bound to encourage Germany in her Machiavellian schemes. The American slump, laying North America itself open to the infiltration of fascist ideas, gave Germany an unhoped-for chance. Might she not make use of the resources which the Anglo-Saxon world had left her, and of the mistakes of the makers of the Versailles treaty, to risk a war of revenge, and to establish her supremacy over the Old World after her eventual victory?

Let us not forget the name of Franklin Roosevelt and the respect which we owe to his work. It is not within our scope to judge the New Deal. But everyone knows the courage and the vigorous optimism of the President, as, supported by the majority of Americans, he took up his hard task upon his election. Supported by an executive armed with exceptional powers, Congress henceforth embarked on a most timely programme of legislation. Once old-fashioned unrestricted liberalism and the over-simplified 'help yourself' policy had disappeared, a new system of industrial relations, infinitely more efficient than the old, resulted from the methods of reconstruction now adopted. The obstinate opposition of the Supreme Court could not defeat either the forward movement of the intellectual *élite*, putting all its talent at the President's disposal, or the loyalty of the working class, grateful to the man who refused to benefit only a privileged minority and made it his concern to achieve a reasonable standard of living for all.

There was at once a stiffening of attitude, and American policy could now make a stand in the face of the Berlin–Rome–Tokio Axis and the Anti-Comintern pact. It was not only a matter of America's influence in Europe. Her supremacy in the Pacific was also a question at issue. When the Republican party regained some seats in 1938 a new wave of isolationism swept over the whole of America. Franklin Roosevelt took up the fight against this serious danger with the utmost energy. Defending the interests of the democratic cause more strenuously than ever, he became deeply involved in the European quarrel, and took his stand against fascist dictatorship with its lawlessness and its police system of delation and terrorism. The Chicago speech of October 1938 and the appeals which followed showed the world what a true idea Roosevelt had of the German menace, and with what insight he tried to draw together the democracies of the west, then divided from one another, in the face of their common enemy. Above all he understood that the U.S.A. could not afford to break her links with Great Britain and her empire. After so many illusions and mistakes the U.S.A. had learned from experience: now that the isolationist phase was over, and while the Axis powers hovered threateningly over the world, she was ready for the role which she was to play in the Second World War. A gulf was fixed between American democracy and European fascism; for the American judged any state deprived of an active opposition to be unworthy of the name. Once more, just when she thinks victory assured, Germany will break her strength, after pushing deep into Russia, against the American Colossus.

(*b*) *South America.* At this juncture Roosevelt had tried to draw Latin America into the organization of common defence against the Axis. That area was, however, under the influence of Spanish-Italian fascism. In addition, powerful German minorities had obtained a foothold there, and after Hitler's victory their propaganda reinforced that of Mussolini and Franco.

The South American republics exported foodstuffs and raw materials and imported manufactured goods in exchange. When, after all the efforts of Wilson, the U.S.A. cut herself off from Europe, she flooded South America with her capital and her goods. Thus dollar diplomacy and free capitalistic enterprise were responsible for the birth of Pan-Americanism. The South Americans, far from seeing in it an imperialist menace, considered the movement from the north to be an agent of prosperity and order. But they were also to show that they knew how to safeguard their independence.

They gave expression to Spanish ideas in the office of the President (the ministers being normally responsible only to the head of the state), who governed as a dictator with the support of the army and the police. The struggle was almost everywhere confined to a duel between the natural conservatism of the whites and the aspirations of the peasants and coloured workers among whom Indians predominated. The movement for racial equality, generally supported by the intellectual *élite*, could only struggle against the capitalist invasion from the north, which spread everywhere except in Argentina, Uruguay, and Chile, that is to say except in the extreme south of the continent.

The 1929 crisis rocked the South American republics to their foundations. In the states of Central America, in the republics of the north-west, in Brazil, and in the countries of the south, almost the same pattern is everywhere to be found.

The recent history of Mexico, the state nearest to North America, was typical. In 1910 she began with a revolution which swept away the old feudal system, upheld the rights of both peasant and worker, and gave rise to a sort of popular democracy with communistic features, which cost the country, in several years of civil war, nearly a million lives. First there was an outburst of exasperated radicalism and violent anti-clericalism; then there came a reaction, led by the Church and the army. But about 1926–8 General Callès came to terms with North American capitalism over oil, the country's chief source of wealth. A little later, from 1934 to 1937, a great agrarian reform was introduced and carried through. Socialism won the day; finally the oil companies were nationalized; and this in its turn caused a break with the Anglo-American world. Economic state-control was victorious, with the motto 'Mexico for the Mexicans'.

The relative success achieved by the Mexican proletariat set up a counter-reaction in the Central American states, where civil and military dictatorship, incorporated in the League of Dictators founded in 1931 by General Ubico, was, however, unable to escape a number of troubles and uprisings in Guatemala, Salvador, Honduras, Nicaragua, and other states. Cuba alone held the balance between the socialism of Mexico and the despotism of the neighbouring republics.

In the north-west of South America, in Venezuela, Colombia, Ecuador, Bolivia, and Peru, dictatorships were more moderate. In Colombia and Bolivia, for instance, concessions were made to liberal socialism; in Ecuador a stand was taken against the Church; but in Peru and Venezuela, on the other hand, the dictators relied on the Church for support. This part of the world did not escape the devastating crisis of 1929, exacerbating the fatal struggle between the ruling classes and the proletariat with its two elements, the industrial and the agricultural.

This is why, from 1929 onwards, Brazil, that vast country of planters and industrialists, passed through the most serious material crisis in her history. Brazil had more European immigrants than any other South American state. Dictatorship, which was supported there by Italians, Portuguese, and Germans, had always been attacked by a liberal, not to say revolutionary, opposition. In 1934 she finally achieved a parliamentary constitution, but the powers of the President were still very wide, and ministers were not responsible to the Chambers. After years of crisis a military rebellion brought the country to the verge of communism. In 1937, to counter these tendencies to the Left, a new constitution replaced the parliamentary system by a corporative form of state, based on a plebiscite and fascist in character, under the aegis of Salgado's Green Shirts, which were modelled on the Italian Black Shirts and the Brown Shirts of Hitler.

The procedure was similar in the southern republics: Chile, Argentina, Paraguay, and Uruguay.

After 1925 Chile, an industrial state rich in iron and copper mines, gave up her normal parliamentary system, which respected fundamental rights but which had very unstable ministries, was hard on the great landowners, and armed itself with social legislation progressive and democratic enough to risk the separation of the Church and the state. The country was moving towards a more active political life. After the *coups d'état* of 1927 and 1931, in the midst of the economic crisis, a dictatorship was set up, backed by the conservative parties and the army. In Argentina the Radical party, having expended all its strength from 1916 to 1928, bore the brunt of the crisis, and had to give way to a civilian dictatorship backed by the Conservative and Moderate parties and also by the army. In Paraguay, where there was a period of prosperity after the victory over Bolivia, a socialist régime was set up in 1936, with the support of students and the working class; but in 1937 it was overthrown by a *coup d'état* and replaced by a fascist dictatorship. In Uruguay, a country in the main democratic until about 1933, the old stable government gave way to a régime also based on force.

With reaction against Mexican socialism in Central America; with moderate dictatorships, occasionally anticlerical, in the north-west republics; with a fascist victory in Brazil; and with military or civilian dictatorships ousting parliamentary democracy in the southern states, we see here, as in Spain and Portugal, fascism gaining the upper hand almost all along the line, thanks to the crisis of 1929–30. We may expect the same in Germany.

It is therefore reasonable to conclude that the whole American continent had undergone a certain hardening. Although the United States, after a period of incredible prosperity, had lived through the most tragic crisis in her history, had recovered under the New Deal, and had supported Roosevelt in his attack on the Axis, she was none the less endangered by the reaction, Protestant or racial in its basis, which was engendered by her hostility to communism and by the excesses of her increasingly powerful plutocracy. With the exception of Mexico, Central and South America favoured a more or less fascist form of dictatorship. The high-powered propaganda organized in the United States by the Nazis, after their rise to power, and their growing influence in Latin America, give the measure of the danger which was involved for the west by Italian and German support of Spanish-Portuguese fascism, and by their encouragement, across the Atlantic, of the reactionary forces in the American world.

§ 2. *Union of Soviet Socialist Republics*

In her own hemisphere America, in spite of financial intervention in Europe between 1924 and 1928, and in spite of the influence of German-Italian fascism in the south of her own continent, remains detached from the Old World, and thus makes the treaty of Versailles not only notoriously impotent, but also at the same time productive of the most disastrous consequences. But if this is the policy of America, Europe too, on her side, isolates herself from Soviet Russia.

(*a*) *The 1917 Revolution.* The 1917 revolution had quickly liquidated both opposition at home and foreign intervention. Once the resistance of the ruling classes and landlords and that of the old republican or socialist elements had been destroyed, and once the capitalist Holy Alliance, with its lamentable ignorance and its capricious and confused tendencies, was out of the way, bolshevism struck root in Russia. It was to determine her new political and social structure.

The result of this tremendous event was that Russia, by her very absence, was part of the system created by the treaty of Versailles. This fact was brought home to the peace conference when, faced by a double menace to their peace, both from defeated Germany and from revolutionary Russia, the principal members realized that they would have to accept the reality of communism without incorporating it in the treaty which they were preparing for Europe. Harassed by fearful difficulties the Old World was forced to acknowledge the absence of America and Russia. Resting uneasily on a disquieted and undeveloped Africa, Europe was caught between two continental units inevitably spreading their tentacles in every direction to become world powers, and coming into conflict with one another in every corner of the globe. Russia could scarcely hide her implacable hatred of the capitalist world; and the insurrection for which she was working took on almost cosmic dimensions, spreading revolutionary ferment everywhere and taking the future for granted in virtue of the successes gained in the U.S.S.R. How could the Comintern, in its nature, be anything but a subversive movement of planetary proportions, bound to awaken the opposing movement of the Berlin–Rome–Tokyo Axis?

A dictatorship of a single party, communism depended for its support upon the peasant and working masses. It brought about a new relationship between the agrarian and the urban proletariat. In theory the peasant freed from serfdom, like the artisan freed from capitalist slavery, became a 'worker'. Order had to be introduced into an unprecedented social chaos, in the face of the west and the east. Russia made a clean sweep, and developed a new idea of man and his existence and activities. The primary unit was the human unit of labour: man who possesses nothing except his hands to work with. Russia claimed to be restoring all his dignity, by making him, and him alone, the cornerstone of the future social order. An improvised *élite*, a sort of restricted and dictatorial high command, was to direct the army of workers both on the land and in the workshops, an army of soldiers strictly so-called, an army of minds united by a single doctrine. Thus Lenin reshaped the elements of an outworn community, melting them in the crucible of his system. After complete disintegration there came the most rigid reorientation.

State capitalism, both local and federal, turned the worker into an officially consecrated being, a soldier of the cause. In this huge sum of collective labour, scientific, agricultural, and industrial, the individual represented a unit of action, placed at the service of a system of thought which had been conceived by the *élite* and was to be realized by it in the name and interest of the whole mass. A close and direct relationship was therefore established between the population's material needs and the body of organized labour. A plan of several years' duration, at once theoretic and practical, was put before the people, especially the young; it guaranteed both work and food. A régime of this kind will consider only the material side of man, with his instincts, his appetites, and his elementary needs. It will be both rational and despotic.

This dictatorship arose out of a situation which was essentially tragic, in that such a mode of government might seem the only conceivable or practicable thing. A classless society, whose only hierarchy was, in essence, that of the one party and the ruling *élite*, matched the vastness of the conception and the plan. Henceforward the worker can only survive if he keeps to the place allotted to him and contributes his modest share to the whole structure. The revolution maintains its force and keeps going by a permanent general mobilization of the national energies. The people must be prepared to make any renunciation: they must sacrifice the present, if necessary, to a future which will, it is hoped, be brighter.

The historic past and the old régime having been rooted out, true history, actual history, must begin with the new society. The Russian calendar, by its very existence, may be said to have destroyed the unity of Europe. Karl Marx claimed to be extending the French Revolution beyond the results it had temporarily achieved in western Europe, where, in the course of the nineteenth century, the middle classes and socialism had never been able to agree in their ideas or their actions. This was why he made of his doctrine an absolute, for which Russia was now serving as a field of experiment. After the clean sweep of 1917 there was nothing now to stop Russia from trying out all the recipes gathered from international science, guiding herself in the process either by orthodox Messianism or by the military and police methods of the fallen tsardom.

By the side of the Revolution of 1789 must be set the influence of German idealism, as Fichte, Hegel, and Marx himself had developed it. One may say that its supreme object was to enclose the whole mass of the people in an organized system from which *a priori* there were to be excluded, along with differences of status and remuneration, all forms of social injustice, Roman law, and the principle of private property consecrated by that law. Thought escaped into the past and the future to solve the difficulties of the present. Interpreting Hegel in a revolutionary sense, the Russians took over all the social theories of the west and the nineteenth century. They in their turn could declare that everything that is rational is, and will be, real. How can a distinction then be drawn between the salvation of the individual and that of the community?

In this light, the humanism of the past, with its transcendent values, was no longer valid. Since culture was only an 'epiphenomenon' compared with economic reality, the culture of a capitalist and bourgeois society could not retain its ascendancy. Industry, by the same token, rose to a status of equality with agriculture. Man needed to rebuild his life both on the land and in the factory. From the Russian state and revolution it was easy to progress to the planetary state and world revolution. Pan-Slavism appeared again in a new dress. Long before the Nazis Lenin believed in the power of the idea when it represents the more or less conscious instinct of the masses.

What was the Russian revolution but a first step on the road which seemed destined to lead human societies towards the organized and rigidly administered state? Lenin was equally horrified by the latent anarchy of the western democracies and the unbridled romanticism of the Germans. He preached not indeed the cruelty of fanaticism but the implacable hardness involved in a necessary system of discipline. The Americanization of Russia, infinitely more far-reaching, followed upon that of Germany. Terror and propaganda were by no means absent in a movement of this kind.

Starting from the frightful situation of 1917, and sweeping away internal reaction and foreign intervention, Russia from 1921 to 1923 lays the foundations of her future economic system of complete state-control. It was first of all necessary to ensure the provision of food supplies by means of coercive methods; and so the régime begins by organizing a far-reaching agrarian reform which breaks up the great estates and shares them among the peasants but leaves them the ownership of the land. When this ownership is threatened, the régime has to be humanized by the formation of N.E.P.[1] in order to prevent a peasants' revolt, and this policy lasts until Stalin lays the foundation of the future collective system. After the Sickle it is the turn for the Hammer, that is to say for the beginnings of industrial reorganization. Finally we have monetary reform, the liquidation of bourgeois habits and practices, the establishment of the frontiers, and the Constitution of 1923, ratified on 31 January 1924 by the Congress of Soviets. Seven years of N.E.P., from 1921 to 1928, secured an indispensable breathing-space for Russia, following a terrible famine.

After 1928 and the defeat of Trotsky, Stalin steers Russian policy, as Bismarck had that of Germany, into the channels of possibility. Henceforth his action is inspired purely by a disciplinarian realism of the most rigorous order.

The first Five-Year Plan, set in motion after October 1928, gave the signal to towns and villages for a huge effort of reconstruction. The problem was to equip a poverty-stricken Russia with an up-to-date economic system, which should also be free from any capitalist influence. While the state, by collectivizing the land, became responsible for all agricultural undertakings, the reorganization of industry followed a pattern similar to that of American super-capitalism, the aim in both cases, in spite of the difference in method, being to build up a gigantic industry in a vast country exceedingly rich in raw materials.

[1] N.E.P. = New Economic Policy.

Towards 1935, when the great effort begins to take shape, Russian communism allows the tension to relax. Democratic trends can be observed. There is, for instance, within a social framework given new life by the reinstatement of family institutions, the equal status of the two proletariats which appears in the constitution of 5 December 1935 and in its astonishing concessions to bourgeois liberalism. In the elections of 12 December of that year a unanimous vote was cast in favour of Stalin; but the government in the Kremlin and the dissensions by which it was secretly troubled remained wrapped in mystery. There are always the methods of purge and liquidation to bring recalcitrants back to the right road. The terrible ordeal of 1941 found a people ready to face and defeat it.

During this period relations with the outside world were strengthened and restored to normal; but this did not result in any real contacts or exchanges between Russia and Europe. With Germany there was the treaty of Rapallo. Trade agreements with several countries followed. Then came the Conferences of Cannes and The Hague in 1922; the recognition of the Soviet régime by the Baltic states; its recognition by England in 1924, followed by serious trouble in 1926–7, and then by a return to normal relations in 1929; recognition by France and Italy, both in 1924; and recognition by Japan in 1925. The treaty of Rapallo was confirmed in 1926, at the very moment when Trotskyism was completely liquidated.

In 1933, when Hitler seized power, the Russian dictator confirmed the treaty of Rapallo once more. While carrying out a policy of non-aggression, the U.S.S.R. was none the less alarmed by the danger of National Socialism. The Nazis, indeed, hardly concealed their designs upon the Ukraine and the east in general. Russia therefore prudently retreated before this scarcely veiled threat. Recognized by the U.S.A. after the election of Franklin Roosevelt, she proposed to France a pact of mutual assistance, somewhat reminiscent of the Franco-Russian alliance of 1891. The Soviet government was obviously anxious for peace, the *status quo*, collective security, and disarmament. In 1934 Russia entered the League of Nations, doubtless in order to take the place of Germany. For before her eyes there now appears on her eastern flank an enemy who is no less dangerous than the Third Reich—Japan. Russia has Axis fascism on her doorstep, in the Far East as well as in Europe.

At this stage it is impossible not to raise the profoundly serious problem whether fascism is not a sort of inverted communism, organized and used by a bourgeoisie which is not afraid to borrow Russia's own weapons and to conduct with left-wing apparatus a right-wing revolution, a 'national' revolution which matches the 'social' and 'international' revolution. If the U.S.S.R. starts with a socialism which seeks to be total and universal, and then moves on to nationalism, the fascist states seem on their side to start with nationalism, and then to turn towards a pseudo-socialism which is, after all, nothing but a massive solidarity, under dictatorial control, within a national framework.

(*b*) *Russia's expansion in the Middle and Far East.* The picture would not be complete without some reference to Russia's expansion in the Middle and Far East. Persia, Afghanistan, and Turkey, being immediate neighbours, had soon recognized the Soviet régime. Although isolated in relation to the European west, the new Russia was still the most western nation of the east. In the Middle East she therefore turned to those peoples who were trying to throw off any foreign control and working for national independence. Her fervent propaganda against the allegedly decadent nations of the west thus gradually became the single front of the colonial or semi-colonial peoples and the communist régime. At the Congress of Baku in September 1920 there was initiated a policy called 'the by-pass for Asia' (*détour pour l'Asie*), which was directed mainly against the British empire, as a delayed revenge for the 1904 defeats.

But just at the moment when Russia, having become westernized in the technical field, turns to the continent of Asia, the east in her turn looks towards the west.

Turkey sets the example. Not, indeed, that she imitates her ally in Moscow. She wishes to have nothing to do with communism, and is simply taking part in a vast Asiatic movement which aims at preparing for Asia a sort of racial revenge on Europe, whose prestige had been partially weakened by the First World War. In protest against the colonialism of Europe, the United States and the U.S.S.R., for different reasons, both take their stand on the 'right of nations to decide their own destiny', the most fundamental of all the Wilsonian principles. As the metropolitan countries had been helped by the natives of their colonies and thus remained in their debt, and as, on the other hand, technical advances spread and national consciousness was awakened everywhere, Islam became marked out for a new role, and one of the highest importance.

The seeds of new ideas and the desire for independence found a favourable ground in Egypt, a country which is indeed part of Africa, but forms a part of the whole that is here under consideration. There is, for instance, the Arab awakening, a real revolution, due to the extension of modern means of communication. The divided nations of Islam have, it is true, to fight for a long time yet against French sovereignty, Great Britain's ambitions, and Jewish hopes in Palestine. But their solidarity grows. In Syria and to the south, French and British alike meet the same desire for independence. We may recall the Assembly of Damascus, the Druse revolt in 1925, the disturbances of 1933 and 1936, and the negotiations which immediately preceded the Second World War. In Iraq, in 1936, the governing cabinet comes under the influence of Turkey, and breaks with British tutelage. As for the problem of Arabia, the most complicated of all, Ibn Saud solves it in his own way as the Arab world comes into conflict with the Christian minorities and with the Palestine Zionists, both hated with equal fanaticism.

In Persia the 1907 and 1919 treaties were denounced, and the work of modernization went on in imitation of Turkey. A similar process is followed in Afghanistan, that harsh country which absorbed the new civilization overnight, thereby setting up a reaction which by its violence seriously retarded the transformation that had begun.

This tremendous movement spreads with amazing speed to the whole of south Asia. India and Burma are already caught up in it. India, loyal to Britain from 1914 to 1918, claims her fundamental rights as a reward. The India Act of 1919, Gandhi's action, English intervention, the struggle between Muslim and Hindu, India's entry into the League of Nations, the London Round Table Conference, and finally the 1935 Constitution granting India a parliament, are so many stages on India's road to independence. Similar events are enacted in Siam, Indochina, the Philippines, and the Netherlands East Indies.

Soviet influence has its part to play. While Turkey fiercely resists communism, and while Egypt, Arabia, and Syria are fired first and foremost by the idea of the solidarity of Islam, Russian influence is most strongly felt in Iran and Afghanistan and the whole of southern Asia. The Soviet government had threatened Teheran since 1920, and after its discomfiture had contracted a sort of alliance with Persia. In 1921 an agreement between Russia and Afghanistan ratified the good relations begun with the accession of Amanullah. Finally, communism tried to stir up against European dominion in India all its different races, united together in the one desire for independence. Since that time the influence of communism seems to have had even more effect in the Netherlands East Indies, Siam, and Indochina.

One great problem remains: the relations between China and Japan.

Immediately after the First World War Soviet propaganda had found favourable conditions in China. In effect, communism was made to appear a national resistance movement against foreign imperialism. Sun Yat-Sen was treated as the 'Chinese Lenin', although in fact he was Americanized to a very great extent. He followed the Russian pattern, extended the Kuomintang to peasants and workers, and reorganized his party by means of rigid centralization. The first Chinese revolution was therefore linked with that of 1917 in Russia. How otherwise would the U.S.S.R. have been able to advance into the heart of Asia? Anti-communist and nationalist reaction, led by Chiang Kai-Shek, afterwards tried to spare China a horrible civil war by breaking away from the U.S.S.R. This policy lasted from 1927 to 1930. It was not until 1932 that China and Russia resumed diplomatic relations.

At this moment, when disorder in China had reached its peak, Japan made her first offensive. It is well known how rapidly she had assimilated western science and technique. A population of more than 70 million inhabitants and the impossibility of large-scale emigration to the U.S.A. were two factors which taken together could only have one effect: to encourage socialism and communist propaganda among the working masses. Until 1923 the U.S.A. and England, helped by the Dominions, had succeeded in controlling Japanese expansion. After 1927 the succession of conquests began. Japan had designs upon Manchuria, north China, Siberia, and the Indies, no matter if her ambitions led her into war with the United States. The first attempt was made from 1931 to 1932. Then in March 1933 Japan withdrew from the League of Nations, and, as he claimed to be fighting communism, Chiang Kai-Shek faced this formidable enemy, risking the most bitter protests against his policy. From 1936 to 1939 the war between China and Japan develops in all its vast tragic proportions. But this time China fights back with desperate strength, at the very moment when the Russo-German pact brings Japan a sad disillusion.

Thus Russian influence, which in Europe was confronted by victorious fascism, was met in Asia by Chiang Kai-Shek's resistance and by Japanese fascism. In reply Russia retreats behind her frontiers. With the Second World War imminent she has to make ready for the great ordeal of 1941 reserved for her by Hitler's Germany in spite of the 1939 pact.

Africa did not escape the infection. Strange movements were felt even in Australasia. In the French colonies, which had served France so well from 1914 to 1918, a vigorous agitation was stirring. North Africa was affected by Pan-Arabism. Tunisians were clamouring for self-government. In Algeria, Arab propaganda tried to stir up 7,000,000 natives against 800,000 Frenchmen. Finally, in Morocco, after the work done by Lyautey, the first troubles coincided with the Abd-el-Krim affair. The symptoms showed themselves before 1924; they defined themselves more clearly between 1924 and the 1938–9 risings, more especially at the time when the Spanish War gave rise to new conflicts in the area. Lastly the Italian colonies were the scene of serious struggles, when Fascism, having checked all Pan-Arab and autonomist attempts, threw her strength into the conquest of Ethiopia.

In Central and in South Africa there was a general spirit of disagreement, in spite of considerable differences in different areas, between whites and coloured workers. And while in Australia a moderate nationalism was the order of the day, in New Zealand a strong Labour majority had been established.

Uncertain of herself after a shattering war; with little support from an Africa seething with revolt; squeezed between America and Russia, between capitalism and communism, both aiming at world domination—a divided and balkanized Europe has to struggle to defend herself against bourgeois fascism and proletarian communism, but without being able to choose or create a new order strong enough to maintain the balance between the great forces engaged in conflict.

II

ITALO-GERMAN FASCISM AND THE EUROPEAN PERIPHERY

HAD Europe, after 1919, any clear picture of the new world which had arisen out of the war, and of the part which she might play in it with what remained of her energy and resources? Far from that, she was conscious at an early stage of her own isolation. The existence of the League of Nations was only a slight alleviation of the extremely precarious nature of her position. Thanks to the essential provisions of the Versailles treaty there was a fatal disequilibrium between a Germany with her unity recovered and the perimeter states with their number increased and their divisions encouraged by a peace which had arbitrarily 'balkanized' Europe. As some shrewd observers noted as early as 1921, Germany was almost ready to start the great game again. This became very clear when Hitler seized power in 1933.

§ 1. *Post-war years*

It was evident that with the armistice of 1918 Germany only interrupted her military programme to take it up again later. Nietzsche did not need to wait for the First World War before prophesying to Europeans that if they could not establish a sound federation they would see rising in their midst a monstrous state which they would have to destroy in order to free themselves from a slavery worse than death; an apocalyptic vision, rapidly dimmed by the optimism of Geneva. Only those who, knowing the German mentality, followed its development closely were able to discern, behind the brilliant façade of the concert of nations, the spectre of the most relentlessly aggressive nationalism the world has ever known.

(*a*) *Confusion in Europe*. After the storm had spent itself, the Old World was a scene of disorder alike in social, economic, financial, and political matters. Before 1914 none of the Great Powers had achieved for itself a real compromise between bourgeois liberalism and the demands of even moderate socialism. If this could be amply demonstrated for Germany, it was even more true of Austria–Hungary and Italy. Neither Great Britain nor France nor Spain, in spite of their democratic traditions, had found a solution acceptable to their respective working classes.

It is true that everywhere, even in Germany, 1914 had witnessed that 'unity of dedication' among the social classes which had marked the outbreak of hostilities, in the aggressor states as well as in those which considered themselves the victims. But it was an alliance which could not long survive the unprecedented difficulties which four years of war had imposed on all the combatant nations.

Once the war was over, increasingly bitter class struggles emerged as the central phenomenon in Europe. In Germany terrible strikes had already preceded Ludendorff's offensive of March 1918. In all the countries of Europe the same feeling of complete insecurity was widespread, contrasting most painfully with the apparently prosperous years before the conflagration. Social displacements of every kind were brought about, no less important than the modification and multiplication of frontiers in a balkanized Europe. Revolutionary tendencies were no longer restricted to a single nation. They were common to victors and vanquished alike.

Germany was destined to undergo the tragic events of 1918–20 and to witness the brutal destruction of revolutionary Spartacism by the Social Democrats, supported by the forces of reaction. In Austria and Hungary socialism was in power, while Bulgaria submitted to a peasant dictatorship and Greece was ruled by a republic. Everywhere socialization was the order of the day. Masses of peasants still under arms were impatiently waiting to return to their homes. Strikes increased among the workers behind the front line. No nation escaped the menace.

Encouraged by the war, vast economic changes were taking place in Europe. They were not unlike those which were on foot in Russia and America.

From this angle, agrarian reform stands out in bold relief. By leaving intact the great landed estates in the east, Germany condemned her bogus political revolution to a complete stalemate; but the small successor states of the Austro-Hungarian monarchy, almost all agricultural in character, carried out, whether victors or vanquished, a reform on the Russian model, and used similar though less radical methods. Feudalism disappeared. Not, indeed, that eastern Europe had thought of introducing, at one stroke, a system of communism based on the peasantry. On the contrary, the land was divided, at the risk of endangering agricultural production, in order to forestall any communist invasion. With only limited credits at their disposal, the new landowners borrowed at high rates of interest, and exchanged the landlord's chains for those of their creditors. While the debts of the peasants mounted up, and agricultural production decreased, trade relations between west and east became seriously involved.

In the field of industry, on the other hand, it was by no means simple to convert war plant to peaceful uses; but while the shortage of industrial equipment was enormous, the demand was enormous too. How was it possible to replace so much destroyed equipment, repair so much neglected property, obtain such quantities of raw materials and foodstuffs? And, especially, how could demobilized workers be absorbed by industries which were working only at half pressure? When production has been increased and geared to meet an unlimited consumption, there is always a risk of under-consumption as soon as the most pressing needs have been met. Mushroom war-time fortunes, bankruptcies and crashes, falling prices and flooded markets, unemployment, Spanish 'flu—how could people cope with so many disasters and dangers at once?

Monetary confusion ranked among the most difficult consequences of the war. It was impossible to resume exchanges and normal previous competition while prices, varying in every country, defied all attempts at any general adjustment. After an exhausting war, with accumulated debts, incalculable pensions to be paid, and unprecedented expenses on reconstruction, there was not a country that was not obliged to borrow incessantly, to issue unlimited notes and Treasury vouchers, in short to use all the measures of bankruptcy and to risk inflation.

The monetary crisis was a symbol of the inevitable collapse of the Triple *Entente*, already severely shaken by Russia's defaulting. There is no doubt that the nations had been inspired by a common ideal of the defence of civilization and the preservation of values. But what was to become of this fine solidarity if the common foundations gave way at the material level? The working classes everywhere were threatened with unemployment, higher prices, and poverty. Out of this situation there sprang up everywhere the 'Fourth Estate', an international proletariat standing above all national proletariats. The destruction of the middle class, and all the resentment implied by it, gave rise to the worst possible political complications. It was the main cause of fascism.

(*b*) *The Treaty of Versailles*. A number of monarchies having disappeared, a bridge of transition had to be built between the old order and some system of republican democracy; but this was made more difficult by the social and economic crisis. The older democracies had so many problems to solve simultaneously that in the effort they almost wrecked their most firmly established institutions and nearly wasted the best of their energy.

This means that the whole development of fascism was implicit in the essential features of the situation created by the war—the fear of communism and its deeply aggressive tactics towards bourgeois democracy; the uneasy conscience of the ruling classes, tempted to save their stakes, their privileges, and their future by using dictatorial methods based on the example of communism itself, and by employing (in order to escape from all their accumulated difficulties) devices calculated to inspire the members of the community with a solidarity at once massive and mystical and a nationalism no less violent than ambitious. Hitler's twenty-five-point programme dates from 1920. The march on Rome took place in 1922.

The treaty system adopted by Europe in 1919 was hardly calculated to save her from this mortal danger.

The Allies did not agree amongst themselves. Today it can be seen to what extent the fear of bolshevism overshadowed all the negotiations, making the English and Americans tender to Germany, and leading the French, anxious for their safety as immediate neighbours of the Reich, to make disastrous concessions.

In the attempt to guide the countries of Europe under the auspices of the Geneva system towards the path of democracy, nationalism was encouraged by the conferring on each people of the right to self-determination. With no international army, and incapable of forcing its members to make any sacrifice of sovereignty, the League of Nations collapsed; and with it all the principles of the new world order also fell to pieces, leaving a clear field for that rabid nationalism of which the Nazi Rosenberg said that it was bound to follow fifteen centuries of universalism, thus condemning the nations, as so many 'Fates on the march', to a perpetual struggle.

Although it left Germany her unity and her industrial plant, the pledges of her future power, the treaty still could not fail to displease her. It permitted her to spread against the Versailles 'dictate' the most violent and embittered—and therefore the most telling—propaganda. Determined not to accept her responsibility, Germany was determined to avoid any discriminatory clause, and refused to accept any diminution of her territory. As Bainville so justly said, the peace was 'too strong for its infirmities, and too weak for its elements of strength'. The Germans were able to confuse at their pleasure questionable claims with legitimate demands, and to merge them all together in that optimistic self-indulgence which costs its victim so dear.

Rejected by Russia and America, the Versailles treaty put the continent of Europe into a fatally unbalanced state. Faced with the Reich, which was capable of annulling the consequences of her defeat with a lightning rapidity; encumbered by Franco-British rivalry; threatened by the uncertain attitude of Italy and Spain, by the impotence of the smaller western democracies and the Scandinavian countries, and finally by the balkanization of eastern Europe, the European perimeter states were almost as ineffective as the League of Nations. There was no power in the Old World to keep the stability which would have been the only guarantee of peace. The support of Italy and Spain for Hitler's Reich at once turned the scale in Germany's favour.

Although it extended beyond Europe, and included the British Dominions and other states, the League of Nations was primarily a European organization, for its essential task was to build the unity of the continent. But did Europe at that stage wish to exist as a unified continent? The question for all who feared the proximity of Russia was whether it was not essential to build a united Europe and to solve the problem of Germany's relations with the perimeter states. But had such a desire ever existed in the Europe of the past? Neither the eleventh-century crusade, nor the Mongol invasion of the thirteenth century, nor the Turkish flood of the fifteenth, had succeeded in uniting Europe. Whether we consider the Roman empire and the Church confronted by the barbarians, or the Carolingian empire disrupted by the treaty of Verdun, or the Hohenstaufen, or Charles V, or later still Napoleon, all attempts have failed. Europe has never considered it as her mission to do more than create independent nations. Neither the papal authority nor the nineteenth-century internationals have gone beyond this line of development. Belgium separated herself from Holland, and Norway from Sweden; Bismarck's system was erected against the Second Empire of Napoleon III; it is always the most fervid nationalism that has won the day. In the name of nationalism the herd instinct is glorified, and the intelligence that unites nations is despised. Hitler's Third Reich was the culmination of this fatal process.

§ 2. *Italy and Germany*

In this distracted Europe of the twenty years between the two wars, Italian fascism and German national socialism may be traced to roots which go back to the armistice of 1918.

To the observer who takes a broad view of the happenings in central Europe from 1919 to 1939, Bismarck's Triple Alliance—threatened with collapse on the eve of 1914, and defeated in 1918—may seem to have revived again under the impetus of fascism, and the final stage of its new evolution may appear to be the conquest of Austria and Czechoslovakia. These positions once within her grasp, Germany, in alliance with Italy, might well consider the Balkans an easy prey. But Hitlerism, the German form of fascism, appeared as early as 1919 in Bavaria, inspired by a doctrine that aimed at the union of Austria, Bohemia, and Bavaria. As for Italian Fascism, though it was in existence before Hitlerism, it did not create an ideology for itself until Hitlerism appeared.

(*a*) *Fascism.* Like defeated Germany and the successor states of Austria–Hungary, Italy, although she was among the victors, declared herself dissatisfied with the Versailles treaty. She was against the formation of a Danubian system and any political construction pivoted on Vienna. She did not seem to understand that only this kind of grouping would be able to make any stand against Prussia in the new Europe. The disappearance of the Dual Monarchy had now raised her to the rank of a great power. Assured of the Brenner, of part of the Tyrol, of Trieste, and of several of the Dalmatian islands, she was not concerned, from a national point of view, in the development of any great power beyond the Adriatic. Her self-deception was paradoxical, and sprang from motives of secondary importance. After 1921 she gave vent to her dissatisfaction. Greater Serbia annoyed her. She wanted Fiume. She was irritated by the allocation of colonial mandates. Might she not have been separated permanently from Germany if she had been given a share of the German colonies?

On the other hand her internal affairs bore no relation to her external situation. They provided an excellent opportunity for the extreme Left to throw itself boldly into agitation, to link up in March 1919 with the Third International, and to win staggering successes in the November elections. In this disturbed atmosphere Mussolini's party was formed. It was in Italy that, for the first time, a strong minority, comparable in its solidarity to the Communist party, played the reactionary game, and set itself against parliamentary democracy and a system of government which had become purely passive. The *fascio*, which took over an ancient Italian name though it dated only from 1919, claimed like the Nazis at a later date to be opposing simultaneously both the reactionary Right, afraid of anything new, and the destructive communism of the Left. Though it did not succeed in its first form, it renewed its efforts, and with the help of the Right it succeeded in defeating democracy and socialism—owing much, however, to an organization that was Left Wing and pseudo-revolutionary in character. Between November 1918 and March 1919 two facts emerge with clear force: the violent nature of the social, economic, and political crisis, and the failure of Mussolini's first programme. This last is an important fact, because a similar failure was in store for Hitler in 1923. But the crisis in Italy after the war had reached such a pitch of intensity, and parliamentary democracy functioned so feebly in a country which had only enjoyed universal suffrage since 1912, that the extreme Left had been able to unleash every kind of violence. The disillusionments of peace, and especially the Soviet victory and the state of ferment in the working classes, helped its efforts greatly. Calling for a dictatorship of the proletariat the Left-Wing leaders talked of forcing the Socialist party to take the decisive step and affiliate itself at once to the Third International.

Convinced, and not without reason, that the reactionary Right was afraid of every social innovation, and that communism might lead the country to ruin, Mussolini undertook to meet this double danger. Like Hitler a little later, he attacked big business and bolshevism at the same time. He claimed that his 'fasces' were being mobilized against this double peril.

He outlined their programme of action in fourteen points. It was a mistaken policy, which could only lead to a complete failure.

It is therefore by his relative moderation that the future tribune fails at this early stage. Success will come when he uses the most efficient and brutal methods to deal with the working-class unrest, strikes, the dislocation of public services, the violent socialist offensive against the Church and the army, and the impotent governments of Orlando and Nitti, in the period between March 1919 and May 1920.

The elections of November 1919, returning 273 Socialists, Communists, and Catholic Socialists as against 161 Liberals, provided him with a basis for his anti-communist campaign. D'Annunzio's attack on Fiume, on 12 September 1919, adds a halo to the Blackshirt Organization and strengthens the appeal to national pride and military heroism. The crazy ambitions of the military and naval classes, who had designs on Dalmatia; the economic interests championed by the industrialists and bankers; the financial support given by them to the militia, which was intended to supplant an army believed to be cankered with bolshevism; the firm support of a bourgeois middle class ruined by the war, and of a peasant class growing more and more restive—these were the factors which from June 1920 onwards gave rise to a sort of revolution of the Right, combining a mystical spirit with a rationalist organization, but armed with a formidable technique of the Left which clearly betrayed the influence of Russian communist methods.

From June 1920 to October 1922, and again from October 1922 to January 1923, the political tragedy of Italy unfolds itself with a relentless logic. Giolitti and his successors, misjudging the importance of the movement, allowed the Fascist party to gain a footing first in Parliament and then in the government. In conformity with democratic traditions he was careful not to outlaw it. The extreme Left had provoked a general strike; it had organized the taking over of factories and a mass rebellion of the proletariat; it had not forgotten the peasants and their claims for the abolition of the great estates and the sharing out of the land. This time Mussolini matched the terrorism of the Left with a terrorism of the Right. He attacked Giolitti and Sforza in the field of foreign policy. Faced with the problem of the helpless and paralysed mass of the working class and the peasantry, he brought to perfection his technique of ruthless and cruel dictatorship. The movement ran through the country like wildfire. The march on Rome was the crowning point of this extraordinary process. Power was in his hands when, in January 1923, the militia of 300,000 men was created.

What was the value of Mussolini's doctrine of Fascism? It cannot be denied that for his ideology he was indebted to French sources; to Blanqui, to Henri Bergson, as interpreted by Georges Sorel, to H. Lagardelle and to Charles Maurras. German influences are equally clear—romantic philosophy, Hegelianism, the later works of Nietzsche, and the ideology of Hitler himself; and in addition there are some other Italian and Russian sources. Italian thought, however, could not achieve the breadth or precise significance of that anti-Semitic Pan-Germanism 'ad usum populi' which was the creed of the Nazis. The latter, even at the period of their closest alliance with Fascism, always stressed the differences between their own aims and programme and those of Fascist Italy.

It is more important to note that after 1926 Mussolinism spread like an oil-stain in Europe. There was Pilsudski in Poland, Voldemaras in Lithuania, King Alexander in Yugoslavia, Dr. Salazar in Portugal. In this year too, 1926, was decided the fate of Hitler's party, in the course of the battle between Hitler and the Strasser brothers, when the idealistic socialism of the latter gave way before Hitler's Machiavellianism.

On the other hand, it is not surprising to find in the ideology of Mussolini the essential features of the Nazi doctrine; a return to political primitivism; the concept of the 'Chief' who, as a symbol of communal unity and invested with complete authority, rules with dictatorial power over a so-called 'absolute' democracy, a state-people or people-state, comparable to a sort of mystic body pseudo-religious in its character. This 'Chief' is supposed to know by intuitive divination, and to express in his speeches and his personal acts a will of the masses inspired by their elementary instincts. But this will is above all a will to power. The *imperium* which is to come demands its historic 'place in the sun': it preaches collective greatness, contempt of the old humanism and its humanitarian tradition, constant meditation upon the glorious past, worship of the state and the new Reich.

Like Nazism, Italian Fascism involved a certain social programme. Mussolini, that syndicalist rake, believed that only by imitating communism was it possible to meet the danger of communism. It was a question, therefore, of assuaging adroitly the war of classes, and of including in a single Charter of Labour capitalist employers, workers, and a distressed peasantry. This was done by 1927. Capitalists and trade unionists were to collaborate under the control of the state, and the state was to be very cautiously corporative in character. There were to be large public works, the 'battle for wheat', land reform, the draining of the Pontine marshes, and any other measures which provided the most efficient propaganda for the régime. Well and good; but how were sound financial relations to be established with the rest of the world? How was the *lira* to be revalued? In the meantime unemployment, a high cost of living, and poverty continued down to 1939 and the eve of war.

The régime's foreign policy had much more bearing on the future of Europe.

Before the Third Reich of Hitler Mussolini introduced into Europe that restless and aggressive brand of nationalism, which, mystical and fanatical in character, made the national community a sort of dangerous meteorite. The contrast was striking between the apparently peaceful Europe of Locarno and the array of national dictatorships which grew up about 1926, just after Locarno. All these states vociferously demanded the revision of treaties, movable frontiers, and all the thousand and one new advantages open to nations bold enough to seize them under an international system which was being confirmed in its instability, from 1925 onwards, by the Geneva assembly itself.

Encouraged by German resistance and Franco-British difficulties, the diplomacy of Mussolini flatters Hungary's revisionists, threatens Yugoslavia, works up feeling at home against France, refuses parity of naval armament, exercises a preponderant influence in the Balkans, and covets Tunisia, even if the dictator is styled by Paul Boncour 'the Carnival Caesar'. The Corfu Affair in August 1923 betrays Italy's real feelings towards Greece. And in spite of the concessions made to her, Italy treats Britain high-handedly.

This policy of blackmail, complaints, and intimidation succeeded for the moment. In 1926 Austen Chamberlain gave Italy a free hand in the Adriatic against Yugoslavia, which Fascism was endeavouring to encircle from the south-east. Two years earlier Ramsay Macdonald had ceded to Italy certain territories to round off Italian Somaliland. Even with Germany, in 1926, Italy had a crow to pluck on the question of the Upper Adige part of the Tyrol.

As soon as Hitler came to power, events moved swiftly in central Europe. The two fascist countries looked upon each other at first with some suspicion, but they rapidly came together to form the Axis. By 1934 the Fascist grip on Italy was complete. On 25 July 1934 the Nazis assassinated Dollfuss. The meeting at Venice, the concentration of Italian divisions on the Brenner, the colonization of Albania, and the creation of Libya no doubt cut across German plans. But thanks to Laval's policy of appeasing every dictator in Europe, and thanks to England, incorrigibly easy-going, Mussolini was able to arrange the Stresa Conference, which, following hard upon the reintroduction of conscription in the Reich, appeared for an instant to unite Italy, France, and England against the Nazis. It is well known how much England was stirred by this *rapprochement*, and to what hopes this spontaneous concord of Europe gave rise at Geneva.

Anglo-French dissension, and the unfortunate Anglo-German naval agreement of 1935, soon shook the foundation of this weak edifice. The Ethiopian campaign followed, embroiling Italy irreparably with the western powers and drawing her towards Germany, till finally her disastrous colonial adventure divided France and England over the question of sanctions. This enabled Hitler to attempt and carry through the coup of 1936. When he eventually annexed Austria and Czechoslovakia, his Italian ally had no choice but to congratulate him.

(*b*) *National Socialism.* When we reflect on the signal importance of the evacuation of the Rhineland and on Hitler's success at the 1930 elections, German history between the two wars seems to fall into two clearly defined decades. It is a much more complicated history, and one more fraught with consequences, than that of Fascist Italy. In Italy the parliamentary régime had developed slowly, but soon collapsed before the audacity of Fascism backed by the governing classes. In Germany, on the contrary, the history of the Weimar Republic, during the first decade, runs parallel with that of the Nazi party. From 1918 to 1923, the tragedy of inflation encouraged the early growth of

Hitlerism, but the prosperous years from 1924 to 1928 left Hitler's party in the background, and it used these fallow years to reconstruct and win over north Germany.

The years from 1929 to 1932 may be considered as a great turning-point in the history of the Reich. Here the crisis of 1929 played a vital role. It brought about the final downfall of the proletarianized middle class and placed the old ruling class decisively on the side of Hitler's fascism. After the ruthless purge of 30 June 1934, which disposed of all danger to the party from within, there ensued with lightning rapidity a succession of Nazi break-away measures—in 1935, the reintroduction of conscription; in 1936, the militarization of the Rhineland and the denunciation of the treaty regulating the rivers of central Europe; in 1937, the transference of railways and the Reichsbank to national ownership; in 1938, the occupation by force of Austria and Czechoslovakia; in 1939, the treaty with Stalin's Russia. It needed the attack on Poland to rouse the west against the Third Reich!

A serious study of the German constitution of 11 August 1919 shows that this complex machinery, formed by numerous borrowings from democracies all over the world, lacked the driving power necessary for its operation. After having had, from 1919 to 1925, a Social Democrat President and a series of governments with a majority drawn from the Social Democrats and the Catholic Centre, the principal beneficiaries under the republic, the constitution was doomed the moment that a President from the Right, Marshal Hindenburg, was elected. This ill-fated parliamentary democracy, now become presidential, was bound to meet with speedy ruin.

How can we unravel its history from that of the Hitler party? The party was founded in 1919. On their side the chief political personalities of the Weimar régime had in their own fashion prepared the way for the coming of fascism: Schacht in economy and finance, Von Seeckt in the army, Stresemann in foreign policy. Without their sustained efforts, concealed by the apparent social and political crisis, Hitler would never have seized power.

When they came to power, the Nazis accordingly succeeded to an administrative, economic, and military system more firmly established than was generally believed; to an already advanced stage of national planning; and to the solidly laid foundations of a diplomatic position in Europe. The tragic riddle is that of the social and ideological origins of the movement.

The Reich, whose bureaucratic framework and industrial machinery had maintained themselves through so many vicissitudes, had at the same time undergone a process of material and moral decay, of disruption and disintegration, and a virtual bolshevization which affected the middle and working classes. The ruling minority had safeguarded their essential positions, but the majority of the population had suffered since 1914 a series of ordeals without precedent in the country's history. The result was that by 1932 the German community was vulnerable, unstable, and weak to an unprecedented degree.

In an over-industrialized state such as Germany a clash was bound to occur between the powerful organizations of the oligarchy of landowners and employers, and those of the agricultural and industrial proletariat. The middle classes, ruined by inflation, were in danger of being crushed between these two millstones. Neither a return to the old autocratic monarchy, nor a communist revolution, nor even a parliamentary democracy, stood much chance in these conditions. Besides, this German *Mittelstand* had been attracted at an early stage towards the collective mysticism of the one party, and towards the ideology which Pan-Germanism had already formulated in every detail before 1914, but which had not yet percolated through to the masses. It was reserved for Hitler and Nazism to give the ideology vogue.

The population of Germany, which numbered nearly 70,000,000, was increasing less since the war, and was also ageing. Generations of young people, overwhelmed by defeat and reduced to despair by unemployment, were therefore pouring in a flood into occupations to which the older generations clung obstinately and selfishly. Safety valves that had hitherto operated for the surplus population—emigration, epidemics, and infant mortality—were now lacking. The only outlet possible for the German people was work and new economic activities.

Nothing could be more terrible than unemployment for a people of this kind. The old professional spirit had been partly destroyed by the very triumph of specialization, and the process of disintegration was particularly strong in the industrial cities, where there was a crushing atmosphere of automatism and a depressing intellectual uniformity. Apart from the general impoverishment and the disappearance of private fortunes, there was the enormous transformation which had taken place from great-scale economic enterprises, now dislocated by the economic crisis, to salaried earnings, pensions and allowances, and a mass of small payments dispensed by the state to a population that was growing more and more needy.

The traditional classification of capitalists, middle class, and proletariat seems here too simple. The two opposite poles seem to be: (1) an oligarchy of the great owners, concentrating a great part of the nation's capital and income in the hands of a few; (2) a vast proletariat harassed by want and unemployment. The ruling classes, including all their families, represented only a hundred-and-thirtieth of the population, or about 500,000 persons. Country gentry, industrial magnates, big business and high finance, civil servants, directors, and the large rentiers, were among this number, with their spirit of solidarity and authoritarianism. As for the proletariat, it consisted of about 18 million workers out of a total number of 31 million persons or almost half the population of Germany.

The intervening middle group between these extremes presented a curious picture of diversity. About as large as the proletarian masses, it comprised two clearly different categories: the old class of medium and small owners, and the new class of professional salary-earners. In the first category were peasant landlords, the middling industrialists, artisans, tradespeople, and a number of owners sunk to a proletarian level. In the second, now considerably increased, were employees, civil servants, and the *élite* of the liberal professions. It was this *Mittelstand*, this middle class with its two aspects, that created Nazism. It had its unemployed; it nourished a solid hatred of capitalism and of Marxism; it had for a considerable time been infected with anti-Semitism and enamoured of a vast and efficient solidarity like that presented by fascism. War and inflation had doomed it to a relentless process of levelling down which was calculated to exacerbate nationalism.

To sum up, the social condition of Germany at this time is a sort of magnifying glass in which the essential features of those European societies which were a prey to fascism may be seen with an amazing clearness.

This is precisely the material upon which the ideology of Pan-Germanism, built up by Germany in the nineteenth and twentieth centuries, worked with all the weight of its prestige. A new hierarchy, economic in origin, born of the impoverishment and the levelling process at work in the population, cut across the traditional social hierarchy. The pseudo-revolutionary movement springs from the exact point where these two hierarchies intersect, in the area where the bourgeois mentality comes up against the proletarian tendencies of levelling which it has no intention of accepting.

The only antidote to the levelling process, especially for youth, was in the paramilitary organizations, with their uniform and their badges. The poverty-stricken out-of-work is transformed at one blow into the helmeted, jack-booted agent of an all-powerful dictatorship. Hitler's S.A. and S.S. were waiting the call of the chief to rise out of the horrible social morass in which the German community was engulfed.

The counterpart of disintegration, reducing human beings to the condition of mere atoms, is sudden polarization, or the rapid synchronization[1] of the members of the social system. The explanation of the 'cold revolution', accompanied, paradoxically enough, in Germany more than anywhere else by an incredible mystical fervour, is to be found in the clever organization of Hitler's militia, copied from Italian Fascism and Russian communism, and in the backing which it secured, at the time when it was passing through an almost fatal financial crisis, from the upper bourgeois of the business world and the country gentry. Nazism popularizes and strengthens racial anti-Semitism, and takes over wholesale the diatribes of Pan-Germanism, Nietzsche, and their followers against the humanism of the west. Going back to Houston Stewart Chamberlain, the heir of all the old racialism, the Hitler leaders reshape his ambitious programme, bringing it down to the level of the despairing masses, but stressing continental objectives rather than colonial aims. *Mittel-Europa* for the German *Mittelstand*, and the complete supremacy of the Third Reich in Europe and in the spaces of the Russian east—these are the aims announced in the apologia of the New Order.

It is therefore not a question, as was too frequently said in the trials at Nuremburg, of a simple 'plot' or ordinary 'conspiracy'. The Nazis intended, most fervently and at the same time most rationalistically, to translate into fact a geo-political

[1] The German *Gleichschaltung*.

conception of the world. They wanted to reorganize the world to the advantage of the Axis alone, at the expense and in contempt of the values recognized in the west. Nazi Germany drives a wedge between the capitalist countries and the communism of Asia in order to achieve her ends with the connivance of Mussolini's Italy, Spanish fascism, and Japanese nationalism. After the German offensive against France and England, the invasion of Russia, and the Japanese attack on Pearl Harbour, the U.S.A. at long last realizes that it is time to enter the lists.

What is significant for our purpose is the series of acts, of *faits accomplis*, which the Third Reich threw, as it were, into the balance of Fate between 1938 and 1940, in order to ensure her victory over the western powers and over Stalin's Russia in the east. The Russo-German treaty of 1939 enabled Germany to fight only on the Franco-British front after the conquest of Poland. Who could doubt that Hitler would afterwards turn against Russia? It is a reasonable hypothesis that he had hoped to deal with Russia first, while ensuring the neutrality of England and France. The western powers were not deceived. They had no wish for a repetition of 1918. And, together with America, they saved the world.

The triple conquest, carried out between 1938–9, of Austria, Czechoslovakia, and Poland re-established Bismarck's Triple Alliance almost in its entirety. It gave the Third Reich an opportunity and time to fight France and England, to extend the German frontiers to the west while striking a blow at the heart of the British and French empires, and after that to destroy Russia and seize the Balkan peninsula. After this, with the support of Spain and Italy, it would have been child's play to bring to heel the Scandinavian countries and the small western democracies. The union of Austria with the Reich not only meant that a 'Greater Germany' (Gross-Deutschland), still stiffened by Prussian hegemony, became the successor to Bismarck's 'Little Germany'; it also meant the renewal of the old link between Germany and Italy and the realization of the dream of the medieval emperors.

The annexation of Austria was Hitler's first move. In November 1918 Austria had become a democratic republic. The Allies had always opposed its union with the Reich. Austria had therefore been governed by a sort of political marriage between Social Democrats and Christian Socialists, more or less after the model of Weimar. Cut off as she was from her former territories, Austria was forced to pass through a succession of economic metamorphoses. The two parties carried on perpetual warfare until the attempted Anschluss of 1931. Chancellor Dollfuss then tried to liquidate socialism by setting up an embryo dictatorship and a sort of presidential republic. After his assassination, when Germany and Italy had joined forces, the Anschluss became only a matter of time. Morally it took place in 1936; politically two years later. Henceforth Austria was nothing but a province of the Third Reich.

Czechoslovakia and Poland were the two essential links in the chain of the European perimeter. It now remains to see how, and why, the attitude of the perimeter nations enabled the Reich to risk an offensive against these two states—created by the war and confirmed by the treaty of 1919—which eventually started the Second World War.

§ 3. *The European periphery*

Placed by destiny along the frontiers of the German Reich, and also adjoining Mussolini's Italy, the nations of the European perimeter had to take up their position in regard to central Europe, now become fascist, and they were forced to look for support, in order to insure their future, to the continents beyond Europe.

We may risk from this point of view the following classification. (*a*) The western group, France and Britain, including the small democracies strung out between Holland and Switzerland, looked towards the Atlantic, the U.S.A., and their African possessions. (*b*) The Iberian group, Spain and Portugal, turned to the fascism of the Axis and leaned towards South America. (*c*) The nations of eastern Europe were caught between Germany and Russia; while as for the Scandinavian countries of the north, they seemed to hesitate between east and west.

(*a*) *The western powers.* The two western powers were seriously preoccupied by their own domestic problems.

The social and economic situation in Great Britain was difficult. There were workers demanding the maintenance of wartime rates of pay; there was outworn machinery and a routine system of industrial management; there was a monetary policy which increased production costs in an attempt to raise the pound to parity with the dollar. The problem was to preserve the balance of trade while the U.S.A. and Japan were advancing to the conquest of foreign markets. From 1921 unemployment figures reached 2½ millions. Only able to prosper in a prosperous world, Britain favours, and hopes for, the rehabilitation of Germany.

The political consequences of the crisis led to the victory of the Labour party shortly before the 1929 troubles. MacDonald's first cabinet had emerged five years after the armistice. The Conservatives returned to power by 1925; then came the general strike, followed by the 1929 elections, which brought Labour back into power. MacDonald's second cabinet was supported by a relative majority of his party over either of the other two.

But the world crisis soon forced the Labour leader to form a united national cabinet. The elections of October 1931 gave the Conservatives an overwhelming majority, but MacDonald still retained office. The devaluation of the pound, which dropped by 30 per cent., put a stop to the crisis, and from 1932 onwards Britain began to recover. But she never regained her old position in world markets.

The general situation remained unchanged until 1936. After the dramatic abdication of Edward VIII and the accession of George VI, it was Neville Chamberlain who presided over the country's destinies. He was flattering himself with the hope of settling the quarrel between central European fascism and the democracies at the very moment when an Irish movement of revolt, always a nightmare for Britain on the eve of war, sought to alter the system of the Commonwealth, which was becoming more and more a federation of equal, sovereign, and self-governing states embraced in a single imperial community.

Having settled the problem of war debts in January 1923, Britain had maintained excellent relations with the U.S.A. during later years, but only by undertaking heavy financial responsibilities. Her policy towards Russia, however, remained confused and erratic. During the decade 1929–39 she followed a trend hostile to Russia; the outstanding feature of the period, after the rearmament of Germany, being the sinister Munich affair.

France, partially occupied for four years, and with her 1,300,000 dead, came out of the war of 1914–18 even more exhausted than Great Britain. Her old administrative machine was still functioning normally, and the parliamentary game

The Shell-Mex Building, from the Thames, London

could begin again. But the social crisis was no less serious than it was on the other side of the Channel. Everyone was claiming compensation from the government for the sufferings of the war. The French peasant class was still strong, but it was on the decline in comparison with the industrial working class. The urban population was increasing. A sort of intensive industrialization within a closed circle was developing in France, where the country was not in a position to compete for foreign markets.

This is why the franc fell while prices rose. These difficulties acted as a spur to the communist opposition, which drew strength from the weakness of the moderate socialists and the traditionalist C.G.T. (the French Trade Union movement). Henceforth the Second and Third Internationals divide the energies of French socialism. This communist agitation sharply differentiates France from Britain; it also plays into the hands of the reactionaries. Once again there are violent clashes between extremist parties in the country, giving rise to a series of financial crises which increase in severity until the Second World War. The powerful leftward trend accentuates the depreciation of the currency, encourages the export of capital, prevents the public from contributing to government bonds, and further unbalances the budget. This is the explanation of the instability of the government and the crisis of the franc. Recovery follows between 1926 and 1928, and in spite of the continuing instability of the government the country is able to escape the worst consequences of the world crisis, thanks to an alliance of radicals and socialists.

When Hitler seized power in 1933 and was lavish with promises of peace to France, that country, apparently ignorant of the diatribes against her in *Mein Kampf*, and with her currency now stabilized, continued to turn a blind eye to the deadly danger across the Rhine. The Popular Front of 1936 brought about, it is true, a real republican revival, before the lapse into pseudo-fascism; but all chance of a reconciliation between bourgeoisie and proletariat was dead. How could social reforms have prevented economic depression? It was therefore in tragic circumstances that Léon Blum resigned office in June 1937. Once more a prey to crisis and instability, the country seemed to be adrift. The Spanish War was not of a nature to reconcile the bourgeoisie and the proletariat in France.

The phases of development correspond very closely in Britain and France, in spite of the fundamental differences that remain. But this parallelism is only significant in so far as it explains the attitude of these two countries towards Germany and Europe. Chief beneficiaries after the victory, they defend what they have won through the agency of the League of Nations. They risk nothing new or decisive, and are in fact paralysed by their own quarrels.

American isolationism relieved the British of the obligations they had undertaken in the matter of giving assistance to France. On the other hand, Great Britain, filled with a sense of security by her insular position and the destruction of the German fleet, was led by her indulgent sympathy and chivalrous temperament not to oppose the rearmament of her previous enemy. She also appeared to fear ambitions for domination on the part of France. And of what interest could reparations be to a people, like the British, for which Germany counted only as an exporter nation? The dominions openly encouraged England in this fatal course, while with Clemenceau there disappeared the only Frenchman capable of reminding the Americans and the British of their formal promises. Keynes's famous book was the product of this unpromising situation.

It was in the interest of France that peace should be a sort of continuous process, capable of creating not only a reasonable Germany but also a coherent and stable Europe. France, with her crushing burdens, and with her frontier bordering on Prussia–Germany, could not abandon reparations, which were the guarantees of her security. The premature collapse of the Versailles treaty, the indifference with which her anxious vigilance was met, the encouragement given to German inertia by perpetual Franco-British disagreements; these were the disillusionments which morally broke her back.

From 1920 to January 1922 conferences succeeded each other from Spa to Cannes without achieving any appreciable result. The surprises of Genoa, the Russo-German agreement of Rapallo, the isolation of France after the occupation of the Ruhr, all these set-backs coincided with the anti-French revulsion to be noted on all sides in Britain, the U.S.A., and Germany. The Ruhr attempt ended badly. France had wished to assert her rights, and everything turned against her.

When Austen Chamberlain took over foreign affairs he showed himself to be more understanding. He feared German rearmament and encouraged Franco-British solidarity. He was well aware that the occupation of the Ruhr had stimulated economic activity in Britain. Was a new era about to dawn in the relations between the three greatest powers of the Old World?

The governing idea was the integration of a rehabilitated Germany into a reorganized Europe. But no one followed it up, except in the rarefied and remote atmosphere of the League of Nations. The conciliatory policy of Briand and Stresemann, which brought Germany into the League of Nations in 1926, culminated in 1930, the very year of Hitler's first victory at the polls, in the evacuation of the Rhineland. Germany is once more in the circle of powers. Over realities there is now spread the thin web of ideologies and pacts.

Then came the 1929 crisis, the reawakening of German nationalism, the attempted Anschluss in 1931, the Young plan and the Hoover Moratorium, the complete failure of the Disarmament Conference; and thus France, Italy, Britain, and the U.S.A. had to allow Germany to be treated on an equal footing with her neighbours. This was a providential jumping-off ground for a Hitler!

Here was the crucial turning-point in this tragic succession of events. Germany's achievements between 1935 and 1939 are only four years ahead. She breaks away from Geneva, and tears the net which had been intended to restrain her. A fresh phase of Anglo-French disagreement opens. This time it is Pierre Laval who is responsible. Rejecting the policy of Barthou, he makes friends with Italy and Germany. While British diplomacy is toying with the idea of disarmament, Hitler reintroduces conscription in 1935.

France's negotiations with Russia, which aimed at encircling the Reich by defensive alliances, and the naval agreement, accepted by Italy, of 18 June 1935, combined to break the Stresa front. The attack on Ethiopia put an end to Anglo-Italian friendship; and then, when the problem of sanctions arose, Anglo-French friendship in its turn seemed only a phrase. On 7 March 1936 Hitler remilitarized the Rhineland. He knew beforehand that Britain and France could not lift a finger.

While Britain saw the death of all her hopes of disarmament, France fell a victim to moral exhaustion. The two countries were still to show enough strength to join forces against the Axis and to guarantee support to Poland. But during the night of 29/30

September 1938, along with Italy, they authorized Hitler to annex the Sudeten lands in Czechoslovakia. Daladier and Chamberlain brought back from Bavaria, not peace with honour, but humiliation born of disagreement and their ignorance of Germany's real intentions. The Russo-German treaty followed, with its guarantee for Germany that she would only have to fight on a single front.

There was a certain fatality in this Franco-British policy. England, temporizing and lulled by her illusions, was too late in turning against the Third Reich. Disheartened, France watched the rebirth of German aggression. She retreated physically and morally behind her Maginot Line, the symbol of false security. Nor was there any improvement in Franco-British relations outside Europe, whether towards America or in the Middle East.

Between western Europe and central Europe the chain of small democracies had played a modest, but not negligible role. The blast of the world crisis had, however, struck them too. There had been social struggles of real gravity in Belgium, which had given rise to the fascism of Degrelle. The conflict between Walloons and Flemings laid the country open to a veritable invasion of German influences. Again in Switzerland, a country of direct democracy with little scope for parliamentarianism, there was no lack of social disorders. As communism encouraged these disorders, Switzerland saw fit to break off diplomatic relations with Russia. Otherwise all these small states remained settled and stable. Within the framework of the traditional struggle between the bourgeoisie and socialism, they, like all the others, had their two extremes: fascism and communism. Parliamentarianism functioned as it did in Britain and France. Realizing that they might be an easy prey for the Third Reich, they isolated themselves in cautious neutrality.

(*b*) *Spain and Portugal.* In the Iberian peninsula the social struggle had taken a particularly tragic form. Spain followed the tradition of which South America had already given her an example. She turned to Italy and Germany, who replied by giving a Machiavellian support to the forces of reaction in their bitter war against the Spanish Left, unfortunately divided against itself.

The end of the war of 1914–18 saw the end for Spain of the period of prosperity which she had owed to her neutrality. The great strike of 1917 exposed all the poverty of the masses, which had been concealed behind the façade of economic abundance. For centuries the country had been waiting for a democratic rebirth. But the struggle between the forces of conservatism and revolution was inexorable, with no hope of reconciliation. From 1927 to 1929 the apparently benevolent dictatorship of Primo di Rivera had introduced fascism into the country, creating a sham system designed to dupe the people. But between 1930 and 1931 monarchists and republicans are at each others' throats. The republic wins the day temporarily, but is soon destroyed by its own internal dissensions.

Almost at the moment when Hitler assumed power in Germany, the electoral defeat of the Left Wing Spanish parties brought about the collapse of the constitution adopted on 9 December 1931. The fascist *Falange* and the Popular Front lined up against one another. On 17 July 1936, a few months after Hitler's bold coup, General Franco used Moorish troops in the most horrible of all civil wars. The convenient non-intervention policy adopted by France and Britain enabled Italy and Germany to give support to Franco. With the Third International backing the efforts of the Reds the war took on a symbolic aspect. It ended with the surrender of Madrid in March 1939, on the eve of the Second World War.

Portugal, after an unsettled period, followed in 1923 the example of Italy and Spain. Under the presidency of Carmona, this small country submitted to the flexible and intelligent dictatorship of Salazar. Dispensing with parliamentarianism, he created a sort of National-Christian state, whose objective was to unite the managing classes and the working masses in a well-intentioned corporative system.

This is the picture of western Europe. Alongside the democracies, tolerant of fascism, we find two countries which unequivocally followed the example of Italy and Germany. Meanwhile, across the Atlantic, while U.S. dollars helped the rehabilitation of a Germany preparing to follow her leader, the South American republics more or less copied Franco and the fascist leaders. Between the Anglo-Saxon world, ignorant of Hitler's ambitions and regarding him as the great bulwark against bolshevism, and Spanish-Portuguese fascism, France stands in hesitation, torn as she is between her own fascists and her Popular Front.

(*c*) *Eastern Europe.* What was happening in the meantime to the neighbours of Russia in eastern Europe?

In 1918 the collapse of the Tsarist régime liberated the Baltic states. They formed the first link in a chain of states stretching as far as the Black Sea and Turkey. They were new and rather feeble republics, which had only been able to achieve their desire for independence between Russia on the one side and Germany on the other, and they were thus confronted by two equally redoubtable worlds. Conscious of their weakness, after carrying out an agrarian reform at the expense of the German minority, they all set up an authoritarian régime, fascist in character.

The new Poland, compelled in exceptional conditions to unite in a single crucible three economic systems which had hitherto been separate, had witnessed between 1919 and 1923 an extraordinary resurrection. The people had retained their innate patriotism, and a keen sense of national unity. It was in triumph that Pilsudski entered Warsaw in 1918 after thirty years of conspiracy against Tsarist Russia. The country had had to fight her neighbours, particularly the new Russia. The 1921 Constitution, modelled on that of France, did not prevent the march on Warsaw, imitating the march on Rome. From 1926 to 1935 Pilsudski was the incontestable ruler of Poland. He superimposed his dictatorship on a parliamentary régime ill adapted to meet the needs of the situation. Above all he was an army chief. After him came the so-called rule of the colonels, dominated in particular by the personality of Colonel Beck, who, renouncing the system of Geneva, copied that very Hitler who was preparing to attack his country. Poland was in fact well aware of her danger and did not hesitate to accept the guarantee of Great Britain and France.

In the centre of eastern Europe there was a typical group: on the one hand Hungary, a revisionist nation *par excellence*, and on the other President Benes's Little *Entente*.

In spite of the strength of the conservative classes in Hungary, poverty, unemployment, and the return of prisoners from Russia had encouraged the rise of communism. This explains the tragic and premature attempt of Béla Kun, which made a liberal democracy impossible and, on the contrary, paved the way for fascism. After the ratification of the Trianon treaty, which cost Hungary so dear, Count Bethlen wielded power from 1921 to

1931, postponing agrarian reform, bolstering up the feudal system, and content with observing some constitutional forms. This was why Hungary soon turned to Mussolini's Italy. When Gomboes became Bethlen's successor, there ensued a dictatorship of the firm hand. After the Austrian Anschluss in 1938 the half-million Germans settled in Hungary began to agitate more than ever like the Sudetens in Czechoslovakia. What could a fascist Hungary do, except yield to the imperious pressure of Germany?

It was of course against Germany, and in relation to her, that the Little *Entente* had been formed in 1922–3. Up till 1933 Czechoslovakia was able to grow and develop under the leadership of Masaryk and Benes. The Czech state strengthened itself wonderfully from 1924 to 1929. But Masaryk's retirement, the Sudeten disturbances, and the success of Henlein and his fifth column shook it to its foundations. Hitler's entry into Prague, on 15 March 1939, sealed its doom. It was finally separated from the west, by which it was abandoned in 1938, and the way was paved for its sudden volte-face and the communist triumph of 1948.

Racially more mixed than Czechoslovakia, Yugoslavia, a state of Serbs, Croats, and Slovenes, faced even graver problems. After achieving agrarian reform at an early date, it also in its turn became a dictatorship between 1924 and 1929. Here it was the king, Alexander, who employed this weapon to put down anarchy at home and meet threats from Italy and Macedonia. He dissolved Parliament, suspended the Constitution, and gave to a general the task of forming a government under his own control. After his assassination at Marseilles in 1934 the country reverted to democracy and a free field for all parties. But Yugoslavia made use of the friendship of Italy for her own ends, recognized Mussolini's conquest of Albania, and gravitated towards the Axis. She did not, however, by these gyrations escape the horrors of invasion.

It was not surprising that Rumania attempted agrarian reform after the signature of the armistice. It was the National Peasant party, founded in 1926, which ensured the country's solidarity. But the forms of a constitutional monarchy, laid down in 1923, did not save her from a royal dictatorship. As soon as Hitler seized power, Codreanu's Iron Guards appeared. It required all the king's strength to disband them, and to set up a single party in support of the royal dictatorship.

On every side, therefore, from the Baltic states to the Little Entente, there was the same general trend towards dictatorship, more or less moderated by features copied from democracy.

Bulgaria, like Hungary and Austria, was a conquered country. Here also there was agrarian reform and a peasant dictatorship; and here, as in Rumania, the agrarian party made a stand against bolshevism. After 1933–4 there was here, as there was almost everywhere in Europe, a mixture of parliamentarianism and royal dictatorship. In Greece, after years of perpetual strife, from 1918 to 1925, during which she hovered between monarchy and republic, the partisans of Germany and those of the Allies, King Constantine and Venizelos, the vision of a Greater Greece rapidly faded before the rise of Turkey. After eleven years of a republic that was a semi-dictatorship (1922–33) her king was restored to Greece and his throne to George III. The king dissolved Parliament in August 1936; and after the fall of Albania he tried to forearm against impending Italian invasion and to save the independence of his country.

Who can fail to see the features common to all these countries of eastern Europe? When Russia made her influence felt, after the defeat of Germany, she found, as a result of the general trend towards dictatorship and authoritarianism, the ground already prepared and firmly rooted habits of mind favourable to her own dictatorship.

We find few surprises among the nations of the Scandinavian north. Finland, starting with a democracy in 1919, and carrying out agrarian reforms from 1918 to 1922, nevertheless ends up, after a period under the progressives, with a form of dictatorship closely linked with a 'National Patriotic' movement, peasant in its origin and with marked fascist features.

The other Scandinavian countries had a spell of great prosperity during the war of 1914–18. But after the end of hostilities they had great difficulty in obtaining food supplies. They were all democratic republics, with many socialist trends, even though monarchies were retained. Constituting a little closed world, they did not fight one another, and adopted peaceful means of settling any disputes.

In Denmark the balance between radicals and socialists was preserved until 1939. In Sweden, as is well known, the development of socialism was still more remarkable. Supported by the liberals and radicals Branting's socialists showed themselves to be possessed of practical realism and extraordinary moderation. In this they resembled the British Labour party. Norway, more individualist and bourgeois, was more aggressively socialist; but yet she had developed, up till the outbreak of war, a Labour movement very similar to those of neighbouring countries. Democrats and socialists were united here against the Nazi menace.

In this general sketch of the European perimeter states in the period between the two wars, some fundamental characteristics emerge which seem to have survived the catastrophe. The Spanish peninsula remains solidly fascist. Anglo-French relations are still strained. Eastern Europe has exchanged fascist or semi-fascist for communist dictatorship.

What is obvious is that between the two wars Weimar Germany and Hitler's Germany equally profited from their advantages. After the Polish campaign and the attack on Denmark and Norway the Germany of Hitler had seized almost all the European perimeter. But after temporarily defeating France she broke herself against the three forces of British resistance, Russian resistance, and the help supplied once again by the United States to the nations of the old Triple *Entente*. The Nazi régime was only victorious over its weaker neighbours; it could not carry out the decisive part of its initial programme.

III
PROBLEMS AND CONFLICTS

In a study which recently appeared in *Universitas*, the Tübingen review, Herr Fürtwängler, the famous German conductor, makes an interesting comparison between traditional music based on a tonic system and modern or 'atonal' music. He suggests that while the former expresses to perfection the musical tradition of Europe, closely linked with the essential features of western humanism, the latter is one of the expressions of contemporary disharmony, awakened centuries ago by Copernicus's view of the world, and stimulated by the growing sense of an ever-widening universe, by the scientific inventions resulting from it, and doubtless also by the extraordinary increase in population of which our ancient continent has been the scene.

This kind of interpretation is extremely fruitful. It enables us to link up the various parts of the picture, which must be put before the reader to round off properly this summary of the various questions and contradictions which weigh upon our minds.

We must in fact ask ourselves, in thinking of the period from 1914 to 1945, the period of the new 'Thirty Years War', not only what were the difficulties which confronted men in those days, but also and above all what relations there were between those difficulties. If it is true that the spirit of an age is expressed, in its essential unity, in all the different fields in which its activity is present, we may perhaps succeed in distinguishing, among the apparent confusion of the present day, the main lines of an evolution which has been maturing for centuries, and in doing so we may gain some valuable insight into the development of the near future.

§ 1. *The social and economic problems*

A rapid glance at the new world situation has shown us Europe ravaged by two successive wars and now wedged between the American continent, representing the traditions and methods of the capitalist world, and the continent of Asia, in which communism is spreading its conquests farther and farther afield. In a world in which industrialization, carrying with it the use of all the technical achievements of the past, plays the role of a central phenomenon, and tends to invade the field of agriculture, the problem is to know who will be the masters of the masses, and whether it will be employers of the old style or the leaders chosen by a proletarian revolution.

Is not this the question which Nietzsche put to himself in the penetrating vision of his last years? Were not men asking themselves, across the Rhine, who would be the supermen of the future, capable of organizing production on a planetary scale and of ensuring for the masses the comfort to which they could lay claim?

(*a*) *National revolution.* The great struggle between west and east was reflected, within the limited framework of the small continent of Europe whose population, however, had increased in one century by almost 300 millions, in the war of classes and the growing antagonism between the bourgeoisie on the one side and on the other the proletariat both industrial and agricultural. Yet was it not a French socialist, Jean Jaurès, who in *L'Armée nouvelle* celebrated in dithyrambic terms the achievements of the bourgeoisie and their imperial conquests throughout the world? He lived in hopes that after so many successful efforts they would be able to meet socialist demands and to lay the foundations of a real reconciliation, with a social order worthy of the name, between themselves and the workers who laboured in their service. Assassinated on the eve of the First World War, Jean Jaurès could not foresee to what extent war was yet to inflame social conflicts in Europe.

Reconciliation was not attained in any of the great European nations.

In France, where the middle class, as Bernanos has shown, was at first only a collection of 'upstarts enriched by military contracts, by looting the belongings of the émigrés, and by the vast speculations which preceded and followed the Terror', the bourgeoisie was composed for the most part of men who were sprung from the people. Risen from a peasant class, 'harsh both to animals and the men they employ', the class of employers here retained a stern ruthlessness towards the workers, whom they condemned to a proletarian existence, and above whom they had risen themselves only by the power of money. The machine age from its beginning set two sections of people against one another, the one corrupted by profit and the other degraded by poverty.

In Germany, during the period in which she attained her unity by a process of industrialization as sudden as it was furious, reconciliation failed more completely than anywhere else. In his recent book, *The German Catastrophe*, Meinecke, tracing the origins of European fascism, distinguishes two revolutionary currents in the history of Germany and Europe: the social and the national. The first, originating in the French Revolution, led directly to the idea of a universal proletarian revolution. The other revolution, the national or fascist, sprang from the middle classes both propertied and salaried, the cultivated or merely educated people who, rejecting with horror the idea of a social revolution, refused to break with the established order of things, and on the contrary sought to confirm it by trying to force each country to organize itself internally for the purpose of consolidating the traditional bases of society, and thereby ensuring *their* own strength and *their* own power of expansion. This second form of revolution nowhere attained such vast proportions as it did in Germany, and nowhere else did it assume so tragic a form.

No one will deny that these two revolutionary movements had a common demographic origin. There had been a fantastic increase in the populations of Italy and Germany. For this reason they had been ready to adopt the motto 'justice between classes', as opposed to 'justice between nations'. To achieve that end the ruling caste and the middle classes directed their energies to doping and duping the proletariat in order to harness it to their own selfish aims, with the ultimate object of destroying communism. A desperate attempt to pen socialism within the fold of nationalism! Is this not the true meaning of the terms 'national socialism' and 'fascism'?

The German people are carried along, stage by stage, towards the terrible explosion which shattered Europe into fragments. The national current appeared first, half-a-century before the socialist. From 1815 to 1850 economic development, the success of the Customs Union, and the unprecedented development of Prussian militarism combined to sweep the bourgeoisie to its fate. From 1850 to 1871 Bismarck's successes, crowned with resounding military victories, widened the gulf between the new generation and the old classical liberalism. From 1871 to 1914 the process continues and is completed. Affecting all the country's activities, the spirit of discipline makes nationalism terribly rigid, particularly among the middle but also in the working classes. The temporary and almost miraculous truce of these classes put the seal on the 1914 offensive.

This truce was patched up again after defeat, but with the object of liquidating communism. When the great unemployment crisis succeeded the inflation and the years of false prosperity from 1924 to 1928, and the catastrophe of 1929 descended, the middle classes, backed by the desperate younger generation, now seized control of affairs, grouping themselves around the dictator on whom they pinned their hopes, and forcing him on the old ruling classes.

Henceforth, expressing itself in a social structure influenced and inspired by the example of Italian fascism, Nazism dominated the whole of Germany, and afterwards spread outwards through all the periphery of Europe. It was the day of nationalist revolutions in Europe, until the time when the greatest among them, the German revolution, itself attacked the surrounding nations, both great and small, to swallow them up and inaugurate in Europe the New Order and the hegemony of the 'Master Race'.

Confronting the Russian Revolution, with its tendency to develop into a world revolution which draws into its sweep all the national proletariats, there stands the other or nationalist revolution, which swallows up the working class, and all its political parties and trade unions, in a ruthless dictatorship, and claims to represent the real destiny of the German people.

Nevertheless, this nationalist revolution by no means disdains the other revolution. It is careful not to neglect social problems. The nationalist capture of socialism was achieved by means of the fascist policy of social reform which depended on the idea of a totalitarian autarky or self-sufficiency. The dictator state intervened more and more in the economic field to put an end to the anarchy of unrestricted capitalism. Whether fascist or democratic, the modern state recognizes the principle that everyone has the right to a reasonable standard of life. State socialism or corporative socialism is everywhere installed. When capitalism is attacked, no one seeks to defend it, though everyone wants to preserve it. Even in the midst of this tragedy, it is plain that the conception of social justice is on the march.

But it is sacrificed, none the less, to the idea of 'justice between nations'.

A vast movement, then, was taking shape, immediately after the Armistice, towards the solution of Labour problems. Countries like Britain and Sweden are not a little proud of their legislation in this field; and the Weimar Constitution, in its section on fundamental rights, traced the first, if still very modest, lines of a social democracy. At a later date the dictatorships vied with the democracies in this field. The League of Nations and the International Labour Office gave strong support to labour measures. The eight-hour day and other restrictions, holidays with pay, improvements of the conditions of labour for women and children, and social insurance came into being. While the allied dictatorships of Italy and Germany, with their 'Labour Fronts', attempted social reconstruction on corporative lines, France, with her 'Croix de Feu' and the corporativism of Vichy, imitated her neighbours. But no one in France was at all deceived as to the real objectives of such a programme.

(*b*) *Industrial developments*. Whatever the differences between Italian Fascism, German National Socialism, and the later forms of dictatorship in the European perimeter states, it is easy to see what these movements have in common. The history of the Weimar Republic is already summed up, in its entirety, in one single determining factor: the almost complete disintegration of the German people, brought about by defeat, and especially by the inflation which ruined the middle classes, reduced the working masses to unemployment, and ended by dragging down the standard of living to a uniformly wretched level. As Jakob Burckhardt once argued, any disintegration of this kind leads inevitably to a sudden convulsive 'polarization' of the body social, particularly in heavily industrialized nations where, with a diminished agricultural and peasant stock, the situation in the great cities assumes the dimensions of a catastrophe.

How is it possible to explain the 'synchronization' which in Germany followed the Reichstag fire unless we remember this abrupt transition from relaxation to tension, which Goebbels discusses so complacently, but which is the obvious sign of an unhealthy community? It is the same sort of tension, though less spontaneous, which is to be seen in Italy just before and just after the march on Rome. In both cases the basis is degeneration brought about by post-war conditions.

The more one studies the phenomenon of Germany in all its aspects, the more clearly can be seen, in this strange magnifying glass, the essential features of the social and economic disease which afflicted the whole of Europe in the period between the two wars. First, there were certain transformations in the economic structure of the world and in particular of European societies. We must not forget that, after the Armistice, agrarian reform assumed immense proportions in the whole of eastern Europe except Germany east of the Elbe. Highly industrialized countries encouraged agriculture and high prices by means of protective methods. On the other hand, agricultural countries were forced to become industrialized, and to manufacture part of the goods they had imported so easily before.

World commerce was shrinking while the internal trade of each of the nations revived and capital was being invested in the country of its origin. The international expansion of credit came to an end. The natural system of exchange formerly in operation gave place to a system of nations confronting one another, in a relative isolation, from their different encampments. At the very moment when the peoples of the earth were, and were conscious of being, more than ever in a state of economic interdependence, international trade was suddenly closed down. Like individuals in a period of growing population, peoples found themselves on the top of one another, and seemed to get in each other's way instead of helping one another.

At the same time Europe lost her former monopoly. Everywhere industry, trade, and transport went through a general process of decentralization. As a result of this, a great deal of trade went on outside Europe, and the old world lost valuable markets, to the extent of about one-fifth of its previous share in international commerce. It is true that between 1924 and 1929 Europe regained a little of the ground she had lost. But there was a new recession between 1929 and 1932, and this gave to the United States and Japan the lead which Germany and Italy were trying to achieve, in Europe itself, within the framework of the Axis. Mechanization favoured the young nations, since machines and skilled tools could be handled by unskilled labour. In the field of industrialization Europe therefore tends to become cut off from the rest of the world. The old basic industries decline, while there are growing up and developing everywhere new industries whose appearance had hitherto remained unforeseen. Coal, in particular, gives way to the chemical industries, oil, hydraulic power, and rubber.

What is the effect of this world phenomenon on Europe and especially on Germany?

In Germany, more than anywhere else, a sort of absolute materialism had overthrown spiritual and cultural values. After a war for which Germany bore the chief responsibility, the burning problems were those of technical progress and expanding production. In this primarily manufacturing nation, the mass of the people were largely dependent on industrial prosperity. The big business combinations, horizontal or vertical, of which there were so many in Germany after the Armistice, finally developed into giant cartels which superimposed businesses one upon the other, depersonalized capital, enormously increased some private fortunes, and were totally unlike the combinations in the United States and Russia. They attacked their shattered country instead of serving her. At the same time they introduced a policy of extreme economic nationalism, which, lasting from 1924 to 1928, through the period of foreign loans, was destined to end, when the crisis came, in the terrible unemployment of the years 1929–32.

This divorce between a concentrated system of industry and the general life of the nations, as the parliamentary Weimar republic knew it, was not destined to long duration. Like all European nations in time of war, Germany had learnt to be self-supporting. Nothing could kill economic liberalism more surely than the protectionism due to the exigencies of war. In war every country increases its exports and decreases its imports, trying to maintain its home market on the margin of world markets and to fix its own arbitrary prices. The balkanization of Europe brought about by the peace treaties had the effect of increasing these tendencies towards national self-sufficiency. It was with the thought of revenge and war that Germany and Italy mobilized their resources within their own borders. Thus the nations moved towards an organized, directed, and artificial economy.

In Germany, the Schachts, the von Seeckts, and the Stresemanns had carefully prepared the reorganization of the country by bringing industry, the army, and diplomacy into their programme of reconstruction. The initial combinations, which had wellnigh developed into a feudal system, were turned into a system of intensified state control. The collapse of economic liberalism becomes almost complete. The state takes over endless functions. There is a multiplication of laws and regulations in an attempt to restore the balance of the social system. With the introduction of state control, and owing to the faults of capitalism itself, individual enterprise and competition are in abeyance. The state fights economic stagnation, assists shaky undertakings, and above all lays the foundations of future economic planning. When the masses begin to emerge from their disintegration and to regroup themselves by means of fascism, the planned control of Germany is completed. It only remains to hand over the job to the Nazis so that all may be geared to the dictatorial machine. The parliamentary republic had in fact become presidential and authoritarian before giving way to the Nazi régime.

It was not that no attempts were made to establish an international economic system. A policy of national self-sufficiency could only have the effect of exacerbating conflicts and provoking war. And so men sought at Geneva for means of averting the danger. They emphasized the solidarity of the nations. They multiplied methods of positive collaboration, systems of co-ordination and contact. They tried to demonstrate that one national crisis gives rise to swarms of others all round it. Inter-Allied organizations sprang up on every hand. In 1920 the International Chamber of Commerce was founded in Paris. The League of Nations looked forward to the reorganization of monetary systems. There was even talk of rebuilding Europe, and making it a single market.

A certain sentiment of solidarity was evident even in regard to Austria, Hungary, Bulgaria, and Germany, at the time of the Dawes and Young plans, and again when the bank for the settlement of international debts was created. An Economic and Monetary Conference met in London in 1933. Many industrial agreements were concluded after 1924. But the weakness inherent in the League of Nations was reflected in the movement. Moreover, in the fascist countries it met with bitter opponents.

(*c*) *Financial problems*. Nothing shows the power of economic nationalism so much as the financial concentration proceeding in every country, and notably in Germany. Joint-stock companies swallowed up private banks and the smaller undertakings The impersonal power of the banks in its turn undermined middling and private property. By 1932 the concentration of banking was complete in Germany.

But we must not forget the disorganization that preceded this phenomenon of self-sufficient combinations. The system which was working so well before 1914, when London was the capital of the financial world, was completely out of gear by the end of the war. There were serious disturbances everywhere. Speculation took the place of saving. Irritability increased with each crisis. In a country like Germany the 1921–3 inflation completely destroyed normal relations between debtor and creditor. Later it encouraged the Germans to contract loans which they could neither honour by paying interest nor meet by repayment.

The 1929 crisis only emphasized the general disorder, which more and more restricted international activity in the financial markets. Floating capital, instead of being invested in profitable enterprises, drifted from one country to another to escape devaluation. The nations, reduced to a paper-money currency, found devaluation both a palliative and a menace of catastrophe. Currencies, reduced to anarchy, obstructed the process of trade for which they were intended. Debtor countries could no longer settle their debts by exporting to creditor countries. They paid for the goods they imported with gold and shares, and, reserves being low, they restricted imports. The stability of the national currency was to be assured by its remaining at home, that is to say by the cutting down of foreign expenditure.

Without gold to back currencies, the dictatorships in central and eastern Europe established the most rigid control of exchange to prevent relations with the outside world from upsetting the economic balance established at home within the framework of national self-sufficiency. In Germany, to maintain the high exchange rate of the mark, Dr. Schacht invented the blocked and the registered mark, transforming monetary legislation into a complete maze, managing everything by means of a vacuum, suppressing foreign exchanges, and therefore restricting money to a purely internal function in order to proclaim its soundness. It was only in northern and western Europe that money remained free.

In London, indeed, in 1933 an attempt was made to reestablish an international standard of value. But the great gold question was reduced to the plain and simple fact that it was impossible to reach an agreement between the nations on the stabilization of currencies. Some sort of balance was reached between 1933 and 1936, but it was not kept up between 1936 and 1939. In fact the nations gave up the use of metal currencies. Gold was no longer used for internal payments. The unequal distribution of gold, which in spite of everything still kept its value, created real disorder in the world.

Added to this was the problem of debts, naturally bound up with the monetary problem. With the rates of interest much higher than in 1914 nations were burdened with enormous liabilities, which were incessantly increased by new loans. Public expenditure increased with the taxes. Indebtedness abroad was no less acute than financial embarrassment at home. War debts, international loans to be paid in gold, and grave problems of financial exchange were piled upon one another.

Here again Germany's case is typical. Between 1914 and 1928 no nation had borrowed more than she did after the inflation and the currency reform. Loans contracted by the Reich, the Länder, and the Communes amounted to 103 thousand million francs of that period. The flow of capital between America and Europe was reversed. While Britain, France, and Germany had 33 thousand million dollars in foreign credits in 1914, from 1915 onwards these three nations were in debt to Wall Street, which had in the interval taken the place of London as the financial capital. Between 1925 and 1929, there had been a formidable inflation of loans and credits, giving rise to an extraordinary instability and finally causing disaster. But it permitted Germany, none the less, to make her war preparations.

From this point of view it is easier to understand the supreme importance of the 1929–32 crisis, which immediately preceded the advent of Hitlerism.

The collapse of a prosperity which was nothing but a façade spread through the whole of the world. It shattered the economy of Europe even more than that of other continents. Hardly had the Austrian Creditanstalt collapsed when Germany decided, in July 1931, to close the banks and pursue the policy of a moratorium or a regulation of exchanges. The countries of central and eastern Europe had recourse to methods of chance. Short-term foreign credits were frozen. Conditions were scarcely any better in Sweden, rocked by the Kreuger scandal; in France, embarrassed by the banking crisis; in Britain, which, with considerable credits in Germany, had gone off the gold standard; or in America, which had followed England's example in order to counteract the effects on trade of the fall of sterling. The principal results of this unprecedented disturbance were a sudden fall in prices, the reduction of the total value of world trade by two-thirds, a falling standard of living, a severe crippling of industry, a world-wide unemployment affecting 30 million workers in 1932, and a peasantry which ceased to use manufactured products and renounced artificial fertilizers. 'A tragic economic landscape emerged', writes M. Baumont, 'with industry at a standstill, agriculture in distress, and the banks in danger.'

The most obvious results were economic nationalism, the ruin of international trade, and a system of planned economy within the framework of national self-sufficiency. Germany, more sorely tried than any other country, was on the road to bankruptcy. The last straw was the Young Plan and reparations. The country craved an absolute power. The Hoover moratorium aimed, above all, at saving the numerous American investments which had been risked in the course of the confusion.

How could the moratorium have saved Germany? Foreigners were hastily withdrawing capital which was out on loan, and the country could not count on any foreign credits. The 'Danat Bank' had just shut its doors. What were the Germans to do? They sacrificed everything to monetary stability, particularly their international credit and the prestige of their banks. They shut up exchanges and frontiers, and isolated themselves in a system of self-sufficiency; the export of shares was forbidden, and capital was not allowed to leave the country. By these means they weathered the storm. No doubt their eyes were on France, where Poincaré had before restored monetary stability. No doubt there would be established a Franco-German economic commission. But Germany was, in fact, left to her fate. Brüning's decree-laws prescribed strict economies, increased taxation, and imposed the reduction of wages, salaries, and unemployment benefits. These were described as last-ditch measures, unpopular by definition, and as such they laid the way wide open for the triumph of Hitlerism.

There was a mass sinking into material poverty. From 1920 to 1923 inflation had wiped out the middle classes, and Hitler had profited by it. The eclipse of its fortunes from 1924 to 1928 had given the single party of the future time to gather new strength. The movement broke out again with accumulated violence. Its triumph was an answer to the crisis. Hitler promised work and bread. Demagogy flourishes best among poverty and despair. Although Nazis and Communists were still at war, and the Nazi party itself went through a serious financial crisis, it was completely victorious at the Lippe elections, on 13 January 1933, and its success was ratified by President Hindenburg's decisive act.

Dr. Schacht then entered the lists. His hour had come. What would he do in the period from 1932 to 1938? After handling the funds contributed by business men and country landowners for the elections of 5 March, and after seeing absolute dictatorship set up in Germany, thanks to the full powers given to Hitler, Dr. Schacht, now once more President of the Reichsbank, put himself at the service of the totalitarian state. He used the Reichsbank in order to supply the régime with credit, to carry out the national programme of work, and to encourage rearmament after the building of autobahns. He knew that it was only in this way that Germany would obtain equality of status.

Industrial and financial problems were therefore solved simultaneously. As it was not possible to resort to inflation or increased taxation, recourse was had to the invention of *Mefo-wechsel*, which were drafts drawn by the armament manufacturers on the Me*tallfo*r*schung* company. By this means a free flow of money was started, which set in motion a system of work for the masses. The problem of imports was somehow solved, even if there were grave difficulties in the way of exports. Dr. Schacht personally opposed the régime, or so he tells us, with all his might; he opposed its financial extravagance and the abuses of state control. He made use of barter and bilateral treaties to take the place of the normal system of exportation. South-eastern Europe and South America fell in with these methods. A quarrel broke out in 1938, and Schacht was replaced by Funk.

Within the framework of the national revolution which had ousted the social, a new if artificial reconciliation was achieved between the middling bourgeoisie and the working classes. The ruling class, untouched by agrarian reform, profited from the agreement. Under a scheme of national self-sufficiency Germany set a current in motion which enabled her to harness the whole people to work and to include in the new army the whole of her youth.

§ 2. *The political crisis*

The social and economic crisis clearly led to the weakening of the western democracies, shaken to their foundation and deprived of their old international scope. On the other hand, by an unprecedented paradox, it encouraged the self-sufficient nationalism of central, eastern, and southern Europe. What, then, were the effects of the political crisis?

(*a*) *The elements of the problem.* It is difficult to separate economics and politics. The liberal world falls largely to pieces before the pressure of demographic factors. A new situation thus emerges, stirred by different political passions.

The general process of industrialization reaches the peasant population. The age of the technician and the specialist has arrived, in which the rights of the individual and the values of the inner life are ignored. The machine man, *homo economicus*, appears, and with him emerges a dynamic class of factory workers who confront the static landed class. This development was well-marked even before the war. The war speeded it up, dispatching peasants to the front and workers into factories in the rear. The system of state control turns this to its own advantage.

The state takes into its charge large numbers of families deprived of their heads. Requisitioning and rationing are in full force. War in its turn, like specialization, devalues the individual. In the strict sense of the word, it 'mobilizes' men, and places them at the disposal of an exacting community which may demand the supreme sacrifice from each. Individuals are submerged in the mass. With collective suffering, common interests emerge. The *Massenmensch*, gregarious in character, has arrived. His demands will be essentially material and utilitarian. In this we find repeated the pattern of disintegration, inevitably followed, as we have already noted, by a regrouping on dictatorial lines.

The same causes bring about the same effects both in economics and politics. The same set of social conditions, as we have seen, had led Europe both to social disintegration and to inflamed nationalism. This same paradoxical antithesis is to be seen in the field of politics. Nationalism flares up with great violence, but in a new international setting which contrasts oddly with the struggle of neighbour with neighbour. It seems as if, just when industrialization and war reduced everything to the same level, humanity, and European humanity in particular, has a sort of start in face of the inevitable. How can men possibly return to their former individualism? So they rush into a nationalism which groups desperate men, Nietzsche's *Viel zu Vielen*, in a common effort of collective galvanization which tends to cut them off from all the rest of the world.

With American isolationism on the one side and Russian aloofness on the other, the balkanization of Europe is redoubled by an anarchy of nationalities both great and small. The world is rapidly becoming standardized. Thought is communicated from people to people by means infinitely more varied and rapid than in the past. As a result, it grows daily thinner and becomes more vulgarized. More and more subjected to the influence of mediocre ideas and the harmful effect of slogans produced by the press and propaganda, individuals are lost in gigantic towns which because of their very size have an ever-increasing capacity for expansion and communicate readily with the country through the cinema, radio, and daily newspaper. Middle-class life takes on working-class standards in industrial areas and in the vast public and private services. Inevitable similarities establish themselves in the conditions of life of all individuals. In their everyday life all men are faced with identical problems and similar difficulties.

Local differences, therefore, tend to disappear, and a terrifying 'monism' threatens to engulf the human world. The nations are desperately intermingled at the very moment when they are galvanizing themselves as fascist entities. A materialistic universalism arises, encouraged by inventions; and in the heart of it different nationalisms struggle to take their revenge. War had accustomed men to regard the world as a whole, bringing it, more or less dimly, within everyone's range of vision. People were no longer accustomed to consider their problems solely from a national point of view. This actual internationalism, the fruit of the modern machine age, is the dominating feature of the twenty years between the two wars. But it exacerbates nationalist feelings, which unconsciously revolt against it. Or else, as in the case of the Third Reich, it implants in nations visions of grandeur bearing no relation to their real power.

The results of this development were on the one hand the weakening of the organization created at Geneva by the victorious western powers, and on the other the unleashing of nationalist brutality at its worst, more especially among the defeated nations. Fascism drew the working masses away from communism, and united them in a common attempt at feverish recovery and victorious expansion which was hopelessly artificial and destined to utter failure.

Here again the case of Germany provides us with a typical example, or a sort of magnifying glass. Hitler's Germany, in order to bring about the reconciliation of classes, utilized anti-Semitism and racial feeling, the one a negative and the other a positive ideology, but each complementary to the other and both elaborated long before by nineteenth-century thinkers.

In Germany anti-Semitism, ever since the beginning of the Bismarck era, had always been a sort of barometer of political feeling. It was a weapon adopted by the middle classes and used by them to defend the Christian confessions and the established social order against the militant atheist socialism of that period. Anti-Semitic propaganda originated in the writings of Marx, and started from the idea that in Germany the Jew was all-powerful, and must inevitably, by reason of his natural superiority, gain the upper hand over the German.

Under William II, and just when the influence of Gobineau began to reach Germany, the movement became racial, and developed into a kind of religion, or German paganism, which set up the Aryan, the superior German, the master race, in an opposition which was abstract but all the more effective and deadly, against the Jew. His presence and action were held to be traceable in the priesthood of the time of Jewish decadence; in the idealist rationalism of Greece; in the Christianity of the different confessions; in democratic and parliamentary liberalism; and finally in the socialism of the various Workers' Internationals and in international institutions generally. Against this mysterious and omnipresent enemy, an enthusiastic nationalism was the only possible remedy.

The object of Nazism was, in effect, to destroy the international order by setting up in opposition to it the German nation, mystically envisaged as a racial community. The special complaint against the Jew and his activities was that he originated the struggle between capitalism and the working class, a struggle which could only lead to bolshevism. Were not Karl Marx, Kurt Eisner, and Béla Kun Jews? Here was a theme of propaganda which it was easy to use. It was even possible to point to the Jews' own nationalist movement, the movement of Zionism, now established in Palestine. And it is well known how Germany, through the story of the 'Protocols of the Elders of Zion', tried to pass on to the Jews her own responsibility for the war.

In any case the war and the crisis actually created a formidable movement of anti-Semitism. The position of Jews suddenly became tragic. They lost the offices and the positions which they had acquired; liberalism disappeared everywhere, and among the middle classes Jews were treated quite pitilessly as parasites and foreigners. In this way the Jew became the principal symbol of the *Gegen-Reich*, that is to say of all the elements hostile to Germany. It therefore became necessary to destroy the 600,000 Jews who had made their home there, and about 6 million were actually butchered in Europe at large. The terrible link between anti-Semitism and fascism explains the long martyrdom which the Third Reich inflicted on Israel and which was its shame. From Germany this murderous and aggressive racialism radiated to Italy, Hungary, Poland, Slovakia, Rumania, North Africa, France itself, and even to the United States.

(*b*) *The future of democracy*. Heir to all the racial Pan-Germanism of the nineteenth century, Hitler's dictatorship exactly met the demands of the nationalist drive. Even before the First World War, men had acknowledged the problem, talked of Caesarism on the march, and foretold an era of tyrannies. Just after the Armistice a few prophets hoped for a new selective *élite*. Others, like Spengler and Moeller van den Bruck, ventured on a defence of Prussia. Under Hitler, the German youth followed the example of the young men of Megara, who destroyed books and the constitution. The modern state, armed with far-reaching powers by war, made use of those powers, especially in Germany, to extend its prerogatives on the plea of crisis. Help was given to it by the ruling classes, by an agrarian feudalism which had not been destroyed, and by the industrial world which carried Hitler to power. The nations were not inclined to throw their national individuality into the melting-pot of a world republic. On the contrary they enclosed themselves in this very individuality. They emphasized it and exaggerated it at will. This will explain why Caesarism was everywhere victorious, imitating the Russian Revolution and adopting in Italy and Germany the system of a single party along with the methods of American and Russian propaganda.

To this crude fascism must, however, be added the more or less embryonic dictatorship, with its Catholic tinge, which was to be found in France, Spain, and Italy; a dictatorship with formulae borrowed from Hegel and Marx, from Nietzsche and Pareto, from Bergson and Georges Sorel, from Unamuno and William James. The methods and procedure of these dictators are well known: they included a framework of self-sufficiency, a visionary leader, social reform, and government by number through a system of organized plebiscites.

In 1914 there were in Europe 17 monarchies as against 3 republics. In November 1918 there were 13 monarchies as against 13 republics, and in 1939, 6 monarchies as against 3 democracies. The void was filled by dictatorships of every sort and kind, which evidently awakened new energies. The victory of democracy in 1919 was only temporary and superficial. Universal suffrage was established everywhere; but it was easily converted into a plebiscite for dictatorship.

In the fascist countries, especially in Italy and Germany, it was the young who attacked parliamentary democracy and the traditional parties. They were disgusted with the indefinite and monotonous succession of coalition governments under the Weimar Constitution, and this weariness of the young was common in some degree throughout the whole of Europe. They wanted something new. In German lands especially they had that burning enthusiasm which is a feature of German character, but is not always directed to reasonable ends. Accordingly they ended by regimenting themselves. Carrying the mass of the people with them, they rushed headlong into slavery, setting up the menace of fascism, with its powerful solidarity, against the communist menace. They took a pleasure in facile and purely negative criticism of professional parliamentarianism. They accused it of lack of ideas and intellectual stagnation. They declared that extremist parties always carried the day over the moderate parties by virtue of the cynicism of their violence and brutality; and as they needed a cadre, they enrolled themselves simultaneously in the single party and the *Wehrmacht*.

In spite of some compromises, and in spite of a policy of collaboration which is explained partly by a complete ignorance of German aims and partly by a culpable complicity, parliamentary democracy by no means gave up the struggle in the western nations. The only sections which mistrusted it, and turned away from its principles, were the communists and the elements among the middle classes, in the west as well as in Germany, which had not got definitely clear of fascism.

Not that parliamentary democracy is today more sure of victory, after the Second World War, than it was after the First. Its present enemies are no longer the same as they were in the past. Formerly its opponents were monarchy, aristocracy, and plutocracy. Today the communists and fascism can only employ against it the argument of plutocracy. Even that is threadbare. The chief argument against it now is that of inefficiency. But here the convinced democrat has a good hand to play; he can recall the discomforts of the Soviet system and the follies of fascism; above all he can point out that recent wars have all been won by nations with a more democratic régime than that of their opponents. Democracy, he can say, may be indecisive and slow, but it avoids the monstrous errors of violent dictatorships. The real difficulty today, in a continent like Europe, is to know whether Germany will one day, after recovering her unity, choose a form of democracy which suits her, and escape that embryo dictatorship of 'managers' and technicians described by the American Burnham in his book on the managerial revolution.

While it is easy to show that parliamentary democracy is closely bound up with the European inheritance and that its collapse would mean the death of western humanism, on the other hand it would be folly to ignore the dangers that threaten it today. Communism is with us, ruthless in its will for destruction. Fascism is far from giving up the fight. Critics are legion. Democracy is accused of not having kept its promises, both after 1918 and after 1945. It is reproached for a certain dilettantism, which compromises its doctrine and action. The permanent struggle between capital and labour, and the growing pressure exercised by the working masses under the democratic system, make public opinion weary of the indecisive battles between the political parties.

These parties are often called parasitical. Men mock at their narrow-sighted programmes, which fail to notice the nation's true interest. In the end, the parliamentary system, like the Jews, becomes the scapegoat for all current ills: it is accused of dreary inaction, and of sterile bargaining which undermines the authority of government. Even the elector no longer knows if his right to vote is equivalent to a right to control. He rather despises his representative, whom professional necessity turns into a sort of eager errand-boy at the service of his electors. He knows that the partisan is always trying to usurp the place of the man, and that he diffuses around him a sense of oppression and persecution which is always giving the lie to real democratic traditions. Democracy is and always will be in danger. Its first duty is to realize the fact.

(*c*) *The Churches.* After penning socialism in the fold of totalitarian nationalism, fascism tried, between the two wars, to destroy its dream of a social revolution, at the risk of destroying thereby the ideal of social justice which is and will always be an essential element in western humanism. We have just seen why, and how, fascism also attacked democracy, which defended its traditional doctrines in countries such as England, France, and Switzerland. Rising to a still higher level, we have now to consider its relation to Christianity.

There is no need to dwell on Calvinism; its development is inextricably linked with the history of democracy. Indirectly it inspired the French Revolution, though the Revolution was derived from a movement of free thought which owed its origin to the failure of the Reformation to establish a hold in France. The fate of Roman Catholicism is a matter which touches the future of Europe more nearly. Here, once more, Germany presents what may almost be called a symbolic picture. The war waged by Nazism against the Christian confessions, a war continued today by communist aggression, assumes a vital importance from our present point of view.

The Papacy is both a great spiritual power and a determining factor in world politics. This is true, in particular, because of the part which it plays in social action and in the fate of the distressed masses. After its fashion, it protests against the exploitation of man by man, but in doing so it avoids Marxism and its consequences.

The greatest danger between 1918 and 1940 lay in inflamed

nationalism, which worshipped fatherland, soil, and race, and built up a doctrine and programme whose pseudo-religious character was no insignificant menace to the Christian confessions. What had a Pius XI to set against this fanatical mysticism and mythology except a sort of international liberalism, directed towards the maintenance of peace, and a defence of human individuality? But the influence of the Church was on the wane after 1914. Carried away by a new conception of life and by scientific inventions, secular civilization seemed to be gaining ground on the Church. The era of enlightenment which began about 1750 is not yet at an end. The indifference and intolerance which are engendered by atheism prevent men from believing in that spiritual reality which must never on any account be subdued to the exterior world.

This explains the bitterness of the struggle between oecumenical Christianity and the nationalist states in the interval between the two wars. The Pope defined the issue admirably in a recent encyclical:

> The human race . . . although, according to the natural order established by God, it is divided into social groups, nations, or States, independent of one another in their methods of organizing and directing their internal life, is nevertheless united by mutual bonds of morality and justice in a great community. . . . Who can fail to see that to affirm the absolute autonomy of the State is openly to defy this immanent natural law . . ., to make the stability of international relations dependent on the pleasure of governments, and to destroy every possibility of real unity and fruitful collaboration for the general good?

This could not be better expressed. The Papacy, indeed, in spite of encouraging nationalism by canonizing a Joan of Arc or a Bobbola, sets its face sternly against the excesses of nationalism, whether it be the *Action Française*, or the German Hitler movement, or Italian fascism. On the other hand, it makes concordats with the different states which concentrate the whole of ecclesiastical jurisdiction in the hands of the sovereign pontiff, whose authority over the 1,167 dioceses of Catholic Christianity is absolute.

This is one of the great contradictions of our time. We are witnessing an increasing mobilization of anti-Christian forces, with a general secularization, a materialistic atmosphere, a concentration of learning on the process of critical research, the liquidation of old beliefs, neo-Darwinian theories of evolution, a determinism hostile to any ideas of supernatural intervention, and the destruction of political parties with any Catholic tendencies. And yet, in the face of these dangerous manœuvres, faith seeks to rally its forces. The problems of war and the post-war period arouse religious unrest in every quarter. Against the insecurity of an anxious and fluid world, the Churches set the immutability of Christian values. Everywhere men feel a need for drawing together and unity. Spiritual traditions revive, and men's minds are suspicious of the rigid determinism preached by scientists who are today obliged to recognize the relativity of the laws they promulgate.

The war engaged between the Churches and the totalitarian régime in Italy and Germany acquires from this point of view a very significant bearing. It enables us to differentiate the two fascist régimes.

In Italy, Catholicism saw the defeat of its newly created Popular party. The Church was ready to follow Mussolini in his diatribes against liberalism, socialism, and freemasonry. Did not the Duce attack divorce? Did he not reinstate the crucifix in the schools and the cross over the arena of the Coliseum? The clergy could not but support a régime that granted special privileges to the 'dominant religion' and guaranteed religious peace. The Lateran agreements of 11 February 1929 guaranteed the Church valuable compensations. Only the struggle for control of the young seems to have degenerated into bitter conflicts.

In Germany, the two confessions (Catholic and Protestant) found themselves faced with a conscious paganism, of mystical and pseudo-religious tendencies, which sought to replace the many territorial churches by a single national Church, with the slogan 'One People, one Church, one School'. Futhermore, anti-Semitism created a tragic situation.

Under the Weimar Republic Catholicism flourished. The reasons why it benefited so much under this régime are known. Lutheranism, no longer the state Church, had no authority, international or governmental, on which to rest. The Constitution of 11 August 1919 gave to both confessions the status of 'Corporations under public law'. Now since the Reformation German civilization had developed on a double basis—the actual basis of the different territories or states, and the imaginary basis of a single controlling Reich. After the peace of Westphalia, in 1648, Christianity found itself allied with the territorial powers. Therefore it could not support the fanatical nationalism which made the Third Reich into a sort of racial and biological community. Just as German Christianity had gradually deserted the cause of universalism, so Pan-Germanism in turn deserted the cause of Christianity.

This explains the persecution which Nazism inflicted on both religions. Lutheranism generally, along with the 'German Christians', made a sort of compromise or agreement with the Nazis; but the 'Church militant' section defended itself, as did Catholicism, alike on the ground of doctrine and in the ecclesiastical field. The Nazi method was to discredit and gradually to undermine the Churches, not to destroy them at one blow. But when Hitler attacked the west and Russia, Christians in Germany had to choose between their religious convictions and the total victory, in Germany and Europe, of Hitlerism and a view of the world fundamentally opposed to the essence of Christianity.

In France, the struggle between secularism and Catholicism gradually abated. Portugal and Spain guarded the interests of the Church; and the Church herself maintained her essential positions in central Europe and Poland, made considerable progress in the United States, and preserved most of her mission-fields in the rest of the world.

§ 3. *Culture*

Secular culture did not escape the fundamental conflict which is the tragedy of our age.

(*a*) *General development.* The first years after the war of 1914–18 were a period of inevitable confusion. After so many restrictions, regulations, and sacrifices the European countries were intoxicated with freedom. The people scrambled for the gaiety, amenities, and pleasures of which they had been deprived so long. After being pent up in hopeless repression, their elementary instincts were violently released.

After the slaughter, however, and after so many bereavements and so much effort expended at the front and behind the lines, the continent was weighed down by a burden of weariness. How, in particular, was it possible not to be plunged into melancholy by the undeniable decadence of Europe, with so many unique positions now, it seemed, gone for ever? This indescribable mixture of optimism and bitter pessimism created a new *mal du siècle*. Innumerable individual insolvencies were summed up in the partial bankruptcy of the whole of liberal humanism. Could the west still believe in the direct progress of humanity towards a better world? Reason itself was in question, and with it the principle of abstract universalism which tended to fade before the vision of peoples tragically destined to clash with one another in an ever-recurring struggle.

This was the origin of the irrational fever that took hold of men's minds. It became a universal sickness. In the temporary rout, moral values were obscured. While wickedness and vice were rampant, and the gangster made his appearance, the masses ran after success, ready to bow the knee to the stronger. It was a terrible process of attrition, prolonging the destruction already wrought by the war. The intellectual *élite*, on their side, raised their usual protest against social conventions. There was a general passion for novelty and emancipation. The world had become plastic; it seemed as if man, as Nietzsche had taught, would be able to mould it to his own desires. There was an inevitable anti-bourgeois reaction, which delighted in evoking all the bogies of revolution. Like the Existentialists in their first phase, men were even ready to revolt against human nature itself.

But in 1924 a change took place. Irrationalism did not, indeed, disappear, but it gave ground before a rationalist optimism which seemed to radiate from Geneva over the rest of the continent. There was talk of *rapprochement* between the nations. Germany was silent about Hitlerism. There was a sort of universal rebirth of confidence. In the framework of economic and financial prosperity there emerged a social philosophy which claimed to introduce order into our knowledge of the past. In Germany men like Troeltsch and Max Weber developed a descriptive and positive sociology looking towards a great future and far-distant horizons; and E. R. Curtius exalted the clarity and clean rigour of the genius of France. Even socialist thinkers seemed to prefer continuity to revolutionary change and subversion. Men were seeking a new equilibrium and discipline. Germany proclaimed the new realism, *die neue Sachlichkeit*. She wished to emerge from chaos; and meanwhile in England, America, and France ancient traditions were again seeking the light.

At this moment the crisis of 1929 broke. Stunned, the world awoke from an illusory prosperity. The teaching of Nietzsche was more than ever the order of the day. He was held to be the genius who had first perceived the implications of the irreconcilable contradiction between the Christian vision and the Copernican view of the universe. The order of salvation gave way once more to the actual conditions of the lot of man. The old individualism was at grips with collectivism in all its phases; with socialist tyranny, the corporative state, the racial community. The Fascist and Nazi ideologies, with their myths and their slogans, seemed to have won the victory.

Faced with this mysterious movement, the individual seeks to recover possession of himself. He does not want to lose ground. What he expects of true science, revealing to him true reality, is that it should set him free from his eternal and mortal unrest: indeed he recognizes this permanent anguish of anxiety as the principle of his own nature. Henceforth he makes it his distinguishing characteristic, putting all his trust in Kierkegaard and Existentialism. Apart from fascism and communism, there is nothing left but this, or the tenets of a psychology which gains an increasing hold, for those who reject the Christian doctrine of personality. At all costs, man must find a place for himself in the Copernican universe.

(*b*) *Science*. What does the new science teach us? Encouraged and supported by technology it has gained a real preponderance. Taking its place outside the shelters which man has built for himself throughout the ages, the scientific vision of the world reveals itself to our view as a piecemeal collection of fragments produced by specialization. Each man now cultivates only a single field of knowledge; and yet, none the less, vast syntheses are elaborated, which seek to change the whole of science and our general interpretation of the universe. Scientists are united by a system of international collaboration which leaves each of them, at the same time, in the enjoyment of personal independence. In this respect the scientific nationalism of the Nazis completely fails.

It is the fate of reason itself that now comes into question. Reason reaches its limits even in what seems to be the purely abstract field of mathematics. The concept of scientific law had by now broken down. The 'quantum' theory revolutionized the study of physics by introducing the idea of discontinuity. This was a rude invasion, which changed all previous notions of the celestial mechanism. The theory of relativity shattered the traditional conception of space and time. Man realized that he could not acquire any true knowledge of the universe without thinking of his own position as 'subject' in relation to 'object'. The systems of measurement which he uses for the terrestrial globe are not absolutely valid for other planets or for the galaxies of distant stars. A new formula of gravitation has to be sketched, and Newton's laws have to be re-examined. Nothing is more changeable, more fluid, or more of a riddle, than the victories of science. The world appears to be subject to unknown and unmastered forces, whose boundless fertility surpasses and defeats all the concepts of thought.

The rigid mechanism which seemed to rule the universe, according to the classical system of physics, is shattered. The idea of relative time replaces that of absolute time. The crisis of determinism begins. The theory of relativity implied a development of capital importance in scientific synthesis. From the point of view of relativity, Einstein stated, there was an identity of the two branches of physics—mechanics and electromagnetism—which had incorporated the rest as a result of the work of Newton and Clerk Maxwell. The myth of the two branches of physics thus seems to be exploded. The synthesis of Clerk Maxwell had led to Hertzian waves; the synthesis of Einstein leads us to atomic energy. The synthesis, in itself, is already a source of new energy. In quantitative mechanics, we have now 'relations of uncertainty', or a principle of indeterminacy resulting from the fact that the observer acts on the system observed. One has to be content with laws of probability; and this theory of 'probabilism' implies a spiritual interpretation of the world.

Turning for a moment from the realm of science to that of politics we may say that on the determinist basis we shall sketch in our minds a 'blue print' of a form of human society based solely on calculation and planning, and on the rigorous integration of the individual in a totalitarian state; while on the probabilist basis we shall admit some element of free will and allow that man may be something more than a mere cog in the social machine. Marx founded all his theory on the determinist physics of his day; and Russia thoroughly understands today how science based on the principle of uncertainty leads thought towards a conception of the state which is non-totalitarian.

(*c*) *Literature and the arts.* If we seek to attain a bird's-eye view of literary trends in Europe during the twentieth century, we discover at once that it is difficult to separate European from world literature, and then we find that the old ideas and literary schools have been enlarged and overflowed partly by a new realism, which the war and its consequences served to increase, and partly by a deepening of the inner life which is equally remarkable and no less fertile.

Writers treated the war of 1914–18 both in a heroic and chivalrous style and on a note of defeatism and lamentation. Literature became national and social. In reaction against the individualism of art for art's sake, it delighted in depicting the fighting men and the masses. The scale of events liberated the small middle-class *élite*, by throwing open to the mind, in all their width, the avenues leading into the enormous complexity of society. This is especially true in Russia and America. There were similar tendencies in England, where the Victorian conventions are swept away by the daring works of men like Bernard Shaw, H. G. Wells, D. H. Lawrence, and James Joyce. In France Romain Rolland and Jules Romains played the same role. Germany already disturbed to her depths by too rapid industrialization, broke more violently than her neighbours with the bourgeois past; forcibly, but in a singular isolation, she sought to express an apocalyptic anguish, which is to be explained by the highly vulnerable condition, both pyschological and moral, of the German people.

In addition, the number of historical and political writings increased. The spirit of world solidarity made itself felt in thousands of such manifestations. Archaeology, prehistory, problems of general synthesis, and a curiosity about collective forces all moved men's minds towards a remarkably widened horizon. New life was given to the notion of *Weltliteratur* which Goethe had preached and of which Europe, with her failing spiritual resources, stood more and more in need. No longer afraid of *la trahison des clercs*, writers flung themselves willingly into the social and political mêlée. This explains, in particular, the excesses of Nazi ideology in Germany, ending inevitably in an ardent defence of collective tendencies and a formidable explosion of bellicose passions.

Psychological literature, seeking to escape from the intolerable misery of the present, is equally prominent. Writers of this type ask themselves the question, 'What is to become of western humanism, which is now so harshly called into question?' They tend to romanticize every thing and every happening: they make poetic material take the place of real passion. With them, irrationalism defends its rights against the tyranny of the intellect. Theosophy and the occult; visionary mysticism; the search for a 'paradise lost'; minds haunted by a yearning for the Divine; analyses probing the mysteries of the soul; confessions; endless introspection; surrealism bent on salvaging the treasures of the inner life; all these styles and tendencies are jostling together in a confused mêlée on the field of world literature. All nations alike are exposed to the storm.

The same conflict is engaged, in the realm of the fine arts, between old traditions of the highest value and the new forms which owe their origin to the enormous pressure of events and the influence of the masses.

While in the nineteenth century architecture scarcely underwent any change, the abundance and novelty of certain materials now permit new and unexpected adaptations. The massive designs of Nazism and Fascism have encouraged, in Germany and Italy, a sort of spectacular reconstruction; and here we find an objective architecture which has lent itself to social requirements both in the construction of blocks of flats for workers and in the building of suburban villas and the proper layout of their gardens. In the search for light, styles became bare and linear, with a taste for bare, white walls tending towards a sort of elegant, restrained neo-classicism.

Although the great tradition of French pictorial art continued to flourish in Montparnasse, painting, too, was inundated by an infinite variety of modernist tendencies and by the unrest which was stirring in this as in other fields. The craving for novelty carries the day, and does so, if need be, by pure negation. Foreign painters, like van Dongen, Picasso, Chagall, and many others stimulate new methods of painting. They open the way to innovators who, while they are cautious up to a point, pass beyond impressionism to fauvism, cubism, and other modes of expression more or less unconventional.

The same development is seen in sculpture, where the wonderful inspiration of Rodin is followed by the poetic work of Bourdelle, succeeded in turn by Maillol and Despiau in France, and by Kolbe and Barlach in Germany.

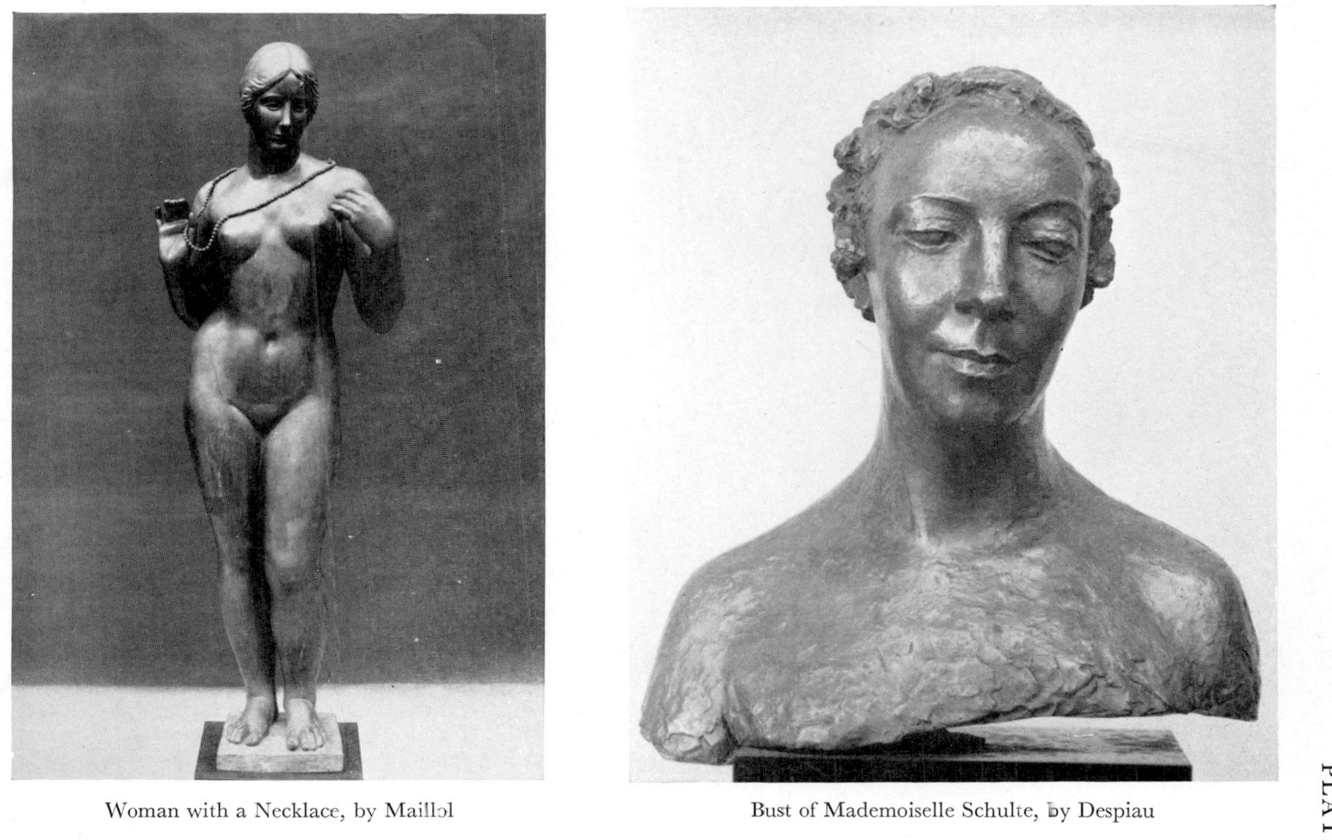

Woman with a Necklace, by Maillol

Bust of Mademoiselle Schulte, by Despiau

But nothing is more revealing than the opposition between tonal and atonal music. The genius of tonality is expressed in a coherent musical interval, which plays a similar role to that of perspective in the plastic arts. A rhythm of life and the alternation of tension and relaxation are the mysteries of this formal music, which can give the listener his bearings and translate for him, as it were, the essential movement of his soul. Here is a wonderful world of independent and fixed forms, on which the musician can play at will. Such music is in its nature entirely a matter of cadence, which binds all the elements together and gives them harmonic significance. There is nothing in the inheritance of Europe grander or more essential than the work of its musicians.

And yet there is also atonal music, first introduced by Schönberg. There is no doubt that it answers an imperious necessity of an enigmatic age. It is completely new, and it shocks the public by its very novelty. With neither rest nor pause, its dynamic quality expresses the unrest and the suffering of our time; and as such music is always attached to some sort of exterior programme, it exposes us to the full force of elementary powers. It obviously springs from the cosmic sense which has come to us since the Renaissance through the discoveries of Copernicus. If tonal music, by virtue of the discipline and solidity of its scheme, is close to Christianity, to classical rationalism, and to western humanism, and if it makes man and his soul the measure of all things, then atonal music carries us into the cosmic spaces which, as Nietzsche was the first to understand, suggest something alarmingly different from, and opposed to, the world which the peoples of western Europe have built—the world which the Germans, fascinated by Nietzsche, have partly destroyed.

If we consider European culture as a whole, we may say that, based on a continent which owes its particular character to the extraordinary diversity of its component nations, it has succeeded in combining an obvious unity of its common elements with the rich variety of aspirations and activities that springs from so many peoples gathered together on so small a space. All in all, the culture of Europe has established and maintained a balance between reason and feeling, between spiritual discipline and human passions both individual and social. That is its achievement and glory.

But this is an equilibrium which is threatened on every side: in the social and economic fields, in politics and religion, in literature and the arts. The masses, with their numbers increased by unprecedented demographic development, not only enter into politics; they penetrate everywhere, claiming still wider provinces for the satisfaction of desires which are incontestably legitimate.

IV
CONCLUSIONS AND OUTLOOK FOR THE FUTURE

THE situation of Europe as it took shape between 1945 and 1950 is the inevitable result of that second 'Thirty Years War' which has been studied, in its essential aspects, in the present section. Between the two wars, Europe was still 'poised' between the United States and Russia. Today she is 'rent' internally by the conflict which pits these two powers against one another. She is cruelly 'partitioned' between their respective influences. The partition which sets western Germany in opposition to eastern is the symbolic expression of this tragic cleavage. The uniformity of treatment prescribed for all the four zones by the Potsdam Agreement has never been carried out. The failure of the Moscow Conference of March and April 1947 has widened the separation; and the result, in Germany and in Europe, is an opposition between the system of 'people's democracy' in the east and the 'parliamentary democracy' of the west. The initiative of the west has in Germany always preceded the measures to which Russia has had recourse. The Prague *coup d'état* of 1948 seems to have been the reply to Marshall Aid and the preparations for the Atlantic pact.

The appearance of Hitler's national socialism and New Order was the chief event of the twenty years between the two wars. Similarly the German problem was, and still is today, the most arduous of all the problems confronting nations and their governments. It is evident that this problem, by its extraordinary complexity, and also, no doubt, in virtue of a general ignorance of its nature, has had an increasingly disorganizing influence on world diplomacy since 1919. In addition, the public opinion and the political parties of the parliamentary democracies continue to be strangely divided and wavering in their attitude to the problem.

The partition of Germany in 1945 was bound to aggravate the difficulty. It discourages the observer who wishes, before he draws any conclusions, to catch some glimpse of the future. It perpetuates what may be called the unreality of contemporary German politics. Neither the system imposed by Russia on the inhabitants of east Germany nor the democratization attempted by the Allies in the west seems to have made any deep impression on a people thrown into unprecedented confusion by a second defeat and its consequences, but still retaining its ardour for work and a firm determination to build again a twice demolished structure.

Germany is trying to find herself amongst the ruins, in spite of her present disintegration. She is dreaming again of national unity, as she did before in the time of her old territorial disintegration, while in actual fact she is still divided. No man can guess what will be the nature of German democracy if the unity of Germany should be restored. One can only remember that by 'democracy' Germans have always meant the integration of their national energies into a coherent Reich. But the great state of Prussia is now no more. That is a crucial fact. There is nothing now to prevent the Germans from building, in the centre of Europe, a true federal state, in which unitary and local institutions would be harmoniously balanced. The Bonn Constitution has sketched the first outlines of such a development.

For the moment, however, we can only consider western Germany; and the question here is whether it will be admitted to the Council of Europe.

When, in the middle period of his career, Nietzsche advised Europeans to unite, he described the monstrous state that would rise up in their midst if they delayed too long, a state which they would have to destroy before they could embark on definite construction. This state came into being in the guise and shape of the Third Reich. It has been destroyed. But its fall has been so great that it has left behind, not only a void and confusion in the centre of the continent, but also the disablement of Europe *vis-à-vis* the monstrous state of the east, the state created by the revolution of 1917, a state which Nietzsche could not foresee.

At the moment, the European idea seems stricken with weakness and paralysis. It was so already between the two wars. In the field of theory, a small minority of vigorous minds had, indeed, elaborated the idea on its political side. But it needed the crisis of 1929 to produce any scheme for the economic reorganization of Europe; and neither Tardieu's plan nor the Stresa Conference achieved the desired result. As for the London Conference of 1933, its result served to prove that Britain preferred her links with the commonwealth to any which she might forge on the continent.

A fresh start has to be made, under conditions infinitely more complex. The cleavage between east and west in Europe is an accomplished fact. Britain seems more cautious than ever. It is a question whether Europe will be brought under a system of planned economy or will return to a free exchange market. It may be that, owing to disagreement among the socialists of western Europe, a free market will win the day. The Netherlands will follow that trend. An unplanned economy has many supporters in Great Britain. Since the formation of the Strasbourg Assembly, the previous combinations of national parties with one another have been broken off. For the moment, western Europe has successfully avoided the risk of being shipwrecked by the clash of socialism and the bourgeoisie. Bourgeois tendencies seem to be gaining ground.

Must we anticipate future developments, consent in advance to some sacrifices of sovereignty, and bow to the super-state of the future? It is a serious problem, but one which is always present in the background of contemporary discussions.

The real question of the day, in our opinion, is whether victory will go to the Council of Ministers at Strasbourg, perhaps more divided than is commonly believed, or to the Consultative Assembly, for which France seems to wish to secure the preponderance. Here everything hangs on the relations between Britain and France—Britain and the continent. The assembly is the driving wheel *par excellence*, but the ministers are there to act as a brake on its driving power.

In the face of so uncertain and confused a situation, the German problem obviously acquires a new and more pressing urgency. As Germany has now sketched the lines of her political reorganization, and as she is now beginning, with the great industrial plant which is still at her command, to tackle the problem of economic reconstruction, all eyes are fixed upon her. She is therefore again in the position which she held between the two wars: she is the mirror in which we can best see the significance and trace the development of the major problems of our day. Everything is shown there in a peculiar light, and with an exceptional magnification due to her tragic difficulties.

From this point of view, the future of democracy in Germany is a matter for anxious and particular consideration. Good observers are of the opinion that, in view of the very limited character of the efforts made by Britain and France in this direction, the American attempt is doomed to failure, in spite of the great resources behind it. America has proposed to guarantee the existence, and to ensure the operation, of German parliamentary institutions and German private enterprise. But Germany herself appears rather to favour the only power that in the view of her most influential elements seems solidly based and sure of the future—the power of finance and industry. There is a serious risk that in the future this power may be wielded by technocrats, 'managers' of the Burnham stamp, who are legion across the Rhine. The conclusion generally reached, after reading the German press and reviews and listening to well-informed Germans, is that the struggle between capitalism and communism is over, and that the future pattern will be a strict organization of social, economic, and administrative activity.

In the same way men of goodwill in the west, who devote their energies to the cause of a future Union of Europe, believe that the continent will somehow or other be one day organized, and that if this result is not achieved democratically, by a full-scale system of parliamentary institutions, it will be achieved by the technocrats—a consummation which might lead Europe into neo-fascism, or into a form of anti-Stalin communism in the style of Tito.

Europe, like Germany—and Germany, like Europe—stands at the cross-roads.

There is one conception, and it is the oldest, which makes man and his personality the real measure of all things. It is a conception which is always recalling the individual to a sense of his own values, which are internal and psychological because they are based on liberty. This is the road followed by western humanism under the guidance of its great tradition: a tradition connected with ancient Hellas by the memory of Ptolemy and the Ptolemaic system; a tradition linked with Christianity in all its many forms; a tradition linked again both with democratic liberalism and with that moderate socialism which does not sacrifice personal values to the demands of social organization.

There is another and more recent conception which dates from the Renaissance, and draws its strength from the tremendous discovery revealed by Copernicus in 1543. It is a conception which attempts to give man his place in a cosmos which appears to him overwhelming because it is not adjusted to his measure and infinitely surpasses his limited powers. It looks at the human lot in the light of ordinary reality: it sees man as a being launched from his birth and without his volition on the full flood of nature, into a world of forces where he struggles and can only survive by dint of vitality and by getting control, for his guidance, of an ever-increasing share of the forces among which he is struggling. It recognizes man as a little thing in comparison with the Universe, which none the less lends him its powers, and yet is ready in a moment to destroy him and all his works.

There is no doubt that Nietzsche was the first European to proclaim the contradiction between these two paths and these two different attitudes towards the Infinite. If this is the case, and if the philosopher whose genius revealed this tragic dilemma was a German by birth, the reason is that Germany herself had reached the cross-roads.

The tremendous demographic growth of humanity in our own age puts this terrible dilemma in its proper setting. On the one hand we find a middle class, with its success and its prestige sanctioned by the old tradition of humanism and the humanist emphasis on personality, but also with a growing tendency to cling to the positions it has won. On the other hand there stands the mass of the people, more and more engulfed by a movement of industrial mechanization, which is diffusing itself all over the world, and extending itself even to the countryside in the shape of agrarian collectivism. The masses, by the act of asserting their claims, tend to absorb the old middle classes. This demographic development thus assumes the character of a cosmic event. It reduces men ruthlessly to a common level. It plunges them into a social environment where personality is threatened with extinction, flattened down by the crushing weight of an omnipotent technology. In every sphere—the social and economic, the political, and the cultural—it seems as if a great human flood were surging up for the attack, and beginning to batter, with its hurrying waves, a civilization whose pride it has been to affirm the greatness of human personality by the creation of strong aristocratic hierarchies.

At all costs the inheritance of Europe must be saved. The social tide must not be allowed to sweep over Europe in a nameless catastrophe, engulfing for ever in its course so many incomparable treasures, some of them inherited by the Old World from still older civilizations. Nor must the middle classes of

Europe, shutting their ears to the demands of the masses, reply to them only by fascism, the newest and the most cruel of all the forms of the exploitation of man by man, and condemned as such since 1945.

Europe, and Germany in the centre of Europe, owe it to themselves to rebuild their life by bringing about a synthesis between these basis tendencies. They also owe it to themselves to replace the will to power, which Nietzsche held to be the only method of solving the contradiction, by a will for human solidarity, so as to save simultaneously and in the same breath both the rights of personality and of man's free spirit and also the rights of the people at large, who will never henceforward cease from demanding the standard of well-being which is now in principle open to all.

Otherwise, social disaster will bring bourgeois conservatism down to the ground: and that, if it finally falls, may involve in its ruin a civilization possessed of genuine treasures which ought to be preserved and kept intact for the benefit and the delight of future generations.

1914–50

DOCUMENTS

I

Treaty of Versailles (1919)

(a) *Articles Relating to Germany*

Article 42. Germany is forbidden to maintain or construct any fortifications either on the left bank of the Rhine or on the right bank to the west of a line drawn 50 kilometres to the east of the Rhine.

Article 43. In the area defined above, the maintenance and the assembly of armed forces, either permanently or temporarily, and military manœuvres of any kind, as well as the upkeep of all permanent works for mobilization, are in the same way forbidden.

Article 44. In case Germany violates in any manner whatever the provisions of Article 42 and 43, she shall be regarded as committing a hostile act against the Powers signatory of the present Treaty and as calculated to disturb the peace of the world.

Section V. Preamble. The High Contracting Parties, recognizing the moral obligation to redress the wrong done by Germany in 1871, both to the rights of France and to the wishes of the population of Alsace and Lorraine, which were separated from their country in spite of the solemn protest of their representatives at the Assembly of Bordeaux, agree upon the following article:

Article 51. The Territories which were ceded to Germany in accordance with the Preliminaries of Peace signed at Versailles on February 26, 1871 . . . are restored to French sovereignty as from the date of the Armistice of November 11, 1918. . . .

Article 80. Germany acknowledges and will respect strictly the independence of Austria within the frontiers which may be fixed in a Treaty between that State and the principal Allied and Associated Powers; she agrees that this independence shall be inalienable, except with the consent of the Council of the League of Nations.

Article 81. Germany, in conformity with the action already taken by the Allied and Associated Powers, recognizes the complete independence of the Czecho-Slovak State which will include the autonomous territory of the Ruthenians to the south of the Carpathians. . . .

Article 87. Germany, in conformity with the action already taken by the Allied and Associated Powers, recognizes the complete independence of Poland. . . .

Article 119. Germany renounces in favour of the principal Allied and Associated Powers all her rights and titles over her overseas possessions.

Article 159. The German military forces shall be demobilized and reduced as prescribed hereinafter.

Article 231. The Allied and Associated Governments affirm and Germany accepts the responsibility of Germany and her Allies for causing all the loss and damage to which the Allied and Associated Governments and their nationals have been subjected as a consequence of the war imposed upon them by the aggression of Germany and her allies.

Article 247. Germany undertakes to furnish to the University of Louvain . . . manuscripts, incunabula, printed books . . . corresponding in number and value to those destroyed in the burning by Germany of the Library of Louvain. . . .

Article 377. At any time the League of Nations may recommend the revision of such of these Articles as relate to a permanent administrative régime.

(b) *The Covenant of the League of Nations*

EXTRACTS

Article 8. The members of the League recognize that the maintenance of peace requires the reduction of national armaments to the lowest point consistent with national safety and the enforcement by common action of international obligations.

The Council, taking account of the geographical situation and circumstances of each State, shall formulate plans for such reduction for the consideration and action of the several Governments.

Such plans shall be subject to reconsideration and revision at least every ten years.

After these plans shall have been adopted by the several Governments, the limits of armament therein fixed shall not be exceeded without the concurrence of the Council.

The Members of the League agree that the manufacture by private enterprise of munitions and implements of war is open to grave objections. The Council shall advise how the evil effects attendant upon such manufacture can be prevented, due regard being had to the necessities of those Members of the League which are not able to manufacture the munitions and implements of war necessary for their safety.

The Members of the League undertake to interchange full and frank information as to the scale of their armament, their military, naval and air programmes and the conditions of such of their industries as are adaptable to warlike purposes.

Article 10. The Members of the League undertake to respect and preserve as against external aggression the territorial integrity and existing political independence of all Members of the League. In case of any such aggression, or in case of any threat or danger of such aggression, the Council shall advise upon the means by which this obligation shall be fulfilled.

Article 11. Any war or threat of war, whether immediately affecting any of the Members of the League or not, is hereby declared a matter of concern to the whole League, and the League shall take any action that may be deemed wise and effectual to safeguard the peace of nations. In case any such emergency should arise, the Secretary General shall, on the request of any Member of the League, forthwith summon a meeting of the Council.

It is also declared to be the friendly right of each Member of the League to bring to the attention of the Assembly or of the Council any circumstance whatever affecting international relations which threatens to disturb international peace or the good understanding between nations upon which peace depends.

Article 16. Should any Member of the League resort to war in disregard of its covenant under articles 12, 13 or 15, it shall *ipso facto* be deemed to have committed an act of war against all Members of the League, which hereby undertake immediately to subject it to the severance of all trade or financial relations, ... and [to] the prevention of all financial, commercial, or personal intercourse between the nationals of the covenant-breaking State and the nationals of any other State, whether a Member of the League or not.

It shall be the duty of the Council in such case to recommend to the several Governments concerned what effective military, naval or air force the Members of the League shall severally contribute to the armed forces to be used to protect the covenants of the League.

II

The Views of Masaryk and Benes

(*a*) *Thomas G. Masaryk: 'The New Europe'*

DEMOCRATIC PEACE AND ITS TERMS

The Pan-German alliance was concluded not merely because of geographical and historical reasons, but because of deep inner relationship: Russia, Austria, and Turkey are in their substance dynastic, militaristic, aggressive, anti-national and anti-democratic. Turkey has fallen. Austria is following Turkey, and Russia will fall immediately after and through Austria.

The programme of the Allies is in its consequences also a programme for the liberation and humanization of the German nation.

Democracy is the political organization of society resting on the official foundations of humanitarianism; aristocracy (oligarchy-monarchism), as it developed historically, is based on theocracy, on religion and church. European States have not yet freed themselves, all and to the fullest extent, from medieval theocratism.

(1938)

(*b*) *Eduard Benes: 'My Fears and my Hopes'*

EXTRACTS

. . . But this unbelievable cynicism [of Germany] goes much farther: not only does it publicly announce that it does not intend and will not keep its pledged word and the treaty it has signed when that is inconvenient to it; at the same time it demands that its opponent or partner should keep this same treaty, in so far as it has aspects that are favourable to Nazism. Otherwise it declares him to be a traitor, a swindler and a rogue. Germany destroyed everything that was inconvenient to her in the Versailles Treaty and demands from others that they should respect those parts of it that are advantageous for Germany. She destroyed the Locarno Treaty, and furiously attacked Great Britain when she came to an agreement with France and Belgium to keep the intact sections of Locarno. She destroyed Austria, and furiously attacked those who asked whether they were not authorized or obliged by their Geneva obligations to defend the existence of Austria. At the same time, she demanded all Austria's assets all over the world and refused to pay Austria's debts. She destroyed the Munich Agreement by means of the most shameful deceit and violence, and at the same time demanded that Britain and France should keep that agreement in a number of matters.

She promised not to touch Czechoslovakia if her wishes were satisfied in the matter of the Czechoslovakia-Germans, and appealed to the principle of justice for all nationalities, and immediately afterwards she occupied this state and introduced there the greatest national terror and oppression that it is possible to imagine. She concluded a treaty of friendship with Poland for ten years, and then in the most dishonourable manner prepared war against that country and made an agreement with Poland's neighbour for the partition of Polish territory.

. . . That which is most insupportable of all for this our present age, that which most offends our twentieth century and which really reduces this Nazi régime to the same level as the ages of ancient barbarism, is that this is a whole *doctrine*, worked out as a political system; that it is the real faith and the accepted system of principles of Nazi policy, the Nazi order, the Nazi State, the Nazi world, developed in peace as in war against friends and foes alike; it is simply Nazism's political confession of faith.

These principles, the most immoral that the world has ever seen, are the real essence, the intellectual and moral basis of the Nazi world. Violence, power, terror, military force, the dagger and the rifle; that is the basis of Nazi theory and practice on which the whole system rests. In the moral sense, Nazism means the end of the civilization of the twentieth century.

Those are the reasons, ladies and gentlemen, why we are at war. Not only in order to stem the expansion of Pan-Germanism . . . not only in order that Austria, Czechoslovakia, and Poland may be free again, but above all in order that all I have just spoken of may be done away with and may be made impossible ever again in Germany or anywhere else. The life which the Nazi ideological and political system has brought to Germany and Europe means spiritual and moral death; such a life is not worth living. That is why we are fighting.

And now . . . what are my fears for the present situation? My fears are that Europe, belligerent Western Europe, might not see the whole essence of this struggle; that it might not see that it is necessary mercilessly to do away with this whole Nazi régime; that it might not see that with this Nazi world and its helpers in Germany neither agreement nor co-existence is possible; . . . that it might not see that it is necessary to put an unconditional and definitive end to this whole system and its military machine. No decent discussion, no acceptable compromise, no agreement was ever possible with Nazism or will ever be possible. This is the essence of Nazism. That is what I am striving for, that no decent man in Europe should ever forget this.

(1939–40)

III

Briand on the Organization of a System of European Federal Union

The proposal submitted for study by twenty-seven European governments was justified by their acute feeling of collective responsibility in face of the danger threatening European peace—from a political as well as from a social and economic point of view—in consequence of the lack of co-ordination still existing in the general economy of Europe. The need to establish a permanent system of *de jure* solidarity for the rational organization of Europe is, in fact, a result of the essential conditions of the security and welfare of the peoples who are required by their geographical position to be partners in a *de facto* solidarity in this region of the world.

There can be no doubt today that the lack of cohesion in the grouping of the material and moral forces of Europe constitutes, in practice, the most serious obstacle to the development and efficacy of all the political or juridical institutions which are likely to form the basis for the first attempts at a universal peace organization. This dispersion of forces limits no less seriously, in Europe, the possibilities of extending economic markets, the attempts to intensify and improve industrial production, and, thereby, all guarantees against labour crises, which are a source of political as well as of social instability. The danger of such disintegration is further increased by the extent of the new frontiers (over 20,000 kilometres of customs barriers) which the treaties [of 1919] have had to create in order to do justice to national aspirations in Europe. Even the action of the League of Nations, whose responsibilities are all the heavier by reason of its universality, might be gravely hampered in Europe unless this territorial arrangement were promptly compensated for by a bond of solidarity which would allow European nations to become conscious at last of the geographical unity of Europe and to realize, within the framework of the League, one of those regional *ententes* formally recommended by the Covenant.

In other words, the quest for a formula of European co-operation in connexion with the League of Nations, far from weakening the authority of that body, must only, and can only, tend to increase it, since it is closely related to the views of the League.

It is not a question of constituting a European grouping outside the League of Nations, but on the contrary of harmonizing European interests under the control and in the spirit of the League, by integrating within its universal system a system which is limited and thereby more effective. The realization of a European federal organization would always be put to the credit of the League of Nations as a progressive measure, arising from its activity, from which the non-European countries themselves might benefit.

Such a conception could leave no room for ambiguity, any more than that which gave rise, on an even narrower regional basis, to the collective negotiations for the Locarno agreement, which inaugurated the real policy of European co-operation.

In fact, there are certain questions of specific interest to Europe, for the solution of which the European states may feel the need to take appropriate action more immediately and more directly, in the interest of peace itself, and for dealing with which, moreover, they are particularly qualified by reason of their ethnical affinities and their common civilization. The League of Nations itself, in the general exercise of its activity, has more than once had to take into account the fact that Europe constitutes a geographical unity for which certain common solutions may be suitable that could not be applied to the world at large. One of the particular tasks of the proposed association would be precisely that of preparing and facilitating the co-ordination of the strictly European activities of the League of Nations.

Far from being a new organ for the settlement of disputes, the European assembly would not be qualified to deal with the substance of the particular problems which have been remitted by the Covenant or by treaties to a special procedure of the League of Nations or to any other expressly defined procedure; in such matters it could only be called upon to exercise its good offices in a purely consultative capacity. But even in cases where some essential task reserved for the League of Nations is in question, the federal link between European states would still play a very useful part, by preparing an atmosphere favourable to a peaceful settlement by the League, or by facilitating the execution of its decisions in practice.

BRIAND's Memorandum of 9 September 1929.

IV

Passages from the Writings of Lenin

(*a*) *On Dual Power*

The strikingly original feature of our revolution is that it has created *dual power*. This fact must be realized first and foremost; without understanding it, we can make no advance. For instance, we must know how to supplement and correct the old formulas of Bolshevism. For although they have proved themselves sound in general, their concrete application has shown itself to be different. *Nobody* hitherto thought, or could have thought, of dual power.

Wherein does this dual power consist?

It consists in the fact that side by side with the Provisional Government, the government of the bourgeoisie, another government has arisen, weak and embryonic as yet, but nevertheless undeniably a government that exists in fact and is growing; the government of the Soviets of workers' and soldiers' deputies.

What is the social composition of this other government? The proletariat and the peasantry (in soldiers' uniforms). What is its political character? It is a revolutionary dictatorship; that is to say a power based directly on a revolutionary *coup de force*, on a direct initiative of the popular masses coming from below, and *not on the law* laid down by the power of a centralized State. This new power is of quite a different sort from that generally found in parliamentary bourgeois democratic republics of the usual type, which has hitherto been predominant in the advanced countries of Europe and America. This fact is often forgotten, and not sufficiently taken into account. Yet it is the essential point. The new power is of the same type as the

Paris Commune of 1871. These are the characteristic features of the type: (1) the source of power lies not in laws previously discussed and voted by a Parliament, but in the direct local initiative of the popular masses, coming from below, or in a *coup de force*, to use a current phrase; (2) the police and the army, institutions divided from the people and opposed to the people, are replaced by the direct arming of the whole people, and thus under such a power order is maintained in the State by the armed workers and peasants *themselves*, the armed people *itself*; (3) the body of officials, the bureaucracy, is also replaced by the direct power of the people itself, or at any rate placed under special control; not only do they become simple elected agents, but they are also subject to recall at the first demand of the people. From being a privileged body enjoying remunerative 'sinecures', and from being bourgeois in character, they become a special branch of workers, whose salary *does not exceed* the usual pay of a good workman.

Published in *Pravda*, No. 28, 22 (9) April 1917.

(*b*) *Extracts from 'The State and Revolution'* (*1918*)

1

For instance, when, in the Revolution of 1917, the question of the real meaning and role of the State arose, in all its importance, as a practical question demanding immediate action on a wide mass-scale, all the Socialist-Revolutionaries and Mensheviks rattled down, suddenly and without reservation, to the lower-middle-class theory of the 'conciliation of classes by the State.' Innumerable resolutions and articles by publicists of both these parties were saturated through and through with this purely middle-class and philistine theory of conciliation. That the State is the organ of domination of a definite class which *cannot* be reconciled to its social antipodes—this the lower middle-class democracy is never able to understand. Their attitude towards the State is one of the most telling proofs that our Socialist-Revolutionaries and Mensheviks are not Socialists at all (which we Bolsheviks have always maintained), but only lower-middle-class democrats, with a phraseology very nearly Socialist.

The State and Revolution, chap. i, § 1.

2

In its first phase or first stage Communism *cannot* as yet be economically mature and quite free of all tradition and of all taint of Capitalism. Hence we see the interesting phenomenon of the first phase of Communism retaining 'the narrow horizon of bourgeois law'. Bourgeois law, in respect of the distribution of articles of consumption, presupposes inevitably the capitalist State, for law is nothing without the organization for *forcing* people to obey it. Consequently, for a certain time not only bourgeois law, but even the capitalist State may remain under Communism without the capitalist class.

Ibid., chap. v, § 4.

(*c*) *Report on Peace. Speech on the Closure of the Discussion 8 November (26 October) 1917*

I am resolutely opposed to our demand for peace taking on the character of an ultimatum. . . . We must not, by refusing to yield on an unimportant point of our demands, enable the imperialist governments to say that our intransigence prevented them from entering into peace negotiations. . . .

We will confront all governments with our peace proposals. Let them be answerable to their peoples.

There is a further point, comrades, to which you must pay close attention. The secret treaties must be published. The clauses dealing with annexations and contributions must be annulled. . . . We do not bind ourselves by these treaties. . . . We reject all clauses involving depredation and violence, but we cannot reject the clauses establishing good-neighbourly relations and economic agreements; we will accept them joyfully. We propose a three months' armistice; we are in favour of a long breathing-space because the nations are exhausted, and because they yearn for rest after the three years and more that this bloody slaughter has lasted. We must understand that the nations ought to discuss the conditions of peace and to express their will through the medium of parliaments, and that this will take time. But we do not reject proposals for a shorter armistice; we will examine them and we ought to accept them, even if we are offered an armistice of one month or six weeks. . . . Our proposal for an armistice, too, must not assume the character of an ultimatum, for a government which rejects an armistice is criminal.

. . . The strength of a State, in our view, lies in the consciousness of the masses. . . . We need not fear to speak the truth about our weariness. Indeed, what country is not weary today; what nation does not openly confess it? Look at Italy, where this weariness has given rise to a prolonged revolutionary movement demanding an end to the slaughter. Do we not see in Germany mass workers' manifestations taking place under the slogan of an end to the war? Is not weariness the cause of the mutiny of the German fleet, ruthlessly repressed by the butcher William and his lackeys? If events of this character can take place in a country as disciplined as Germany, where men are now beginning to talk about weariness and bringing the war to an end, we in our turn need not fear to speak openly of such things. For this is something as true for us as it is for all the belligerent and even for non-belligerent countries.

Published in *Pravda*, No. 171, 10 November (28 October) 1917.

V

Extracts on National Socialism

(*a*) *The Views of Hitler in 'Mein Kampf'*

1. EDUCATION IN THE RACIAL STATE

The State that is grounded on the racial principle and is alive to the significance of this truth will first of all have to base its educational work not on the mere imparting of knowledge but rather on physical training and development of healthy bodies. The cultivation of the intellectual faculties comes only in the second place. And here again it is character which has to be developed first of all, strength of will and decision. And the educational system ought to foster the spirit of readiness to accept responsibilities gladly. Formal instruction in the sciences must be considered last in importance. Accordingly the State which is grounded on the racial idea must start with the principle that a person whose formal education in the sciences is relatively small but who is physically sound and robust, of a steadfast and honest character, ready and able to make decisions and endowed with strength of will, is a more useful member of the national community than a weakling who is scholarly and refined. A nation composed of learned men who are physical weaklings, hesitant about decisions of the will and timid pacifists, is not capable of assuring even its own existence on this earth.

ADOLF HITLER, *Mein Kampf*, Vol. II, chap. ii (1927).

2. THE WEIMAR REPUBLIC

The chief characteristic difference between the policy of the present Reich and that of former times lies in this: The old Reich gave freedom to its people at home and showed itself strong towards the outside world, whereas the Republic shows itself weak towards the stranger and oppresses its own citizens at home. In both cases one attitude determines the other. A vigorous national State does not need to make many laws for the interior, because of the affection and attachment of its citizens. The international servile State can live only by coercing its citizens to render it the services it demands. And it is a piece of impudent falsehood for the present régime to speak of 'Free citizens'. Only the old Germany could speak in that manner. The present Republic is a colony of slaves at the service of the stranger. At best it has subjects, but not citizens. Hence it does not possess a national flag but only a trade mark, introduced and protected by official decree and legislative measures. This symbol, which is the Gessler's cap of German Democracy, will always remain alien to the spirit of our people. On its side, the Republic, having no sense of tradition or respect for past greatness, dragged the symbol of the past in the mud, but it will be surprised one day to discover how superficial is the devotion of its citizens to its own symbol. The Republic has given to itself the character of an intermezzo in German history.

Ibid., chap. x (1927).

3. THE FOREIGN POLICY OF GERMANY

The future goal of our foreign policy ought not to involve an orientation to the East or the West; but it ought to be an Eastern policy which will have in view the acquisition of such territory as is necessary for our German people. To carry out this policy we need that force which the mortal enemy of our nation, France, now deprives us of by holding us in her grip and pitilessly robbing us of our strength. Therefore we must stop at no sacrifice in our effort to destroy the French striving towards hegemony over Europe. As our natural ally today we have every Power on the Continent that feels France's lust for hegemony in Europe unbearable. No attempt to approach those Powers ought to appear too difficult for us, and no sacrifice should be considered too heavy, if the final outcome would be to make it possible for us to overthrow our bitterest enemy. The minor wounds will be cured by the beneficent influence of time, once the ground wounds have been cauterized and closed.

Ibid., chap. xiv *ad finem* (1927).

(*b*) *Rosenberg's views in 'The Myth of the Twentieth Century'*

None of the nations of Europe is racially homogeneous, not even Germany. On the basis of the most recent investigations, we may assume five races, which show marked differences of type. Now it is an indubitable fact that the Nordic race has been the first and foremost for Europe as a vehicle of genuine culture. It is from the blood of this race that the great heroes, artists and founders of States have sprung: it was they who built the sure strongholds and the religious fanes; it was Nordic blood that produced poetry, and created the works of music which we honour as our greatest revelations. It was this blood, too, which more than any other formed and shaped German life. Even those circles in which it only shows itself in scanty proportions today are rooted and grounded in it. To be German is to be Nordic; and this element has acted on the Western, Dinaric, and East-Baltic races in the creation of their culture and type of civilization. Even a type which may appear to be predominantly Dinaric has often been inwardly shaped by Nordic influence. To emphasize the importance of the Nordic race is not to sow 'race-hatred' in Germany: on the contrary, it is the conscious recognition of a *bond of union* among our people which is a bond of blood. Without this bond of union, as it has been formed by the course of history, Germany would never have become a German *Reich*: German poetry would never have arisen; and the idea of honour would never have controlled and ennobled our law and our life.

Pp. 576–7 in the German original, published in 1930.

VI

Mussolini on the Doctrine of Fascism

Fascism is a religious conception in which man is seen in his immanent relationship with a superior law and with an objective Will that transcends the particular individual and raises him to conscious membership of a spiritual society. Whoever has seen in the religious politics of the Fascist régime nothing but mere opportunism has not understood that Fascism besides being a system of government is also, and above all, a system of thought.

Fascism is an historical conception, in which man is what he is only in so far as he works with the spiritual process in which he finds himself, in the family or social group, in the nation and in the history in which all nations collaborate. From this follows the great value of tradition, in memories, in language, in customs, in the standards of social life. Outside history man is nothing. Consequently Fascism is opposed to all the individualistic abstractions of a materialistic nature like those of the eighteenth century; and it is opposed to all Jacobin utopias and innovations. It does not consider that 'happiness' is possible upon earth, as it appeared to be in the desire of the economic literature of the eighteenth century, and hence it rejects all teleological theories according to which mankind would reach a definitive stabilized condition at a certain period in history. This implies putting oneself outside history and life, which is a continual change and coming to be. Politically, Fascism wishes to be a realistic doctrine; practically, it aspires to solve only the problems which arise historically of themselves and that of themselves find or suggest their own solution. To act among men, as to act in the natural world, it is necessary to enter into the process of reality and to master the already operating forces.

Against individualism, the Fascist conception is for the State; and it is for the individual in so far as he coincides with the State, which is the conscience and universal will of man in his historical existence. It is opposed to classical Liberalism, which arose from the necessity of reacting against absolutism, and which brought its historical purpose to an end when the State was transformed into the conscience and will of the people. Liberalism denied the State in the interests of the particular individual; Fascism reaffirms the State as the true reality of the individual.

BENITO MUSSOLINI, *The Doctrine of Fascism, Fundamental Ideas*, §§ 5, 6, 7 (published in the Italian Encyclopaedia, in 1931).

VII

Paul Valéry on the Spiritual Crisis

Who, then, are Europeans?

I venture on this ground with many reservations; with the infinite scruples that one must have when one attempts a provisional definition of something which is not susceptible of really exact description. . . .

Well, I shall consider as European all the nations which have undergone, during the course of history, the three influences I am about to name.

The first is that of Rome. Wherever the Roman Empire has held sway and wherever its power has been felt, and even wherever the Empire has been feared, admired, and envied; wherever the weight of the Roman sword has been felt; wherever the majesty of Rome's laws and institutions, and the structure and dignity of its magistracy, have been recognized, copied, and sometimes freely imitated, —there something European will be found. Rome is the eternal model of organized and stable power.

I do not know the reasons for this great triumph. It is useless to seek for them now, as it is idle to wonder what Europe would have become had it not become Roman.

The fact alone matters for us; the fact of the amazingly enduring impression made on so many races and generations by that superstitious and yet rational power—that power so curiously imbued with the spirit of jurisdiction, the spirit of war, the spirit of religion, and the spirit of formalism—which was the first to impose on conquered peoples the benefits of tolerance and good administration.

Then came Christianity. You know how it gradually spread within the very sphere of the Roman conquest. If we except the New World, which was not so much Christianized as populated by Christians, and if we except Russia, the greater part of which never knew the laws of Rome or the rule of Caesar, we see that the extent of the Christian religion, even today, almost exactly coincides with that of the authority of the Empire. These two conquests, although so different, have nevertheless certain points of likeness, and this likeness is important to us. The policy of the Romans, which became ever more flexible and ingenious, and whose flexibility and facility increased as the central power weakened, that is to say as the Empire grew vaster and more heterogeneous, introduced into the system of the domination of nations by a nation a most remarkable new element. . . .

But we are not yet finished Europeans. Something is lacking to complete the picture, a certain marvellous modification which did not give us our sense of public order and our respect for citizenship and temporal justice, nor yet the depth of our souls, our absolute idealism, and our sense of eternal justice. The thing that is lacking is that subtle and powerful action to which we owe the best of our intelligence, the delicacy and strength of our knowledge, as also the clarity, purity and *distinction* of our art and literature; these *virtues* came to us from Greece.

Once again we must admire here the part played by the Roman Empire. It conquered in order to be conquered. Permeated by Greece and by Christianity, it offered them a vast field, already pacified and organized; it prepared a site for them, and formed the mould into which the Christian idea and the thought of Greece were to flow and intermingle so curiously.

It is perhaps what we owe to Greece that distinguishes us most profoundly from the rest of humanity. We owe to her the discipline of our mind, the extraordinary example of perfection in every sphere. We owe to her a method of thinking which tends to refer everything to man, to the complete man; man becomes in himself the system of references by which everything can eventually be measured. He must therefore develop every part of his being and maintain them all in a harmony as clear, and even as evident, as possible. He must develop his body and his mind. As for the mind itself, he will safeguard himself against its excesses, its fancies, and its vague and purely imaginative productions, by a meticulous criticism and analysis of its judgments, by a rational division of its functions, and by a regular observance of its forms.

From *Variété: Édition de 1924*, Note 1.

VIII

Strachey on the Theory and Practice of Socialism (1936)

It is reasonable to expect that the far wider area of sexual choice open to every citizen of a homogeneous, classless society will, over a few generations, have a markedly eugenic effect, and so increase the mental and physical powers of the race. It would, I fancy, be dangerous in the present state of our ignorance of the science of eugenics to regard this as more than a reasonable expectation. But it is, at any rate, an incomparably more rational hypothesis than is the monstrous nonsense of 'eugenics' as that infant science is taught in capitalist states today. I say nothing of the delirium of fascist 'race theories'. But in England and America a bastard eugenics is current in which the fact that the working class which is permanently ill-nourished, ill-housed, ill-clad, and deprived of adequate medical attention, or the knowledge of modern hygienic principles, necessarily suffers in physique, is used, not as an argument for improving the workers' conditions, but in order to prove that the workers are 'inferior stock' to the capitalist! (P. 102, note 1.)

. . . . . .

Now most people when they use the word dictatorship have in mind the absolute, irresponsible and uncontrolled rule of one man over the rest of the community. . . . The Fascist régimes of Hitler and Mussolini are its contemporary prototypes. The undesirability of this type of government is so well established that we need not discuss it. Is this the kind of government which we should have in a socialist Britain and America? It is not. When we speak of the necessity of establishing 'the dictatorship of the proletariat', as a condition for the achievement of socialism, we mean something totally different. (P. 150.)

. . . . . .

Every year of fascist despotism serves to destroy those qualities in a people which are most useful for the building of socialism. Hitler and Mussolini, for example, have devoted their not inconsiderable energies to stamping out the independence, the self-reliance, the initiative and power of self-government of the German and Italian peoples. Fascist régimes gradually reduce the whole cultural level of a people. They begin by the destruction of its art and literature. Then the educational system is drastically curtailed, and what is left perverted to narrowly military ends. . . . (P. 167.)

. . . . . .

The swirling stream of world events, is now beginning to have its effect in Great Britain. In less than a year it has set up a remarkably strong current of opinion in favour of the accomplishment of the unity of the British working-class movement by the acceptance of the

British Communist Party's recent application for affiliation to the Labour Party. As the situation develops, this current of opinion will flow more and more strongly. And it will extend itself to America. Events themselves will convince the workers of Britain and America that peace, liberty, and a relatively tolerable standard of life are becoming more and more incompatible with the existence of capitalism. . . . (Pp. 448–9.)

IX

Winston Churchill's Speech of 14 July 1940

Let us think rather of the future. Today is the 14th of July, the national festival of France. A year ago, in Paris, I watched the stately parade down the Champs Élysées of the French Army and the French Empire. Who can foresee what the course of years will bring? Faith is given to us to help and comfort us when we stand in awe before the unfurling scroll of human destiny. And I proclaim my faith that some of us will live to see a 14th of July when a liberated France will once again rejoice in her greatness and her glory, and once again stand forward as the champion of the freedom and the rights of man. When the day dawns, as dawn it will, the soul of France will turn with comprehension and with kindness to those Frenchmen and Frenchwomen, wherever they may be, who in the darkest hour did not despair of the Republic.

In the meantime, we shall not waste our breath or cumber our thought with reproaches. When you have a friend and comrade at whose side you have faced tremendous struggles, and your friend is smitten down by a stunning blow, it may be necessary to make sure that the weapon that has fallen from his hands shall not be added to the resources of your common enemy. But you need not bear malice because of your friend's cries of delirium and gestures of agony. You must not add to his pain; you must work for his recovery. The association of interest between Britain and France remains. Duty inescapable remains. So long as our pathway to victory is not impeded, we are ready to discharge such offices of goodwill towards the French Government as may be possible and to foster the trade and help the administration of those parts of the great French Empire which are now cut off from captive France but which maintain their freedom. Subject to the iron demands of the war which we are waging against Hitler and all his works, we shall try so to conduct ourselves that every true French heart will beat and glow at the way we carry on the struggle, and that not only France but all the oppressed countries of Europe may feel that each British victory is a step towards the liberation of the continent from the foulest thraldom into which it has ever been cast.

All goes to show that the war will be long and hard. No one can tell where it will spread. One thing is certain, the peoples of Europe will not be ruled for long by the Nazi Gestapo, nor will the world yield itself to Hitler's gospel of hatred, appetite and domination.

And now it has come to us to stand alone in the breach, and face the worst that the tyrant's might and enmity can do. Bearing ourselves humbly before God, but conscious that we serve an unfolding purpose, we are ready to defend our native land against the invasion by which it is threatened. We are fighting *by* ourselves alone, but we are not fighting *for* ourselves alone. Here in this strong City of Refuge which enshrines the title-deeds of human progress and is of deep consequence to Christian civilization, here, girt about by the seas and oceans where the Navy reigns, shielded from above by the prowess and devotion of our airmen—we await undismayed the impending assault. Perhaps it will never come. We must show ourselves equally capable of meeting a sudden violent shock, or what is perhaps a harder test, a prolonged vigil. But be the ordeal sharp or long, or both, we shall tolerate no parley, we may show mercy, we shall ask for none.

I can easily understand how sympathetic onlookers across the Atlantic or anxious friends in the yet unravished countries of Europe, who cannot measure our resources or our resolve, may have feared for our survival when they saw so many States and Kingdoms torn to pieces in a few weeks or even days by the monstrous force of the Nazi war machine. But Hitler has not yet been withstood by a great nation with a will-power the equal of his own. Many of these countries have been poisoned by intrigue before they were struck down by violence. They have been rotted from within before they were smitten from without. How else can you explain what has happened to France, to the French people, to the leaders of the French people?

But here, in our island, we are in good health and in good heart. We have seen how Hitler prepared in scientific detail the plans for destroying the neighbouring countries of Germany. He had his plan for Poland and his plans for Norway. He had his plans for Denmark. He had his plans all worked out for the doom of the peaceful, trustful Dutch—and of course for the Belgians. We have seen how the French were undermined and overthrown. We may therefore be sure that there *is* a plan—perhaps built up over years—for destroying Great Britain, which after all has the honour to be his main and foremost enemy. All I can say is that any plan for invading Britain which Hitler made two months ago, must have had to be entirely re-cast to meet our new position.

X

Declaration by the United Nations including the Text of the Atlantic Charter

Signed at Washington. 1 January 1942

The governments signatory hereto; having subscribed to a common programme of purposes and principles embodied in the Joint Declaration . . . dated August 14, 1941, known as the Atlantic Charter;

being convinced that complete victory over their enemies is essential to defend life, liberty, independence and religious freedom and to preserve human rights and justice in their lands, and that they are now engaged in a common struggle against savage and brutal forces seeking to subjugate the world, DECLARE:

1°) Each government pledges itself to employ its full resources military or economic against those members of the Tripartite Pact and its adherents with which such government is at war.

2°) Each government pledges itself to cooperate with the governments signatory hereto and not make a separate armistice or peace with the enemies.

The foregoing declaration may be adhered to by other nations which are or which may be rendering material assistance and contributions in the struggle for victory over Hitlerism.

Done at Washington. January, 1 1942.

The Atlantic Charter

The President of the United States of America and the Prime Minister representing His Majesty's Government in the United Kingdom, being met together, deem it right to make known certain common principles in the national policies of their respective countries on which they base their hopes for a better future for the world.

First. Their countries seek no aggrandizement, territorial or other.

Second. They desire to see no territorial changes that do not accord with the freely expressed wishes of the people concerned.

Third. They respect the right of all peoples to choose the form of government under which they will live, and they wish to see sovereign rights and self-government restored to those who have been forcibly deprived of them.

Fourth. They will endeavour, with due respect for their existing obligations, to further the enjoyment by all states, great or small, victor or vanquished, of access on equal terms to the trade and to the raw materials of the world which are needed for their economic prosperity.

Fifth. They desire to bring about the fullest collaboration between all nations in the economic field with the object of securing for all improved labour standards, economic advancement, and social security.

Sixth. After the final destruction of the Nazi tyranny, they hope to see established a peace which will afford to all nations the means of dwelling in safety within their own boundaries, and which will afford assurance that all men in all lands may live out their lives in freedom from fear and want.

Seventh. Such a peace should enable all men to traverse the high seas and oceans without hindrance.

Eighth. They believe that all the nations of the world, for realistic as well as spiritual reasons, must come to the abandonment of the use of force. Since no future peace can be maintained if land, sea or air armaments continue to be employed by nations which threaten or may threaten aggression outside of their frontiers, they believe, pending the establishment of a wider and permanent system of general security, that the disarmament of such nations is essential. They will likewise aid and encourage all other practicable measures which will lighten for peace-loving peoples the crushing burden of armaments.

January, 6, 1942.

XI

Extracts from the Charter of the United Nations, 1945

CHAPTER I

Purposes and Principles

Article 1

The purposes of the United Nations are:

1. To maintain international peace and security, and to that end: to take effective collective measures for the prevention and removal of threats to the peace and for the suppression of acts of aggression or other breaches of the peace, and to bring about by peaceful means, and in conformity with the principles of justice and international law, adjustment or settlement of international disputes or situations which might lead to a breach of the peace;

2. To develop friendly relations among nations based on respect for the principle of equal rights and self-determination of peoples, and to take other appropriate measures to strengthen universal peace;

3. To achieve international cooperation in solving international

problems of an economic, social, cultural, or humanitarian character, and in promoting and encouraging respect for human rights and for fundamental freedoms for all without distinction as to race, sex, language, or religion; and

4. To be a centre for harmonizing the actions of nations in the attainment of these common ends.

Article 2

The organization and its members, in pursuit of the purposes stated in Article 1, shall act in accordance with the following principles:

1. The organization is based on the principle of the sovereign equality of all its members.

2. All members, in order to ensure to all of them the rights and benefits resulting from membership, shall fulfil in good faith the obligations assumed by them in accordance with the present Charter.

4. All members shall refrain in their international relations from the threat or use of force against the territorial integrity or political independence of any State, or in any other manner inconsistent with the purposes of the United Nations.

5. All members shall give the United Nations every assistance in any action it takes in accordance with the present Charter, and shall refrain from giving assistance to any State against which the United Nations is taking preventive or enforcement action.

CHAPTER II

Membership

Article 4

1. Membership in the United Nations is open to all other peace-loving States which accept the obligations contained in the present Charter and, in the judgment of the organization, are able and willing to carry out these obligations.

2. The admission of any such State to membership in the United Nations will be effected by a decision of the General Assembly upon the recommendation of the Security Council.

CHAPTER III

Organs

Article 8

The United Nations shall place no restrictions on the eligibility of men and women to participate in any capacity and under conditions of equality in its principal and subsidiary organs.

CHAPTER IV

The General Assembly

Article 13

1. The General Assembly shall initiate studies and make recommendations for the purpose of:

(*a*) Promoting international cooperation in the political field and encouraging the progressive development of international law and its codification;

(*b*) Promoting international cooperation in the economic, social, cultural, educational, and health fields, and assisting in the realization of human rights and fundamental freedoms for all without distinction as to race, sex, language, or religion.

CHAPTER VI

Pacific Settlements of Dispute

Article 33

1. The parties to any dispute, the continuance of which is likely to endanger the maintenance of international peace and security, shall, first of all, seek a solution by negotiation, inquiry, mediation, conciliation, arbitration, judicial settlement, resort to regional agencies or arrangements, or other peaceful means of their own choice.

CHAPTER IX

International Economic and Social Cooperation

Article 55

With a view to the creation of conditions of stability and well-being which are necessary for peaceful and friendly relations among nations based on respect for the principle of equal rights and self-determination of peoples, the United Nations shall promote:

(*a*) Higher standards of living, full employment, and conditions of economic and social progress and development;

(*b*) solutions of international economic, social, health and related problems, and international cultural and educational cooperation; and

(*c*) universal respect for, and observance of, human rights and fundamental freedoms for all without distinction as to race, language, or religion.

Note. The translation of some of the documents from the French—Briand's Memorandum (III), two of the passages from the writings of Lenin (IV*a* and IV*c*, in a French version of the original Russian), and the passage of Paul Valéry's from *Variété* (VII)—has been made by one of the editors (E.B.), who has also translated from the German the passage from Rosenberg's *The Myth of the Twentieth Century*. All the other passages are printed either from the English original of the texts quoted or (as regards IV*b*, V*a*, and VI) from published English translations of the original Russian, German, or Italian.

VIII
REVIEW AND EPILOGUE

By

SIR ERNEST BARKER

I

SPACE

§ 1. To the Greeks, who invented the term, Europe meant the 'wide prospect' or 'broad field of vision'. But the wide prospect on which they looked, twenty-five centuries ago, was still a narrow field. They had begun by applying the term only to central Greece; they had then extended it to cover all the mainland of Greece; finally they had used it to denote the whole of the northern land-mass of which Greece, like Italy, was a part and a projection. Even so, their 'Europe' signified an area which was both vague and limited: vague, in the sense that the dark northern area beyond the Balkans was unsurveyed and uncircumscribed; limited, in the sense that to be a European, and to have European ways, meant primarily and particularly to be an inhabitant of the sunnier countries which bordered the northern shores of the Mediterranean Sea.

This mention of the Greek view of Europe may remind us that it is still possible, after 2,500 years, to regard Europe from two points of view: the southern, which was that of the Greeks and their successors the Romans, and the northern, which has established itself since the end of ancient history, and more particularly since the beginning of what we call modern history some 500 years ago. From the southern point of view, or the point of view of antiquity, Europe is in effect the Mediterranean basin; and if it primarily means the northern shores of that basin, it also includes the eastern and the fringe of the southern shores. From an early date the Greeks had moved into and made their settlements in Asia Minor; they had begun to affect, and to be affected by, the interior of western Asia; and the conquests of Alexander, surviving in the Hellenistic kingdoms established by his successors, had carried the culture and institutions of Europe to the Tigris and even the Indus. Rome inherited and continued the work which had thus been begun: she drew the north coast of Africa into the circle of the Europe of antiquity; she settled farmers and built towns, with temples and theatres which may still be traced, along the African littoral; and affecting it deeply by her action she was affected in turn by its influence when her African provinces gave her emperors, Fathers of the Church, and men of letters who had mastered the art of a rich, if exotic, Latinity.

From the southern or ancient point of view Europe is thus a sea, with its surrounding shores and their hinterland. From the northern or modern point of view Europe is something different. It is a long horizontal peninsula, stretching from west to east (or from east to west, according to one's choice), which is physically an annexe or outcrop of the vast land-mass of Asia. This peninsula is generally narrow, at any rate in comparison with the land-mass to which it is joined; it is also deeply indented, with a great length of coastline and an easy access to open sea-water. The line of its junction with the land-mass is a shifting borderland which has wavered and oscillated in the course of history. At one time it is a line drawn far away to the east, along the Ural mountains and down to the Caspian Sea; at another it is a line pushed back towards the west, and running down from the east of the Baltic to the west coast of the Black Sea or even still farther west. Indeed it may almost be said that neither from the southern nor from the northern point of view is Europe a fixed quantity or a determinate area. From the southern point of view it spills into west Asia and North Africa; from the northern it spills into the mass of Asia, as that mass in turn spills back into it. History does not move according to continents or geographical divisions. It follows a way of its own in time which is not tied to categories of space. The distinction between Europe and Asia is difficult to draw even in terms of space. It is far more difficult to draw in terms of time and history. To consider the matter simply from the point of view of language, apart from other expressions of man's culture and mental activity, is to be reminded that a single family of related languages, the Indo-European, runs almost uninterrupted, and without a definite break, from western Ireland and the Highlands of Scotland to the Ganges and beyond.

§ 2. Yet we must also remember that, both from the northern and from the southern point of view, there is a division too in the idea and nature of Europe. Neither the Europe of the southern nor that of the northern mind is essentially and intrinsically one. On the contrary each would appear to be essentially and intrinsically two. This is perhaps less true of the Europe of the northern mind than it is of the Europe of the southern. But even the northern idea of Europe admits—indeed we may even say postulates—

a line of division at the point where the peninsula joins the land-mass; and when this line of division is pushed by the pressure of Asia backward towards the west until it runs through the middle of geographical Europe, as it did in the days of the Mongol and the later Turkish invasions, we may say that two Europes emerge in the north, the Europe of the west and north-west and the Europe of the east. Archaeologists report the existence of two such Europes far back in man's development. In upper palaeolithic art a distinction may be traced between a western province, including the countries of the Atlantic sea-board and part of central Europe, and an eastern province stretching from Moravia into the Ukraine and beyond; and it has been noted that when Magdalenian art was flowering in the western province, there was still a dearth of invention in the eastern. It is curious to reflect that our twentieth-century division between the two Europes of the north has already some sort of parallel in the early days of pre-history.

But the division of the Europe of the southern mind is even clearer and still more striking. The Europe of the Mediterranean basin, the Europe of antiquity, was not a unity. It, too, had its west and its east: it was, and it has long remained, even to the present day, a system of duality. If a line is drawn from the head of the Adriatic south-eastward to the Straits of Otranto and thence southwards past Sicily to the northern coast of Africa, we may say that on one side of the line there is the Latin world of Rome, and on the other the world—originally Hellenic, then Hellenistic, and finally Hellenistic-oriental—of Athens and Alexandria, Antioch and Istanbul. This division already began to emerge at the beginning of the second century B.C., when Rome, mistress of the western Mediterranean after the Second Punic War, confronted with her legions and law the Hellenistic kingdoms of the east. Her legions and law were victorious: she eventually united, or seemed to unite, the two halves of the Mediterranean in a single Roman empire; and soon after the end of the second century A.D., or within a space of 400 years from the time when Rome first confronted the east, one citizenship ran from Cadiz to Antioch and even farther than Antioch. By the edict of Caracalla (A.D. 212) all free inhabitants of the Roman empire were embraced in the fold of the same *civitas Romana*, and the theory could thenceforth be held that Rome was the *communis patria* of all the civilized world of the Mediterranean basin. But the old division still persisted beneath the apparent unity; and within the course of a century, during the reigns of Diocletian and Constantine, it declared itself in new forms, which were destined to endure for more than a thousand years, and whose relics and survivals may still be traced even today.

Two causes combined to renew and revive the old division of the Europe of the Mediterranean basin during the fourth and fifth centuries of our era. The first of them was a matter of politics and secular order. The burden of the administration of a huge empire, threatened by decay within and the rude assaults of vigorous invaders without, was too great for a single centre: a single Atlas could no longer bear on his shoulders the 'too vast orb' of the fate of Rome. The new centre of Constantinople was made by Constantine the capital of the east; a new senate arose on the Bosphorus; and eventually, by the end of the fifth century, an east Roman or Byzantine empire divided itself from the west, and established itself in the 'second Rome' for the duration of the next ten centuries. The other, and perhaps even greater, cause which helped to produce the division of the Europe of the south was a matter of religion and ecclesiastical order. Christianity had at one time seemed likely to weld all the Mediterranean world together in a new form of unity, and to add the cohesive force of a common religious allegiance to the binding ties of a common citizenship in a single secular empire. But just as the single secular empire soon divided itself into two halves, so Christianity, too, soon divided itself into two forms—the Catholic form of the west and the Orthodox form of the east. The schism was long in becoming overt and final; but from the first the more legal and pragmatical west, interested in discipline and organization, and concerned with liturgical forms and the external decencies of public worship, had distinguished itself from the more metaphysical and subtle spirit of the east. In the course of the eighth century, with the outbreak of the Iconoclastic controversy, due to an eastern movement away from material images, the distinction had become more pronounced; and eventually, by the middle of the eleventh century, schism became open and irreparable. Meanwhile, as early as the middle of the seventh century, a new divisive force had been added by the emergence of Mohammedanism and its establishment in large areas of the eastern Mediterranean. The unity of the old Graeco-Roman civilization of the Mediterranean basin, never absolutely firm, might seem to be entirely disrupted in the age of the Carolingians, when Islam had swung round the southern half of the basin in a great arc which stretched from Bagdad to the southern Pyrenees; when the Papacy had blessed (in A.D. 800) a new western empire, with its capital in the Rhineland, to watch and challenge the eastern empire entrenched on the Bosphorus; and when it was also beginning itself to challenge, in the course of the struggle between Nicholas I and Photius (*circiter* 860), the title and the authority of the patriarch of Constantinople.

§ 3. The general course of the argument thus brings us face to face with two parallel and similar conclusions. The first is that if we look at Europe from the northern point of view we find a continuous impact and counter-impact—a recurrent oscillation and a permanent tension—between the western European peninsula and the eastern Asiatic land-mass with which it is connected. This is a perpetual motif or theme; but it recurs in different forms, and is expressed in new variations, at different stages of history. At one stage, which may already be traced in the fifth century of our era, in the days of Attila or even earlier, and which lasts till the days of the Mongol empire of the thirteenth century and even of the Turkish empire of the sixteenth, there is a thrust from the turbulent centre of Asia which carries its conquering cavalry to the very centre of Europe. Whatever the causes of this thrust—whether it was due to geographical factors, such as progressive desiccation, driving swarms of migrants in search of food towards more fertile areas, or (as is more probable) to personal factors such as the feuds and fiery passions of warlike chieftains, resulting in volcanic eruptions and the projection of some victorious horde on a far-flung career of conquest—the menace which it brought to Europe was constant for many centuries. Western Europe might be secure after the victory of the Emperor Otto I over the Magyars at the battle of the Lechfeld in 955; but Russia in the east was to know the pressure of the Golden Horde in later centuries, and the lands of the Danube to the south-east were to be overrun still later by the armies of the Ottoman sultans. The tide turned, and a counter-impact began, when the Slav peasantry of the Russian plains, advancing relentlessly as frontiersmen in search of new farms, moved steadily eastward from the beginning of the seventeenth century, and eventually reached the shores of the Pacific Ocean. Europe thus moved *overland* into north Asia (as about the same time, with the navigations of the Portuguese, the Dutch, and the English, it also began to move *overseas* into south Asia); and a new epoch began in the relation of the European peninsula to the Asiatic land-mass. A great power, European in the racial origin of its people, and continuing to draw on Europe both for the inspiration of ideas and the secrets of technique, Russia became a Eurasian colossus, bestriding the north of Asia as well as the east of Europe, and adding a new and fateful ingredient to the general European amalgam. Russia-in-Europe is not all Russia (any more than the British in Britain are the whole of the British Empire and Commonwealth); and the general Eurasian mass of Russia, apart from all questions of dogma and ideology, is a complication of Europe at one end as the overseas diffusion of Britain is a complication at the other. In any case the old problem of the relation of the peninsula to the land-mass—the problem of settling where the one ends and the other begins, and at what point the line of division should be drawn—is a problem which has not been settled but perhaps has been even accentuated by the development of Russia.

The other and parallel conclusion to which we are drawn by the course of the argument is that if we look at Europe from a southern point of view we find a similar clash of impact and counter-impact, and a similar system of oscillation and tension, between the countries of the western and central Mediterranean and those of its eastern shores and their hinterland in western Asia. Here again the line of division at which impact happens and tension is felt may vary from age to age, according as it is pushed far back to the west or moved in turn far into the east. About 500 B.C. the line may be said to run through the Aegean; and we may regard the Persian Wars and the thrusts of Darius and Xerxes as an attempt to push it still farther westwards and to absorb Greece in the eastern world. The attempt failed; and a century and a half after its failure the Greek civilization of the west, under the leadership of Alexander of Macedon, swept eastward in turn in a long movement of expansion which carried it far into southern Asia. One of the wonders of history is the spread of Greek art and Greek coinage, Greek cities and even Greek kingdoms, as far as the valley of the Indus and the Afghan highlands of Bactria; indeed Greek art, in its

Graeco-Buddhist form, may be traced even in the deserts of Turkestan and on to the borders of China. But the Hellenistic phase of Greek history meant a fusion of Greece *with* the Orient even more than an extension of Greece *into* the Orient; and the civilization of Hellas became in the process Hellenistic-oriental instead of Hellenic and western. Meanwhile a new and more westerly power had arisen in Rome; and the power of Rome, victorious over the Phoenician immigrants from Syria who had established eastern influence in the west of North Africa and the south of Spain, began to draw, or suggest, a new line of division, henceforth permanent, which runs down the Adriatic and across to Tunisia. This is the line of division which was for the future to separate the two parts of the Europe of the south; and though it is true that Rome united both parts for a time in the bonds of her empire and the fold of a common citizenship, it is none the less true that in language and culture, in the general trend of religious belief, and eventually even in political structure, the two parts were destined to remain distinct. Rome carried, indeed, her empire and her law, and with them all her material and social engineering (she was essentially a great 'engineer', in the largest and fullest sense of the term), through the whole of the Mediterranean basin; but the eventual legacy which she bequeathed was a legacy of the two parts rather than of a single whole. There was no united Europe even in the days of the Antonines. There was only an interaction and a mutual influence of two really separate halves; and at the end of the ancient world, by the fifth century of our era, the separation had become even greater than the interaction and mutual influence.

§ 4. Living in the west of Europe, we are naturally prone to emphasize the part which the west has played in the history of the interaction between the west and the east; and we are all the more prone to do so if we belong to the great and numerous branch of the Christian Church which looks to Rome for its guidance. But if we reflect on the whole course of history, and particularly on the thousand years, from A.D. 500 to 1500, which lie between the end of the ancient and the beginning of the modern world, we shall recognize that the great stream of influence has often run from the east to the west, and that the east has again and again been the inventor, or at any rate the disseminator, of many of the treasures of civilization. Wherever the home may have been of the original Aryan community which invented the parent form of all the Indo-European languages (whether it was in Asia, or in the south of Russia, or somewhere near the Baltic), it seems certain that the priceless gift of the alphabet came to Europe from the region of Syria and Palestine, and that here was the clearing-house of thought which standardized a form of letters and transmitted it through Greece and Etruria to Rome and the western world. This gift and its transmission both go far back in time—possibly as far as the second quarter of the second millennium B.C. A whole millennium later—at a time when Greece was just beginning to emerge into the light, and Rome was still in darkness—a far greater gift, destined to issue in a far greater and more momentous transmission, began to be made by Palestine. The Hebrew scriptures begin with the writings of Amos and the other prophets of the eighth century B.C.; they rise to their glory in the great creative age of the middle centuries (especially the sixth) of the first millennium B.C.; they pass into a later 'Wisdom' literature of profundity and power; and translated during the third and second centuries B.C. into the Greek form of the Septuagint they are transmitted to the western world and become a part of its inheritance. This was the 'preparation of the Gospel'; and in this preparation, and in the Gospel, the eastern Mediterranean gave its transcendent gift to the whole of the Mediterranean world and ultimately to northern Europe. The religious thought of our continent, in the ancient phase of its history, long drew its light and inspiration from the east. Not all the light was white and clear, nor all the inspiration true. If the Hebrew scriptures and the Christian Gospel came from the east, there also came the various worships of Isis, of Mithras, of Cybele, and of 'the unconquered Sun'. Those were dubious gifts. But we may thank the east for Stoicism, that Spartan creed of the educated pagan, founded by the Cypriot Zeno, which nourished a theology as well as a cosmology, and transmitted to Christianity its idea of the common 'law of nature' and its belief in the principles of liberty, equality, and fraternity which sprang from the idea of that law.

It was not only in the classical period, and down to A.D. 500, that the east flowed into the west as an active influence and stimulus. The thousand years which followed the close of the classical period, A.D. 500–1500, show an interaction between the east and the west of the Mediterranean basin in which the east was the giver even more than the receiver. It is true that the west discharged the exaltation and the lightning of the Crusades into the east, from the end of the eleventh century onwards; and it is true that the Crusades not only issued in a Latin kingdom of Jerusalem, but also brought the west into direct and regular contact with eastern life upon eastern soil and under eastern skies. But it is also true that the Latin kingdom fell before Saladin in less than a century after its foundation; and it left little trace in the east except the ruins of deserted castles. Again it is true that during the course of the thirteenth and fourteenth centuries the Papacy sought to establish religious missions in Asia, and to revive the Christian tradition established centuries before by the Nestorian missionaries; but again it is also true that these efforts were eventually lost in the sand. The permanent and seminal influence, during the Middle Ages, was the influence of the east on the west rather than that of the west on the east. This influence of the east on the west was partly that of Mohammedanism and partly that of Byzantinism; and the latter was the greater.

The influence of Mohammedanism, radiating from Bagdad and Syria, and moving along the coast of North Africa into the south of Spain, resulted in commercial and cultural connexions which stimulated western Europe. The Italian cities benefited by the commercial connexion; the nascent learning of medieval Europe, and its budding universities, benefited by the cultural. If the architecture of Granada could show an astonishing beauty, the learning of Cordoba, in the days of Averroes, during the second half of the twelfth century, had a depth of scholarship and philosophy which made western Europe its debtor. The Arabic Aristotle, and also the Arabic Plato, became part of the inheritance of Europe; and though by the middle of the thirteenth century, after the Fourth Crusade had carried the Latins into the Levant, St. Thomas Aquinas could use Latin translations of the *Ethics* and *Politics* of Aristotle made in Greece directly from the Greek, an Averroistic school continued to preserve and cherish an Arabic interpretation of the philosophy of Greece down to the sixteenth century. But the influence of Byzantium, and the Greek art and scholarship of the east, gave more to the development of western Europe during the Middle Ages than ever Mohammedanism did. The scholarship of Byzantium not only contributed texts of Aristotle for transmission in translations to the studies of Paris, Cologne, and Oxford during the thirteenth century: it also contributed Greek teachers, as well as Greek texts, to the Italian Renaissance of the fifteenth century; and it thus led western thought back to the fountains of Greek philosophy and the original language of the New Testament. The art of Byzantium also gave an impulse to the development of the art of the Italian primitives, such as Duccio and Giotto: the birth of western painting owes a debt to Greek iconography; and as late as the sixteenth century 'the last Byzantine', El Greco of Crete, could carry to Venice and Rome, and eventually to Spain, the tradition of Greek portraiture, Greek treatment of landscape, and Greek use of colour and light.

But even at an earlier date, and on a still larger scale, Byzantium had made great gifts to another and different part of Europe—the Balkans and Russia. This was one of her greatest services: to link the eastern half of the Europe of the south with the eastern half of the Europe of the north. Here her influence no longer moves westward, but towards the north; and here she contributed her chief gifts to the civilization of Europe. The brothers Cyril and Methodius, in the ninth century, were the apostles of the Slavs in Macedonia and as far afield as Moravia; they constructed a Slavonic liturgy, in the face of the opposition of German bishops; and Cyril also invented an alphabet (or it may be even two alphabets, the Cyrillic and the Glagolitic) based on the Greek uncial alphabet of his time, for the expression of Slavonic sounds. It was thus two Greeks, born in Salonica, who evangelized and 'alphabetized' the mass of the Slavs (apart from the Poles, the Czechs, the Croats, and the Slovenes, who adopted both Latin Christianity and the Latin alphabet); and it was from this source that the Russians, the Bulgarians, and the Serbs drew the religion of Greek Orthodoxy, the alphabet in which they wrote, and with it the first possibility of a native vernacular literature. Already under the unsaintly St. Vladimir, at the end of the tenth century, the Russian principality of Kiev had accepted the religion of Greek orthodoxy and the Slavonic liturgy; and the Church thus founded in Russia was subject to Constantinople and staffed by a hierarchy largely Greek. Eventually the centre of political primacy passed from Kiev northward to Moscow; and under Ivan III of Moscow, 'lord of all Rus' in the latter half of the fifteenth century, a great new power began to emerge on the horizon of Europe. When Constantinople fell before the Ottoman Turks in 1453, and the last of its emperors perished in the sack, the Russia of Ivan III became the inheritor of the east Roman empire and the patron and head of Greek orthodoxy, now overwhelmed by the Turkish flood in all other countries. Ivan, in 1472, married the niece of the fallen emperor, Sophia Palaeologus, and with her hand he claimed as her dowry the Byzantine titles of autocrat and Caesar (or 'Tsar'), thus annexing the Byzantine imperial tradition and making Moscow the 'third Rome'. Byzantium died on the Bosphorus (except in so far as her tradition and ceremonial survived in the system and protocol of the Sublime Porte); but she left her inheritance, political and ecclesiastical, to the Russian Tsars and the Russian Church.

§ 5. Hitherto the course of the argument has been concerned with Europe as so much land; with Europe as a continent, a continuous and connected tract of the surface of the earth, impinging upon and interacting with another and greater tract called the continent of Asia. But Europe is sea as well as land: indeed it is sea in a sense, and to an extent, which is not matched by any other continent. Deeply and uniquely indented—enclosing the Baltic Sea on the north, and containing the far greater part, and almost every port, of the coast of the Mediterranean Sea on the south—Europe has always been maritime; close to the sound and scent of the sea; inevitably impelled, even if reluctantly (the ancients had no love of the sea), to navigations and the sea-borne movement of men and their commodities. Before the record of history there were the prehistoric voyagings, which we can only guess from the archaeological traces they have left in surviving monuments and relics, of the 'beaker folk' and the builders of megalithic tombs who carried their culture from the middle of the Mediterranean as far as the British Isles. Later, by the eighth century B.C., there were the tradings, explorations and settlements of the early Greeks, and the long seafaring of the Phoenicians which carried them both to Britain and down the coast of Africa. Then, at a far later date, from the eighth to the eleventh century of our era (and even later still) there were the sea-raids and adventures of the Scandinavian Vikings, which led them far into the Mediterranean (to Micklegarth and Jorsala—Constantinople and Jerusalem) and even, according to tradition, across the Atlantic to the gulf of St. Lawrence and 'Vineland'. The one parallel to these European navigations is the navigations of the Arabs of southern Arabia, sailing in their dhows down the coast of East Africa to Zanzibar, as they did over a thousand years ago, and across the Indian Ocean to the Malay peninsula and Java.

But the European navigators, down to the close of the Middle Ages, were either 'prospectors' and traders (such as the Phoenicians of antiquity, or the medieval Genoese who ventured out into the Atlantic in the days of Dante) or sea captains and freebooters of the type celebrated in the old Norse sagas. A new epoch began, and Europe took to the sea in earnest, from the later half of the fifteenth century onwards. It was now no longer a matter of prospectors and freebooters; it was a matter of organized states. The powers of the Atlantic seaboard—first Portugal, then Spain, then England, then the Netherlands, then France—dived from their spring-board into the sea, and made their way westwards, southwards, and eastwards into the oceans of the world. This was a new and great phase in the general history of Europe. It was the beginning of 'Europe overseas': of European settlements which peopled new continents, and of an organized movement of European trade which took European governments and merchant companies round Africa to the Indies and to the Spice islands of the Far East. This new and great phase in the history of Europe marks a revolution in its life. It is partly a revolution in size—Europe is henceforth greater than metropolitan Europe—but it is also a revolution in character. The new Europe overseas is not only affected and conditioned by Europe; it also affects and conditions Europe. Europe henceforth no longer lives to itself alone. It goes out of itself into other lands and comes back into itself transformed, or at any rate changed, both by their influence and its own experience.

The revolution which produced Europe overseas was part of a general revolution. The sixteenth and seventeenth centuries of our era are a great divide in history. It is not merely a matter of the three new *R*'s—the Renaissance of classical learning, spreading from Italy to western Europe; the Reformation of Medieval Christianity, producing a new religious life in central and northwestern Europe; the Reception of Roman law (purged and clarified by the general idea of natural law) as a motive force in the transformation of the jurisprudence of France, Germany, and the Low Countries. There were also three other new things—the discovery of the western and the southern hemispheres, vitally and integrally connected with the development of Europe overseas; the emergence of the principle of nationality and the idea and practice of the nation-state, also connected with the same development, since it was the nation-states that went overseas and accentuated their nature in the process by the national rivalry of their voyages and settlements; and finally the rise of modern natural science, again connected with the same development, for as we may gather from the thought and writings of Bacon it was the discovery of a new physical world which suggested to men's minds the idea of discovering a new mental world of knowledge by new inductive methods. ('This proficience in navigation and discoveries', Bacon wrote, 'may plant also an expectation of the further proficience and augmentation of all sciences; because it may seem they are ordained by God to be coevals, that is, to meet in one age.') But a new epoch of this magnitude, illuminated by so many new stars, deserves a separate inquiry; and that inquiry may properly be reserved for the later section of this review and epilogue which deals with the category of time.

II
STOCK

§ 1. Before we turn to the category of time, and proceed to consider the phases and stages of the history of Europe, there is something to be said about stock, or in other words the human material, in all its different forms and with all its different gifts, which has contributed to the shaping of the European inheritance. Already, in our treatment of the category of space, we have had reason to note the divisions which chequer the unity of Europe—the division between the Europe of the north and the Europe of the south, and the further line of division (a moving line, swinging now to the right and now to the left) which separates each of these Europes into a western and an eastern part. This division, and the impact and counter-impact between the divided parts, has made the whole of the continent a peculiarly fertile field of development and, since about 1000 B.C., the great nursing mother of civilization.

Civilization began, indeed, outside the periphery of Europe. It began in south-west Asia and in north-east Africa. It began in the river valleys leading down from the mountains of eastern Anatolia to the Persian Gulf and up from the highlands of Abyssinia and equatorial Africa to the eastern Mediterranean; it began with valley-cultivation, the management of valley-irrigation, and the growth of 'civility' in civic communities attached to temple-centres or gathered round princely courts. But these early civilizations, while they radiated their influence far afield, were by their very nature enclosed in their river-valleys; and though they attempted expansion and conquest, their peoples were managed multitudes rather than free communities, nor had they the salt of the open sea to invigorate their life and stimulate their motion. It was otherwise with the peoples of the Mediterranean basin and the lands to the north of that basin. The sea was about them for a highway; and the land was a space in which border areas marched with one another, inducing contact or provoking conflict, but always offering a challenge and demanding some sort of response. Whether or no, as the philosopher Berkeley wrote,

> Westwards the course of empire takes its way,

we may say that the course of civilization had moved westward by the end of the second millenium B.C., and was setting up its rest by the open seas and among the border areas of a congenial continent.

The Mediterranean Sea has always been fertile of contacts—contacts which have been the spurs and the incentives of civilization. Its islands are a sufficient example, with their layers on layers of successive immigrants imposed on and fusing with one another: Rhodes, for example, with its revolving cycles of civilization, now Greek, now Roman, now Byzantine, now Frankish (during the days of the Hospitallers), now Turkish, and now again once more Greek; or again Malta, with all its vicissitudes, from the prehistoric tomb-builders to the English occupants of the nineteenth century; or yet again Sicily, with its succession (which has also been inter-mixture) of Greek, Carthaginian, and Roman, Arab, Byzantine, and Norman, Angevin and Aragonese. Almost as fertile of contacts have been, too, the borders or 'marches'. There is a long and stirring story of the different marches of Europe, a story deeply embedded in ballads and *chansons* and even epics, from the *Iliad* to the *Song of Roland*, from the *Nibelungenlied* to the ballad of *Chevy Chase*. The story, as it survives in literature, is a story of Heroic Ages, and of attacking and defending peoples led by great warrior chieftains: it is, in a word, a story of conflict. But conflict is not the whole story, though it is the story celebrated in literature. The many marches of Europe—the Spanish; the English marches on the Welsh and Scottish borders; the march of the Rhineland, or middle kingdom; the marches of east Germany, between the Teuton and the Slav; the marches of east Russia, between the Slav and the Tartar—all these have been areas of contact as well as areas of conflict. It is on the marches that we may trace the cross-fertilization of cultures.

But it is not only on the marches. The history of the cross-fertilization of cultures is a history which may be traced through the whole of the length and breadth of Europe, and not merely along the line of division where a wall or a ditch or some form of *limes* once marked the presence of a 'debatable land'. It is a history, too, which is old in time as well as broad in sweep; indeed it had already begun, as we know from archaeological remains which show us the faience beads of the east mixed with the tools of the west, in the Bronze Age of prehistory. In the age of recorded history—the age beginning, let us say, about 800 B.C., when the Hebrew prophets were already writing and the

Homeric poems were being recited—there are three elements or ingredients in this process of cross-fertilization which command particular attention. They all appear, and enter gradually into combination with one another, in the course of ancient history, between the year 800 B.C. and the year A.D. 500. The three are Israel, Hellas, and Rome: Hebrew religious thought, Greek humanism and philosophy, and the Latin power of ordered drill and legal organization. If we sought to express each element in a single word which served as a key or clue to its nature, the Hebrew word would be *Yahweh*, the personal God who is and who acts as a person in time; the Greek word would be *Logos*, the rational principle shaping an ordered, intelligible cosmos, and enabling man, by its presence in the core of his being, to 'measure all things' in its own light; the Latin word would be *Jus*, the engineered system of law and order 'joining together'[1] and binding the members of a human society, as an engineered system of roads and bridges joins place to place by its links.

The Hebrew seer, the Greek philosopher, and the Roman engineer are all different from one another. They may, and they did, conflict. But the notable thing, at the end of the count, is not their conflict: it is rather their combination. That combination produced the general Christian tradition as it stood at the end of antiquity. There were many centres in which the elements were mixed and blended. There was Rome itself, where nobles like the Scipios were already listening to Greek philosophers in the second century B.C., and where Syrians and Jews from the east were already at home in the days of Juvenal. There was Lyons, a great centre of latinized Gaul, where Irenaeus, a Greek from Smyrna, was bishop and metropolitan at the end of the second century A.D., and where he wrote in Greek, was immediately translated into Latin, and habitually talked to his people in Celtic. Above all there was Alexandria, the great meeting-place of Jew and Gentile, and the seething centre of religious philosophies during all the centuries from the time of Philo, at the beginning of the Christian era, through the age of Clement and Origen and the later age of Arius and Athanasius, down to the decline and degeneration of the great turbulent city in the fifth century A.D.

In all these centres and others (the African province in which

[1] The root notion of *Jus* is that of 'junction', and the word would appear to be derived from an Indo-European original which takes the Latin form of *jungere*.

St. Augustine could write *The City of God* must not be forgotten) a process of natural syncretism united the different ingredients. The Christian tradition, at the end of the process, was at once Jewish, Greek, and Roman. It had its own Palestinian scriptures, where already, in the 'Wisdom' literature of the Old Testament and in passages of the New Testament, *some* Greek influences may be traced; but in the time of the early Fathers of the Church it united to its own scriptures the *general* thought of Greek philosophy, and then proceeded to add to the union something of the legal discipline, and much of the organization, of Roman *Jus* and Roman *imperium*. We may say that Alexandria was the particular centre of the union of the Hebrew and Christian Scriptures with the philosophy of Greece; we may count Rome itself as the centre where the pattern of Roman discipline was superimposed on the amalgam. The Roman legal discipline, represented by the Roman Papacy, was becoming the dominant element in the mixture, at any rate in the west, during the last days of antiquity. In the Middle Ages that discipline dominated much of the life of western Europe; and it only began to lose its predominance when the Renaissance and the Reformation combined to bring men back to the originals of Greek philosophy and the original Greek of the New Testament. In the east, however, even under a system of Caesaropapism which exalted the lay power of the eastern emperors, the Byzantine Greeks of the Middle Ages continued still to cherish the old Greek metaphysical genius: Byzantine art had its spiritual glories in its mosaics and its paintings; and Byzantine philosophy kept something of the spirit of Plato alive, ready for transmission when the day came to Italy and the west.

§ 2. There are other elements in the general inheritance of Europe besides the Hebrew, the Greek, and the Roman elements of the Mediterranean south. There are also, if we may take them in the order of their appearing and offering their different gifts, the Celts, the Teutons, and the Slavs of the northern peninsula of Europe. Each of these names is linguistic, and not a name or term of race. None of them signifies breed or blood, or any of the physical facts which are studied by anthropologists: each of them indicates language, and with it the culture contained in and carried by that vehicle; and each is thus a term relative to the spirit of man and the achievements of his spirit, and not to the human body and its physical structure and features. The Celtic-speaking peoples today are a mere fraction of Europe, numbering no more than two millions, and found only in Brittany, Wales, the Scottish Highlands, and parts of Ireland. But if we go back to the origins of the Celts and their early diffusion in time, we find them a numerous, widely diffused, and singularly gifted people. Their original home was in what is now the south of Germany; and there, closely associated with the Italic tribes to the south, they had already developed, early in the first millenium B.C., a language closely akin to Latin. From their original home they spread far and wide, both westward and eastward, but more particularly westward. Westward, they moved into Gaul, spreading their language and culture as they went; and thence they moved southward into Spain, about the seventh century B.C., and northward into Britain in successive waves till the beginning of the Christian era. Eastward, they occupied Bohemia and conquered Transylvania: they even penetrated, in the third century B.C., into Asia Minor, and here they established themselves in Galatia. The period about 300 B.C. marks the height of their power. By that time they had already settled in the valley of the Po, and under a leader Brennus (perhaps a Celtic royal title) they had attacked Rome and put it to ransom: a little after that time, under another Brennus, they invaded Greece and reached Thermopylae. They thus anticipated, in the first millenium B.C., what the Teutonic tribes were afterwards to do in the first millenium of our era; but their career was halted and checked, first by the growth of Roman power, and later by the surge and spread of their neighbours and rivals the Teutons.

What the Celts contributed to the inheritance of Europe was two successive cultures—the Hallstatt culture of the period 650–500 B.C. (so named from an Austrian village where its relics have been excavated), and the La Tène culture of the period 250–50 B.C. (similarly named from a Swiss village). Both of these Celtic cultures, like the Celtic language, are closely connected with Italy and the development of the Italic tribes. The growing civilization of north Italy, itself affected and fed by influences from the southern and eastern Mediterranean, affected and fed in turn the art and imagination of the Celts to the north of the Alps; and they in their turn developed, especially in their metalwork, a sense of form and design which still excites admiration and which served in its day as an artistic stimulus in many lands and for many centuries. In its early, Hallstatt phase the art of the Celts, always tending to geometrical patterns, had still a certain rigidity; in its later, La Tène phase, borrowing more and more from the classical style of the Mediterranean area, and even learning (possibly through the Scythians) an east European style which ran to animal designs, their art acquired a grace of flowing curves and spirals which perhaps reached its height in Celtic Britain. Here the triumphs of Celtic art may be traced, from the third century B.C. onwards, in wonders of gold- and bronze-work on decorated shields, mirrors, and scabbard-mounts; here again, in the days of that Celtic Christianity which flourished and spread from the sixth century A.D. onwards, and rendered so great a service in the evangelization of Britain, we may trace still finer triumphs of the Celtic genius in the illumination of manuscripts, such as the *Book of Kells* of the late seventh and the *Lindisfarne Gospels* of the early eighth century, and perhaps also in the great series of stone crosses (such as the Ruthwell and Bewcastle crosses of about A.D. 700), with their sculptured figures and the running spiral of their scroll-ornament, which are a unique feature of Britain.

The art of the Celts was the most widely diffused of all the gifts which they made to Europe; but it was not their only gift. Their imagination was not only the inspiration of art; it was also the inspiration of literature; and it poured itself into their religious faith. There is a Celtic strain in some of the beauties of Latin poetry; the eager imagination of Catullus and the musing melancholy of Virgil remind us that they were both born in the parts of northern Italy which the Celts had touched and settled. The 'matter of Britain'—the legend of Arthur and his Knights—is a Celtic 'matter' which haunted the poetry of the Middle Ages; and the prose-literature of the later Celts, in Ireland and in Wales, has a gusto and an imaginative sweep of decorative treatment which may sometimes remind us of the flowing curves and graces of earlier Celtic art. The glow and enthusiasm of the religious faith of Celtic Christianity, radiating from Ireland, inspired the lives of saints, and diffused missions and monasteries not only in the British Isles, but also as far afield as Switzerland and northern Italy.

§ 3. The influence of the Celts, far-flung but fitful and too often transitory, was an influence of art and imagination, and added a decorative grace to the ages and areas upon which it acted. The influence of the Teutons was not so widely diffused; but it was more massive and profound. On the whole they were late entrants on the European scene. Settled originally in Scandinavia and the north of Germany, where they may be traced at the beginning of the first millenium B.C., they only began their great movement of expansion about 250 B.C., when they pressed down on the Celts of southern Germany and sought to establish their hold along the course of the Rhine. Involved, or involving themselves, in hostilities with the Romans, in the days of Marius and Julius Caesar (100 to 50 B.C.), they were afterwards kept for some centuries behind the Roman *limes*, which ran from the Rhine near Coblenz to the Danube near Ratisbon; but entering in time the Roman empire, first as mercenaries in auxiliary regiments, and then about A.D. 400 as invaders, they eventually flooded the west of Europe, including England and part of Scotland; and they even established themselves for a time in an empire of the Goths which embraced much of the east of Europe and could boast its own Gothic Bible in its own Gothic alphabet. The Gothic empire was transitory; the flooding of western Europe was permanent, and the remnants of the Celts were finally driven into the west of the British Isles. The Teutonic tribes which remained in their old seats to the east of the *limes* maintained their Teutonic speech and something of their Teutonic tradition; though even they, in the process of time, were drawn towards and affected by their western neighbours. But the victorious tribesmen who had invaded and occupied the Roman empire of the west soon underwent a change: they ceased, in large measure, to be Teutonic, and became Romance. They were mainly war-bands, settled among and imposed upon a large indigenous population; they adopted, or were adopted into, the framework of life which they found; with the one exception of the Anglo-Saxons in England they became latinized in speech, and thereby they entered more and more into the cultural inheritance of the ancient past conveyed in and transmitted with the Latin language. Converted to the western form of Christianity, they were drawn into the obedience of Rome and into a close connexion with the Papacy; and by the year A.D. 800, with the imperial coronation of Charlemagne at Rome, that connexion had issued in a new Roman empire, eventually called Holy, which lasted in the west, at any rate in form, for the space of a thousand years.

What was the contribution made to the inheritance of Europe by the Teutonic leaven and ferment? The early Teutons of Scandinavia and northern Germany had developed no great original culture in their original home: on the contrary they had borrowed from, and been influenced by, the Celtic culture first of the Hallstatt and later of the La Tène period. What they brought with them, when they moved southward to the Alps and westward across the Rhine, was a hardy physique and its two allies—a pertinacious habit of agriculture and a military prowess superior to that of the Celts and the later Romans. It was they, at any rate in Britain, who cleared the forests and brought under cultivation the heavier soils of the valley bottoms, where the earlier Celts had been content with the easier soils of the downland chalk; who used the heavier and more effective Teutonic plough; and who, abandoning the rectangular system of the old Celtic fields, introduced the system of long strips scattered in three open village fields. The range of their conquests attests their military prowess; and the subsequent development of the feudal system, in the countries in which they settled, shows a form of government and society based on military considerations and the idea that military service was the chief duty to the community.

An old interpretation of history, dominant in the nineteenth century, ascribed a love of personal liberty, and with it the origins of modern democracy, to Teutonic origins. The early Teutonic village communities were regarded as composed of free kinsmen, who cultivated in common the lands which they owned in common; and on this democratic substructure it was held that there arose a similar superstructure first of free moots in hundreds and shires, the parents of local self-government, and then of a free moot of the whole folk, the parent of later parliaments and parliamentary democracy. This line of interpretation began in the Arcadian pastoral of Tacitus' *Germania*, a pamphlet lauding the Teutonic tribes as so many 'nature' peoples, superior, as such, to the sophisticated and degenerate Romans; and it found favour with German historians of the middle of the nineteenth century, writing under the influence of the liberalism of their age. But it is not an interpretation which suits a heroic age of warrior kings and chieftains engaged in forays and conquests. We should more naturally expect what may be called a 'chieftain culture', with warrior chiefs concentrating land and wealth and governing power in their own hands. That is a culture already attested by the richly furnished burial-chambers under the barrows of the Bronze Age; it is the ancient culture which new discoveries of treasure trove still continue to attest. Only on the middle Danube, in the cemeteries of ancient settlements, is there evidence of some equality of wealth among the village communities; and the peaceful peasant culture of the Danubian region is something very different from the military aristocracy of the tribes of western Europe.

In their military character the Teutons did not differ from the Celts, except in the fact of superior strength. The Celts, too, could sing themselves into battle; and they, too, had their warrior chieftains. In the gifts of art and beauty the Celts transcended the Teutons; but the Teutons, too, had a literature which matched and sometimes surpassed the literature of the Celts. It is a literature more varied and diverse than that of the Celts; but this is because the Teutons, in the course of time, became varied and diverse themselves. In Scandinavia, where they remained unmixed, they produced the Edda and sagas. In Germany itself, where they were little mixed, they produced about A.D. 600 heroic lays written by bards for war-chiefs (now almost altogether lost); and later, in the days of the Hohenstaufen emperors, they made stylized and feudalized redactions of the old heroic themes, such as we find in the *Nibelungenlied*. In Anglo-Saxon England they created a religious and reflective poetry which, though Teutonic in style and temper, drew much of its inspiration from Latin Christianity and the Roman Church. Elsewhere the language and literature of the Teutons was merged into Latin; and even in England, during the Middle Ages, the old English language was so mixed with Latin that it became a 'language of the bridge', destined to carry a literature equally mixed and composite. Indeed it was perhaps in the sphere of politics, rather than in that of art and culture, that the pure Teutonic genius made its peculiar contribution to Europe. Not only may we associate the Teutons with the development of feudalism and the institutions of feudal government: we may also ascribe to a Teutonic origin the institution of kingship which crowned the feudal polity and eventually corrected its defects. The warrior chieftain of a tribe, consecrated by the Church, became an anointed king who swore at his coronation the triple oath to maintain peace, to repress rapacity and wrong-doing, and to enjoin equity and mercy. The institution of kingship, erected on this basis, played no small part in the development of medieval and modern Europe. It served as a centripetal and consolidating force which was more than the formal apex of a feudal hierarchy, and it thus drew together, in common membership of a common *regnum*, all the inhabitants of the territory in which it was able to make its power felt, including the clergy and commons as well as the feudal nobility. The territorial *regna* thus created were the precursors and the preparation of the national states of modern Europe; and kingship in this way cleared the ground for the existence of the modern nation and the action of the modern state.

§ 4. The third element or ingredient besides the Celts and the Teutons, an element at once the easternmost in space and the last to appear in time, is the Slavonic peoples. Today the Slavs, numbering almost 200 millions (if we include Asia as well as Europe), are the most numerous of European peoples. In their origins, which are obscure, and hidden, as it were, in a blanket of grey mist, they seem to have been domiciled near the Pripet marshes, in the basins of the Vistula and the Upper Dniester. Here they touched the Germans on the west and the Iranian peoples of the steppes of Scythia on the east. Linguistically, like the Teutons and Celts, they belonged to the Indo-European group of languages; but their affinities are said to be less with the western branches of that group (the *centum* branches, so called because they began the word for a hundred with a guttural) than with the eastern or Indo-Iranian branches (the *satəm* branches, which started the word with a sibilant). Enclosed at first in a limited and barren territory, a flat expanse of indistinguishable plains, they multiplied fast in the course of time and diffused themselves far afield. There is no evidence of their movement before the Christian era; indeed it is not till the sixth century A.D. that we first find them mentioned under the name of Slavs by any historical authority. They appear to have come for a time under the transitory empire established by the Goths in the east of Europe, and this is said to explain the Teutonic words which are to be found in Slavonic languages. The empire of the Goths was supplanted by a Hunnish Empire, as the Goths in time moved southward and westward (about 400 B.C.); the Hunnish empire collapsed in its turn, and a vacuum was thus created which the Slavs began to fill. They spread at some time to north-east Germany, perhaps left vacant by the movement of the Teutonic tribes into the Roman empire, and here they settled on the Oder and as far west as the Elbe. They were in Bohemia by the latter half of the sixth century; at about the same period a southern section had penetrated into Greece, and during the course of the seventh century the southern Slavs were diffused over much of the Balkan peninsula. By A.D. 700 the Slavs had thus, in the course of their wide diffusion, moved out of their primitive mist into the light of the surrounding world: they were the neighbours of the Teutonic tribes, now established in the Roman empire and among the Latin tradition; they were also, and even more closely, the neighbours of the Byzantine empire and the Greek Orthodox Church.

It was the Byzantine empire and the Orthodox Church by which they were destined to be mainly influenced. The nature of their own native culture is as obscure as their early history, and no less shrouded in mist. By themselves, and by their own genius, they tended to a life of small communistic groups; they had little instinct for obedience to any central rule, unless such rule were imposed by an alien authority capable of profiting by their indiscipline; they loved their farms, and were given to agriculture; they had a natural zest for music and singing. These traits have lasted through the ages; but in themselves they cannot be called a culture or a contribution to the general culture of Europe. In the main the Slavs drew their culture from the legacy and the mission of the Byzantine Greeks. Something has already been said of the gifts of Byzantium to the Slavs who came within the ambit of her influence: the gifts of an alphabet (or alphabets) and of a liturgy, and, over and above these, the further gift of reception into the circle of Greek Christianity and the still further, but more dubious, gift of inheritance of the imperial tradition and the Caesaropapism of Constantinople. This was the influence which was to survive till the days of Dostoievsky, the Slavophil prophet of the spiritual supremacy of Slavonic Orthodoxy in the Christian world. But it was the tragedy of the Slavs, in the course of more than a thousand years after their original spread and expansion in the seventh and the eighth centuries, to become and to remain a split and divided stock. They had diffused themselves only too widely. They were in touch with the Teutonic and Latin west as well as the Byzantine east; and in their plastic and primitive state they succumbed to, and were divided between, the two different influences. If Byzantium was the greater magnet, and drew into its orbit the southern Slavs of the Balkans and the eastern Slavs of what was to be Russia, the Teutonic and Latin west was also another magnet, and it drew the Poles, the Czechs, the Croats, and the Slovenes towards western culture and the Roman obedience. The division is already apparent at the end of the ninth century: if Cyril and Methodius carried the Greek Church into Moravia, their presence and their mission were resented by the German clergy of the Latin rite, and their work was eventually undone. A difference of religion, of liturgy, and even of the very alphabet henceforth divided the Slavs; in a word they became a stock not of one homogeneous culture, but of two different cultures, both largely borrowed.

There was still another cleavage which the process of history imposed on the Slavs. A geographical division was added to the cultural. In the course of the tenth century the Germans, advancing from the west, established an *Ostmark* which developed later into the duchy of Austria; and in the same century the Magyars, advancing from the east, founded in the steppelands of the Theiss and the middle Danube a kingdom of Hungary which met and adjoined the German *Ostmark*. The iron bar of Austria–Hungary was thus thrust among and between the Slavs, who were henceforth divided into a northern and a southern group. These divided groups, which might not have acted together even if there had been no bar of division between them, became in their separation the prey of two different movements of expansion. In the north, from the reign of Henry the Fowler onwards (919–936), there was a German process of eastward advance, a *Drang nach Osten*, which lasted, with intermissions, for more than a thousand years, and has only been checked and reversed, in our own day, by the results of the last world war, which has brought the Slavs back to the line of the Oder and the Neisse. In the south, from 1350 onwards, there was the flooding of the Ottoman Turks into the Balkans, and the subjugation of the southern Slavs to Mohammedan rule for the next five centuries. Russia alone, in her own vast spaces, was left intact; and even Russia, during the thirteenth and fourteenth centuries, lay under the Tartar yoke and paid tribute to the Khans of the Golden Horde. Apart from Russia, and apart from some periods of Polish glory and the Czech renaissance of the late fourteenth and the early fifteenth century, the Slavs were a submerged stock till the nineteenth century.

At the end of the count it is difficult to assess the Slav contribution to the development of Europe. It is almost a question of the future rather than a matter of the past. Prophecy is not history; but the present mass of 200 million Slavs, with its fertility of reproduction, and its new if compulsory cohesion under the aegis of Russia, is bound to tell more in the balance than did the less numerous and far more divided Slavs of the past. Meanwhile, if we look back on the twelve centuries, or more, which have elapsed since the Slavs first entered into the light of history, it would seem that they have been hitherto mainly borrowers rather than lenders. Their great borrowing in the past, which was mainly that of the southern and the eastern Slavs, was the borrowing from Byzantium, and especially from the Greek Orthodox Church. A more recent borrowing—so recent that it belongs to the twentieth century—which seems to have taken the place of the old historic loan from Byzantium and Greek Christianity, is the borrowing of the philosophy of German Marxism. Perhaps the greatest achievement of the Slavs, made possible by the genius of Lenin, who may possibly come to be reckoned the greatest figure in their history, is the achievement of turning Marxism into a practicable and working system, and of vesting this system with the form of consecration and the quasi-religious ardour which are symbolized in and by the mausoleum of Lenin in Moscow. The world has still to judge the quality of that achievement. Was it a continuation and extension of that late flowering of the Slav genius which had already begun in the nineteenth century and expressed itself in great novelists such as Tolstoi and Dostoievsky and musicians such as Glinka and Borodin? Or was it the petrifaction and end of all that flowering, and the substitution for it of a flat and drab monotony of thought like the physical monotony of the great east European plain? No answer can yet be given. Slavonic history began in a mist, and today the Slav world is shrouded again in a mist which withdraws it from the sight and the comity of the rest of Europe.

§ 5. Such are the main elements and ingredients in the inheritance of Europe—the Hebrew, the Greek, and the Roman; the Celtic, the Teutonic, and the Slavonic. They are not, indeed, the only ingredients. Over and above the contribution of the

Lenin's tomb in the Red Square, Moscow

Hebrews, there is also the contribution of the general Semitic world to which the Hebrews belonged. It has already been noted that the Semites of the region of Syria and Palestine transmitted to Europe, at an early date, the priceless gift of the alphabet; and the Arabic gift of numerals was another great, but far later, gift, which came to Europe during the twelfth century of our era. But the Arabs not only gave Europe the science of numerals (or, as it was once termed, 'algorism'), and along with it the science of algebra and the pseudo-science of alchemy: they gave other and still greater gifts. Settling in the south of Spain, where they held their ground from the beginning of the eighth century till the beginning of the thirteenth, and even, in diminished strength, till the conquest of Granada in 1492, they left permanent memorials of their architecture in Andalusia; and during the thirteenth century they began to transmit to the rising universities of the west, through Latin versions of Hebrew versions of their own paraphrases and commentaries, some sort of interpretation of the philosophy of ancient Greece. Nor was this all. In agriculture and in industry, and in the arts of commerce, the emirs and caliphs of Cordoba gave an example and an incentive. They applied irrigation to improve the soil; they encouraged the cultivation of the olive, the vine, and citrous fruits; they promoted the mining of silver; their artisans made Toledo blades and Cordoba leathers; and their merchants carried on trade, through Seville on the west and Malaga on the east, with many countries. In the middle of the Middle Ages, from A.D. 1000 to 1200, the Arabs of southern Spain, like the Byzantines of east Europe, had lessons to give to north-western Europe in the art of civilized life.

When we think of all these elements contributed by these different stocks, some at one time and some at another, and when we reflect on the mutual interaction between all the elements and all the stocks, we realize that the inheritance of Europe is not the inheritance of a single legacy, steadily transmitted in a single family with some little addition in each generation, as the estate of a landowner used to be transmitted with occasional increase from father to son. On the contrary it is an inheritance of many different legacies; and these many different legacies are not so much added to one another mathematically as fused with one another in a biological process of mixture and mutation which produces new results at stage after stage of the process. In a word, the inheritance of Europe must not be conceived on the analogy of a legal estate in land or any other such 'hereditament': the true analogy must be drawn from biology and not from law. The transmission of the inheritance is a matter of marriage and crossing; of the interaction of factors and the results of cross-fertilization; of the blending of different strains and the historical selection of cultures. The wealth of Europe, in the course of its past development, has consisted in the variety of its many emergent strains. But there is even more to be taken into account than the variety of the different strains which have emerged in Europe itself or been transmitted to Europe from the adjoining south-west of Asia. We have also to remember the fact that in the course of its modern history, and during the last four centuries, Europe has moved overseas and made settlements in other continents. Overseas Europe is a projection of Europe, but it is a projection which is different from Europe, and it reacts in its difference upon the Europe from which it has been projected.

We may see the results, in different forms, in the two parts of the American continent. In the north of America, in the United States, there has been a reblending of European strains in a new amalgam on a new soil; and this reblending, with the peculiar culture and form of economy which it has produced, is now engaged in reacting upon, or interacting with, the Europe which provided its different original strains. In the Latin America of the south, and also of the centre, there has been a new blending of a strain predominantly Spanish with the native strain of the Central and South American Indians; and this new blending, though different in its proportions in different parts of the area, is a general force which reacts upon, or interacts with, the Spaniards of Europe. What has happened in the United States and Latin America has its parallels—but parallels combined with difference—in other areas of the world. There is the action and reaction between Great Britain, as a part of Europe, and the countries and territories of the British Commonwealth and the British colonial empire; and this action and reaction is all the more profound, so far as concerns the Commonwealth countries of India, Pakistan, and Ceylon, because it is based on an historic contact between a west European people and the peoples of southern Asia, numbering hundreds of millions, who are seeking today to unite some of the political ideas and institutions, and something of the language and literature, of the west with the ancient and indigenous civilizations of the east. Again there is the action and reaction between metropolitan France and the overseas territories and 'associated States' which are joined with it in the French Union; and there is also the action and reaction, which has long affected the economy and the social structure of both, between the Netherlands and Indonesia.

These actions and reactions, in their sum, constitute a new process of cross-fertilization over and above the process at work in Europe itself among its own different strains. It is a process which crosses the temper and character of 'colonial' lands with the temper and character of 'metropolitan' countries. That process may be traced in the history of ancient Greece, and in the interaction between the Greek colonies of Asia Minor and Sicily and the old cities of the Greek mainland. It is a process which has repeated itself, with a difference, in the four centuries of modern history. The Greek colonies were independent and sovereign; the colonies of modern history were for a long time subordinate to the metropolitan states of Europe under a system of imperialism. Imperialism was dying at the end of the nineteenth century; it is being replaced, in the twentieth, by a system of equal, or more equal, partnership. But even imperialism, with all its defects—its domination, its profit-making, and all its attendant wars—served a purpose higher than itself. It fostered a contact and crossing of cultures which fostered in turn the development both of metropolitan Europe and of its colonial territory. The one of them ultimately learned that its mission was not exploitation but guidance; the other learned that its destiny was progress and not stagnation. Even at the price which has been paid in the past—and it has been heavy—the contact of Europe with the overseas peoples and territories beyond its bounds may yet be justified by its fruits, not only for Europe (that is only one, and perhaps the lesser, side of the account), but also for the world beyond it.

III
TIME

§ 1. The plan of this history, as it was originally drawn by a committee of Allied historians meeting regularly in London during the last two years of the war (1943–5), and as it has since been achieved, with some slight revision of details, by the editors then appointed and the contributors whom they invited, is a chronological plan which divides the history of Europe into seven periods of time. The periods are of unequal length, tapering up as it were from the base to the apex: the first of them is a period not of centuries but of millennia, and even more than millennia; the last of them is a period of less than half a century.

The first three periods may be taken together for the purposes of this review and epilogue. They extend in time from such beginnings of man as have left any form of memorial down to the beginning of the sixteenth century and, with it, of modern history. The first period is that of prehistory, or the period anterior to written records. It begins with the first beginnings of our race; it ends in Europe (though not in the Middle East, where written records are already to be found at a far earlier date), in the first quarter of the first millennium before our era. This was the period of the great fundamental inventions which are the first and original items of the European inheritance: fire and flint; tools and weapons, first of stone, then of bronze, and finally of iron; the domestication of animals; the use of the plough and the practice of agriculture. But it was also a period of the discovery of art as well as of useful arts. The cave paintings, the megalithic monuments, the painted pottery and the patterned beakers, the decorated metal-work of the Bronze and the early Iron Age—all these show the growth and flowering of an artistic impulse, partly in the service of magic and religion, but partly also in order to gratify the simple desire for beauty.

On this first and prehistoric period there supervenes, after 800 B.C., the first historic period, which may also be called the classical period. This is the period of the Hebrew, the Greek, and the Roman contributions, which have already been considered, if only with a rapid and cursory glance, in a previous passage of the argument. Two things may be said of this period. First, it laid the 'foundations'—alike in religion and philosophy, in literature and art, and in law and institutions—on which our civilization is still very largely based; and this is the reason why we must always return, in each new generation, to the study of the Classical Age and the inspiration of its original splendours. Secondly, it may also be said, and it deserves to be remembered, that the Classical Age produced for a time, in the course of the second century A.D., the first glimmer of a 'United Europe'; and though it was only a glimmer—limited in its extent; fragile in its own nature, because it lacked the cohesion of free consent and the cement of a common purpose; precarious in its existence, because it had no stable scheme of defence against the pressing masses beyond its frontiers—it still left a memory which survived through all the succeeding centuries, and not least in the Middle Ages.

But the medieval period, the third in this brief survey, though it cherished in name during its thousand years (A.D. 476–1494) the idea of the unity of Europe, was none the less a period of division, and this division increased as it drew towards its end. It is true that the Celts, the Teutons, and the Slavs were now drawn into the community of Europe; and if during the classical period the Hebrews, the Greeks, and the Romans were the great contributors to the inheritance of Europe, it may be said that these three other stocks, and particularly the Teutonic, now added their contributions to the common treasure. It is also true that the uniting and cohesive conception of empire was still present in men's minds during the course of the Middle Ages, and that a common Christian fund of ideas pervaded the whole of Europe. But there were two empires and not one—the Roman empire of the west, renewed by Charlemagne and continued by the German Ottos and their successors, and the Byzantine empire of the east with its succession of dynasties—and the common Christian fund increasingly became, especially from the eleventh century onwards (the century of the final breach), the two separate and divided funds of the Latin and the Greek Churches. Nor was this all. Western Europe might nominally acknowledge the overshadowing of the 'gold wing' of the Roman Church and the 'silver wing' of the Roman empire; but already in the Middle Ages the actual fact of its internal division, destined to become so startingly clear in the sixteenth century, was emerging more and more. Universalism was the theory: particularism was the fact; and the actual form which particularism took may be called by the name of 'territorialism'. The territorial prince, ruling independently some territory of his own in his own way and by his own motion, becomes the nucleus of life, whether in the kingdoms of France and England and Castile and Aragon, or in the Habsburg duchy of Austria, or in the Hohenzollern electorate of Brandenburg; and the tendency grows for the territorial principality to be accompanied by something in the nature of a territorial or regional Church. The principle of nationalism, and with it the idea of the nation-state and the national Church, is foreign to the thought of the Middle Ages proper; but the territorial principle is clearly apparent in the two last centuries of the Middle Ages, and that principle, if it is not nationalism, is the nursing mother of nationalism.

§ 2. When we leave the first three of our seven periods, and come to the fourth—the period of the sixteenth and seventeenth centuries—we come to a 'great divide'; a 'divide' or watershed in the landscape of history as salient, and as momentous, as that to which we have come in our day and generation. (The historians of the future may well account the century through which we are struggling now as one of the great divides and watersheds of time.) During the Middle Ages, in spite of territorialism and transcending all the forces of division, there had survived in western Europe the common tradition of an old and inherited civilization, of which the Roman Church was the guardian, and which she transmitted and inculcated through common and international agencies such as the clergy, the monastic orders, and the universities. That common tradition had been fundamentally and essentially Latin—Latin not only in the sense that the Latin language was the vehicle of its teaching, but Latin also in the further sense that the substance of knowledge was a substance drawn either from Latin authors or from a limited range of Latin translations from the original Greek. The beginning of the change which marks the 'great divide' and the transition to modern history was the intellectual movement called the Italian Renaissance. It was not, indeed, the first appearance of the spirit of renaissance. If by renaissance we mean a passion and an endeavour to recover and renew the freshness and the fullness of the classical inheritance, we may say that that passion and endeavour had already shown themselves in the Carolingian revival of the ninth century, in the classical revival of the twelfth century in the school of Chartres and the nascent university of Paris, and again in the revival and recovery of the general philosophy of Aristotle during the course of the thirteenth century. But the Italian Renaissance of the fifteenth century went farther, as it went deeper, than any of the previous revivals; and it did so in two ways. First, it was in the main a movement of secular scholarship, which sought to wrest from the church and the clergy the monopoly which they had hitherto enjoyed. Secondly, it was an attempt to recover and reinterpret the whole of the Greek contribution to the tradition of Europe: the whole of the art and literature as well as the philosophy of Greece. It was a reversion, or an ascension, to the Greek element in the inheritance of Europe; it was a turning away from, or rather a going beyond, the Latin element which had so long been dominant and had so long overlain the Greek.

Reformation followed upon Renaissance, and in some respects it went the same way. It went back behind the Latin Vulgate to the Greek New Testament; it went back behind a religion of works and organized institutionalism, constructed and operated with the engineering skill of Rome, to a spirit of faith and free fellowship in a freely formed Christian polity. In this sense the Renaissance prepared the way for the coming of the Reformation; and the Reformation, when it had come, continued to draw on the spirit of the Renaissance for the comfort and countenance of scholarship, and for the recovery and revival of the original tradition of the early Church and the doctrines of the early Fathers. But the Reformation was a great and complex thing; and if it was mixed with the Renaissance, it was also mixed with other and even greater movements of the age. It was allied, for instance, with that movement of simple and untaught piety which had already inspired the English Lollards, the Czech Hussites, and the followers in the Netherlands of the Brethren of the Common Life. But it was also allied, or rather it came to be mixed, with another and more material factor which also played its part in the making of modern history. That factor was the New Monarchy of the sixteenth-century type.

It has already been noted that the territorial principality was a growing force in the later Middle Ages, and that there was an increasing tendency for this growing force to draw religion into its orbit, and to move towards the system of a territorial Church congruous with its own nature. This growing force gathered new and overwhelming power in the course of the sixteenth century.

It rose majestic above the ruins of a feudalism exploded both by its own excesses and by new developments of the art of war; it enlisted the support of the growing commercial classes, assisting their rise, borrowing their capital, and using what it borrowed to support a new type of professional army and a new class of professional administrators. Upon this basis, and with this support, the new monarch of the age of the Reformation was able to establish within his territory a close politico-ecclesiastical system, claiming supremacy alike in secular and ecclesiastical affairs, and turning the people he governed into an exclusive group, with a peculiar character of its own informing its general life. Here we begin to see the emergence of the principle of nationality, at once inheriting and expanding the legacy left by the older principle of 'territorialism'. The new principle of nationality is a pervasive leaven: it affects economies as well as politics, and religion as well as both. It inaugurates modern history and divides the world after 1500 from the world before that crucial date. Constant in its operation, it is Protean in its forms. Allied with and fostered by absolutism in the sixteenth century, it becomes in the course of the nineteenth the ally of liberal democracy, under the guise and plea of the right of national self-determination; and then in the twentieth century, swinging round as it were on itself, and returning to its earlier alliance, it takes the form of totalitarianism and weds itself to the fascist mysticism of the magnetic 'leader' and his magnetized followers. In all its forms it is at once and simultaneously both a force of division and a bond of union: it unifies a people, but in the same act it divides the peoples. It encourages a people to develop its own way of life and type of civilization—and that is all to the good; but it may also encourage a people to forget the common inheritance which underlies all the different ways and types, to think itself unique, and even to seek to impose itself as the one true way and type—and that is all to the bad. The problem which the principle still poses to Europe today is whether, and if so by what means, the good can be preserved and the evil conjured away.

Besides the Renaissance, the Reformation, and the emergence of the nation-state, the sixteenth century also brought to Europe, or at any rate to western Europe, an era of overseas discovery and overseas colonization. There was a setting and hardening of the west in the form of nation-states; but concurrently with it there was also a flowing of each of the sea-board states across the Atlantic and into the Pacific. The two things were interconnected: the newly formed nation-states stood poised and ready for expansion, and the voyages of the discoverers drew each of them into policies of expansion which took them over strange seas and into far distant lands. The result of these policies of expansion—Portuguese, Spanish, English, French, and Dutch—was to make the 'great divide' still deeper and more momentous, and to separate modern history still more sharply from medieval. There had been expansion and exploration in the course of the Middle Ages; but it had not been conducted by states, and it had only carried the French nobility, and the burghers of Venice and Genoa, to settle on the coast of Palestine or among the islands and on the shores of the Aegean Sea. The expansion of the sixteenth century was an expansion of states: it was an oceanic expansion, far beyond inland seas; and it resulted in something new and hitherto unparalleled in history—the formation of what may be called 'maritime empires', totally different in kind from the old land-empires of Alexander and Rome.

The history of Europe becomes vastly different when it is connected with, and affected by, the history of other continents. For one thing the wars of Europe begin to assume the character not only of internal wars, whether based on dynastic claims or on religious differences, but also of colonial wars, resulting from overseas claims and ambitions. They became more and more in the nature of wars of maritime empires; their results are registered in terms of the conquest or cession of colonial territories; and if it is not till the eighteenth century that this registration is obvious, we may trace already the underlying motive of a struggle for trade and a colonial sphere in the English and Dutch hostilities with Spain at the end of the sixteenth century. There is also another new factor in the development of European history which is due to its connexion with the history of other continents. Europe ceases to be affected solely by what happens within its own confines: it begins to be affected, sometimes deeply, by what happens overseas. One simple example of this effect is the rise of the level of European prices which resulted from the discovery of precious metals in South America, and which, in its turn, produced both economic and political difficulties in the countries of western Europe. Landlords, finding their rents worth less, either raised them to the detriment of their tenants or evicted the tenants of arable holdings and followed the new and more lucrative method of the great sheep-run and its thousands of sheep; governments, equally finding that their revenues had depreciated in value, resorted to new financial exactions and provoked discontents or even rebellions. Whether for good or for evil—and both ingredients were mixed—the world into which Europe had overflowed flowed back again into Europe and affected its development.

There is still another new force in the making of modern history which must be added to our reckoning. The conjunction of the four forces of Renaissance and Reformation, the nation-state and the 'maritime empire', does not complete the tale; and the account must finally include the birth of modern science, destined in turn to give birth to modern technology and invention, and thereby to produce a revolution in the arts of life unparalleled since the original inventions of human prehistory. The birth of modern science, as we have already had reason to notice at the end of the first section of this review, drew some of its inspiration from the age of geographical discovery and the foundation of maritime empires. But the first great achievement of modern science—an achievement which created a new picture of the heavens—is an independent achievement, coeval with the beginning of the age of discovery. Nicolaus Copernicus, a Polish scholar of the university of Cracow, and like Newton a practical reformer of the coinage as well as a discoverer of the 'principles of natural philosophy', had already worked out by 1530 his theory 'of the revolutions of the celestial orbs' which revolutionized men's view of the universe. The seventeenth century carried farther what had already been begun in the sixteenth: Galileo and Newton continued, and Newton crowned, the work of Copernicus: Harvey, with his theory 'of the motion of the heart', founded a new physiology, as Copernicus had founded a new astronomy, and thus inaugurated a new era of the science of physic as the astronomers had inaugurated a new era of the science of physics.

There is a sense in which these discoveries are something utterly new in the history of the inheritance of Europe. For centuries men had lived in the past, regarding it as the accumulated storehouse of all wisdom possible to man; and the farthest reach of their effort had been some renaissance or recovery of the past. With the birth of modern science the general view is changed: the 'antiquity of time' is now regarded as the 'world's youth', and men think of the treasure to be gathered in the future rather than of the stores accumulated in the past. From this point of view it has been said that 'the most momentous innovation since the spread of Christianity was the scientific revolution crowned by the work of Sir Isaac Newton'. From the same point of view it may also be said, with a different emphasis, (as it is said by the last of the contributors to this work), that the Copernican revolution ushered into the world a new conception of man and of man's place in the universe, divergent from, and in conflict with, the traditional humanism of the west.

We are here confronted by a problem. Was modern science so entirely new? Is it something different and divergent from the general tradition of the inheritance of Europe: a new revolutionary force which sweeps man away from old moorings into the eternal silence of infinite space and the dance of innumerable atoms? Some forms of modern science—the materialist and the determinist, especially when they are allied, or proceed to ally themselves, with a particular social doctrine—may seem to suggest an affirmative answer. But on a just view of history we have to concern ourselves with the general trend and action of the whole spirit of modern science. From that point of view we may say that the nature of modern science, in the course of the last four centuries since the publication of Copernicus's *De Revolutionibus*, is neither entirely new nor utterly discrepant with the general tradition of ancient and medieval Europe. The natural and physical science of the Greeks was science, even if it was little backed by experiment: Aristotle had already followed the method, and left the lesson, of patient induction based on careful observation; and the theory of Epicureanism, as it was expounded by Lucretius, already involved a view of the universe which anticipated modern physics and affected thinkers of the seventeenth century such as Gassendi. We may even say that the alchemy and the astrology of the Middle Ages, perverted as they were by magic and fantasies of the miraculous, were also attempts to discover the real nature of things, and actually helped in some measure to foster real discoveries. The birth of modern science is a rebirth, as well as a birth: a revival or a renaissance, rather than an absolute novelty. It was indeed the fashion of the seventeenth century to reject the long 'tyranny of the Stagirite', and to turn its back on the authority of

Aristotle; and there was some reason and justice in claiming emancipation from the formalized and schematized Aristotelianism of the medieval schools. But the rejection of such Aristotelianism was also the recovery of the true spirit of Aristotle; and it was not only Epicureanism, but also Aristotelianism (and also the tradition of Hippocrates), which presided at that rebirth of natural philosophy which we are apt to call by the name of the birth of modern science.

The true revolutionary force of our modern development is perhaps less modern science (which fits into and grows out of the tradition of the past) than modern technology. What has swept men from their moorings and utterly altered their lives has been technology, with its mass of mechanisms, rather than the spirit of science; and if technology is a child of science, it is a child which, once adult, acts on its own account and produces its own results. But these results belong to a later period than that of the rebirth of science in the sixteenth and seventeenth centuries. It was in the eighteenth century, in the England of the Industrial Revolution, that technology began to spread its conquests. Spreading to the continent in the nineteenth century, and triumphant now in North America, it is the modern giant, producing gigantic instruments both of peace and war, and breeding great populations, born of its own abundance, to use—or misuse—those instruments. Here is our present problem. It is the Industrial Revolution, rather than the Copernican, which involves us in our dilemma.

§ 3. The fourth of the seven periods included in the plan of this history inevitably invited, and has accordingly received, a particular measure of review. The three succeeding periods—that of the eighteenth century, a century of 'enlightenment' and clarity, of solid sense and Palladian architecture, ending and exploding in an eruption of romanticism and revolution; that of the nineteenth century, with its technical triumphs and its nationalist movements, its oscillations between reaction and revolution (neither of them notably violent, according to the standards which our later experience has brought us), its general appearance of progress and its seeming promise of peace and a permanent system of Europe; and that of the first half of the twentieth century, with more and still greater technical triumphs, new and more strident movements of nationalism, new and far more tremendous revolutions, and (above all) new and far more gigantic wars—these three later periods, and especially the last, are too packed with a varied and shifting significance to permit a synoptic view. It is only possible to attempt some brief and imperfect reflections, necessarily scattered and even disjointed, which are suggested to the mind as it seeks to survey the succession of shifting phases.

The sixteenth and seventeenth centuries, along with their other legacies, had bequeathed to a later age a system of developing nation-states, at any rate in western Europe, and along with it a rivalry between contending monarchies, each eager for power, economic and military, and each anxious to win prestige for its court and its general culture. The eighteenth century accentuates the division and carries it across the world into the field of colonial wars, waged on the seas and in North America and the Asian sub-continent of India. England, thanks to her navy, was generally victorious in these wars; but she paid a price for her victory in the secession of her North American colonies and the foundation of the American republic. This was destined to prove, in its eventual results, the most momentous of all the events of the eighteenth century. Immediately, it produced a democratic federal state, basing itself on the Law of Nature and declaring its allegiance to the Rights of Man, which worked as a fermenting leaven in Europe and helped to cause the French Revolution. Ultimately, the example thus set was a liberal influence in the development of the British empire, and served to promote its transformation into a free Commonwealth of freely associated sovereign communities. Ultimately, again, it brought into Europe, as the twentieth century was to show, a great state destined to aid in defending the cause of liberty and the conjoint cause of peace.

But the eighteenth century was not only a century of wars and of the momentous, if unintended, results produced in their course. It was also a century which was moved by ideas that rose above, and served to assuage, the brute facts of division and war. One of these ideas was that of Balance. The original form of this idea was that of a 'balance of power'. In this form the idea was as old as the sixteenth century, when the threat of Habsburg predominance drew other states together to form a counterweight; and it was even more active in the last quarter of the seventeenth century, when the new threat of Bourbon predominance reversed the grouping but strengthened the principle.

The eighteenth century formally enunciated the principle (under the style of *justum potentiae equilibrium*) in the treaty of Utrecht; and it also extended its operation, hitherto mainly a matter of southern Europe, to the northern area of the Baltic, thereby creating, or seeking to create, a general *modus convivendi* for the whole of the continent. In its measure this notion of a balance of power was a service to the cause of peace and a remedy of division; and the notion attained such vogue that it came to be extended from the area of foreign relations to the field of internal politics. Men began to feel and to argue (as Montesquieu did in *L'Esprit des Lois*) that there ought not to be a predominance of the executive power, but that it ought to be balanced by the legislative; and in this way the idea of balance, in addition to serving the cause of peace between states, came also to serve the cause of liberty, and to encourage the limitation of power by constitutional checks, inside the state itself.

Another idea by which the eighteenth century was moved was that of enlightenment. A common cult of cool reason united the cultured intelligentsia of all countries, and created a common climate of the mind not only in Paris and London, but also in the Berlin of Frederic II, the St. Petersburg of Catherine II, and the Vienna of Maria Theresa and Joseph II. Voltaire became a prophet: the 'philosophers' of the *Encyclopédie* diffused the temper and the discoveries of the founders of modern science, and sought to extend to the moral world of human institutions the planned design and the rational system which their precursors had traced in the world of space and matter. Bentham expressed the prevalent feeling of the century in which he was born when he argued in 1776 that 'correspondent to discovery and improvement in the natural world' there was, or should be, 'reformation in the moral'. This feeling produced two allied and yet divergent results. One of them was a vogue of benevolent or enlightened despotism: a readiness to expect reformation at the hands of absolute monarchs, enlightened by the doctrines and acting on the advice of publicists and philosophers. Plato, in his day, had hoped for the conjunction of a philosophic legislator with a young and bold, but teachable, tyrant; Bentham, before he was disillusioned and had turned to democracy in dudgeon, cherished a similar hope. The other result of the sanguine rationalism of the eighteenth century was a hope of attaining the very same end by means diametrically opposite. There were those of the intelligentsia who were ready to act for themselves; and these, enlisting the aid of the bourgeoisie, which had its own hopes and desires, preferred and took the way of revolution. They carried the day in France; and thus the century of balance and enlightenment ended in turbulence and cloud. Yet it did not end without the affirmation of a principle of unity, in a form more positive and heartening than the idea of balance, and more concrete and specific than the idea of a common enlightenment and a common cult of cool reason. This was the affirmation of the fraternity of the peoples of Europe, based on their common pursuit of the common ideals of liberty and equality. It is true that the affirmation was made as it were *ex cathedra* by the leaders of a single people, and made by them to suit their own interest; it is also true that the fraternity affirmed was compulsory rather than voluntary, and was supported by armies and guns even more than it was by persuasion. But the fact remains that an old idea of the European inheritance—an idea proclaimed by Alexander of Macedon and preached by the Stoic philosophers of antiquity—was brought once more into the light of day and charged once more with electric force.

The immediate issue was something the opposite of fraternity. Armies and guns proved far more powerful than the principle which they were supposed to support; and Napoleon, the master of strategy and artillery, imposed for some years a compulsory unity on central and western Europe. The Napoleonic system was an imperialism of a new type. In form it was a marriage of autocracy to democracy by means of plebiscites; in substance, it was charged with revolutionary energy, and it proved a reforming force which permanently altered the states of Europe, partly through the internal reforms which it produced or provoked, and partly by the reshaping of territories and the redrawing of boundaries which it left behind as a legacy. But the course of the nineteenth century was determined less by the system of Napoleon than by reaction against that system. The essence of the reaction was a new and ardent nationalism, of which the seeds had already been sown by the Romantic movement of the later years of the eighteenth century, but which grew to its maturity in the course of the nineteenth.

§ 4. The enlightenment of the eighteenth century had been a conception, or set of conceptions, common to Europe at large, and it had found its basis in a common cult of cool reason and good sense. The romanticism which begins to develop in the last quarter of the eighteenth century is something predominantly German, and its basis is subjective emotion, or personal intuition, rather than the common 'bank and capital' of reason. The development of German romanticism, from the days of Herder onwards, tended to encourage the notion that each people, or 'folk', was endowed with a common fund of feeling, peculiar to itself, which issued in a common but peculiar literature, a common but peculiar law, and, generally and all round. a common but peculiar *Weltanschauung* and way of living. On this basis, it was argued, a people must always look inward, into its own self-consciousness; it must recover its own unique past and control its own unique present; it must interpret the world for itself, by means of its own outlook on life, and project itself into the world through its own institutions and culture. This fashion of thinking, or rather feeling, became widely spread in the nineteenth century: it poured a new mental content into the vessel of nationalism and affected not only politics, but also the arts and literature, and even historical and legal scholarship. Strong in countries such as Germany and Italy, which had still to achieve some form of political unity, the spirit of nationalism was also strong, in a different way and with an opposite operation, in the countries of the Austro-Hungarian and the Turkish empires. Here it tended to dissolve an existing but imposed system of political unity, and to substitute in its place a system of national political units each nationally self-determined. But whether it sought to create a new form of political unity or to dissolve an existing form, the spirit of nationalism, as it showed itself in the nineteenth century, produced by its operation a Europe different in nature from that of the eighteenth century and indeed of all previous centuries.

Hitherto, in some form or other, the notion of the unity of Europe had been prevalent if not predominant. In the Middle Ages that unity had been conceived in religious terms, and men had regarded Europe as the home of a common Christendom. The sixteenth and seventeenth centuries had indeed altered that conception: they had introduced nation-states on the scene, and they had split the west of Europe into opposing camps of the Roman and the Reformed Churches; but even during these centuries the notion of a common Christendom still survived in men's minds, and even if there was a period of religious wars, down to the peace of Westphalia, the very fact that the wars were wars between different branches of a common Christian religion attested the surviving strength of the notion. The notion had then been threatened, or we may even say displaced, by the growth of the scientific spirit and the vogue of a secular enlightenment which marked the eighteenth century. But the enlightenment which threatened, or even displaced, the old notion of a common Christendom was itself a common notion, and whether it encouraged benevolent despotism or fostered revolutionary movements, it was based on a common and general belief in the law of nature and reason. The new nationalism of the nineteenth century, with its new, self-conscious nations each immersed in its separate spirit and each treasuring its separate past, was a new phase in the history of Europe.

There was a difference, however, between the operation of nationalism during the first half of the century and its operation during the second. Down to 1848 the insurgence of nationalism, directing itself in the main against any form of absolutism, Napoleonic or other, which prevented its expression, was allied with the general cause of a common liberalism, and issued in revolutionary movements which had international dimensions and assumed an international character. In this phase of its operation nationalism might appear to be a new bond or principle of unity, rather than a force of division. One nationality might appeal to and concert its action with another; a common sympathy might unite the populations of different capitals; a common cause of liberalism, and a common policy of democratic self-government, might seem to promise a new union of Europe. The promise was not fulfilled. Nationalism could also wed itself voluntarily, or be compulsorily harnessed, to the cause of absolutism; and liberalism might thus find itself defeated by the force which it had imagined to be its ally, but which proved, in the issue, to be a separate, self-centred, and stronger power. This was the experience of Germany during the Bismarckian era. At once the centre and the laboratory of Europe, Germany showed in the latter half of the nineteenth century, and was destined to show on a greater and more terrible scale in the first half of the twentieth, that a heady spirit of nationalism can not only be yoked to absolutism, but can itself become an absolute which knows no allies and acknowledges no principle other than its own sovereign self.

There was another great force at work in the Europe of the nineteenth century besides the spirit of nationalism. This was a force of matter; the force of a new technology; the force of a great revolution in methods of production and transport and the whole economic apparatus of life; the force of the factory and of urban aggregations of factories, accompanied by the further force of a vastly increased population and the mechanization and urbanization of the life of its many millions. The Industrial Revolution, as has been noted, had already established itself in England in the course of the eighteenth century; and by the resources which it provided, at whatever human cost, it had sustained England in her colonial wars and carried her through her long struggle with revolutionary and Napoleonic France. The new technology spread to the continent in the course of the nineteenth century; it brought with it all its concomitants and consequences; and by the middle of the century it had produced the philosophy of Marx and the Communist Manifesto. European socialism had entered the stage; and with it there had been added to the drama a new actor of the first magnitude. What was to be its role, and what were to be its relations to the other two actors already on the stage, liberalism and nationalism? Liberalism was the legacy of the revolutionary wing of the enlightenment of the eighteenth century: it still drew on the old tradition of the European inheritance, and cherished the idea of a fraternity of Europe in the common enjoyment of political liberty and political equality; it believed in the civil rights of individual men and the political right of the whole of a people to democratic self-government. Nationalism, in the form which it had now assumed, was the heir of the romanticism which had emerged at the end of the eighteenth century and grown to full flower in the beginning of the nineteenth; it had shown itself ready, in the first half of the nineteenth century, to act as the ally of liberalism, but it was about to begin a movement towards the iron arm of an absolute authority which would secure its hold and ensure its expansion. Would socialism ally itself with liberalism or with nationalism, or would it act independently of both, and, if so, how would it act?

The answer to these questions is an answer which is still in debate. So far as any answer was given in the course of the nineteenth century, it was still, in the main, academic: no socialist party had attained such strength, in any country, that it could give an actual and practical answer. The academic answer given in the Communist Manifesto is an answer against any alliance with nationalism: the workers of all nations are bidden to unite together in a cause which is common to all. In this sense it may be said that socialism began by offering Europe a new principle of unity; a principle other than Christendom or balance or enlightenment: the principle of a new fraternity, no longer based on the liberal foundation of political principles, but resting (as its votaries claimed) on the economic rock of the common interest of workers in their common capacity of workers. The foundation of 'internationals', which sought to be European organizations of the representatives of workers across and above the lines of national and political division, was designed to promote the new fraternity and to establish a new form of European unity. But the design was built upon paper, and not on the solid ground of mass feeling and mass support. The solid fact at the end of the nineteenth century, at any rate in central and western Europe, was the solidity of national states and their hardening political systems, each gripping an increased population and its increased economic activity with a growing strength of administrative regulation, and each finding itself absorbed in itself and its own consolidation. Socialist 'internationals' beat idly against national solidities; and when war came at last in the beginning of the twentieth century the socialist parties of the different states engaged in hostilities were ranged in line with other parties on behalf of their nation's cause.

It may thus be said that neither liberalism nor socialism provided a scheme for the unity of Europe in the course of the nineteenth century. Liberalism had offered some promise in the first half of the century, when a common hope of liberal progress had sometimes run like a fire from the capital of one state to another; but the promise dwindled and died after the failure of the liberal movements of 1848. Socialism might seem to offer a new form of promise in the latter half of the century, but its 'internationals' proved visionary and spasmodic, and Bismarck, even before Hitler, could invent a form of 'national socialism' which was to draw socialists into the camp of the nationalist absolute state. In this state and posture of the affairs of Europe, there remained only the old idea of balance to supply some principle of unity, or at least some alternative to chaos. Indeed it had seemed at one time, after the end of the Napoleonic wars and the new settlement of Europe which followed, that the idea of balance might rise and be sublimated to that of concert, and that the states of Europe might plan their future relations together in common session and agreement. But there was no common fund of agreed ideas on which a concert could rest; the states of eastern Europe had a different philosophy from those of the west; and in any case the insurgent spirit of nationality, in the various forms which it assumed in Germany and Italy and in south-east Europe, was too set on itself and its objects to be concerted and planned by any common authority. Concert soon fell back into balance; balance, in its turn, slipped down into a precarious equilibrium, only to be maintained, as the age of Bismarck showed, by a system of insurances and reinsurances against the risk of a general war; and eventually, by 1914, a precarious equilibrium became patent disequilibrium, and Europe went into the melting-pot in which it is still immersed.

It cannot but seem a tragedy that at the height of its material achievement, when it appeared to set the pattern to all the rest of the world, the civilization of Europe should have been subjected to such an ordeal. Developing pure and applied science to ever greater heights; pushing farther and farther the arts both of war and of peace, in multiple production and the multiplication of every form of transport; producing new treasures of literature and the arts, alike in Russia at the one end and in France at the other—Europe by 1900 was greater in many ways than she had ever been before. Then, after 1900, she cracked internally; then, too, she found that new and great powers had been maturing without, both in the continent of America and in the continent of Asia; then, to end the account, she found that, far from having a primacy or setting a general pattern, she was not even adequate to herself or sufficient for her own problems, but needed the aid of the new and great powers outside herself to sustain her economy and ensure her defence. Here, for the moment, we are only concerned with the internal collapse, the cracking within, which came at the beginning of the twentieth century. What had been wrong, or amiss, in the Europe of the nineteenth century, and what had been the flaw that led to the cracking and rending? It had been, in a word, the dissolution of two empires, first the Turkish and then the Austro-Hungarian; it had been the emergence of new national forces and factors in their areas; it had been the disturbance which that emergence caused to Germany and Russia, and the tension which it caused between them. The unsolved problem of the nineteenth century in Europe, which led to the wars of the twentieth century, and is still unsolved today, is the problem of the settlement of that great tract of territory, mainly Slavonic in its population, which lies between Germany and Russia (wherever Germany ends and wherever Russia begins), and which stretches down from the Baltic to the Aegean Sea. Not that this unsolved problem stood, or stands, alone. It drew in its train, for instance, and still in some measure draws, the problem of the relation between France and Germany. It draws in its train today the far greater problem of the boundaries and the relations between Russian soviet socialism and the parliamentary liberalism of the states of western Europe. But the fact remains that the debatable land which the nineteenth century left as a problem to the twentieth, and which still vexes the twentieth century, is the land of eastern Europe.

§ 5. The twentieth century, at the end of the war of 1914–18, sought to solve the problem of the debatable land on the lines of national self-determination (thus extinguishing Austria-Hungary and practically eliminating Turkey from Europe), in the expectation that each of the new self-determining nations would adopt a policy of internal liberalism. The expectation was optimistic; and the solution also left out of the account the probable reaction both of Germany and Russia to the creation on their frontiers of new national states, partly carved at their expense and possibly acting to their detriment. But the twentieth century, if it thus gave a new and larger vent to nationalism, also sought to establish a League of Nations, and thus to provide a 'concert', of a new type, which would act as a principle and organ of unity among the nations and provide some sort of solution to the problem of rival nationalisms. But here again hope was too large; and here again the solution provided left great and grave factors out of account. The League of Nations was an aspiration, or a sum of aspirations, rather than a union of wills and powers actively and effectively devoted to the cause of unity; in any case, it was conceived so widely, and stretched so far, that it was addressed to the world at large rather than to the immediate problem of the co-ordination of Europe; and even at that, and with all its width and extension, it left out of its original scheme the new Union of Socialist Soviet Republics in eastern Europe, as it was also forced, by the American decision to abstain from joining, to leave out the United States of America.

The war of 1914–18, which had been finally settled only by American intervention, had already shown, though the lesson had not yet been taken to heart, that a system of Europe could be established only with American co-operation. Deprived of that co-operation, and depriving itself, willy-nilly, of any clear understanding and co-operation with Russia, Europe drifted into a chaos. Deep social and economic trends added themselves to political defects to increase and hasten the drift. The after-swell of war was heaving in the depths, and producing unexpected and even unsuspected consequences. Great wars are in their nature revolutions as well as wars; and the revolutions last far longer than the actual wars themselves. The war of 1914–18 had given a giant's strength to technology; it had increased the mechanization of life, and caused a new massing of men in still greater aggregations; it had provided, or suggested, new possibilities of mass-control, issuing in new techniques of human manipulation by means of astute management. There had thus emerged, especially in central Europe, a 'managerial revolution' in the broadest sense of the term—a revolution which affected politics as well as industry, and could be made to include in its sweep the whole of human life. Concurrently with this movement there was also a grave disturbance of the old equilibrium of classes; and in Germany, in particular, the middle classes, and more especially their lower strata, were displaced and almost submerged. Here 'managerial' technique found its peculiar material; and here a new nationalism arose which had the monstrous character of a Frankenstein. Created by manipulation; confounding race with nation; compounding memories of the heroic age of tribalism with an alleged new gospel of national socialism—the new nationalism became a portent. It made a deep cleavage in the middle of Europe; and a rift appeared which seemed fatal to any form of the idea of the unity of Europe.

On the eve of the war of 1939–45 the three forces which had stirred Europe in the nineteenth century—liberalism, nationalism, and socialism—seemed arrayed for a triangular duel. In the centre was the new nationalism, called by its opponents fascism, whether it took the Wagnerian form of a new 'Ring' of heroes under an Aryan banner of so-called 'national socialism', or preferred, as in Italy, to travesty Mazzini and to mimic the glories of ancient Rome by the theatrical pomp of a new Augustus and the hollow cult of a new *concordia ordinum* under the style of 'corporativism'. In both countries there was a recurrence and an explosion of what may be called historical romanticism; in both it was mixed with the latest methods of modern management; in both the amalgam suggests, in retrospect, the notion of an induced and almost theatrical nationalism, more pompous and less real than the nationalism of the nineteenth century, but bent, none the less, on realizing its own deep and calculated ambitions. This nationalism of the centre stood between the two other main European forces—the old parliamentary liberalism of the west, and the new socialism, now called communism, which had established itself since 1917 in the east. The liberalism of the west inherited its tradition from the nineteenth century, though it was adding the new ingredient of public social services and moving towards the conception of the general welfare state; it had not the novelty or the hot gospel either of the nationalist centre or of the communist east, and it stood perplexed by the problem of determining its relations to both. The communism of the east was from one point of view an astonishing novelty: few men would have prophesied, in 1900, that the Russia of the Tsars would leap at a bound from the most belated of autocracies to the most radical form of socialism. But there was an old tradition among the Slavs of life in communistic groups; there was an old messianic fervour which had once found vent in the cult of Orthodoxy and the proclamation of the 'third Rome', and now found vent in the cult of Marxism and the preaching of a new and secular gospel; and there was, by 1917, a general disorganization of state and society which opened the door to the audacity of a new and resolute builder prepared to act in the style of an Ivan the Terrible or a Peter the Great. In any case the great leap was made; and communist Russia now stood by the side of western liberalism and the new nationalism of Germany and Italy.

The result was a triple Europe. The three forces of liberalism, nationalism, and socialism, which had each been spread, in the nineteenth century, through the whole of Europe, and had vied or allied with one another in almost every country, forming a common if tangled web, were now as it were localized and divided, each in its own separate enclave. Instead of working as general leavens, in a general connexion and rivalry, each force was cantoned out in a province, and grew to a greater intensity in it. Liberalism, in particular, ceased to act everywhere, as it had once done, if in different forms and different degrees in the different countries in which it acted: there was no room for it in the centre or the east, and it could only live in the west. Once it had been a general force which had made for the general unity of Europe; now, unable to count on any general support and sympathy, it could no longer make for unity but only increase division. It might thus seem that Europe, as it stood by the end of 1938, was no longer the home and residence of a common civilization, and no longer a family united in the possession and enjoyment of a common inheritance. Europe could not be one, or act together as one, when it was split or splitting into three—three different ways of life and types of civilization.

Then came the war of 1939–45. The war was originally a war between the liberal states of the west and the nationalist states of the centre, with the communist state of the east watching and profiting—or seeming to profit—while others fought; it eventually became a war in which the liberal states of the west were joined, on the basis of a temporary and *ad hoc* alliance, with the communist state of the east in a common struggle against the centre. The temporary alliance dissolved, in reality if not in form, in the hour of victory; the result of the struggle was to eliminate the new nationalism of central Europe, and even, for the time being, any vestige of a German state; but it was also to bring the western states into direct and immediate contact with the communist state of the east, along a line drawn down the middle of Europe from the Baltic to the Adriatic. The issue of the war was thus the elimination of the three Europes, but also, and at the same time, the establishment of two Europes. Two different civilizations are now standing face to face in a posture of doubt and distrust, if not in a state of hostility. Two different interpretations of the nature of democracy and the true character of popular government are involved in this confrontation; the one civilization claims that popular government means the government of the workers (or rather of their party, or rather, in the last resort, of the leaders of their party) in the interest of the workers; the other claims that it means the government of all, with no respect or regard to class, by free discussion among all, in the common interest of all. Behind this division of civilizations, and this opposition of politics, there lies the cardinal fact of geography which has already been mentioned in the beginning of this review. This is the fact of the division and tension between the peninsular part of Europe, with all its coasts and indentations, and the great Eurasian landmass which it adjoins and on which it impinges. Our present social and political division, new in its immediate form, has an older and even more stubborn division for its background.

But the war of 1939–45, and the results which it has left behind, are more than a matter of Europe. The problem of the future of Europe is a problem which stretches farther than Europe, and cannot be settled merely by Europe. The Second World War, like the first, was only finally settled by American intervention; and in it, as in the earlier war, Europe found that it could not even emerge from war—let alone make any firm peace—by its own unaided resources. But the second war has gone farther than the first in bringing home to Europe the need of outside help to maintain the balance and secure the peace of a stable equilibrium. In 1919 and afterwards the United States left Europe and disappeared across the Atlantic. In 1945 and afterwards the United States has remained in Europe, and has become (as one of the occupying powers in Germany, as a giver of economic aid to the liberal states of the west, and as a partner in their collective defence) a part, which seems likely to be permanent, of the general system of Europe. In one sense this is a proof that Europe has ceased to be, or ceased, at any rate, to be self-sufficient. In another sense, and when we remember that the United States is in its nature a projection and offshoot of Europe, inheriting its tradition and continuing its principles, it is not a sign or symbol of the dissolution of Europe. The new world has been called in before, and it needs to be called in again, to redress the balance of the old. The reason why Europe is not sufficient to itself is the simple fact that Europe has expanded beyond itself, and that its balance and system accordingly depend, and inevitably depend, on its outgrowths as well as itself.

IV

CONCLUSION

If we seek to look in conclusion at the tendencies of the times, it might seem at first sight as if Europe, unable to remain European, were dubiously poised in the balance between the U.S.S.R. and the U.S.A., and were destined either to be Russianized or cut to the American pattern. It is true that a highly variegated Europe is standing at the moment between two massive uniformities; and the odds may be held to be in favour of the great uniformities. But the variegation of Europe is a strength as well as a weakness, and a strength even more than a weakness. The many nations of peninsular Europe, with their many languages and literatures, and all their various schemes both of social life and political structure, provide a rich sum of patterns and types which are not only a stimulus to one another but also serve as a store of examples on which the rest of the world can draw. The different common forces at work in this variegated system—the force of nationalism, the force of liberalism, the force of socialism—enter here into various combinations which make peninsular Europe a laboratory for the world. Great Britain, for instance, has been attempting, in the course of the last few years, a combination of liberalism and socialism, and a reconciliation of nationalized production with private enterprise, which is something new in its kind; and similar movements have been afoot in other parts of western Europe. There is something here which is precious in its kind. Can we say to it *Esto Perpetua*, and, if so, on what conditions is its perpetuity possible?

We have to begin by admitting that the Great Europe of the geographers—the Europe which stretches from the west coast of Ireland to the Urals, and from the North Cape to the south coast of Sicily—has always been a spatial rather than a mental and historical unit. It has already been noticed, in the first section of this review, that whether we look at Europe in terms of the south and the Mediterranean or whether we regard it from a northern point of view there has always been a cleavage between an eastern and a western half. This cleavage is still with us; and it weighs the more heavily on our minds today because it is newly deepened for us by the ideological difference of communism and liberalism, and because we feel it freshly accentuated by the demographic factor of the great growth of population in the Slavonic east. But there is some comfort in the reflection that there is nothing new in kind, even if there is a difference of degree, in a cleavage between two Europes which is almost as old as time. There is a further and greater comfort in the reflection that a process of cross-fertilization between its different elements has always been a great factor in the general inheritance of Europe and the transmission of that inheritance. It is true that there is little contact today along the 'marches' of the border-area which runs down through the middle of Europe; it is true that a curtain seems to have descended, and that an ancient instinct of xenophobia seems to be stronger than ever in the east; it is true that the eastern land-mass appears to be drawn together in a common aversion from the west. Even natural science has lost its fraternity, splitting as it were into different species; and if there is still some exchange of commodities, it is almost a grudging exchange. The omens are not propitious. But it is one of the lessons of history that adjoining civilizations must in the long run come into contact and even begin to 'cross'. The process, when it begins, will naturally be strongest in the debatable land between the eastern Baltic and the Aegean Sea. The west will be wise to be patient. That is one of the conditions of its own perpetuity. If its liberalism and its nationalism and its socialism, each mixed with and each moderating the other, have something to give to the border-area of eastern Europe, they will give it in time, and by virtue of patience, when once there is any desire to receive. And that desire may emerge, even sooner than we expect.

There is a still further and greater condition of the perpetuity of western Europe. Eastern Europe has drawn itself together, or at any rate it has been drawn together by its directing centre, in a common scheme of policy and structure which runs through all its states. The U.S.S.R.—itself in form a federal state, if in fact a centralized mechanism—has imposed the fact of a semi-federal direction on the associated states of eastern Europe, though it has left them the form and status of independent sovereigns. Here, therefore, the new force of federalism has been added to the three old forces of nationalism, liberalism, and socialism which have hitherto directed the movement of Europe. That new force has also to be added, and indeed is now being added, in the Europe of the west, which is thus beginning to answer the integration of the east by a similar, and yet different, integration of its own. The growth of 'Western Union', which in its broader form has already moved to the idea and practice of a 'Council of Europe', began in 1947, and is proceeding steadily if slowly. It differs from the integration of the east in being a voluntary movement, based on the free adhesion of each consenting state. It differs again, and in consequence, in not being inimical either to the idea of nationalism or to the principles of liberalism: on the contrary it can include and enlist both, as it can also include and enlist the ideas and principles of socialism—not indeed as a *sine qua non* which all states must adopt (though some statesmen have sought to follow that line), but rather as a possible ingredient which may or may not be added in each particular case by the free choice of each participant. This growth of 'union' and this institution of a common 'council' is not, in itself, the adoption of a federal system or the constitution of a federal state. Such a consummation is unlikely in view of the different national traditions and the general variegation of pattern which distinguishes western Europe from all the regions or territories which have hitherto adopted the logic of a full federal system. What is happening is rather a movement of the guiding idea of federalism than an adoption of actual federalism; but already the movement has gone far enough to result in proposals for a bicameral European legislature, making 'rules' for Europe (the Europe of the west) with the assent of all member states, and for an executive organ connected with the legislature which would give effect and force to those 'rules'.

Europe—the peninsular Europe of the west—can endure and prosper, and maintain the perpetuity of her inheritance, if she can mix some new and experimental form of federalism, suited to her own peculiar needs, with the other forces which have been, and still are, active in determining her life. On this condition she can retain the riches of a variegated pattern of different national idiosyncrasies; on this condition she can remain the laboratory of the world, searching out new ideas and new combinations of ideas; on this condition she can offer and inspire resistance to that movement towards a drab technological (or 'technocratic') universalism which might otherwise overwhelm the whole of the human race. There remains, indeed, the peril which must always be present in a system of two Europes: the peninsular Europe of the west, and the Europe of the eastern land-mass which is Eurasian as well as European. The peril may seem to be accentuated if each of these Europes draws itself together, federally or quasi-federally, and the two thus confront one another as separate collectivities growing more and more collective. But the idea of balance is an old idea in Europe, which has done some service in the past, and may, in new forms and with a new grouping of forces, do service in the present and the future. There have been two Europes in the past, and they have managed to live together, or at any rate side by side. There has been a Holy Roman empire of the west by the side of an east Roman emperor, and a Latin Christianity by the side of Greek Orthodoxy. The form and substance of the old division have both changed greatly in our generation; but however different both in form and substance, the old division still remains. Our predecessors faced the division. We can only do the same.

Meanwhile the great fact remains—and it is consoling as well as great—that Europe is something more than the peninsula of Europe. Overseas Europe—the Europe that has crossed the oceans since the beginning of the sixteenth century—is still a part of Europe, and still helps to determine its balance and system. To think merely in terms of the land-space of Europe is to think in terms far too narrow. Europe exists and acts in all the continents—no longer in the guise of a conqueror, or as an imperialist power, but rather as a habit of mind and a tradition of civilization. Old political bonds between Europe and its offshoots beyond the seas have either now been broken or are now being steadily loosed. But politics is not everything, and other bonds remain—the firmer and more enduring just because they are looser. The two Americas, that of the Anglo-Saxon north and that of the Latin centre and south, belong to Europe as well as themselves; and if they are separated from it both by the Atlantic Ocean and by a century and more of political independence, they are still connected with it by their civilization and culture. The British Commonwealth—so broad and so mixed in its nature that it now begins to shed the appellation of 'British' and to style itself simply 'the Commonwealth'—carries Europe into every continent, and mixes, in the south of Asia, European traditions of language, literature, and government with the ancient and indigenous traditions of eastern civilizations. The continent of Africa, in the course of the last hundred years, has been drawn into the orbit of Europe; it is being stirred into self-conscious development by the parliamentary methods and the political ideas of Europe; and it is bringing its resources and its economic weight into the general maintenance of a European system and balance.

The connexion of the two Americas with the peninsula of Europe is real, and yet also difficult. The difficulty is not only geographical: it is also a matter of the development of another temper—go-ahead, confident, inventive, electric—under the conditions of a new life, moving at a rapid pace, on a new soil and among new resources. Under such conditions, as ancient Greece had already learned, a difference naturally develops between the more static character of the old metropolitan centres and the more mobile and experimental quality of the new overseas communities. In the United States this difference has been further accentuated both by the fusing of different stocks in the crucible of one nation, producing a new mixed national type, and by a great technological development of unique dimensions and strength. It may thus appear, on the surface, that the 'New World' is a different thing from the 'Old World' of the European pattern; and while the New World may feel that the Old World is frozen and fixed in an outmoded pattern of traditional varieties, the Old World may feel, on its side, that the New World, in spite of its marvels and mechanism, is still fluid, still in the making, and still in search of a pattern. It is necessary to face and feel these differences of outlook. Unless they are faced and felt, there can be no true understanding, and no full co-operation. But the differences are only differences within a fundamental identity. The settlers in the New World have always carried with them the inheritance of Europe; and they still retain that inheritance. That is the bond which must always connect them, whatever their differences may be, with the fate and the fortunes of the Europe from which they brought the inheritance.

The British Commonwealth, in its expansion, has carried Europe far overseas, and it is still, in its measure, a link between Europe and other continents. Today, at its present stage of development, it is particularly a link between Europe and the continent of Asia. That link has been drawn all the closer since the end of the war of 1939–45, by a policy which, at first sight, might seem to be a policy of separation. The Indian empire, as it was once called, has ceased to be an empire: it has become the three sovereign and independent states of India, Pakistan, and Ceylon. But these three states remain, by their own choice and election, in the circle of what is now styled 'the Commonwealth'; and one of them, India, while preferring to be a sovereign democratic republic, with no acknowledgement of the British monarch as in any sense or form the head of its political structure, has also chosen still to remain a member of the Commonwealth, and to acknowledge the British monarch as the head of the Commonwealth in which it remains. Thus, through the Commonwealth, India has chosen to remain in contact and connexion with Europe; and the value of that connexion and contact in linking Asia with Europe has already been proved in practice in the dealing of the United Nations with the affairs of Far East Asia, and is likely to prove itself still further in the future development of Asia and of the relations of Asia with Europe. In another way also, no less notable, India has chosen, by her own free election, to draw on the inheritance of Europe and to join in its enjoyment. The Indian Constitution of 1949, made by a constituent assembly acting for the people of India, adopts the European system of parliamentary democracy, based on universal suffrage, in territorial constituencies irrespective of religion, race, or caste, as the general pattern of political life. This is a remarkable surrender of ancient Indian ideas and practices, and a no less remarkable tribute to some of the basic values of the European inheritance. But if India has thus drawn on Europe, by her own free choice and election, she can be a giver, along with Pakistan and also Ceylon, as well as a borrower. There is an ancient inheritance of southern Asia as well as an inheritance of Europe; and either can draw on the other. There may be a bridge between them which carries a mutual commerce of ideas; and southern Asia, in the act of adopting European ideas and institutions, may also adapt them to her own needs and her own traditions, and thus add from her store something new to the inheritance on which she draws. In any case all southern Asia, from the Middle East to the Pacific, is now drawing together in a new sense of common interests and the necessity of a common policy; and if a bridge for the mutual commerce of ideas between Europe and southern Asia is maintained, this new sense of Asiatic community may be an asset and reinforcement to the Europe of the west.

Finally, and at the conclusion of the account, there is the relation of Africa to Europe. European states in the past have tended to regard the African continent as so much space to be partitioned between them, if necessary at the cost of war, and as a quantity of material resources to be added to themselves for the enhancement of their own power. Europe was indeed projected into Africa, but the Europe projected was a materialistic or imperialistic Europe, and it was projected in a division and rivalry of its parts. True, this was not the whole of the matter; there was also unselfish missionary enterprise, and there was also some idea that the African territories of each power should be held by it as a 'trust', both for the particular benefit of the indigenous peoples and for the common benefit of the rest of the world. But the general picture, none the less, was a picture of exploitation. In the twentieth century the question no longer presents itself as a question of the projection of Europe into Africa. It is rather a question of the drawing of Africa into the circle of the European inheritance and the enjoyment of its benefits. It is a matter not of the gaining of resources but of the giving of help—help in the field of economic development, help in the field of education, help in the field of politics and in the acquisition of the difficult art of self-government. The French Union (as it has been newly organized since 1946) and the British colonial empire are both mainly centred in Africa; and the effort of both is now being directed to the drawing of their African territories not into European rivalries, but into the European inheritance. The French Union has now developed a central representative organ, the Assembly of the Union, in which representatives of Africa (and of other French colonial territories) sit side by side with the representatives of France for consultation on colonial problems; and the representatives of Africa (and of other territories) in the assembly are drawn from elected local assemblies sitting in the different areas. The British colonial empire has been latterly developing representative assemblies, and something in the nature of cabinet or responsible government, in the colonies of western Africa; it is developing secondary schools and universities both in the east and the west; it is encouraging and aiding plans of economic progess in the interest of native agriculture. The problem of the future for Africa—but it is a hope as well as a problem, and a hope for Europe as well as Africa—is concerned with the drawing of Africa into the inheritance of Europe without any loss or impairment of its native vigour and culture. It is the problem, at once difficult and inspiring, of grafting a new shoot upon an ancient stock. If it is solved, another asset may be added to the resources of western Europe, and the vigour and resources of Africa may help to ensure its stability.

But whatever hopes there may be outside the continent of Europe, the strength and the stability of the inheritance of Europe must depend in the last resort on the exertions and the example of Europe itself. The peoples of the peninsula of Europe live upon ancient ground. Considered in terms of demography, they may not matter greatly in comparison with the rest of the world; regarded in terms of mineral and agricultural resources, or even in terms of technology, they do not stand in the forefront; viewed in terms of politics, they have hitherto been divided and vexed by recurrent wars which now, in the twentieth century, involve not only themselves but also the rest of the world. But they live, none the less, upon ancient ground, and they have a peculiar duty to guard its ancient treasures which have been accumulated, preserved, and augmented for nearly thirty centuries of European history. The treasures are rich and various; they include a religious faith, a code of morals and manners, systems of law, structures of government, the various arts, the different sciences. None of these many elements is the peculiar prerogative of Europe: religion has its homes and forms elsewhere: there are other codes of morals and manners: there are other and different expressions of man's artistic sense. But Europe has developed, in the course of a long and continuous history, a unique and peculiar complex of all the different elements, which is at once peculiarly rich and peculiarly interconnected by the mutual sympathy of its ingredients. The complex has for its centre the religion of Christianity, founded in Palestine, influenced by the thought of Greece, shaped in its structure by Rome, and enriched in the process of time by the contributions of all the stocks and nations of Europe. Attached to this centre, or revolving round it, the complex includes a code of morals and manners to which the ethical ideas of the Greeks, Roman notions of 'probity', medieval conceptions of honour and chivalry, the Puritan sense of 'vocation', and the humanitarianism of a later age, have all added their contributions: it includes a system of law, and of the rights and duties of man before the law and under the law, largely based on the jurisprudence of Rome and now spreading in various forms (whether that of the French or German Codes or that of the uncodified English Common Law) to continents outside Europe; it includes a method of government, in the form of parliamentary democracy, which, though it goes back to ancient Greece in its first beginnings, is mainly the product of western Europe during the last two centuries. Finally, this complex of elements which forms the inheritance of Europe includes a general tradition of art (in literature, architecture, sculpture, painting, music, and all its expressions) which, beginning in Greece, has spread through Italy to inspire and adorn all Europe; and it includes, last of all but by no means least, the cool calm spirit of science, which again beginning in Greece, but long dormant after its first beginning, awoke again in the course of the sixteenth century and has since spread its conquests farther and farther.

This is the general complex, rooted in its ancient ground, which Europe has to preserve for its own and the general benefit. Political and economic policies may well be needed for its preservation: some measure of political federalism, and some mode of economic co-operation, may be the conditions of maintaining the spiritual inheritance of Europe. A system or complex of culture must command respect not only in virtue of the values which it includes, but also in virtue of the political strength which is at its command and the economic weight which it carries. It is one of the sad lessons of history that a culture which is not supported by political strength and economic weight is a culture which loses vogue, and may even lose its own vigour. There is therefore a duty laid upon Europe to increase the strength of its political structure and to augment in co-operation the weight of its economic resources. But that duty is not the end or final good of Europe. It is only a means to the end; and its value is only that of a means. The end is the preservation and increase of each element in the complex which forms the inheritance of Europe. It is, in the central realm of religion, to maintain by *personal* allegiance and service the cause of Christian belief and the action of Christian Churches; it is equally, in each of the other realms, to render *personal* service to the maintenance,

The switching tower and aerials of the B.B.C. short-wave Station at Skelton in Cumberland. The aerials, serving all parts of the world, are connected to the circular frame, and the tower serves as a 'selector' switch to bring groups of aerials into use as required

in its purity, of the essential tradition of each. The scientist will render such service if he keeps his pursuit of scientific truth pure from any 'idols' such as the idol of race lately worshipped in Germany or the idol of class now worshipped in Russia: the artist, too, will render such service if he keeps the process of artistic creation free from a worship of the idols of oddity and eccentricity, remembering that he is the heir of the past even more than the prophet of the future. So it is in each realm, and for each of us in our place and sphere: the duty upon us is a personal and individual duty of maintaining in ourselves, and of illustrating to others, the permanent standards of faith and conduct, law and government, art and science, which have been deposited in the long process of the development of Europe. New times may demand new creations; but they do not abrogate old standards. Our age may be a great age of revolution; and the first half of the century in which we are living may prove itself to be one of the great divides in the history of our kind. But if the inheritance of Europe is a fact and not merely a phrase, we have still much left from the past which we have to maintain in the present and to transmit unimpaired to the future.

INDEX

Dates of monarchs are those of the years during which they reigned; dates of other persons are those of birth and death.

PRINTED IN
GREAT BRITAIN
AT THE
UNIVERSITY PRESS
OXFORD
BY
CHARLES BATEY
PRINTER
TO THE
UNIVERSITY